Advance praise for the book

'A beautiful journey through India's cricket history. With stories of India's finest Tests and cricketers told with such warmth, it is a book to cherish.' – **V.V.S. Laxman**

'In a cricket-crazy country, a book to celebrate the eternal romance of the sport.' – **Rajdeep Sardesai**

'A must-read for cricket lovers and enthusiasts of all ages, especially the younger generation who would come to know of the exploits of Indian cricketers of the past and their glorious achievements. The authors must be complimented for their exhaustive, painstaking research and analysis. The book revived a lot of fond memories from the past.' – **S. Venkataraghavan**

'It's a magic carpet ride into the halcyon days of India in Test cricket, its characters brought out like the heroes they were. Nostalgic action replay time casting the best light on players, events and people. A must-read for every fan and student of cricket.' – **R. Mohan**

'This is as much a labour of love as it is a chronicle of Indian cricket's halcyon years. It's been researched with the sort of meticulousness once associated with the batting of Sunil Gavaskar and Rahul Dravid, both of whom feature prominently in these chapters. By speaking to those that were the architects of these great moments, and to those that had a ringside view, the authors have managed to recreate the excitement and sense of wonder from times like no other.' – **Dileep Premachandran**

Praise for *Mid-Wicket Tales: From Trumper to Tendulkar*

'This is a great compilation straight from the hearts of two cricket romantics. It makes you fall in love with cricket, all over again.' – **Rahul Dravid**

'Over the years of loving and following cricket it has been such a great joy to read various cricketing books captivating the essence of individual players and their respective eras… *Mid-Wicket Tales* is a wonderfully put together book. This book will ensure that its readers never forget the traditions of cricket and the players who have gone to painstaking efforts to uphold the culture of our great game.' – **Matthew Hayden**

'I loved reading about so many fantastic players who played the great game of cricket. It is so well researched and there are so many fantastic statistics throughout. I particularly liked the section on sublime lefthanders.' – **Mike Hussey**

'The book has left me bowled over… I applaud the special effort the authors have made to feature many brilliant cricketers who were just not lucky [enough] to become stars. Analytical and insightful, thought provoking but not controversial, this book brings both smiles and tears.' – **Javagal Srinath**

'This book is for all genuine lovers of cricket… The narrative brings alive the game to the reader, animated cricket as I would call it, with such a unique warmth that you will go back again and again to your favourite passages.' – **E.A.S. Prasanna**

'Giri and Raghu brought a lot of erudition to their essays. As cricket lovers they researched assiduously, they crunched numbers, analysed data, tested hypotheses, challenged viewpoints…they did all that but they also had a feel for the history of the game, its characters, its romance.' – **Harsha Bhogle**

From Mumbai to Durban

India's Greatest Tests

S. Giridhar and V.J. Raghunath

JUGGERNAUT BOOKS

KS House, 118 Shahpur Jat, New Delhi 110049, India

First published by Juggernaut Books 2016

ISBN 9789386228079

Typeset in Adobe Caslon Pro by R. Ajith Kumar, New Delhi

Printed at Manipal Technologies Ltd

To my mother Rukmani – Giridhar
To Chander, who taught me how to hold a bat – Raghunath

Contents

Foreword

Gideon Haigh

My favourite cricket T-shirt features a Test match scene from India photographed by Patrick Eagar. In the middle, stooping dourly forward, is an out-of-focus Chris Tavare – in the background, sharply defined, are row upon row of tightly packed spectators, composed almost symmetrically, in a state of concentration almost as trance-like as that of the batsman. The match in question is not included in *From Mumbai to Durban: India's Greatest Tests* – perhaps thanks to Tavare, who took five and a half hours to make 35. But perhaps the spirit is there. In no other country is cricket so intensely observed, is there such communion between player and watcher. And although the Indian Premier League has redefined these relations, making of them an atmosphere of carnival and delight, they continue to exist in a bedrock of seriousness whose origins lie in Test match traditions of mass concentrated observation.

Which makes this book by S. Giridhar and V.J. Raghunath an invaluable addition to cricket's library. It is about India watching, and also about India being watched, for it is as a cricket country and cricket team that numberless outsiders have had their first encounters with its culture. Ashis Nandy famously posited that cricket was an Indian game accidentally discovered by the English. Certainly the country tends to scales that suit a game big, complex and demanding: the Test match values the endurance and patience integral to daily Indian life; the Test match is cricket's epic poem, in which Indian literature is rich. Indian

Test cricketers, their strivings and struggles, their feats and failures, resonate uniquely with the nation's story.

In putting this book together, the writers have also shown Test match temperament. It is no trifling matter to put a book together of such detail and size, imbued with such passion and commitment. As a partnership, it is perhaps still more redolent of the game: after all, nothing in cricket can we accomplish alone. All the eminences are here: Hazare, Mankad, Bedi, Chandra, Gavaskar, Kapil Dev, Dravid, Tendulkar, Sehwag, Laxman. So are many personal favourites: Mohinder Amarnath (all tenacity), Gundappa Viswanath (all charm), Anil Kumble (all guts), Syed Kirmani (we share birthdays is all, but that was enough for me to embrace him way back then).

More controversially, perhaps, the authors have divided their survey into four periods defined by great games. This is Test history rather than cricket history per se, an altogether separate timeline, in which, for instance, Melbourne 1981 looms larger than Lord's 1983, Calcutta 2001 larger than Johannesburg 2007. Perhaps that reflects the capacity of the Test match to make time seem to stand still. Yet it moves on quickly enough. India's inaugural wins in the World Cup and the World T20 probably had a greater influence on the trajectory of Test match cricket than any Test match, while cricket of all varieties is still coping with the consequences of the Indian Premier League.

The survey concludes with the Durban Test of 2010, trailing off into more or less an ellipsis. There have been noteworthy Indian Test performances since: Dhoni's triumph against Australia at Chennai in 2013, Ashwin's against South Africa at Nagpur in 2015. But is the message here that the Test match is less of an event, something less than unifying, with a cricket public increasingly smitten with clubs and franchises? In the promise of Virat Kohli, Murali Vijay and Ajinkya Rahane, there's hope, in defiance perhaps of economic trends, that a second volume of *India's Greatest Tests* will be justified a few years down the track. But they will have their work cut out. In any event, I wish them, and the authors, every success.

Preface

For connoisseurs of the game, great matches are not merely those that their country won but those with drama, heroic moments, tight finishes, tremendous display of skill and acts of sportsmanship. Everyone knows that the most excitable, involved and noisiest crowds are the ones at Indian stadiums. Our memories of watching Test matches from the 1950s are of the gaiety of a festival that pervaded Indian grounds, when an international team came to an Indian city. Drums and music, wisecracks and repartee, home food – each region of the country has its distinctive flavours and aroma – all these were indelible elements of a Test match in India.

Yet, for some years now, expectations of a victory every time India take the field have assumed jingoistic proportions. An opposing batsman's boundary or the fall of their own hero's wicket are met with deathly silence. Is spectator sport only about watching one's team win?

We believe tolerant objectivity and respect for the Test cricketer – whichever era or nation he may represent – is the lens that provides the balance and perspective to appreciate the heroic, gallant loser, even while according an exalted position to the victor. That is why a cricketing nation's history is much more than its great victories; and even a celebratory chronicle of its finest moments must include unyielding draws and gallant defeats.

The 28 Tests we've selected in this book celebrate not just great victories, but also hard-fought games that demonstrated courage and a never-say-die spirit; heroic fourth-innings efforts which were testimony to both character and skill; and matches where India bucked all odds and rose as a team. Our selection therefore also includes nail-biting draws, a memorable tied Test as well as a game lost after brave combat. We have consciously ignored one-sided victories as also Tests won against weaker sides. For any team, playing well overseas has a much greater value than feats in one's own backyard, which is why we've selected 15 'away' Tests. Beginning with the Bombay 1949 Test match against West Indies and culminating with Durban 2010 where they beat South Africa as India rose to become the No. 1 Test team in the world, these 28 Tests represent India's finest cricketing moments and describe the ebb, flow and growth of Indian cricket.

We begin with the drawn fifth Test against West Indies in February 1949; for the first time in its cricket history, India almost pulled off an impossible victory (it had to wait for three more years before it won its first Test against England in 1952). The game at Sabina Park in 1971 might have been a draw but it was a watershed moment in Indian cricket. The psychological victory of a follow-on gave India the belief and confidence to go on to win the next Test and the series.

Three games against Pakistan make our list for different reasons. The second Test at Feroz Shah Kotla in December 1979. Bundled out in the first innings, India were staring at a fourth innings target of 390 but spearheaded by Vengsarkar, played so memorably that towards the end they almost pulled off an improbable victory. The Chennai Test of January 1999 was a heart-breaking defeat of 12 runs despite one of Tendulkar's greatest centuries. An emotionally drained Chennai crowd was in tears, but they found within them the largeness of heart to give a standing ovation as the Pakistan team went around in a victory lap. The game against Pakistan at Multan in April 2004 was admittedly a one-sided game, but it was India's first victory on Pakistani soil, and featured India's first triple century after a Test history of 72 years. The defining overseas victories at Headingley in 2002, the Bullring in Johannesburg in 2006 and in Trent Bridge in 2007 proved India could win against the toughest teams in alien conditions.

These 28 'greatest Tests' also seem to define the four distinct periods of Indian cricket history since 1947. During the first two decades after Independence, we played a game bequeathed to us by a country that had just left our shores with a heady feeling that came with being a free, democratic republic. This era was one of hope and romance, of pure amateur sport. To watch Subhash Gupte and Vinoo Mankad bowl to Dexter and Sobers, or see Tiger Pataudi go out for the toss, cap pulled low over his head, with the gait that is almost the unique preserve of a cricket captain, was rapture enough for the Indian cricket lover. That era ended with India's first overseas Test victory in 1968, perhaps the harbinger of things to come.

The 1970s belonged to our spin quartet – Bishan Singh Bedi, Erapalli Prasanna, Srinivas Venkataraghavan and Bhagwat Chandrasekhar – as they held the cricketing world in thrall. One remembers an unforgettable photograph of a laughing Bedi flanked by his spin comrades, holding up the ball between the fingers of his left hand as if to suggest that our spinners held the world in their hands. These four were so good that they often helped paper over the fragility of the batting that relied too heavily on the peerless Sunil Gavaskar and the support he received at various times from Gundappa Viswanath, Dilip Vengsarkar and Mohinder Amarnath. India learned to fight and not to yield.

In 1978, a tall, athletic Haryanvi teenager called Kapil Dev burst upon the scene. Each country's cricket history has its turning point, and for India, it was that summer evening at Lord's in June 1983 when Kapil lifted the World Cup. The game now captured the Indian imagination like never before. One-day cricket took firm hold and influenced the way Test cricket was played. The quality of fielding, running between wickets and the pace of run-scoring improved dramatically. The concept of neutral umpires was tried out for the first time in 1987 and came to be firmly and irrevocably established. After the economic reforms in India in 1991, media boomed, television channels started beaming every match live and money started pouring into the coffers of the Board of Control for Cricket in India (BCCI). Major technological changes and innovations swept through the game. On-field umpires could now access help from a third umpire seated in the pavilion in front of the television to adjudicate on stumpings and run-outs. Players' earnings through advertising and their cult status became an accepted phenomenon. Cricketers now received for a day's efforts what Bedi and Chandra would not have earned in their entire careers. Cricket was religion and opium both, and the barometer of a people's mood.

The 1990s marked the arrival of some of India's best cricketers ever – Sachin Tendulkar, Rahul Dravid, V.V.S. Laxman, Sourav Ganguly, Anil Kumble and Javagal Srinath. During the 1990s India won only at home, and it would be a few years into the new millennium before their collective exploits put India on top of the cricketing world. But the 1990s ended with the game sullied and tarnished by the scandal of match-fixing. The cricket lover felt betrayed.

A new era, however, was just around the corner. As Ganguly became captain and Dravid, Tendulkar, Laxman, Virender Sehwag, Kumble, Zaheer Khan, Harbhajan Singh and M.S. Dhoni made up a formidable phalanx, India began its thrilling climb to the summit. They won Tests in every country; they were not invincible, but were feared by every opponent. It is no surprise that we round off our list with a clutch of amazing performances by this once-in-a-lifetime team between 2001 and 2010. They left their imprint on the first decade of the new millennium.

~

When we decided to write this book, we knew we had watched only a few matches 'on the ground', while the rest were followed on radio, television or the press. To attempt to recreate the ebb and flow of those matches meant a thrilling pilgrimage into India's Test history. Match reports by the best writers of their times – S.K. Gurunathan, K.N. Prabhu, Ron Hendricks, Rajan Bala, R. Mohan, Sharda Ugra, Sambit Bal, Dileep Premachandran, Ram Mahesh and Anand Vasu from

India; Jim Swanton, John Woodcock, Jack Fingleton, Peter Roebuck, Robin Marlar, Vic Marks, David Hopps and Ted Corbett from the UK, Australia and New Zealand; Tony Cozier, B.R. Jones and Dicky Rutnagur from the West Indies; Qamar Ahmed and Osman Samiuddin from Pakistan. Resurrected memories of radio commentary: Alan McGilvray, John Arlott, Brian Johnstone, Tony Cozier, Reds Pereira, Pearson Surita, V.M. Chakrapani, Dicky Rutnagur, Ananda Rao, Devraj Puri, Berry Sarbadhikary and many others. Talking to India's leading cricket writers was not only a pleasurable experience but an acknowledgement that cricket's historic narrative owes a lot to them. How much our cricket writers were emotionally engaged with the game we gauged from Rajan Bala's moving lines as he mourned the passing of some stalwarts: 'In my life, people like Ghulam (Ahmed), Dattu Phadkar and M.L. Jaisimha have meant a lot. With their passing, a little bit of me has gone too.' This bond between cricketers and correspondents was the norm across the world in those years. Mike Atherton in a fascinating article on Woodcock, his most illustrious predecessor at *The Times*, tells us how Woodcock, now 90 years old, felt so close to the players that 'we were like a family, really'. When Cowdrey was recalled at the age of 42 to play the fearsome Lillee and Thomson in 1974, Woodcock confesses to Atherton that he was shaking as if Cowdrey were his own son. Our own freewheeling conversations with some of the dramatis personae and heroes of these matches, such as Chandu Borde, Bedi, Salim Durani, Mohinder Amarnath, Kris Srikkanth, Sunil Joshi, Venkatesh Prasad and Venkataraghavan, provided us the precious groundside view of those contests, undimmed by the passage of time.

Our earlier book taught us our reader could be anyone – young or old; the knowledgeable that understand the skills required to survive on a fifth-day pitch, as well as those curious to know why life in India comes to a standstill during an international game. Our challenge is to engage each one of them. We are writing this at a time when India's Test cricket under a young new captain, Virat Kohli, is showing great promise. They are proving to be invincible at home and have the potential to win regularly overseas. The ambitious young captain must certainly be aiming for a series win in Australia and South Africa, something India have not achieved yet.

Acknowledgements

This book, even more than our earlier one, has been a humbling experience. We could not have moved one page without help and support that came from every quarter. People opened up to us, they shared generously and willingly. We have experienced only kindness and friendship.

Gideon Haigh, who has a packed writing schedule, found the time to write the foreword for us. For one of the busiest and most respected cricket historians in the world to so readily write, moved us immensely. Sharda Ugra, one of India's most gifted cricket journalists, was such a friend; she introduced us to cricketers and journalists and then, very sportingly, wrote the 'Last word' where she looks at what the future holds for Indian cricket. She can cheer up anyone in five minutes and we were re-energized after every conversation with her. Sidhanta Patnaik of *Wisden India* was marvellous – helping to create the statistics sections, organizing them for us in the book, and proof-reading the entire manuscript, to make sure facts and figures were right, to make sure Kasprowicz was spelt correctly.

The Hindu, the *New Indian Express*, and the *Times of India* provided us reports of the Test matches that feature in this chronicle; R. Mohan offered us his precious books. When it came to collecting rare photographs and images of memorabilia, we were overwhelmed by the generosity of friends. Sunandan Lele, Clayton Murzello, Aloke Mitra, R. Mohan, V. Ramnarayan, Syed Kirmani, Venkatesh Prasad, Nandini Sardesai and many others – often all it needed was just a mail or a call and these would arrive in our inbox. Given our otherwise full days at the university, we could not have moved without this generosity. The ESPN Cricinfo website was the source for all statistics, for the *Wisden Almanack* reports and many wonderful essays. All these are listed in the reference section.

Our publishers at Juggernaut were enthusiastic and supportive and the book owes a great deal to their editor Amish Raj Mulmi. His attention to detail and suggestions have been invaluable. Our families have cheerfully coped with us as we went through periods of feverish work and bouts of doubt. At the university, colleagues were not only indulgent but came forward to help. Especially Shishir Bail, Mathew Idiculla, Karopady, Utkal Mohanty, Sujatha Puranik, Rajashree and Varadarajan – who helped with accessing reports, creating the reference list, the graphs and reading the manuscript to spot errors. We cannot thank our family and office colleagues enough.

And so we have received help, information, insights and advice from various people – cricketers, cricket writers, academics, family and friends, at various times. We thank them for their kindness and friendship:

Mohinder Amarnath, Shishir Bail, V. Balaji, Bishan Singh Bedi, Anurag Behar, Raju Bharatan, Harsha Bhogle, Chandu Borde, Theo Braganza, Abhishek Chopra, Shamya Dasgupta, C.N.K. Dhaveji, Rahul Dravid, Salim Durani, Ramachandra Guha, Gideon Haigh, Mathew Hayden, Michael Hussey, Mathew Idiculla, Arjun Jayadev, Sunil Joshi, D.D. Karopady, Syed Kirmani, Sudhir Krishnaswamy, V.V. Kumar, V.V.S. Laxman, Sunandan Lele, Proteep Malik, Manoj P., Suresh Menon, Reshmi Mitra, R. Mohan, Utkal Mohanty, Rahul Mukhopadhyay, Clayton Murzello, Krishnaswami Narayanan, P. Nataraj, Pankajam, Sidhanta Patnaik, V. Prasad, Venkatesh Prasad, E.A.S. Prasanna, Dileep Premachandran, Sujatha Puranik, L. Ramanath, Aditya Ramani, V. Ramnarayan, Dileep Ranjekar, B.S. Rishikesh, Rajashree S., Rajdeep Sardesai, Satyaki Raghunath, Nandini Sardesai, Satyamurthy, Colonel Vembu Shankar, Krishnamachari Srikkanth, Javagal Srinath, Sridhar Srinivasan, Sharda Ugra, Yogesh Vajpayee, N. Varadarajan, Anand Vasu, Sudheesh Venkatesh, S. Venkataraghavan and others.

PART 1

1947 to 1969

Hope Takes Root

It was the beginning of a new era in Indian history. Jawaharlal Nehru's 'Tryst with Destiny' speech was on everyone's lips. In a couple of years, 26 January 1950 to be precise, India would also declare itself a sovereign democratic republic with its own constitution – a vision of justice, liberty, equality and fraternity enshrined as the core ideals of our nation. For many years after, our National Anthem would be played or sung at every public function; our cinema halls would reverberate with 'Jana gana mana...' at the end of every movie screening. The largest democracy in the world held its first general elections in 1952 and every adult over the age of 21 had the right to exercise his or her franchise. Those early days were filled with hope, brimming with the idealism of a young nation.

It was against this backdrop that free India played sports – hockey, very well and as world champions; football, unrecognizably better than what youngsters today can imagine. At the Melbourne Olympics, India not only won their customary gold medal in hockey, but also reached the semifinals in football. We were decent in badminton while in tennis, Ramanathan Krishnan did the country proud by reaching the semifinals of Wimbledon twice, taking India to the Challenge Round of the Davis Cup and also giving the world an abiding memory of Indian sportsmanship and cultured behaviour every time he stepped on court.

Cricket, of course, was a passion in our cities and with the middle class. The British mischievously formed teams on the basis of religion and race for the Quadrangular and Pentangular tournaments in pre-Independence India. Even then, Indian spectators by and large concentrated on just the game and the players. A growing voice demanded that a tournament among geographic zones of the country was more appropriate, and the Ranji Trophy tournament began in 1934. India had a Test team even before Independence and played its first Test at Lord's in 1932. For every undeserving person like the Maharajkumar of Vizianagaram who sported the Indian blazer, we also had true sportsmen and heroes like C.K. Nayudu, Vijay Merchant, Lala Amarnath, Mushtaq Ali and others to represent the nation. It was India's good fortune that many of these players were still active to help form India's cricket team after the country attained independence.

Independent India's first cricket series was their tour to Australia in December 1947. Their first home series a year later was against West Indies, the ultimate team of entertainers. Over the next 21 years – for this section covers India's cricketing exploits up to 1969 – India played 106 Test matches, 66 of these at home and 40 away. Till the 1950s, teams would travel for weeks by ship to reach another country. Tours would be played over months. But India's cricket itinerary was not very even. For example, after its visit to Australia in 1947–48, India waited 20 years before playing again in that country. During all these years, in this first era of India's post-Independence cricket, New Zealand visited India thrice but we visited the country only in 1968. England and India exchanged tours thrice. West Indies visited India thrice, and each time their fast bowlers and batsmen had the crowds in a fever of nervous excitement. India visited them twice and on the second visit, in 1962, nearly lost Nari Contractor. Our memories of the tragic death of Phil Hughes in Australia in November 2014 are fresh, but those of us who read about Contractor being struck on the head by Charlie Griffith at Barbados know that it was a tragedy just a hair's breadth away from fatality. Contractor miraculously pulled through. Fast bowlers were clocking great speeds – no speed guns in those days, of course – while batsmen faced them bareheaded. They wore no chest guards, no thigh guards; why, even as late as the 1970s, as Kirmani the inimitable raconteur told us, our batsmen would stuff their pant pockets with spare gloves to protect their thighs! India played some of their early Test cricket on matting and the grounds were not the smooth billiard green of modern days. A humble tailor from Pune became a well-known sight, as he would run on to the ground every time an Indian hit a century to give him a gift that his meagre purse would allow. Middle-aged ladies in Mylapore would plan a week in advance for the kind of lunch boxes they would provide their husbands and sons when they went to watch the Test match at the Chepauk. Everyone would know when the commentary would begin, because All India Radio would commence proceedings with its beautiful signature tune in Raga Shivaranjini (interestingly, composed by Czech Jewish refugee Walter Kaufman when he worked with All India Radio). Yet, all this was when other countries visited India. Test matches played in England and Australia would be followed with ears glued to the ball-by-ball commentary that would be aired from both these countries. However, when India visited West Indies, there was no radio commentary and one had only newspapers to tell us what had happened more than a day later. The first time India heard live radio commentary from the Caribbean Islands was only in 1976.

Of course, everything was not rosy and innocent. The worst of it was the intrigue over selection of both players and captains. The administration of the game, from the beginning, was always in the hands of self-important men who treated the players shabbily. The petty-minded administrators got away with something as crass as omitting Vinoo Mankad, the world's leading all-rounder, for the tour of England in 1952 and then shamelessly asking him to join the team midway during the series. The caprice and pettiness of selection during this period continues to rankle. Little wonder that in those 20 years, India tried out as many as 101 players. Of these, 31 played three or fewer than three Tests. Some of these 31 ought not to have played even one, while some ought to have played many more. India had as many as 12 captains for the 90 Tests during these years. The nadir was the home series in 1958–59 against West Indies, where India had four captains for five Tests. It was unedifying.

It was not just the administrators but the players too who were
responsible for this atmosphere of intrigue and mistrust. Teams in the
pre-Pataudi era were riven with rivalries and jealousies. If Mankad
disliked Amarnath, then Vijay Hazare was not fond of Mankad either.
Hazare was extremely uncomfortable with the abusive, intemperate
language Mankad would use to berate the youngsters. In *A History
of Indian Cricket*, Mihir Bose says, '[Mankad] could swear in every
language and once swore continuously in Hindi for a full two minutes'.
Players from the South felt marginalized by the dominance of Bombay
and the West. Gopinath from the South was made to feel unwelcome
because he did not know Hindi. People like Merchant, Madhav Mantri
and Polly Umrigar wanted to ensure there were as many players as
possible from Bombay in the Indian team. Players from the East, such
as Pankaj Roy despite playing for a long time, never felt at home. Why,
even two Parsis, Umrigar and Contractor, could not fully trust each
other. How could India then field its best team and play consistently?
If there were a few players who stayed above and beyond such politics,
they were men like Ghulam Ahmed and Dattu Phadkar. Instability and
suspense were always on the mind till around 1960, when Contractor
was appointed captain. He seemed set for a stable reign but was felled
by Charlie Griffith in 1962 in a near-fatal injury. After him, Pataudi –
at 21 – became the youngest-ever Test captain in cricket history.

Pataudi brought about a complete change in the team culture,
emphasising that the players were not representing Bombay or Madras
or Calcutta* but India. A lid was put on dissensions and factionalism;
working together, merit and performance on the ground became
essential criteria. It was clear that Pataudi valued fielding and famously
said he wanted to see grubby trouser-knees at the end of the day. He

---

* The names of a number of Indian cities have been modified or changed in the last
twenty years. Thus Madras, Bombay, Bangalore and Calcutta are now Chennai,
Mumbai, Bengaluru and Kolkata respectively. In this book, while describing the
cricketing events or narrating anecdotes that occurred before the names of these
cities and states were changed, we have retained their older names.

tried to persuade self-serving administrators and selectors to give him teams that he believed had the best chance and though he met with mixed success, the administrators knew he was his own man. Not everyone may have felt that he was a great tactician but everyone agreed that he was the best thing to happen to Indian cricket. Pataudi received valuable support in his initial days from Umrigar and Vijay Manjrekar and he always remembered them with gratitude. Whether it was Phadkar, Nadkarni or Bedi, they all spoke of Pataudi's captaincy and his impact on team culture in the most glowing terms. Much like Mike Brearley let his academic scholarship rest lightly on his shoulders, so too did Pataudi have the wisdom to treat his own royal background with unconcern. The result was that he was very much one of the boys, be they older stalwarts like Manjrekar or younger ones like G.R. Viswanath. While playing for Hyderabad, he travelled and stayed with the squad in the modest manner that state teams could afford. All this endeared him to his teammates. Pataudi captained India in 36 Tests till 1969, but the change he initiated was to remain forever. Such was his impact that when Indian cricket hit turbulence in 1974, he came back to lead against West Indies, even though his batting and reflexes were on the wane.

We have chosen just four matches from the 106 India played in this period. All four are home matches, of which India won two and drew two. The two wins were against top Australian sides; the two drawn matches were nail-biting finishes as though scripted by a master storyteller. A win in both these drawn matches was just one step away. The draw against West Indies in 1949 was one where India could justifiably feel hard done by. The other, against New Zealand in March 1965, was one where the Indians were forced to follow-on but played so well they nearly delivered a knockout punch. This match bears an uncanny resemblance to the more famous 2001 Test against the world-conquering Australians in Kolkata. Two other matches almost made it to our list: one, when India lost at Brisbane against Australia in 1968, but encapsulated the spirit of fighting till the end. India was valiant in defeat, chasing 395 and falling short by 39 runs. The 1968 Brisbane Test has a startling resemblance to the match that Virat Kohli's team lost at Adelaide in December 2014, going down by an almost identical margin chasing an almost identical target. The second Test that could have made our list is the draw against the mighty West Indies in Madras in January 1967. We were in the stands on the first day as Farokh Engineer nearly hit a hundred before lunch and also on the final day when India, just three wickets from victory, were thwarted by Sobers' brilliance, pad play by Griffith and a couple of dropped catches.

Quite a few of the cricketers who played for India during this period were household names. Immensely popular, they were invited by the high and mighty of the land to grace many a public function. The few who were articulate also became commentators after their playing days were over. Stalwarts like Merchant and Lala were just winding down on glorious careers as this post-Independence era began. Both lost their best years of cricket to World War II as did Mushtaq Ali, Rusi Modi and Vijay Hazare. India was lucky that these fine representatives of Indian cricket from pre-1947 were there to help the Indian team find its feet after Independence. The younger players, Gupte, Mankad, Phadkar, Umrigar and Manjrekar, were wonderful representatives of this era. As India completed its first twenty years after Independence, young cricketers like Bedi and Viswanath had begun taking early strides and people were predicting a great future for the next generation of cricketers who were sprouting from parts of India other than Bombay and western India.

You could not have two more contrasting cricketers than Merchant and Lala. Merchant: serious, technically perfect, not a stride out of place, his visit to the batting crease like a visit to the sanctum sanctorum of his favourite temple. In his book *Porbander to Wadekar*, N.S. Ramaswami, who watched and reported on cricket from the 1930s to the 1980s, observed: 'Merchant batted much as classical authors wrote. He was in fact to be evaluated not in terms of mere cricket, but of the highest arts. At his best, his batsmanship was as the sculpture of Mahabalipuram, pure, flawless, breathing the spirit of classicism.' Lala, on the other hand, 'was a pure romantic, the Byron of Indian cricket'. Ramaswami wrote, 'He was a full-blooded cricketer. He would taste all the experiences of the game, he would explore its depths. At the wicket he was less a batsman than a storm.'

Sujit Mukherjee in *The Romance of Indian Cricket* wrote that Lala played three of the greatest innings by an Indian of those times, adding, 'When all memories of his other strokes have faded, his off-driving will remain imprinted indelibly in the memory. Not to have seen Amarnath drive was like not having heard the Prince of Denmark soliloquize.' Lala's bowling was even more natural, for he bowled brisk medium pace off his 'wrong foot'. Pipe in mouth, a kerchief around the collar, sola 'topee' on his head, it was as if cricket had bestowed an image of the 'shikari' upon him. He was perhaps India's most aggressive and imaginative captain ever. After their playing days, both Merchant and Lala provided expert commentary on radio. Merchant, even on the mike, was one for statistics, engaging more in conversation with Anandji Dossa the statistician than with the commentators. Lala on the mike was irascible; when a commentator kept asking him about a ball that had dismissed an English batsman, Lala put him down witheringly: 'It was just an ordinary ball and a stupid shot and nothing more.'

Lala also had a great eye for talent. In the late 1950s he would select a team called Indian Starlets and pick promising young cricketers and quite a few of them later played for the country. Rajdeep Sardesai in an essay on his father in *Wisden India Almanack 2015* mentions that it was Lala who gave Dilip Sardesai a break. If Amarnath was a dynamic selector good at spotting young talent, Merchant, contrary to expectations, turned out to be an adventurous selector. For one, his impatience with Pataudi became quickly apparent – it coincided with Tiger's loss of form – and in the three years that he was chairman of selectors, he brought in a number of youngsters, giving them breaks in a whirlwind fashion. Whatever his methods, Merchant selected the teams that won India the series in West Indies and England in 1971.

When young Vijay was asked in school what his family name was, he stated instead his father's occupation – 'Merchant' – and that is how his name became Vijay Merchant. He was actually the scion of the Thackersey textile mills family. In the 1970s, a popular Thackersey Fabrics-sponsored Sunday afternoon programme on All India Radio was 'Cricket with Vijay Merchant'.

The others, such as Hazare, Umrigar, Manjrekar and Borde, were all top-class batsmen. Till the 'Fabulous Four' of Tendulkar, Dravid, Laxman and Ganguly happened to Indian cricket, these batsmen could walk into any all-time Indian team. Courageous and technically sound, they scored centuries against the best teams and had a batting average of around 40. They were devoted to Indian cricket and served it in various ways after retirement.

There were also some haunting cases of fine players who were either not given enough chances or squandered them. Deepak Shodhan, Kripal Singh, Hanumant Singh, Abbas Ali Baig and Madhav Apte are five such names that come unbidden to mind; ironically, four of them scored a century on debut. In fact, till Viswanath scored his second Test century, there was a jinx on Indian cricketers who scored a hundred on debut – they never scored a hundred ever again!

There are occasions in this book where we speak of Hazare, Manjrekar and Borde. We may not have that opportunity with Umrigar, and therefore right here, we offer a nostalgic mini-tribute to this wonderful cricketer. Umrigar was a favourite with us from the time we started watching cricket, simply because he was the only Indian cricketer of those times who had a majestic personality and bearing. Polly was six-foot plus and the only brilliant fielder in a side that was sadly lacking in that skill. Many people kept harping about how Umrigar was running away against Trueman in 1952, but all we saw was the same person facing the fearsomely fast Roy Gilchrist and Wes Hall without flinching in 1958. Umrigar and Manjrekar were the only ones who made runs against the deadly pair in that series. We saw his catching expertise too, when he took a full-blooded slash from John

Reid of New Zealand, full stretch over his head, leaning to the right, and he did not even fall down as he recovered his balance. Much after he had retired, the elder amongst us played twice against him and sat at the same table at lunch in Cricket Club of India (CCI), hearing him speak in his booming voice and laugh heartily.

Spin was always India's strength. To those who marvel at the famed spin quartet of the 1970s, one might well ask, was the combination of Mankad, Gupte and Ghulam Ahmed in the 1950s any less? It was just that they did not have the kind of catching support the spin quartet got. With the new ball, Dattu Phadkar was a good medium pacer. Then there was Ramakant Desai, a small-built but dynamic new-ball bowler. India had its share of handy all-rounders too. Phadkar and Bapu Nadkarni were bowling all-rounders while Umrigar and Borde were batting all-rounders. Nadkarni kept going over after over with his accurate left-arm spin and batted tenaciously at all times. He was a sharp close-in fielder, too.

Then finally, there was Mankad, who is without doubt one of the best all-rounders in cricket history. He was the quickest to reach the double of 100 wickets and 1,000 runs, until Ian Botham broke his record. He bowled India to its first Test win, took ten wickets in a Test twice and hit hundreds in Australia and England. Mankad could be the swashbuckling buccaneer or the grim professional as his mood dictated. Against the great fast bowling of Lindwall–Miller in Australia or Bedser–Trueman in England he played the attacking opener and along with Hazare was the only Indian batsman who made an impact. At home against lesser attacks, he could grind and play long innings; his two double centuries as an opener against a mediocre Kiwi attack bear adequate testimony to this facet of Mankad.

Salim Durani, that supremely gifted cricketer, also had the potential to have been a great all-rounder. Also in this mix of all-rounders was Rusi Surti, the Parsi who quit cricket in India to settle down in Queensland. He bowled and batted left-handed and was a top-class fielder, both in the outfield and close-in.

Where India suffered during these 20 years was in their fielding. The best fielders could be counted on one's fingers. Umrigar, Ghorpade, D.K. Gaekwad, Hemu Adhikari, Madhav Apte, Rusi Surti, Pataudi, Nadkarni, Borde and a few others. Some were safe but many were abysmal. The poor quality of fielding during this phase is the reason figures do no justice to Gupte, the greatest orthodox legspinner India has produced. A wonderful spinner with a rich variety, Gupte was one of the greatest leg spinners in cricket history, a connoisseur's delight, drifting, flighting and spinning the ball, asking the batsman questions even on the most placid of pitches. His action was captivating and his repertoire included two googlies and the top-spinner. The three 'Ws' of West Indies (Frank Worrell, Clyde Walcott and Everton Weekes) considered him the greatest spinner of their time. Only Neil Harvey, the Australian left-hander, played him well with his amazing footwork, dancing down the wicket to nullify Gupte's drift, flight and turn.

But the biggest tribute must be reserved for the Indian fan. Their team won only the odd Test at home and almost never abroad. And yet they were there at the ground to watch their heroes play – Tests, first class matches or even festival games. For sure they would be frustrated, because often the team played below its potential. Yet, they kept their faith – in the game and their country's cricketers. The reward for such unconditional love of Indian cricket was to come sooner than they would have expected.

1

Fourth-Innings Heroes

India vs West Indies, fifth Test, Brabourne Stadium, Bombay, 1949

Brabourne did not have even standing room as over 40,000 spectators chewed their nails and shouted themselves hoarse while the shadows lengthened that final evening. India had incredibly reached 355 for 8, chasing 361 to win against the mighty West Indians. History was one big blow away from the trusted bat of Phadkar. Then, to the utter disbelief of the expectant multitude, the umpires, overcome by the unbearable tension, ended the game with two minutes still remaining. Those were the days when a match finished at a stipulated time and not upon the completion of stipulated overs. Indignation, disappointment, anger and an utter fatalistic helplessness gripped the spectators as the players walked off. A historic win had been aborted into an unbelievably thrilling draw. India would have to wait to record its first Test win...

These were the final moments of the five-match series against the much fancied West Indies between November 1948 and February 1949. India had restricted West Indies to a 1-0 lead after four games, and could draw the series by winning the final Test. India had just returned from Australia playing their first tour after Independence, a five-Test series in 1947–48. Lala's men had lost four of those games to

Bradman's Invincibles and also endured the trauma of Mahatma Gandhi's assassination just before they played the final Test in Melbourne. Daunting as it was, that Australian tour had notable benefits and some wonderful feats that gave cause for hope. Hazare, with a century in each innings at Adelaide, announced himself as among the most accomplished batsmen in the world. Among the youngsters, 23-year-old Dattatreya Gajanan Phadkar, a tall and handsome all-rounder, made a name for himself by first forcing his way into the team, then opening the bowling for India and also providing spine to the middle order with forthright batting. Along with Mankad, he formed a bowling combination that was both workhorse-like and wicket-taking. This home Test series against the Windies though, was, not without reason, being labelled a battle between two strong batting sides and two relatively weak bowling sides. Everton Weekes had showed how formidable he was by carrying forward his form from a preceding tour of England. After a hundred in the final Test against England, Weekes knocked three hundreds in the first three Tests against India and could have had a fifth consecutive ton but was run out on 90. For India, Hazare carried on from where he left off, scoring 543 runs with two centuries in this series.

On 4 February 1949, the two teams squared off at the lovely Brabourne Stadium for the final Test. John Goddard, the West Indies captain, won the toss for the fifth consecutive Test; just the fourth time in cricket history that a captain had won five tosses in a row. It was a good toss to win, and Goddard chose to bat first. Theirs was a solid line-up, and the thought of Clyde Walcott and Weekes at No. 3 and No. 4 was daunting. But young Phadkar swung the new ball extraordinarily well to quickly get rid of Allan Rae and the redoubtable Clyde Walcott. It is no secret that India had a very ordinary fielding side, but by some divine benediction, India got its first breakthrough when the difficult chance that Rae gave went to Mushtaq Ali. Now, Ali was not only a cavalier batsman but also India's best fielder, and he took that sharp catch at short-leg. Walcott's wicket was special and the effusive cricket correspondent of *The Hindu* described it thus: 'Walcott, after a lucky snick through the slips, was bowled by a magnificent ball from Phadkar, who hurled himself into this delivery like a human catapult. The ball swung out very late, made lightning pace off the wicket, and uprooted the offstump, with Walcott having shaped to meet it between the middle and the legstumps… it was a rare ball. Walcott said later that if that ball should come again he would be out once more.'

Although the stylish Jeffrey Stollmeyer hit 85, the West Indians were forced to earn every one of their 286 runs. Phadkar, Mankad and Ghulam did most of the bowling and got nine of the ten wickets between them. Their fielders let them down yet again as at least three catches were dropped, the costliest being the ones off Stollmeyer. Weekes too profited and helped himself to a half-century before falling to the off spin of Ghulam. Amidst all this, India's wicketkeeper Probir 'Khokhan' Sen dislocated his shoulder and Lala donned the gloves. How versatile he was, for in this match he bowled, batted, captained and also kept wickets. Lala would in fact snap up three catches behind the stumps in the innings!

Having done well to dismiss the Windies for 286, India surrendered substantial ground when they folded up for just 196 in their first innings. Every batsman in the impressive line-up – Mushtaq, Lala, Hazare, Modi and Mankad – got out after getting starts. In a terse description of Hazare's knock, *The Hindu* called it a bad dream. On the other hand, Lala made a sparkling start to his innings but was bowled by fast bowler John Trim's pace. Mankad too looked in good touch but ran himself out needlessly. Phadkar, after making 25, was another victim of Trim's vicious off-cutter that uprooted his legstump. Wicketkeeper Sen was not fit to bat and India's first innings were finished. With a lead of close to 100, West Indies tried to grind India out of the match by batting long in their second innings. By end of day three, the Windies had a lead of 245 with seven wickets in hand.

On the fourth day, India, marshalled shrewdly by Lala, battled hard. They began the day well and took three wickets for just 40 runs. Mankad pegged away with his left-arm spin while Phadkar and debutant Shute

Banerjee kept at it from the other end with pace. But Allan Rae, the opener, hung on and went into his 90s while Goddard, in the words of Gurunathan, 'presented a barn-door defence and was difficult to dislodge'. When the Windies were finally done on the fourth evening, they had scored 267, a potentially match-winning position. India had to get 361 runs or survive 395 minutes.

They began terribly, and were 9 for 2 in no time. Amarnath joined Modi, one of India's finest middle-order batsmen, to rousing cheers from the large crowd. Lala launched a thrilling counter-attack with a couple of daring late-cuts, a sparkling cover-drive and another lovely offside boundary, racing to 39, when a beautiful ball from Denis Atkinson took his offstump. In walked Vijay Samuel Hazare and soon the day's play ended, with India 90 for 3.

What unfolded on the final day made this match memorable. S.K. Gurunathan, describing the start of that final day in *Sport & Pastime* of 12 February 1949, wrote, 'Every inch of available place was taken up when the match was resumed on Tuesday morning and the Brabourne Stadium looked amphitheatrical.' What a show Hazare and Modi put up on the morning of the final day! They were solid, firm and assertive and in the two hours to lunch they added 85 runs. Seeing their assured batting, Lala sensed a chance for a famous win and sent in a chit to Modi saying, 'We are behind the clock', exhorting him to score faster.

After lunch, both players opened out with a flurry of boundaries. Their century partnership was rich in self-belief and by the time Modi left for a wonderfully made 86, India had reached 221, requiring just 140 runs with six wickets in hand. Sujit Mukherjee recalls, 'On that unbearably tense morning of the last day of the final Test at Bombay, he matched Hazare stroke by stroke in India's great bid to win.'

Meanwhile, Hazare batted and batted – to his century and more. Hazare was a man of few words, but his dry humour was very much evident. He once said, 'It was in 1915 that cricket lost two of its legends in W.G. Grace and Victor Trumper. Maybe they decided to wind up their innings on hearing that I had arrived into the world!' Hazare had already brought the cricketing world's attention upon himself when he hit centuries in both innings in Adelaide. He lost the best years of his cricketing life to World War II. By the time he made his debut for India in 1946, he was 31. Yet, in the seven years and 30 Tests that he played, Hazare scored over 2,000 runs at an average of over 47 with seven tons and nine half-centuries.

Chandu Borde was Hazare's foremost pupil and it was natural that we asked Borde about his mentor. Borde, now past 80 but with a clear recall, was only too happy to do so. As a young cricketer, Borde went to Baroda and stayed at Hazare's home for a year while training with him and playing Ranji Trophy for Baroda. Two things remained etched in his mind: Hazare always middled every ball and was rarely beaten even if the pitch was not good; and although past 41 and retired from Test cricket, Hazare would himself every evening, without fail, clean his shoes, bat, pads and kit. Borde said that when he was India's captain in the 1967 Adelaide Test, it was a tradition for the visiting skipper to sit next to the chairman of the Australian Board. At that time it was Sir Don Bradman and the first thing Bradman asked Borde, was, 'How is Mr Hazare?' Such was the esteem in which Bradman held Hazare. Hazare had monumental patience and unfailing courtesy. Sledging was prevalent even in those days, but Hazare would never retaliate; only his bat would do the talking. Borde rounded off the tribute with this gem: 'Services are playing Baroda at Motibagh Ground, and Col. Adhikari is their captain. You know the military people, they plan everything pucca. They had a plan for Hazare. We were 24 for 2 and when Hazare came, Adhikari told their fast bowler Surendranath to bowl a bouncer on offstump first ball. Surendranath bowled that ball as planned, Hazare mistimed the hook and the catch went to mid-on. Unfortunately, the fielder dropped it. Adhikari went to the fielder and said, "Major, do not feel sad you dropped the catch. Hazare will give you another catch but after he has scored 200 runs." And that is what actually happened!'

Hazare was a fighter, and his 122 in this match was a fighting innings too. He was steely of resolve, and even as he was pushing back the West

Indians, he was taking India closer to victory. To understand the way Hazare played, one can do no better than read Sujit Mukherjee's book, *The Romance of Indian Cricket*. In a detailed analysis of Hazare's batsmanship, Mukherjee wrote, 'Like a piece of precise long-range artillery, he moved inch by inch into position before firing the next accurate salvo.'

Those were the days when 'mandatory overs' had not been conceived. There was also no rule that a minimum number of overs should be bowled in a day. So in essence, it was the sporting conscience of the fielding side that determined the spirit of the game. Sporting captains bowled their overs without resorting to any dilatory tactics, while some were not above such gamesmanship if it gave them even a tiny advantage. At Brabourne that evening, West Indian skipper John Goddard encouraged these tactics. Gurunathan in his report noted, 'Prior Jones was barracked by the crowd for bowling outside the legstump and twice Jones did not complete his bowling action after running up to the crease!' Hazare, recalling the negative tactics, said, 'Walcott, the wicketkeeper of all people, went to the fine-leg boundary to fetch a ball. One can understand the old cricketing adage that if a match cannot be won it must not be lost. But no side is supposed to violate all canons of fair play.' Steven Lynch, coming upon the unpublished diary of Jeffrey Stollmeyer, wrote a delightful essay describing Stollmeyer's contempt for his captain. Drawing from jottings in the diary, he remarked, 'There are frequent digs about Goddard's captaincy style, particularly his tendency to let the game drift: at one point our indisposed diarist hurries down to the boundary from the cool of the dressing room to suggest some tactical changes, and elsewhere he implores Goddard to instruct the batsmen to get a move on.' How different all this was from the sporting spirit that the West Indians would display under Frank Worrell, immortalized by the way they played the final overs of the famous tied Test in Brisbane.

With the score at 285, and India 76 short of the target, Hazare was bowled attempting a big hit off Jones. His dismissal was the turning point. India lost its seventh and eighth wickets in quick succession, still 40 short of victory. With the injured Sen unlikely to bat, Ghulam Ahmed and Phadkar were effectively India's last pair at the crease. With the evening shadows lengthening, Phadkar, robust of method, fearless and clear in mind, was going for the runs. Incredibly, the pair put on 34 runs, almost all of them from Phadkar's blade, and the crowd was on its feet, cheering every run.

Despite Goddard's tactics, India reached 355 for 8, just 6 runs from victory. Then in an act as bizarre as tearing off the last three pages of a whodunit, Mohoni and Joshi, the umpires, called off play with two minutes still remaining. Apparently they were overwhelmed by the unbearable tension of the climax, but it was an inexcusable error. As the players trooped back, the crowd booed the West Indians for their negative tactics and some of their catcalls were also reserved for the umpires. Indians had to accept that their first-ever Test victory had not yet been achieved. What would we not give to know what Lala told the umpires when they came back!

This match was an early indicator that Indian teams in the future would regularly make a real fist of big targets in the fourth innings. Indian cricket history has more than a handful of valorous fourth innings. Lala's men had shown the way. Over the next few decades, as India did much better in its second innings on a number of occasions, it became a common joke to say that India ought to play their second innings first!

Test No. 311: Brabourne Stadium, Bombay, 4–8 February 1949: **West Indies** (Toss) 286 in 104.2 overs (Jeff Stollmeyer 85, Everton Weekes 56; Dattu Phadkar 4-74, Vinoo Mankad 3-54) and 267 in 107.3 overs (Allan Rae 97, Weekes 48; Shute Banerjee 4-54, Mankad 3-77) drew with **India** 192 in 88.4 overs (Vijay Hazare 40, Rusi Modi 33; John Trim 3-69, Gerry Gomez 2-30) and 355/8 in 107 overs (Hazare 122, Modi 86; Prior Jones 5-85).

Captains: Lala Amarnath (India) and John Goddard (West Indies)

2

Beating the World's Best

India vs Australia, second Test, Green Park, Kanpur, 1959

Richie Benaud, terrific statesman-captain and all-rounder, was also blessed to radiate good cheer. And so when the Australians came to play a five-match series in 1959–60, all of India prepared as though it were a carnival. The elder between us was 13, a budding left-hander who idolized Neil Harvey. The younger was just three years old at that time, blissfully unaware. Yet when he started following cricket a few years later and was gifted a whole pile of photographs from sports magazines for his cricket scrapbook by his kindly school teacher, the best pictures in that pile were the amazing close-up photographs from this tour: Norman O'Neill playing the on-drive, Umrigar buckling up his pads, Gordon Rorke and his infamous dragging foot at the bowling crease. Little wonder that even photographers caught up with the spirit of the series when it came to capturing warm and cheerful vignettes of Benaud and his team.

Indian cricket needed this tonic. The preceding few years had been awful: a sorry spectacle of four captains for five Tests against West Indies at home in 1958–59; a 3-0 drubbing at their hands; an unseemly atmosphere of palace intrigue and whimsical selections; then losing every match in England in the summer of 1959 to the pace of Trueman and the seam and swing of Statham.

Now in the winter of 1959, Benaud's team arrived as overwhelming favourites, after annihilating England 4-0 in the Ashes. Benaud's team had a formidable line-up in Neil Harvey, Norman O'Neill, Colin McDonald, Les Favell, Alan Davidson, Ian Meckiff, Ray Lindwall, Lindsay Kline, Wally Grout, Peter Burge and Ken Mackay. The sturdy Gulabrai Ramchand had been nominated India's captain for the series and allied forces with Lala Amarnath, the chairman of selectors now, to form a team. Lala was not merely the chairman of selectors but a hands-on strategist. He travelled with the team, and was at the ground every day, watching and observing and would not hesitate to give his inputs to Ramchand. Ramchand was more than a bits-and-pieces all-rounder. He was an attacking batsman and a businesslike medium pacer endowed with a cricketing brain. His demeanour was much like an army major's – well built, upright, confident, moustache, firm handshake and brisk of intent. N.S. Ramaswami in *From Porbander to Wadekar* pronounced: 'Ramchand, a rugged cricketer, fought to the last ball.'

The series began badly for India as they were trounced in the first Test at Feroz Shah Kotla by an innings. There seemed to be no light at the end of the tunnel. India had now gone through more than three years and 14 Tests without a win, and also lost 11 of those. The Indians had folded up for just 138 in the first innings and 206 in the second innings. While India's batting showed no spine, their bowling seemed toothless. The signs were ominous.

The caravan moved to Kanpur for the second Test. The selectors retained faith in the batting of Roy, Contractor, Umrigar, Borde and Baig but made three interesting changes. They brought in Naren Tamhane as the keeper in place of P.G. 'Nana' Joshi. The young promising fast bowler Ramakant Desai made way for Ramnath Kenny to strengthen the batting and Lala's very own masterstroke was to bring in 35-year-old Jasubhai Patel, the off spinner, in place of the Services cricketer V.M. Muddiah. Green Park had a newly laid turf pitch that Lala believed would turn. Second, he felt that the Aussies would find an off spinner more difficult to handle. Yet, Jasu Patel? He was a rabbit out of the hat, but Lala reckoned his accurate flat offbreaks were best suited to this Green Park track.

Patel had sporadically played four Tests previously with moderate success. He would go on to play only two more Test matches after Kanpur. In all, he played only seven Test matches spread over five years and took 29 wickets. But of these, he took 14 at Kanpur! One monumental performance and he was catapulted to folklore for all time.

When the Kanpur Test began, the early indications were of one more rout. Ramchand won the toss and batted first, but the Indians made a mess of their first innings, collapsing for just 152. From 38 for 1, it was a regular procession. Roy, Contractor, Baig, Borde, Ramchand and Nadkarni all got starts but did not go on to score anything substantial. Davidson took 5 for 31 and Benaud 4 for 63 as the Indians were rolled over in just 70 overs. In reply, as Australia raced away to a good start, it began to look like a repeat of the first Test. McDonald and Harvey were batting comfortably and crossed their fifties.

It was at this stage that the 'miracle at Kanpur' began. Lala, puffing away at his pipe outside the ground, observed that Patel was bowling from the 'wrong' end. He wanted Patel to bowl from the other end into the footmarks outside the right-handers' offstump, left by the spikes of the Aussie left-arm fast bowlers Davidson and Meckiff. Lala got his chance to talk to Ramchand when the players came back to the pavilion for lunch, with Australia 128 for 1.

Ramchand effected that change immediately upon resumption, and the game turned upside down in the matter of a few overs. Patel clean bowled McDonald first, 128 for 2. The stylish right-hander O'Neill joined the left-handed Harvey and they pushed the score to 149. Old-timers who heard the commentary swear that in the time it took them to return from the restroom, the score had collapsed to 149 for 5. First, Harvey was bowled by Patel. In the following over, O'Neill stepped out to drive Borde and was beaten and bowled. Then, 'Slasher Mackay' fell lbw to Patel. From there, the innings subsided without even a whimper. Patel took the next five wickets in a row; he needed no assistance for four of them as he clean bowled Davidson, Benaud and Lindsay Kline and trapped Barry Jarman leg before. Only for the wicket of Gordon Rorke did he need the help of Abbas Ali Baig to take the catch. Bowling 35.5 overs, Jasu Patel had taken 9 for 69! Australia's last nine wickets had fallen for just 91 runs, and Patel had taken eight of those wickets bowling from the end Lala had suggested. Jimmy Amarnath told us, 'I am not speaking as his son, but as a fellow cricketer. Lala was very knowledgeable, positive and a great judge of the game. He was outspoken, confident, a strong personality and his cricketing acumen was marvellous. People looked up to him, they listened to him.'

The previous season against the formidable West Indies, Subhash Gupte, one of the greatest legspinners in the history of the game, had taken 9 for 102. When we spoke to Borde about Jasu Patel's nine-wicket haul, the veteran first paid tribute to Gupte's magic: 'You should have been there in Kanpur in 1958. On a placid wicket in Kanpur, against a very strong West Indian side, he made the batsmen dance. 9 for 102. I'll never forget that day. Patel could not have emulated a more distinguished bowler.'

Despite Patel's magical spell, Australia still had a lead of 67 runs as India began their second innings. Pankaj Roy and Nari Contractor carefully negotiated the new ball and India ended the second day at 31 for no loss. They were still 36 runs behind Australia and would have to bat really well the next day. After Roy was dismissed, Umrigar stayed with Contractor till the deficit was wiped out, but departed immediately afterwards, falling to Davidson. Abbas Ali Baig now joined Contractor. Baig had become a sensation by scoring a ton on debut at Manchester earlier that summer. Later in this series, a girl would come running on to the ground to kiss this batting star. So here was this handsome 20-year-old, the youngest Indian to hit a century, an Oxford Blue, joining forces with Contractor to keep Australia at bay. The two batsmen were building the Indian second innings patiently, when the left-handed opener was out to a freak catch by Harvey off Davidson. As the batsman pulled a short delivery, Harvey turned around at short-leg to avoid injury, and the ball stuck between his legs. When Contractor was dismissed for 74, India was 121 for 3, and in effect, ahead by only 54 runs. Twenty-six runs later, Baig fell for 36 to the wiles of Benaud. Skipper Ramchand followed immediately and India was once again floundering, five wickets gone and a lead of just 86 runs. At this stage, Lala's second selectorial change proved his worth. Ramnath Kenny came to the crease to join Borde. Kenny's presence was most reassuring and the two forged a valiant partnership. A little before close of play, Borde fell to Meckiff and India ended the day at 226 for 6, a lead of 149 with Kenny and Nadkarni at the crease. Next day, these two batsmen proved to be priceless. Englishmen refer to Trevor Bailey as the 'Barnacle' in recognition of his obdurate occupation of the crease. Nadkarni was every bit as stubborn in his batting while his bowling was miserly. That day, Nadkarni scored 46, Kenny scored 51 and the two took the score to 286 before being separated. Shortly thereafter, the innings ended for 291. India had batted a marathon 144 overs. The big, broad Davidson had bowled a massive 57 overs, mostly slow orthodox left-arm spin on a wearing wicket, very effectively (like his predecessor Bill Johnstone used to do for Bradman) to return figures of 7 for 93, finishing with 12 wickets in the match. Since he had also scored a fighting 40 in their first-innings collapse, this was a great all-round effort from the big man and was perhaps a forerunner to his performance in the tied Test against West Indies in Brisbane next year, where he scored 44 and 80 and took 11 wickets. Davidson, people say, was a bit of a hypochondriac but he and Benaud had a special relationship. Davidson would do anything for Benaud.

The Aussies faced a target of 225 in the fourth innings on a wearing wicket. Surendranath and Ramchand bowled a few perfunctory overs with the new ball before Ramchand called on Jasu Patel and Umrigar, both bowling offbreaks. Before play ended on the fourth day, Patel had dismissed Stevens and Umrigar had got the vital wicket of the dangerous Harvey, caught by Nadkarni at slip, as the ball broke away sharply from the left-hander at an ideal length. The day ended with India needing eight wickets and the Australians requiring 169 runs. It seemed that the match would go all the way to the wire on the fifth day. S.K. Gurunathan described Harvey's dismissal with great relish but ended his dispatch with the words, 'There is yet O'Neill.'

The next day, even as spectators were just settling into their seats, O'Neill was gone, caught by Nadkarni at leg-slip off a sharply turning offbreak from Umrigar. Nadkarni was India's best close-catcher before the famous days of India's close-in cordon of Solkar, Venkat, Abid Ali and Wadekar. Stationed at slip or leg-slip to the spinners, Nadkarni held quite a few catches but perhaps none as important as the two he took at Kanpur. Continuing his memories of the match, Borde, thrifty as ever with superlatives, told us, 'Nadkarni was a safe close-in fielder. Don't ask me if those two catches were difficult. Every catch is important and those two catches were very important.' We reminded him that Patel might have taken all 10 wickets in the first innings if Borde had not claimed the wicket of O'Neill. He laughed and said, 'I think I bowled him with a googly or faster one. There is no clip on the Internet. I just cannot remember, baba!' Incidentally, Borde peaked as a bowler against Dexter's MCC in 1961 and in tandem with Durani, bowled India to victories in the last two tests. Borde had a funny action – left arm raised to the sky and hop, hop, hop on his right foot before delivery. Unfortunately, he picked up an injury to his shoulder and that curtailed his bowling career.

Within no time, Davidson, Benaud, Jarman and Kline had been dismissed, and a short while later the match was over. Indeed, that final morning, it was a procession. Borde narrated this gem: 'The Australians were staying with industrial magnate Singhania in his mansion. It had a swimming pool. Many Australian players were relaxing in the swimming pool on the final morning when they got the message that wickets were falling. They literally rushed to the ground in their towels.' We were

The triumphant Indian Test team who beat the stro ng Australians by 119 runs in the Kanpur Test. (Top row): G. S. Ramchand (captain), P. R. Umrigar, P. Roy and N. J. Contractor. (Centre row): A. A. Baig, C. G. Borde and R. B. Kenny. (Bottom row): Jasu Patel, N. S. Tamhane, R. G. Nadkarni and R. Surendernath.

INDIA'S GREAT TRIUMPH IN KANPUR TEST

———◆———

PATEL AND UMRIGAR SKITTLE AUSTRALIA OUT FOR 105

From S. K. Gurunathan

KANPUR Dec 24

Patel this morning claimed four wickets for 23 runs, while Umrigar obtained his three wickets for 17 runs. Both bowled superbly, taking advantage of the wicket as well as motion.

To Ramchand, who has been a fighter all his career, has thus fallen the unique honour of leading India to victory against the redoubtable and champion cricketing country, Australia. Captaincy is something which cannot be described. It can only be seen and

THE SCORE-BOARD

The Hindu, *perhaps for the first time, carried a sports story on its front page with a full banner headline, 'India's great triumph in Kanpur Test'. (Used with permission from Kasturi & Sons.)*

travelling that morning from Madras to Nellore, a drive of just a few hours, and as we halted midway for a coffee, we found out the match was over well before lunch. The innings had lasted just 57.4 overs. Apart from those first few overs with the new ball, Patel and Umrigar had bowled unchanged. Patel finished with 5 for 55 and Umrigar with 4 for 27. Australia had been bundled out for 105 and the Indians had recorded their finest victory ever, beating the world's best side by a comprehensive margin of 119 runs. Jasubhai Patel, that off spinner from the textile town of Ahmedabad who had been called suddenly to play this Test, had match figures of 14 for 124. Borde recalled, 'Overnight dew had freshened the wicket. Patel bowled beautifully. Apart from offbreaks, he was cutting the ball away.'

It was not India's first win, but all their previous wins in the past 27 years had been against a fledgling Pakistan, a second-string MCC and a weak New Zealand. This was therefore India's finest win at the time, achieved against an all-conquering Australia. *The Hindu*, perhaps for the first time, carried a sports story on its front page with a full banner headline, 'India's great triumph in Kanpur Test', and for good measure also printed photographs of all 11 members of the victorious team. When Ramchand passed away in 2011, Yajurvindra Singh wrote a moving tribute to the stalwart: 'A few months ago Ramchand showed me his cricket album after a fair amount of persuasion. He was particularly proud of a photograph that showed him being showered with garlands of marigold after India beat Australia for the first time in 1959 at Kanpur in the second of a five-Test series that would be Ramchand's only stint as captain. The joy and satisfaction on his face sent a frisson of excitement down my spine.'

What this win meant for Indian cricket can be gauged when one reads two excerpts of the match, one written the day India won and the other 40 years later. S.K. Gurunathan, flush with excitement after the win, wrote, 'Kanpur has effaced old memories of other defeats. People who witnessed the match, when they grow old, will talk of this victory with eyes lighted.' Partab Ramchand, a veteran journalist, reminisced 40 years later: 'To old-timers like me and to keen cricket followers of a later generation, the mere mention "Kanpur, 1959" will make eyes sparkle, even though a full four decades have elapsed since that memorable day.'

Test No. 483: Green Park, Kanpur, 19–24 December 1959: India (Toss) 152 in 70.1 overs (Bapu Nadkarni 25, Nari Contractor 24, Gulabrai Ramchand 24; Alan Davidson 5-31, Richie Benaud 4-63) and 291 in 144.3 overs (Contractor 74, Ramnath Kenny 51; Davidson 7-93) beat **Australia** 219 in 77.5 overs (Colin McDonald 53, Neil Harvey 51; Jasu Patel 9-69) and 105 in 57.4 overs (McDonald 34, Harvey 25; Jasu 5-55, Polly Umrigar 4-27) by 119 runs.

Captains: Gulabrai Ramchand (India) and Richie Benaud (Australia)

3

Cliffhanger

India vs Australia, second Test, Brabourne Stadium, Bombay, 1964

As transistor radios excitedly blared out the live commentary from Brabourne Stadium, every Indian cricket follower was hopping from one foot to the other as India crept agonizingly close. Finally, when Borde belted the winning runs, Patel Nagar in Delhi and Triplicane in Madras united in a crescendo with the 40,000 spectators, and millions of others who were listening intently. Bat aloft in triumph, Indrajitsinhji and Borde ran back to the pavilion, as the entire stadium gave them a standing ovation that never seemed to stop. K.S. Indrajitsinhji was the most unlikely supporting hero for this edge-of-the-seat thriller. If he had not played in this Test, even diehard cricket fanatics in India would have found it difficult to recall his name. It is the glorious turn of the fortune wheel that even 50 years later, a man who scored a modest 23 and 3 not out in a game is remembered! Kumar Shri Madhavsinhji Jadeja Indrajitsinhji, for that was his princely name, was a grand-nephew of Ranjitsinhji and a nephew of Duleepsinhji. He was an above-average wicketkeeper-batsman, but his playing days unluckily coincided with those of Farokh Engineer and Budhi Kunderan, which meant that he played for India only when these two players were injured or unavailable.

Of the four Tests that he played, three were in the 1964 series against Bobby Simpson's Australia.

After five days of pulsating cricket, India were 224 for 8 chasing 254 for victory, when our supporting hero joined Chandu Borde. As Borde ratcheted up a flurry of runs, Indrajitsinhji, a competent batsman in first-class cricket but untried at the highest level, put his head down and kept his end safe. There was only Chandrasekhar to follow and the whole world knew that Chandra was the quintessential No. 11. So everything depended on this ninth-wicket pair. How nerve-racking as well as pleasurable this victory was can be gauged from the ingenuous report by P.N. Sundaresan for *The Hindu*: 'As one sits limp and tired after one of the most throbbing day's play, one feels unequal to the task of describing the tense, bitter struggle that Pataudi and his side waged against superlative fielding, accurate bowling and a turning wicket till final success came.'

This match was the second of a three-Test series hastily put together as Australia returned home from their Ashes series in England. India had lost the first Test in Madras after fighting all the way. We watched from the stands as India matched the Aussies every step of the way on the first four days. We can never forget how Nadkarni and Durani spun Australia out in their first innings. At the end of the first innings, India had a lead of 65 runs. Talking to us one evening in 2008, Durani went down memory lane, his face lighting up as he described the first innings: 'Flat, dead Nehru Stadium first day wicket, Nadkarni and I just ran through them. We reduced Australia from 99 for no loss to 211 all out. They were unable to pick my change of pace and length.' But the Aussies, helped hugely by their lower order, did very well in their second innings and set India a target of 333 runs. Disconsolate, we watched India capitulate and lose by 139 runs.

A lot of talk leading up to the second Test was about the new brick-laid pitch at Brabourne Stadium. It was a reddish-tinged strip without a blade of grass and no one was sure how it would behave over the five

days. Whoever won the toss would bat first. Bob Simpson won the toss
and batted first. And soon it was clear that the pitch was benign and
amiable for batting.

Australia, by mid-day, however, were stuttering. India had a huge
stroke of luck when Norman O'Neill fell ill immediately after the
match began and could not bat in either innings. Australia thus were
reduced to playing with ten men. Chandrasekhar bowled superbly
and claimed Brian Booth and Bob Simpson with his flipper, which
the batsmen failed to spot. At 53 for 3 the 35,000-strong crowd was
in a happy mood. Peter Burge, the Queenslander coming off a strong
century that helped Australia win the Ashes in England, however, had
other ideas. He played Chandra with care but was brutal with the other
bowlers. He was a well-built aggressive batsman and his straight-drives
were like pistol shots while his cover-drives left fielders standing. He
had raced to 80 in quick time and a century was his for the asking
when Chandra superbly caught him on the square-leg boundary off
a full-blooded pull that he played against Borde. With his dismissal,
Australia were five down for 146 and in strife again. That is when
the pair of all-rounder Tom Veivers, riding on the confidence of his
earlier innings in Madras, and wicketkeeper-batsman Barry Jarman
took charge and put up a terrific 151-run partnership for the sixth
wicket before Jarman was dismissed just before stumps. At close of
play, Australia had recovered to a healthy 301 for 6, which for those
days was a very good run rate. Sundaresan, reporting for *The Hindu*,
described this crisply: 'Twice during a splendid day's cricket India
struck sharp blows, but on both occasions Australia fought back and
restored its position, not by stubborn methods but by a forthright
attack on the bowling.'

Chandra and Nadkarni polished off the last three wickets (O'Neill
was not fit to bat) next morning and Australia finished with a score of
320. When India batted, they tested the patience of the crowd with
their dour and defensive approach. After losing Sardesai and Durani

(30 for 2), Manjrekar and Jaisimha closed down the hatches. They put on 112 runs before Veivers, bowling offbreaks, dismissed the duo after tea. In the last hour, Hanumant Singh and Pataudi played excruciatingly slowly – just 33 runs from the last 29 overs of the day – as India ground to 178 for 4 at the end of the second day's play. People trickled out of Brabourne in a sour mood.

The third morning belonged to a transformed Pataudi. He was in an attacking, confident mood and changed the tone and tenor of the match. Though Hanumant Singh and Borde were dismissed cheaply, Pataudi found an able ally in left-handed Rusi Surti. Pataudi, from 1964 till 1968, was brilliantly consistent and led from the front. Whether it was Delhi, Madras, Leeds or Melbourne, he was imperious against pace and spin. When one considers that Pataudi played almost all his Test cricket with one eye, one can only marvel at the man. Yet, Tiger made light of this and would modestly brush off the praise that people heaped on him. While reiterating this, V. Ramnarayan, Pataudi's teammate in the Hyderabad team, in his book *Third Man,* also adds, 'In rare moments, he however admitted that with two eyes he might have equalled the great batsmen of the game.'

Here at Bombay, Pataudi led the way with 86, and though the crowd was disappointed that Graham McKenzie caught him at mid-wicket just 14 short of his century, they applauded him as he walked back to the pavilion. Sundaresan wrote, 'For the first time the Stadium crowd had seen the Nawab in full splendour and it gave him a royal ovation.'

The team that Pataudi commanded was a talented bunch. They could bat down to No. 10 (our friend Indrajitsinhji). Jaisimha and Manjrekar had contributed patient and responsible fifties, Pataudi had struck 86 and the lower middle order of Surti, Nadkarni and Indrajitsinhji, who batted with a plaster over his right eye after suffering a cut while wicketkeeping, added valuable runs that helped India post 341, giving them a lead of 21 runs. The Australian openers quickly wiped off this deficit and by the end of the third day, the visitors were 112 for 1 – a lead of 91 runs with nine wickets in hand. Not a bad position to be in, with the added advantage of bowling last on a newly laid pitch.

Though India had not bowled well on the third evening, Pataudi knew he had a bowling combination with teeth. While pace was non-existent, his spin bowling resources were rich. Nadkarni and Durani, the left-arm spinners, were at the peak of their bowling prowess. Chandrasekhar, that wondrous legspinner, had arrived, and Chandu Borde's legspin was always effective. The bowlers were to do their skipper proud on the fourth day. The day began with Chandra striking twice, first claiming Bill Lawry leg before and then comprehensively bowling Peter Burge. Australia slipped to 121 for 3. The ball that bowled Burge was said to be the best leg break bowled till then, so we asked Raju Bharatan, perhaps the only living Indian journalist who has reported on cricket since 1951, to give us a first-hand account of this dismissal. Bharatan said, 'There is no knowing what Burge played for, but the ball was pitched up on or around leg. From there it leg-broke like a viper to take the top of the offstump. Peter Burge put up his right hand in acknowledgement of Chandra having got him with a gem. It is a sight etched in my mind-frame. A word with Burge, later, revealed that the ball made such haste, off the pitch, that it was all over before the burly Aussie could get down his bat.'

Chandra had made his debut the previous year, pitchforked into Tests, at the age of 18, as people saw in him a match-winning bowler. In his book *The Covers Are Off*, Rajan Bala quotes Pataudi telling him that after facing Chandra for the first time in 1963 in a domestic tournament he felt '(Chandra) was the most incredible bowler (he) had faced till then'. When India forged its famous spin quartet, Chandra was the one whom batsmen feared the most.

But after Chandra's twin strikes, there followed a period of over two and a half hours when the fleet footed vice-captain Brian Booth and Bob Cowper – not half as elegant as Booth but of equal determination – put up a partnership of 125 runs. Australia were now in a position of strength, for at 246 for 3, they had a lead of 225 with seven wickets in hand. It was at this point that the innings unspooled most dramatically as Chandra and Nadkarni combined to destroy the rest of the batting for just 30 runs. First Nadkarni got rid of Cowper. Then Chandra dismissed Veivers and Jarman, who had proved to be a nuisance in earlier innings, for ducks. Sundaresan provided an insight into the thought that went into Chandra's bowling: 'He followed two flighted deliveries with his quicker one and Veivers was trapped lbw. Two more flighted balls followed by a similar quick one and Jarman's stumps were wrecked.' Nadkarni then polished off the innings, claiming the last three wickets – Booth stumped by Indrajitsinhji and then McKenzie and Johnny Martin caught by Rusi Surti. The defining difference between this Test in Bombay and the previous game in Madras was that while at the Nehru Stadium India had allowed Australia to recover from 237 for 6 to 397, here at Brabourne, they bundled out Australia from 246 for 3 to 274 all out. Chandra had eight wickets in this match, an even four in both innings. Quite deservedly, *The Hindu* carried the headline 'Nadkarni and Chandrasekhar spin out Australia'.

India now needed 254 to win. Time was not a problem as they had more than a day to score these runs but fourth innings targets are always tricky. India created problems for themselves as they began the chase badly, losing Jaisimha for a duck. Durani and Sardesai seemed to have restored order by taking India to 70 for 1. But Durani, after a graceful 31, gave his wicket away to Simpson's legbreak and then Nadkarni, sent in as nightwatchman, failed in that task as he was dismissed by Veivers. Pataudi sent another nightwatchman, Surti, to see out the day. India now needed 180 runs to win on the final day, with seven wickets in hand. The target might not have looked large but Sundaresan in his dispatch tempered the hopes of his readers by saying: 'The pitch is dusty and taking turn and Simpson will spearhead his attack with his stocky off spinner, Veivers. It will certainly not be an easy job for the home team.'

Forty-five thousand spectators packed into Brabourne Stadium on the fifth day in a holiday mood, for it was the Hindu festival day of Dussehra (Vijayadashami). The vibrancy and heightened excitement at the grounds in India on festival days is indescribable and can only be felt or experienced. Many spectators, dressed in their best, came early to the stadium to watch the players at the nets before play began, such was their enthusiasm for the game. But Sundaresan's foreboding seemed to be coming true that morning and the crowd's good cheer evaporated into serious anxiety. India lost Surti, Sardesai (after making a valuable 56) and Hanumant Singh in quick succession to be left floundering at 122 for 6. The target suddenly seemed a lot farther away but it was at this stage that India's long batting line-up proved its worth. Even with six men back in the hut, India had Pataudi and Manjrekar at the crease, with Chandu Borde still to come. Was it some kind of intuitive move by Pataudi to keep his big guns for the end while releasing lesser batsmen like Nadkarni and Surti ahead? Manjrekar and his captain, batting beautifully and with a little luck, strung together the most invaluable partnership of 93 runs. Pataudi was emphatic that Manjrekar was the best Indian batsman of his time while Sujit Mukherjee declared that 'Manjrekar now remains the undisputed sovereign of Indian batsmen today'. In fulsome appreciation of Manjrekar, *The Hindu*'s correspondent asserted, 'With supreme confidence and a masterly defence he kept the Australians away and swung the fortunes again to his side... Like a solid oak he weathered the storms and stresses of the exciting day, unmoved and laid the foundations for victory. Throughout the combat between bat and ball, Manjrekar shone on a pedestal of his own.'

In a freewheeling chat with us, journalist Rajdeep Sardesai told us that his father Dilip idolized Vijay Manjrekar, and greatly admired his hooks and cuts. Ajit Wadekar in his autobiography said, 'No Bombay cricketer, who has made the grade in recent times, will deny the debt he owes Vijay Manjrekar for his help, encouragement and guidance.' Apart from his technical excellence, Manjrekar was a batsman of courage, something we could personally attest to.

On the final morning of the first Test at Madras, Manjrekar, who had injured his thumb while fielding, came out to bat because India was in trouble. He had cut off part of his glove since his swollen thumb could not go into the protective covering. We watched from the stands as Manjrekar played the rampaging McKenzie, injured thumb exposed, wincing with pain every time the ball hit the bat. He batted beautifully through the entire morning session but was finally dismissed at the stroke of lunch. Once Manjrekar left, the rest of the batting caved in.

Pataudi narrates another example of his courage. In the game at Barbados, in which Griffith felled Contractor, he also smashed Manjrekar's nose, who took no further part in that innings, but in the second innings, he hit a magnificent century. Pataudi wrote, 'As a fighting gesture, this must rate as one of the greatest I have been privileged to witness on the cricket field.' Manjrekar might have become a portly figure in his later years but he was a slim youth in 1952 when he toured England and faced 'Fiery' Trueman at his fastest. Borde, Contractor, Pataudi, Sardesai – all his contemporaries had seen him tackle the fastest bowling with aplomb and were certain he was technically the soundest Indian batsman of their time. In his younger days he was a wonderful hooker of the short-ball; knee trouble made him give up the hook and the pull and concentrate on the offside strokes. 'Tatt' Manjrekar could pierce the cordon with precision as he drew away and cut the off spinners with impunity time and again, however many fielders you placed in the point region. In his later years, since he could not throw due to a suspect shoulder, he lobbed underarm to the keeper from third-man and yet drew great cheers from the Chepauk and Brabourne crowd.

The score had moved to 215 for 6 and with just 39 to get, India seemed to be holding the upper hand when the pendulum swung again. In the space of nine runs, Alan Connolly dismissed both set batsmen

and suddenly India were 224 for 8, staring down the barrel, when the
unlikely pair of Borde and Indrajitsinhji stood resilient and registered
a rare victory against Australia. Borde had taken on the assertive role
in the partnership, playing his cuts and flick shots with confidence.
The crowd was wildly cheering every run. Describing that final victory
charge, the correspondent of *The Hindu* wrote, 'In the pavilion, Pataudi
was restless in his chair. But Indrajit defended an over from McKenzie...
then Veivers bowled to Borde who just patted down the first two balls.
He then lay back and square cut him to the boundary. The crowd rose
to its feet sensing victory. Borde moved swiftly down to the next ball
and clipped it to the unguarded mid-wicket region. As the ball was
speeding to the boundary Simpson and his men turned back towards
the pavilion and the crowd let go the biggest roar. India had won.' The
crowd could not have enough of their heroes who had pulled off this
great win and so the entire team went up to the balcony to wave to
the spectators. Rajdeep Sardesai remembers that his father's collection
of memorabilia has a lovely photograph of the team rejoicing on the
CCI balcony after the victory. Pataudi in *Tiger's Tale* stated, 'I regard
our victory by two wickets at Bombay as the most satisfying I've known
as India's captain.'

The newspapers in Australia were generous in their praise. Jack
Fingleton in a brief message from Canberra informed readers that
'India's win in the second Test over Australia was given wide publicity
in the Australian newspapers yesterday, despite the counter attractions
in Khrushchev's retirement, the British general elections and Olympic
Games.'

Borde, reliving those tense moments as he batted India to victory,
told us, 'The tension and stress is outside the ground. Once you step
in, you forget everything except the ball you face. Though I went in
seven-down, I was a top-order batsman and strokeplayer. My partner
Indrajitsinhji was an all-rounder, so he could bat too. We did not waste
scoring opportunities. Later many people told me that they were very

tense but I tell you the tension is more among the spectators than the players.' We asked Borde what was the thinking behind sending a top batsman at No. 9. Borde replied, 'Only Pat could have answered because he did not consult anybody when he sent two nightwatchmen. But it worked and we won, *na*? In our days we just followed instructions.'

Of Borde the cricketer, more must be said. Many in South India pronounced Borde as 'board' in his first few Tests, thinking the 'e' in his name was silent, till the commentators corrected them. His first appearance at Madras was against West Indies in his third Test. He scored a duck in the first innings and would have probably been dropped if he hadn't scored a lovely unbeaten 56 in the second, with some brilliant cuts, drives and flicks in that knock. As it transpired, this gave him a place in the final Test at Delhi, where he scored 109 and 96 and was regarded as a regular from then on. He became the backbone of India's middle order. Mentored by Hazare, he imbibed the sturdiness from his coach but retained his penchant for strokeplay. His technique was tight but he did not go into any period of self-denial. He scored over 3,000 runs in 55 Tests at an average of 36. He regaled home audiences but unlike his mentor, Borde could not do justice to his abilities abroad. He was also a good legspin bowler till a shoulder injury in 1964 curtailed his bowling. He was an excellent fielder too. Borde told us, 'Fielding was my first love. As a young boy at the club ground I would keep running around the boundary, picking and throwing back the hits because that was all I was allowed to do.' The memories of his strokeplay – the cuts and firm drives – are as fresh in our mind as though we saw him bat yesterday. After Manjrekar, he was India's most assured player of fast bowling. He was senior to Pataudi but once Pataudi became captain, Borde knew he must give up his dream to captain India. Borde captained India just once, at Adelaide in 1967, when Pataudi withdrew because of an injury. Later, in 1970, when the captaincy stakes opened up (Pataudi was on his way out and Merchant and his team of selectors were looking for a replacement), Borde briefly harboured some hopes. By then he was 36, and his best form was well behind him. As he failed in a couple of Duleep Trophy games, Borde knew that not only would he never get a chance to captain India, but he would never play for India again.

Test No. 567: Brabourne Stadium, Bombay, 10–15 October 1964: Australia (Toss) 320 in 103.5 overs (Peter Burge 80, Barry Jarman 78; Bhagwat Chandrasekhar 4-50, Bapu Nadkarni 2-65) and 274 in 99.4 overs (Bob Cowper 81, Brian Booth 74; Nadkarni 4-33, Chandrasekhar 4-73) lost to **India** 341 in 152.3 overs (M.A.K. Pataudi 86, M.L. Jaisimha 66; Tom Veivers 4-68, Alan Connolly 3-66) and 256/8 in 128.4 overs (Dilip Sardesai 56, Pataudi 53; Connolly 3-24, Graham McKenzie 2-43) by two wickets.

Captains: M.A.K. Pataudi (India) and Bobby Simpson (Australia)

4

Rising from the Dead

India vs New Zealand, third Test, Brabourne Stadium,
Bombay, 1965

Very few sides have come back to win after following-on to turn the tables. In over 2,200 Test matches, there have been just three instances. In 1894–95, England defeated Australia after being forced to follow-on; 86 years later, England won at Headingley in what came to be known as Botham's match, and then Kolkata 2001, etched in gold as the Laxman, Dravid and Harbhajan saga. One match that came within a whisker of creating such history was the India–New Zealand match in 1965 on a freshly laid Brabourne pitch. Shot out for under 100 and forced to follow-on, and under the cosh for three days, the Indians sprung a coup in the last few hours of the match.

Perhaps because the match ended in a draw, this Test is not easily recalled. Immortality may have eluded this game, but make no mistake, it had every twist and turn that has marked the most exciting Test matches. Played a full 50 years ago, this was a four-day Test and the third of a four-game series. It is wicked coincidence that three of the four Tests we've chosen from this period were all played in Bombay's Brabourne Stadium.

The visitors consumed 129 overs, while batting first, to put up 297 in laborious fashion. There were long somnambulant phases on the opening day, and the Kiwis were just 227 for 5 at stumps. Local boy Ramakant Desai, India's premier pace bowler, dismissed Sinclair and Bevan Congdon with sharp inswingers in the morning. Small built – hence his nickname Tiny – Desai had a smooth run-up, a lovely leap at the point of delivery and an effective bouncer. Pataudi in his *Tiger's Tale* recalls, 'The wicket, we found, at Bombay was the greenest and quickest ever produced at the Brabourne Stadium, and Desai welcomed these conditions with a good spell of fast bowling.' Ross Morgan came out to the middle at the fall of the second wicket and joined Graham Dowling, to first repair the damage with cautious defence and then, as the bowlers tired, build a good foundation. For once, Chandrasekhar was off the boil and he provided Morgan scoring opportunities off some short deliveries. The two put on a century but again went into a crawl, driving spectators into mid-afternoon torpor. By then Chandra had recovered his length, and off the last ball before tea he got rid of Morgan with a googly. Soon after, Bert Sutcliffe was run out as he could not make his ground after Dowling refused a single. Spectators who wanted to see Sutcliffe and John Reid bat were disappointed by their early dismissals. Sutcliffe, already 44 years old, and Reid in his late 30s, were in the winter of their careers and well past their best.

Meanwhile, the opener Dowling kept going at one end and batted through the day to score a dour century. Vic Pollard, the bits-and-pieces cricketer, his fifth-wicket partner, was intent on ensuring that nothing would enliven proceedings and the pair plodded to take the score to 227. With 20 minutes to go for stumps, Pataudi took the new ball and India dismissed Pollard off the last ball of the day. P.N. Sundaresan gave Pataudi credit for this dismissal in his report for *Sport & Pastime*: 'As the bowler slouched back to the top of his run, Pataudi made a clever move by posting Durani at silly mid-off to Pollard, who was obviously unhappy against swing. This did the trick, for the batsman showed his irritation by swishing wildly at the ball and edged it towards the slips.'

On the second day, India finished off the remaining five wickets for the addition of just 50 runs, thanks to an incisive spell by Desai who finished with six wickets for 55 runs in 25 overs. It left many wondering why the Indian selectors had ignored Desai during Australia's tour of India the previous year when he was clearly India's best new-ball bowler.

Having put the Test to sleep with their batting, New Zealand most unexpectedly shook it to life with their bowling. Well-built Dick Motz with his aggression and the talented Bruce Taylor with his pace, well supported by the utilitarian Bevan Congdon bundled India out for just 88. *Sport & Pastime*'s report of that day's play said, 'Motz and Taylor were really at our batsmen from the first ball. Jaisimha was the first victim of pace and tactics based upon speed.' Durani was rattled by a bouncer which he edged, Sardesai was consumed by one that moved away, and Hanumant Singh trod on his stumps when he went too far back to play a ball. Congdon bowled a beautiful off-cutter to the left-handed Nadkarni and by tea on that day, India were on their knees at 48 for 6. There was to be no respite after the break. Sundaresan summarized the sorry closure of India's innings: 'Any speculation as to whether India would avoid the follow-on ended within half an hour after tea, with the end of the innings at 88.' One can see an undercurrent of vexation in this tempered statement. It was a sorry procession and barring Borde, none of the batsmen stayed even briefly. India faced just 33 overs. Bruce Taylor, the tall all-rounder, had a fairy-tale start to his Test career. Just the previous week, he had made his debut against India at Eden Gardens and celebrated that with a century and 5 for 86. Now in his second match here in Bombay, he had a five-wicket haul in India's first innings. Few all-rounders have ever announced their arrival in such an emphatic fashion – a ton and a 'five for' in their first match and a 'five for' in their second match. Reid lost no time in telling Pataudi that he was enforcing the follow-on and immediately the New Zealanders piled on the agony by removing Farokh Engineer, who opened for India in the second innings. Sixteen wickets had fallen on the second day and India had lost 11 of them. Never had Brabourne seen so many dismissals in a day. It seemed there was only one way the Test could go.

The third day began badly for India once again. Taylor dismissed Durani as soon as play started, with Morgan taking his catch in the slips. No run had been added to the overnight score and India were now 18 for 2. It seemed curtains for India but this was when their incredible fight back began. Jaisimha joined Sardesai and stayed with him till India crossed 100. Valuable as that partnership was, India were still 100 runs adrift when Jaisimha was dismissed. Sundaresan pays tribute to the wicketkeeper and to the sporting spirit of Jai while describing the dismissal: 'A brilliantly anticipated catch by wicketkeeper Ward ended his stay. Ward darted across even as the batsman shaped for a glance and snapped up the catch off the bat. Jaisimha paid his tribute by walking away without waiting for the appeal to be upheld.' A collective sigh went up in the stadium as Jai walked off but they did not know that Dilip Narayan Sardesai would take it upon himself to play a monumental innings to ensure India's safety. Sardesai always had an appetite for big scores and demonstrated that best with his wonderful exploits in West Indies in 1971. Here, with India fighting to save the match, Sardesai was to provide more than a glimpse of what he would do six years later in West Indies.

Borde walked out to join Sardesai and the two batsmen then proceeded to bat India to safety. India first crossed the dreaded threshold of an innings defeat and once that ignominy was averted, Borde stepped up his scoring and completed a most enterprising century. The two complemented each other beautifully: Sardesai watchful and vigilant, Borde assertive and confident. They may have batted in the most contrasting styles but their value was in the long and unbroken partnership they put together. In praise of Borde's brilliant innings on that third day, Sundaresan wrote, 'Faultless to a point Borde's was really a superb knock... (He) found his touch with a springing cover-drive off Pollard. From that moment he kept everybody in the 30,000 crowd thrilled with a series of sparkling drives to cover and to straight field and rippling shots off his toes to mid-wicket. Played in a crisis, the high tone of his batsmanship lifted the heavy labour of recovery to one of great entertainment.' Rajdeep Sardesai told us that Dilip admired the way Borde played fast bowling. Sardesai, Borde and of course Manjrekar were also superb players of spin and in particular, played off spin brilliantly, drawing away and cutting whenever the bowler pitched even marginally short. When we asked Venkataraghavan to rewind 50 years back to this match, he was nostalgic: 'Sardesai and Borde batted brilliantly. You know, Sardesai could switch from defence to attack and he showed it in the next Test with a very fast hundred to set up a victory. And Borde was one of the best and I would say next only to Manjrekar in those days.'

When Borde was finally dismissed for 109, India had a lead of 52. Pataudi came in just before stumps but could not survive the day, as he was castled by Motz. India were effectively 58 for 5 and with a whole day left to play, again in some bother. Hanumant Singh, the dapper prince of Banswara and a cultured strokeplayer, now joined Sardesai, who was unshakeable at the other end.

Even though it was a Monday, a crowd of 15,000 had come to watch the final day. Sardesai and Hanumant simply took the match away from the Kiwis as they put up nearly 200 between them for the sixth wicket. Hanumant was a talent that India wasted. Nicknamed 'Chhotu', he was all class and sound in technique. It was a treat to watch him bat. The two of us had the pleasure of seeing two of Hanumant's finest knocks: a superb 94 against the Aussies in Madras in 1964 and then an excellent 80 against the Kiwis at Delhi. He ought to have played a lot more for India and it is an abiding regret that he was treated in a cavalier fashion by selectors.

Sardesai had batted for 529 minutes in this innings and when he reached his double century, Pataudi declared. It was already half-way through the session between lunch and tea on the final day. New Zealand were left with 43 overs and the target was – definitely for those days – an unachievable 255 runs at a rate of six an over. All that remained, it seemed, was the most boring formality of playing out the remaining time. Yet, the match sprung to life in the most unexpected manner and the last three hours of this match were the stuff of the highest drama.

What an unbelievable scorecard. Dowling was dismissed by Jaisimha for nought, and soon 0 for 1 became 0 for 2, as Venkat, springing up at gully like a basketballer, caught Sinclair brilliantly. Venkat shared an interesting nugget with us: 'It was my debut series and Pat initially made me field at covers. I had to tell him that I was a good close-catcher. Oh, I enjoyed the Sinclair catch, jumping and taking it in my right hand.' Just before tea, Pataudi brought the spinners on and in his first over Chandra clean bowled the clueless Morgan with a googly: 18 for 3. After a brief period of watchfulness, Reid fell to a splendid catch by Borde in the slips off Chandra. The legspinner struck again, getting Sutcliffe caught by Durani at long-leg. It was now 37 for 5. Narrating the electric excitement for his readers, Sundaresan observed, 'After these two vital wickets India, indeed, smelt victory and Pataudi pressed hard... Congdon was locked in a duel with Durani but after 11 minutes he succumbed when Hanumant snapped up a catch at forward short-leg off a forward prod. 45 for 6 now and one run later Pollard, swinging for a pull off Durani, edged the ball high over slip's head where Borde took a catch.'

Within no time New Zealand had slipped to 47 for 7 and even though less than an hour's play remained, the visiting side was seriously in danger of defeat. For three days, New Zealand were in the driving seat and now suddenly in two hours, the match had turned on its head. It was the Indian side that was now hunting them like a pack of wolves. Crucially, Taylor and Brian Yuile batted out some overs at this time and resisted everything the Indians threw at them. Just as it seemed that was it, India broke through again. With only seven minutes remaining, Pataudi put on Venkataraghavan for Durani and the off spinner bowled Taylor with his first ball. The Kiwis were 76 for 8. Could India pick up those two remaining wickets in the remaining six minutes or dozen deliveries? Would Venkat get them or Chandra? Pataudi now had all the fielders crowding the bat in those last few moments and the crowd howled with every delivery that Chandrasekhar bowled. C.S.A. Swami, veteran sports editor of the *Indian Express* (and also an Olympian who represented India in the 1936 Berlin Olympics), noted that the hunter had become the hunted and 'when the curtain fell 10 Indian fielders were crouched around the New Zealand tail, ready to pounce for the kill'. But Ward and Yuile survived a couple of huge leg before appeals and India could not breach New Zealand. A photograph from the final moments of this Test, with all the Indian players surrounding the New Zealand tail-ender, trying desperately to squeeze a win, is now legendary.

Should Pataudi have declared half an hour earlier? If he had given his bowlers 50 overs, could they have pulled it off? Was it caution or was it the need to let Sardesai reach the personal milestone of a double-century that delayed the declaration? Borde was magnanimous in his appraisal of Pataudi's late declaration. 'This is all ifs and buts, the captain has to weigh what if such a declaration does not click, suppose it backfires?' Just three years later, at the Queen's Park Oval in Trinidad, Garry Sobers set England a target of 215 to get in four hours. It was a sporting declaration but Sobers must have fancied his chances and at the same time discounted England's ability to play adventurously, what with Geoff Boycott and Colin Cowdrey in the English ranks. As it turned out, England hit the required runs in 52 overs at a rate upwards of four runs an over, with both Boycott and Cowdrey playing unexpectedly attacking knocks. Sobers never heard the last of the criticism for his declaration but had no regrets. 'I made the declaration for cricket. If I had not done so the game would have died... Looking back now, what I most remember is that we bowled at about 21 overs per hour throughout the innings.' It is at the very heart of sporting contests that such challenges are thrown – they owe it to the people who come to watch the game, to the game itself. On this issue, however, let the last words rest with S.K. Gurunathan, the doyen of Indian cricket correspondents in those days. In his essay, 'From defeat to glory' in *Sport & Pastime* of 3 April 1965, he wrote:

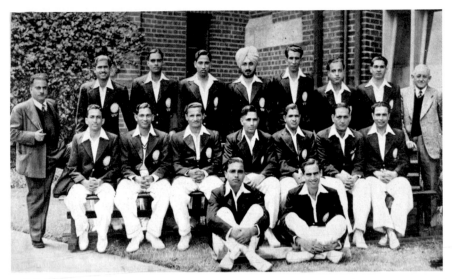

Lala Amarnath's team to Australia for the 1947–48 series – the first cricket tour of independent India. (Courtesy the Melbourne Cricket Club Library)

The charismatic captain Mansur Ali Khan Pataudi, seen here with Garry Sobers at the toss in Eden Gardens on 31 December 1966. (Courtesy Aloke Mitra)

Lovely Chepauk, the venue of many great contests, in the 1960s. For nearly a decade, Chepauk did not host a Test until West Indies played here in 1967. (Courtesy V. Ramnarayan)

English legend Jack Hobbs presenting Polly Umrigar with a cheque for 100 guineas for his century at Old Trafford in 1959. (Courtesy Getty Images)

Vinoo Mankad, one of the game's greatest all-rounders. (Courtesy Getty Images)

Vijay Hazare, one of the finest batsmen of his era. Don Bradman held him in such regard that his first question when the Indians visited Australia in 1967 was 'How is Mr Hazare?' (Courtesy Getty Images)

The West Indies in India

1 9 4 8

Jeffrey Stollmeyer's

D I A R Y

1 9 4 9

A unique piece of writing on cricket: West Indies vice-captain Jeff Stollmeyer's unpublished diary of the 1948–49 tour tears into John Goddard's negative captaincy. Cold comfort for the Indian team which was thwarted by such tactics at Brabourne Stadium. (Courtesy Clayton Murzello)

Sports-loving prime minister Jawaharlal Nehru spent time with rival captains Benaud and Ramchand when the India–Australia series of 1959–60 began in Delhi. (Courtesy Kasturi & Sons)

Cricketers value their peers' approval more than anything else. Vijay Manjrekar's mates unanimously believed he was the best. (Courtesy Getty Images)

Amul's witty hoardings were hugely popular in India. Here they pay tribute to Dilip Sardesai for his exploits in the 1971 Test series against West Indies. (Courtesy Nandini Sardesai)

Farokh Engineer's pivotal role in the 1970s – ebullient keeper, dashing batsman either at the top or middle, morale booster and cheerleader. (Courtesy Aloke Mitra)

Stylish at the crease and stylish at the mike, Jaisimha was famous for belting out Sinatra songs. (Courtesy V. Ramnarayan)

Press and radio commentators – Berry Sarbadhikary, Dicky Rutnagur, K.N. Prabhu, K.N. Chari, Pearson Surita, P.N. Sundaresan – pose for a photo with Tiger Pataudi and Garry Sobers. Before television, we were glued to our transistors. (Courtesy V. Ramnarayan)

The famed spin quartet mesmerized all the teams with their wizardry. They still never miss an opportunity to catch up with each other even decades after their playing days got over. (Courtesy Getty Images)

E.A.S. Prasanna continues to be surrounded by fans nearly 40 years after his last Test. (Courtesy Nagesh Ramamurthy)

'Let no one spoil the beautiful story by suggesting, even remotely, that India might have won the match had Pataudi closed the innings half an hour earlier... Cricket, like life, is full of imponderables and it is in them lies its charm.'

A week later we were at Feroz Shah Kotla, Delhi, when India beat New Zealand. Venkat, not yet 20, took 8 for 72 in the first innings and that same day, a completely possessed Sardesai belted the fastest Test century by an Indian. Dilip had cemented his place and his son Rajdeep tells us that his father always called him his lucky mascot as he was born in 1965! A final vivid memory of that series: Richard Collinge, the six-foot-five-inch fast bowler, bending from waist to half his height to shake hands with the diminutive Prime Minister of India, Lal Bahadur Shastri, when he was introduced to him during lunch at the Willingdon pavilion.

Test No. 582: Brabourne Stadium, Bombay, 12–15 March 1965: **New Zealand** (Toss) 297 in 129.2 overs (Graham Dowling 129, Ross Morgan 71; Ramakant Desai 6-56, Salim Durani 2-26) and 80/8 in 43 overs (Bruce Taylor 21; Bhagwat Chandrasekhar 3-25, Durani 2-16) drew with **India** 88 in 33.3 overs (Chandu Borde 25; Taylor 5-26, Bevan Congdon 2-21) and 463/5 dec in 154.4 overs (f/o) (Dilip Sardesai 200*, Borde 109; Taylor 3-76).

Captains: M.A.K. Pataudi (India) and John Reid (New Zealand)

PART 2

1970 to 1980

A Heady Feeling

The 1970s was the coming of age of Indian cricket. In February 1968, after the 0-4 defeat in Australia, Pataudi and his men travelled to New Zealand to play four Tests, and for the first time ever, India won a series overseas. In fact, India's first three overseas victories came on this tour. Were the Kiwis really a weak team or were the Indians in top form, suitably toughened by the earlier segment of their tour in Australia? One would like to think an important beginning was made in New Zealand. But after that tour, India played no Test cricket for 18 months until the Kiwis paid India a return visit in October 1969. That was a busy winter season as this was immediately followed by a five-Test home series against Bill Lawry's Australia.

By the time these matches began, selectors were convinced that older cricketers needed to make way for young blood. A slew of young cricketers were pitchforked into Test cricket. Chetan Chauhan and Ashok Mankad, Ambar Roy and Ashok Gandotra, Eknath Solkar and G.R. Viswanath, Mohinder Amarnath and Ajit Pai: it seemed that an endless assembly line of new talent was being tried out in the eight Tests in the winter of 1969. There was suddenly no place for Sardesai, Borde or Jaisimha; Hanumant and Durani were already forgotten. Tiger Pataudi remained captain, but his purple patch from 1963 to 1968 was a thing of the past, as he struggled for consistency and his leadership came into question. India barely drew the series with New Zealand and were trounced 3-1 by Australia. The Indian batting was inconsistent, hardly giving anything for the spinners to bowl with. As Suresh Menon wrote in *Bishan: Portrait of a Cricketer*, India seemed easily satisfied with

51

consolation victories while losing a series during this time. He noted, 'India crossed 300 only in the second Test at Kanpur, and 250 only one other time. The only batting spark for India was Viswanath's century on debut in the drawn Kanpur Test.'

We licked our wounds through 1970, then it was time to tour West Indies and England in 1971. No one gave India much of a chance. All that the Indian public wanted was that the team should not lie down and roll over. India, while often driving its countrymen to exasperation, was not a weak team, but it just did not play consistently and determinedly to its potential.

When the team for West Indies was announced, Merchant used his casting vote as chairman of selectors to select Wadekar as skipper in place of Pataudi. His deputy was the combative and confident Venkataraghavan. Old warhorses Durani, Sardesai and Jaisimha wrested back their places with some good domestic performances while youngsters Sunil Gavaskar, Mankad, Viswanath and Solkar brought the vigour of youth to the party. Wadekar as captain got the seniors to become his brains trust. Sardesai, fiercely protective of the youngsters and a motivational hero; Jaisimha, canny and strategic as ever; Durani not moody as he was under Pataudi, but more amenable and willing. Though Wadekar had little of Pataudi's charisma, he managed to get his team together; like beleaguered troops they grouped themselves into a fighting mood. Rohan Kanhai, Garry Sobers, Clive Lloyd were big names but Wadekar and his spinners hemmed them in with close-in fielders.

Although the 1971 tour to West Indies is known as the series that launched Gavaskar, the real hero of the series was Sardesai. The first Test determined the fate of the series and the man who ensured India delivered a psychological blow in this match was Sardesai. For the first time ever, India forced West Indies to follow-on. Forty years later, Venkat had a wide grin on his face as he recounted how Sobers' jaw dropped when Wadekar asked the Windies to follow-on. India won the series 1-0. Bishan Bedi told us they could have even won 2-0. India beat the Windies in Port-of-Spain, fended them off at Kensington Oval in Barbados, and fought and scraped again in Port-of-Spain to preserve the lead. By this time, Sardesai was worn out but Gavaskar had come of age and in a monumental exhibition of classic batting he carried India to safety. It seemed the Indian cricketers had barely time to come home and stretch themselves before they were off again, this time to England. Again, given no chance, Wadekar's team conjured up a series win. The victory came at the Oval in the third Test, but it was the manner in which India played the first Test at Lord's, the way Wadekar counter-attacked and hooked John Snow that set the tempo. India fought England chin to chin, toe to toe right through that summer. The Oval win was only the culmination

This phase was the era when India learnt to fight and win. They copped a few defeats, capitulating when they could have played better, but often they notched up wins – in England, West Indies, New Zealand and Australia. Mihir Bose declared that this period introduced Indians 'to the heady delights of victory and made defeat that much more difficult to accept'. While Gavaskar provided India the batting might of three men put together and Viswanath was truly world-class, the spin quartet had become a terrific attacking force. In India, they were formidable, but even abroad in Sydney, Auckland and Port-of-Spain, Prasanna, Bedi, Chandra and Venkat created stunning and memorable victories. About the quartet, Menon wrote: 'Like characters out of a book they came together: from different cities and with different backgrounds, different approaches to bowling and different temperaments. Somehow the whole was greater than the sum of its parts. Together they scripted one of the most exciting chapters in the history of Indian cricket. Later bowlers claimed more wickets, had a hand in more victories; were statistically more impressive. But none had the charm, the technical mastery, the charisma and the mischief of (the four).'

Mohinder Amarnath and Dilip Vengsarkar joined Gavaskar and Viswanath to add steel and style to India's batting. Syed Kirmani proved to be such a good keeper and stubborn lower-order batsman that India did not miss ebullient Farokh Engineer. How spunky was this team through the 1970s? Very. For evidence, we need look no further than Port-of-Spain in 1976. Only Bradman's 'Invincibles' in 1948 had successfully chased over 400 runs in the fourth innings to win a Test. Thirty-eight years later, Bishan Bedi's team chased 404 and there were centuries from Gavaskar and Viswanath, 85 from Mohinder Amarnath and a rousing 49 not out from Brijesh Patel as India raced to victory.

There were bad troughs too, none more so than the 1974 tour to England. It was an unhappy team, fractious and defeated in the dressing room itself. Bedi says that the '42 all out' at Lord's was the worst moment. Wadekar, unrecognizable as the captain who had led India to a hat-trick of series victories, came home a shattered man and quit cricket. When we told Prasanna that we were writing about some great matches of the 1970s, he told us with a mischievous smile to also write about the horrible 1974 tour 'because a pinch of salt will only enhance the sweetness'.

In 1977, Tony Greig's England beat India in India, a series famous for the 'Vaseline controversy'. In the first Test, replying to England's large first-innings total, India had raced to 40 for no loss, when all hell broke loose. John Lever, the left-arm medium pacer, suddenly started swinging the ball like a demented banana. India collapsed dramatically and lost the Delhi Test. The accusation was that Lever had stuck Vaseline gauze over his eyebrows and touched them every time he bowled to make the ball swing crazily in both innings. Forensic tests on the ball confirmed this. 'Vaseline', howled the crowds every time John Lever touched the ball for the rest of the series but the damage had been done and a badly psyched home team lost the series 3-1. In 1978, India resumed cricketing ties with Pakistan after eighteen years. The Indian team that went to Pakistan under the large-hearted Bedi was told that it was a 'friendship' series, and to remember this at all times. With this kind of diplomatic burden, India was hardly ready when the Pakistan team came at them scrapping and sledging. No one had told the Pakistan team that it was a friendship series. The Indian spinners by now were also past their prime and the Pakistani batsmen feasted on them. Pakistani umpires too were under no illusion of this being a friendship series. India lost 2-0, Bedi's head rolled and Indian cricket once again went into mourning. Bedi commented laconically that the friendship was one-sided. For once he did not have a smile on his face as he spoke to us of that tour.

India played 67 Tests from 1971 to 1980, of which they won 18. There were six commendable victories overseas, perhaps the strongest indicator that Indian cricket had come of age. The finest period in India's cricketing history have been the years between 2001 and 2010, but the years 1971–80 were definitely the next best period. No surprise then, that we have seven Tests from this period, with five of these played overseas in West Indies and England. Three of the seven were drawn matches, each a classic.

The four victories in this selection will perhaps not be contentious: the first-ever victory over West Indies on their soil in 1971; the first-ever win in England, Oval 1971; that spectacular chase of 404 in April 1976 and the magical come-from-behind victory in Kolkata against Clive Lloyd's men in January 1975. Why the Kolkata Test? Firstly, India were down 0-2 in the series, and it was a series played immediately after the miserable 1974 tour to England. Indian batsmen seemed to have no answer to the fiery pace of the red-hot Andy Roberts while the batting might of Roy Fredericks, Gordon Greenidge, Vivian Richards and Clive Lloyd seemed to be pulverizing the spinners. In such a scenario, Viswanath played a career-defining innings, Pataudi led inspirationally, Chandra bowled a Houdini-like spell and suddenly West Indies crumbled to defeat. For India, it was a huge affirmation of their potential and the belief that they could still fight with the best.

Yet again, while selecting the Tests from this era, a couple of great matches could not be accommodated. The 1971 draw at Lord's in the first Test, where a confident and attacking India set the tone for the series. Chasing 183 to win and finishing at 138 for 8, when Wadekar was interviewed at the end of the match, he said, 'We were trying to beat the rain to get there!' The other Test that missed out is a gallant defeat, while chasing a huge fourth innings target of 493. At Adelaide Oval in February 1978 – admittedly against a second-rung Australia shorn of all its star cricketers who were banned for aligning with Kerry Packer – India went after the target like men possessed, only to fall short by just 47 runs. To score 445 runs in 141 overs must surely rank among the greatest fourth innings performances of all time. By 1978, India had also reached a stage where we could send English and Hindi commentators for the radio. As the series, tied at 2-2, was careening towards its final denouement, Anant Setalvad, suave, polished, public school-accented English and Sushil Doshi, poetic and fluent in Hindi, as one can only be in one's mother tongue, were commentating in English and Hindi every alternate ball. It was the most mind-boggling bout of mike passes and when both commentators finally quietened down, Bedi's team had lost all ten wickets and the team finished 47 runs adrift.

Two important aspects will complete the picture of the decade Indian cricket came of age. One, India had at last forged a world-class catching outfit comprising Solkar, Venkat, Wadekar and Abid Ali, which helped the spinners regularly bowl out the opposition. Two, this period consolidated on the stability gained in the Pataudi era. The whimsical Russian roulette of selection of players and captains in the 1950s was a thing of the past. Thus, in the 1970s, we saw extended runs at the helm for Ajit Wadekar and Bishan Singh Bedi. Pataudi came specifically for the 1974–75 series against West Indies under dire circumstances. Venkataraghavan as a one-day specialist was chosen as captain for the World Cup in 1975 and 1979. He also led India on the tour to England in 1979 and that was the only interruption in Gavaskar's long reign as captain after he took over from Bedi in 1978. One also saw greater consistency in player selection. Of the 39 players who represented India in the 1970s, there were 19 players who played a minimum of 30 Tests during their Test careers. Eleven of them were batsmen who scored over 1,500 Test runs while nine of them were bowlers, of whom six were spinners – the famed spin quartet plus Dilip Doshi and Shivlal Yadav. India's approach to pace changed forever towards the end of this period when the peerless Kapil Dev made his debut against Pakistan in Faisalabad in 1978. Before Kapil's arrival, India at least had Abid Ali, Madan Lal and Karsan Ghavri doing new-ball duty, a far better state of affairs compared to the 1960s when they used Jaisimha and Budhi Kunderan to take the shine off the new ball. In 1967 in England, Kunderan was asked by the press, 'What do you bowl?' He replied, 'I will have to find out when I bowl.'

5

'Garry, we are enforcing the follow-on'

India vs West Indies, first Test, Sabina Park, Kingston, Jamaica, 1971

The Indian skipper pushed open the door of the West Indies dressing room, walked in and caught their captain's eye. There was a pause, and once he had everyone's attention, he announced loudly, 'Garry, we are enforcing the follow-on.' Sobers was left speechless, even as the West Indians froze in their seats. There was consternation in the dressing room. Rohan Kanhai walked up to Wadekar and asked if he really meant it. Neither he, nor the rest of his team, was aware that in a Test reduced to four days, a follow-on could be enforced with a 150-run lead in the first innings, as opposed to the 200-run lead in a five-day match. Wadekar, in the first Test of what was expected to be a very tough five-Test tour, had landed the first blow, and India never looked back from there, with the players showing a combination of skill and steel never seen before in any Indian team.

Indian cricketers were known to be poor tourists, and invariably began tours on a losing note. The rest of the tour would feature either more losses or playing catch-up to overcome the deficit. The 1971 tour is famous because it was the first of a hat-trick of series wins for Ajit Wadekar and his team, but the first Test of this defining period in Indian cricket history is the point when India turned the corner in the way it approached its tours. A new captain after a decade, Ajit Wadekar, from the hard-nosed school of Bombay cricket, had been elevated to the position by the casting vote of the chairman of selectors, Vijay Merchant. Middle-class upbringing and values, a degree in Mathematics, a secure job in the State Bank of India, all amalgamated by the serious work ethic of Bombay cricket, was what Wadekar brought to his job. While in the 1960s he had made runs by the bucket – very stylishly too – in domestic cricket, he was experiencing a rough time in international cricket.

Wadekar was thus under pressure on two counts. One, he was the plebeian replacing the aristocratic and charismatic Pataudi who had skippered India for a decade with a panache that had left a deep imprint. Two, Wadekar's own form was shaky and he would have to bat well to hold his place in the team. He was also inheriting a bunch of players who had played and grown under Pataudi's leadership.

Wadekar had a new deputy, Venkataraghavan, and three old warhorses had made a comeback – Durani, Jaisimha and Sardesai. He had a new wicketkeeper too; Engineer was not available and a neat stumper from Hyderabad, P. Krishnamurthy, was making his debut. Among the youngsters, Viswanath had already shown in his debut series that he was destined for glory. Solkar brought guts, temperament and outstanding close-catching quality to the Indian team. Gavaskar was on his maiden tour, earning his place through some remarkable batting in university and first-class cricket. But no one would have even remotely guessed that a legend was about to be born. In Prasanna and Bedi, Wadekar had two world-class spinners but they were their own men, and would later prove more than a handful. It was a good team, a nice mix of youth and experience, but the captain was just finding his way.

The first Test was at Sabina Park in Kingston, Jamaica. Generally West Indian pitches would be hard and bouncy and have a glass-like sheen. Yet Durani, one of the veterans on his second visit to the Caribbean, immediately saw that the pitches were different this time; not as hard and pacy as those he had played on in 1960–61. Moreover, this time, there was no Hall, no Griffith, nobody as fearsome to face. Wadekar doing his own homework, got Jaisimha, one of the finest tacticians in Indian first-class cricket, to be his advisor on strategy and tactics. Jaisimha was known to be Pataudi's buddy and close friend. Yet, the two forged a partnership that was crucial for the team's planning. V. Ramnarayan, our good friend, who played with distinction in the 1970s for Hyderabad and South Zone, in his book *Third Man*, said, 'Eye for detail and unusual memory marked every shrewd move Motganahalli Laxminarasu Jaisimha made as captain of Hyderabad… Jai was the most feared captain of his time in Indian cricket.'

Wadekar entrusted Sardesai with the task of looking after and nurturing the youngsters. Sardesai was good at this, fiercely protective of them and at the same time helping them realize that they were as good as anyone else. Wadekar also did something that Pataudi had never been able to – getting the moody Durani involved, engaged and feel wanted. So, with some licence, we could say that Wadekar had managed to create a core group with a form of collective leadership.

Of course, all this needed to come together on the ground. The first day of the first Test was washed out, reducing the match to a four-day affair. Never had an entire day's Test cricket been washed out in the history of the Kingston ground. B.R. Jones, the West Indian sport scribe, described the start of the series for *The Hindu*: 'The toss, which was made shortly before 11 o'clock, followed hours of feverish preparations by ground staff who were watched by Wadekar, Sobers and a number of West Indian officials… The West Indies skipper Sobers won the toss and put India in to bat. If Wadekar had won he would most certainly have done just that.'

Meanwhile, Jamaicans were protesting at the exclusion of their all-rounder Maurice Foster from the side and also objecting to the Trinidadian Ralph Gosein umpiring in this Test. So there was a flurry of activity even before a ball had been bowled. When Sobers asked India to bat he was certain that the pitch would behave badly because of the rains. Jones stated that a patch at the southern end of the pitch looked damp and held the key to the Test. In no time, India had lost half the side for 75. Their unremarkable opening pair – makeshift opener Abid Ali and debutant Jayantilal – went with just 13 on the board. Jayantilal was suckered into playing for a bouncer and taken brilliantly at slip by Sobers. Gavaskar in his *Sunny Days* recalled that the ball 'came back sharply, got an edge and travelled like lightning between second and third slip. There was a flash of movement and Sobers came up laughing with the ball clutched to his chest.' 'My tour is made,' he wrote in complete admiration for the world's greatest all-rounder! Abid Ali snicked Shillingford to Steve Camacho in the slips and soon thereafter, Wadekar too was gone, showing that his form was still suspect. He attempted an ill-advised hook to Vanburn Holder and mistimed it so badly that he was held at short-leg. Durani, after playing for some time, got out as he misread a googly from Barrett. When Jaisimha was dismissed playing on to an in-cutter from Holder, India were reduced to 75 for 5. The same Jones who had spoken ominously of the damp pitch, now commented, 'The early Indian batsmen lost their wickets not because of the difficulty of the pitch, but due to some timid play. They were psychologically affected by the pitch.'

In these dire circumstances, as Jaisimha walked back to the pavilion, out came Eknath Solkar to join Sardesai. If either of them had lost their wicket the innings would have folded up and maybe the match and series. For Solkar, cricket was the gateway to a better life and future. Son of the groundsman at PJ Hindu Gymkhana, and educated up to high school, everything in life depended on how he did in cricket. For Sardesai, this was the opportunity to resurrect his Test career. It was also now or never for him. Both came from the same club in Bombay, both knew all about fighting cricket. It was said that among Indian batsmen, Sardesai was the only one who would sledge fielding sides to fluster them into bowling what he wanted. His self-confidence was contagious and his incessant banter while at the crease unbelievable. He gave the elder of us a personal exhibition of this trait, as he loudly sang 'sixer' even as he smote him for a six in a league match! Rajdeep told us that because his father was a nervous starter, he liked to talk at the start of his innings to everyone in the field!

Together, the two had the partnership of their lives that day at Sabina Park. Dilip told Eknath to forget the opponents and play as though it was a club match at home. They went on and on. More than three hours later, with India having crossed 200 and after he crossed his fifty, Solkar departed to the bowling of Sobers. The runs they scored, the time they consumed, the message they sent to the dressing room – all these had tremendously positive implications. Throughout that series there were several times when the Indian team found a way out despite being on the back foot, because Sardesai and Solkar had shown them the way.

~

On the third day, Sardesai was far from done. He found in Prasanna an unlikely partner and they added more than a hundred runs for the eighth wicket. Sardesai accelerated after his century and did the bulk of the scoring. He spent around eight hours at the crease and when he was finally dismissed, he had hit 212. The newspapers carried a most interesting box item the next day: 'Sardesai cracks press box panes & cricket records'. The reasons were twofold, one of course to do with his double-century and partnership records, but the other was about one of his ferocious lofted shots that smashed the glass panes of the press box. Describing the event, Jones wrote: 'Journalists plucked splinters of glass from their typewriters and documents. The ball crashed the half-inch thick glass panes and landed into the lap along with splinters of one of the West Indian writers. Sardesai waved "apologies" to the pressmen and play continued.' Rajdeep Sardesai told us that at a condolence meeting after his father passed away, Ashok Mankad said that Dilip Sardesai played flawless, perfect knocks in that series which he had not seen bettered by anyone, not even Sunil Gavaskar who scored more runs but with a number of 'lives' on that tour.

The 1971 series in West Indies is remembered as 'Gavaskar's series' for the 774 runs he scored but the series must be remembered equally for Sardesai's contribution. There were two more centuries from him to come and he would end up with a tally of 642 for the tour, just 122 runs behind Gavaskar's phenomenal tally. He was Indian cricket's 'renaissance' man. Gavaskar in his autobiography *Sunny Days* has said how much of a protective father figure he was to the younger batsmen and how important that was to batsmen like him as they were taking their first steps in international cricket. Sardesai was a great supporter of the young Gavaskar and predicted great things for him even before the tour. Over the years Sardesai always marvelled at Gavaskar's concentration and focus though he considered Viswanath a superior batsman on bad surfaces. One evening, reminiscing about old times, Bedi told us among all the Bombay cricketers Sardesai was the one who would always invite teammates to his home for a sumptuous lunch or dinner. When he scored well, he would come back and tell everyone in the dressing room that there was nothing in the bowling, nothing in the pitch and everyone could go and have a good knock. But if he were to get out early he would talk of demons in the pitch and one would get the impression that Lindwall, Larwood, Hall and Trueman had combined to bowl at their fiery best. The dressing room was soon able to take both these 'Sardesaisms' in the right spirit.

In reply, Camacho and Fredericks put on 73 for the first wicket for the Windies, and there was no inkling of the drama that was to unfold. Then, when Sobers and Kanhai (what a combination to savour!) got together and took the score to 183 for 3, one would have expected a run feast. But that is when Venkataraghavan dismissed Kanhai. From 202 for 4, the next six wickets tumbled for just 15 runs as Venkat and Bedi consumed them. Prasanna, who had taken the initial wickets, finished with 4 for 65 while Bedi had 2 for 63 and Venkat 3 for 46. It was the lowest ever total by West Indies against India. The Indian fielding was flawless with the skipper himself taking two fine catches. The field placing showed that the captain had given a lot of thought to it.

The foreign press was captivated. While Jones wrote 'Magnificent spin bowling by Prasanna, Venkataraghavan and Bishan Singh Bedi humiliated the much-favoured West Indies', John Woodcock, cricket correspondent of *The Times*, said he was seeing the best spin bowling of his time, with special praise for the mesmeric quality of Prasanna's off spin. India's close-in catching too came for praise from Woodcock who wrote, 'India's catching at short-leg was of the kind one associates with the best English counties employing the best close fielders to the best off spinners'.

Bowled out for 217, West Indies had conceded a lead of 170 and were blissfully unaware of the rules which state that if a Test is a four-day affair, the follow-on can be enforced if the lead is 150 or more. Venkat the vice-captain, always on top of rules in cricket, immediately informed Wadekar that he could ask West Indies to bat again. And Wadekar did it in style. Instead of merely informing the umpires, he purposefully walked up to the West Indies dressing room and announced it to Sobers. Rajdeep Sardesai said of Wadekar: 'He may not have had the charisma or the tactical acumen of Pataudi, but he was a calm man, he gave confidence to players; that reduced their tensions and they could come together and perform at or even above their best. Even my father played his best when he was captain. These traits were also evident when he was the manager of the Indian team in the 1990s.'

The impact of a visiting Indian side enforcing the follow-on upon a team that had Sobers, Kanhai, Lloyd and Fredericks was such that the upper hand irrevocably shifted. When the Windies followed on they were 71 for 2 when play ended on the penultimate day. Summarizing the situation quite correctly, Jones wrote, 'West Indies was not yet out of danger, however. A good deal of restraint, dedication and application was needed from Sobers, the new batsman, and Kanhai.' And next day, Kanhai and Sobers proved to be saviours with brilliant, responsible batting. The two all-time legends batted out the match with Kanhai scoring a big unbeaten hundred, while Sobers fell seven short of a ton. Normal service had been restored but for Wadekar and his men this game was not merely a moral victory but a mighty realization that they had the potential to compete against the best. The Indians drove home the advantage immediately in the next Test in Port-of-Spain and it is for the kind of long-term impact it had on Indian cricket that we consider the Test match at Sabina Park as one of India's most important games.

Test No. 680: Sabina Park, Kingston, Jamaica, 18–23 February 1971: India 387 in 158.4 overs (Dilip Sardesai 212, Eknath Solkar 61; Vanburn Holder 4-60, Garry Sobers 2-57) drew with **West Indies** (Toss) 217 in 93.5 overs (Rohan Kanhai 56, Roy Fredericks 45; Erapalli Prasanna 4-65, S. Venkataraghavan 3-46) and 385/5 in 136 overs (f/o) (Kanhai 158*, Sobers 93; Solkar 2-56).

Captains: Ajit Wadekar (India) and Garry Sobers (West Indies)

6

A New Era Is Born

India vs West Indies, second Test, Queen's Park Oval, Port-of-Spain, Trinidad, 1971

The pitch at Queen's Park in Port-of-Spain, unlike the one at Kensington Oval in Bridgetown or Sabina Park in Kingston, was not known to favour fast bowlers; it was a spinners' pitch. Now, as the Indians arrived in Port-of-Spain, all that could be said was that, based on the evidence of the first Test, they would certainly compete and come hard at the West Indies and they would have the support of the spectators of Indian descent. Trinidad's large population of Indian origin has always been most enthusiastic in its support of Indian teams. When India visited the Caribbean Islands for the first time in 1953 and played their first Test there, over 22,000 spectators of Indian origin packed the stands. Mihir Bose explains this emotional connection in *A History of Indian Cricket*: 'As though the Trinidadian of Indian descent saw the visit of the Indian side as a chance to rediscover a lost land.'

Gavaskar, who had missed the first Test because of a whitlow in his finger, was now fit and he replaced Jayantilal in the team. Mankad was drafted at the expense of Jaisimha and thus India had a new opening pair. Viswanath was still unfit but at this point of time the Indians seemed to have a good combination in place. A huge crowd gathered

66

before start of play to watch the match, and the interest generated was not in little measure due to India's superb performance in the first Test. Sobers won the toss and the rudest shock awaited everyone. India opened the bowling with Abid Ali, that utility all-rounder from Hyderabad. Many have wondered why Abid ran in 15 yards to bowl at his pace but that morning he delivered the mother of all deliveries. His first ball pitched around or just outside legstump but never rose. Hugging the ground, the ball scooted through like a rat to hit Fredericks' pad and went on to rattle the stumps. There is nothing more treacherous in cricket than to be bowled by a shooter. A wicket-taking ground grubber, the first ball of a match – if this was not a divine roll of the dice for India then nothing else ever was.

West Indies played in a trance for the rest of that day. Camacho the other opener, departed at 42, caught excellently by Solkar off Bedi. Kanhai attacked, but after making a scorching 37 and with the score at 62, he was dismissed. It was again a catch by Solkar, this time off Prasanna. Then the pitch played its tricks again. Jones in his column for *The Hindu* wrote, 'Another shock was a moment away, as with the total still on 62, Lloyd was clean bowled by a ball from Abid Ali which never lifted from the pitch.' V. Ramnarayan, in his memoir, affectionately says that Abid 'was great company while travelling with the Hyderabad team, taking part in crazy card games devised by Pataudi or singing calypso songs he learnt in the Caribbean. His favourite line was "Great India bowler Abid Ali" which he sang with gusto. Few cricketers exploited their talent better.'

West Indies did not recover and were all out for 217 after tea, having played less than 73 overs. They lost Sobers with the score at 102 when Venkat bowled him. Only some lusty blows from Shillingford the tail-ender helped them cross 200. All this while one man, Charlie Davis, held his end up resolutely to prevent a collapse, with a battling unbeaten 71. Prasanna took four wickets, Bedi took three and Venkat chipped in with the key scalp of Sobers. Davis who was at the crease during much of that innings recalled in an interview with Nagaraj Gollapudi the attacking mindset of the Indian spinners. Nothing epitomized it more than the fact that Venkat bowled at Garry Sobers without a mid-on as protection: 'He bowled tight, flat offbreaks, pitching them on middle and leg, and he once caught Garry in no-man's land, but since the bounce was uneven, the ball pitched and jumped over the offstump. So in the next over Venkat brought the mid-on fielder to gully to force Garry into doing something stupid. He bowled the exact same ball, and seemed to catch Garry again playing half-and-half. But at the last minute Garry got back and hit it to the mid-on boundary. He then came up to me and said. "This man must be mad to bowl to me without a mid-on." I laughed and said, "You were definitely gone to the cleaners in his last over." But that was Garry: he could do anything. Eventually Venkat bowled him in that first innings to have the last laugh.'

Venkat had another tale to narrate of the battle between him and Sobers: 'Something similar happened in 1966 when West Indies toured India. In the first Test at Brabourne, Pataudi brought me on as soon as Sobers came in. I asked for a slip and a short-leg and Pat gave me the field I wanted. Sobers was grinning widely but soon he was groping and didn't have a clue about the first few balls I bowled. I had him plumb lbw in my next over but umpire Mamsa ruled him not out. Sobers confided to Pataudi in the evening that he was out. I clean-bowled Sobers in that innings but after he had made 50.'

When India's turn to bat came, the world had its first glimpse of Gavaskar. The young man had his stroke of luck, too. Sobers dropped him early. In fact, he dropped Gavaskar more than once in that series. Wadekar narrated a story where Sobers came to the Indian dressing room to congratulate Gavaskar, and Wadekar warned him not to shake hands with the Windies skipper because his good luck would get transferred to Sobers!

Mankad and Gavaskar gave India a sound start, and then Gavaskar had another substantial partnership with Sardesai. He crossed fifty in his maiden innings but fell to Jack Noreiga after making 65. Off the very next ball, Wadekar was dismissed for a duck. At 186 for 4, the heroes of Sabina Park – Sardesai and Solkar – were reunited and forged their second successive century partnership. Solkar hit his second fifty on the trot and the phenomenal Sardesai hit a century. The West Indies fielding, ragged that day, was particularly kind to Solkar who got a couple of lives. For Sardesai, stroking freely now, and for Solkar, it was like an extension of the work they had done at Sabina Park a fortnight earlier. They carried India to 300 before Sardesai fell. Emphatic about the impact Sardesai had on this tour, Raju Bharatan wrote, '...scores can never tell the full story of this montage in courage'. Sardesai features in four of the Tests in this book, and plays stellar roles in three of them. Rajdeep said that on the tour to West Indies in 1962, although his father was a middle-order batsman, he put his hand up to open after Contractor was injured. There were only two other overseas tours before the tour of 1971 – to England in 1967 and to Australia in 1967–68. But it was here that Sardesai got to play as a middle-order batsman. He added, 'My father said that when he was batting at his best in 1968–70, Merchant would not select him and in fact dropped him after just one Test in Bombay. He missed his best years as a middle-order bat. As an opener he might have averaged around 30 but as a middle-order bat he averaged nearly 50.'

The rest of the batting added 50 more runs and India finished with a significant first-innings lead of 138 runs. Noreiga, the tall off spinner, had taken nine Indian wickets, bowling a marathon 49.5 overs. Even then, Durani was convinced that West Indies had blundered by dropping Gibbs to accommodate Noreiga. It was interesting to hear this perspective from a batsman who had played both bowlers.

West Indies began their second innings impressively and by the end of the third day, which was preceded by a rest day, they had wiped out the deficit and still had nine wickets in hand. Kanhai who opened the innings with Fredcricks – Steve Camacho was nursing a bruised finger – was the lone wicket to fall, for 27, Venkat snapping him up at slip off Bedi. The dangerous Fredericks was not out on 80 and giving him company was Charlie Davis on a confident 33. To compound matters, Prasanna had injured his bowling hand after Davis the non-striker trod on his fingers as he tried to field a ball off his own bowling. Wadekar was acutely aware that even a modest fourth innings target would challenge India as the pitch would progressively spin more and misbehave. What do cricketers discuss at dinner or in the dressing room at such times? We got an insight into this from Wadekar himself during his discussion with the Indian community at Houston in September 2015. Recalling the 1971 tour, Wadekar said that a highlight of that tour was the discipline and punctuality at team meetings. 'Initially, punctuality for team meetings to discuss and plan strategy was not a feature, but we fixed this without upsetting the chronically late players. The results were outstanding.'

On the fourth morning, West Indies suffered a setback even before play began, when Davis was struck over the eye in the practice nets. He had to go away to the hospital to get the gash stitched. So Fredericks came out with Lloyd. But as soon as play began, Fredericks was run out. Dicky Rutnagur in his report for the *Indian Express* commented, 'Fredericks ran himself out rather foolishly, hitting straight and hard to cover and attempting a single. Jayantilal, a hundred per cent better fielder than when he arrived, was fielding there as substitute for Sardesai, and he made no mistake with his return to Krishnamurthy.' Sobers came out to join Lloyd and there were now two left-handers at the crease. Then came the magical moment. In an inspired move, Wadekar summoned Durani to bowl. Those who have watched Durani bowl will remember he was a different kind of a left-arm spinner. He was tall, came off a longish run-up and delivered with a high arm, bicep quite close to his ear. Durani was a canny bowler and varied his pace, spin and length extremely well. Wadekar recalled Durani's match-winning spell, in his book *My Cricketing Years*: 'In the matter of a couple of overs the game swung dramatically in our favour. Sobers played over one, which spun into him and was comprehensively bowled for a duck. Noticing Lloyd pushing balls that broke into him towards mid-wicket, I moved over to short mid-wicket. I had barely taken up position when Lloyd, as expected, hit the ball to me.' Rutnagur, in his column remarked, 'He bowled a spell as beautiful as any he bowled. Sobers played six balls without scoring and then, in pushing defensively, aimed around and over a delivery of beautiful length.'

We asked Durani about this spell, when we spoke to him a few years ago. He said, 'The wicket was slow and unresponsive to the flighted deliveries of Bedi, so they needed someone like me to hit the deck and make it spin. I also had the ability to vary the pace and that added another dimension to my bowling.' Some weeks before we wrote this, we asked Bedi why Wadekar had decided to bring on Durani. Bedi, quick as ever on the retort, said, 'Nah, not Wadekar's idea. It was Jaisimha's idea.' Then our chat with Bedi turned for a few minutes towards Jai. 'Great thinker of the game. Lovely man. He was a huge help to Wadekar on that tour. Stylish and classical, Jai was such a genteel player.' Then after a pause, Bedi leaned back in his chair, put his arms above his head, and said with a loud guffaw, 'But (the) chap was always so bloody nervous before batting. Padded up, he would smoke like a chimney, cigarette *chhodta hi nahin tha!*'

So much has been said about Durani's two magic balls but what of Venkat? That fourth day in Port-of-Spain, Venkat held one end after Durani had removed Sobers and Lloyd and proceeded to take the next five wickets in a row – Camacho, Barrett, Findlay, Holder and Shillingford – to ensure the Windies did not recover. Rutnagur wrote, 'Venkat spread terror making his offbreaks turn and lift.' Jones was clear that 'Venkataraghavan was the star of the Indian attack'. He had bowled 36 overs in that innings and finished with 5 for 95. A reserved man, he must be feeling somewhere within that his five-wicket haul has been forgotten. To set the record straight here, he was magnificent on that tour. Throughout the five Tests, Venkat bowled unflaggingly, took the most number of wickets by any bowler on that tour (22), concentrated on his close-in catching, made crucial contributions with the bat and made himself indispensable in that team. Venkat, of course, has fond memories of this tour: 'Sardesai was in a zone, batting brilliantly through the series. His double hundred at Sabina Park gave us a psychological advantage, which we capitalized on. Bedi and I carried a great load and we both bowled well throughout the series. The fielding from this series onwards made a huge difference to the spinners' striking ability. Mankad and Gupte were very good earlier but poor fielding let them down.'

Venkat's prowess with mental maths and numbers is legendary. When team prize money first came in the late 1960s, Pataudi entrusted Venkat with distributing it amongst all players. Mihir Bose has written

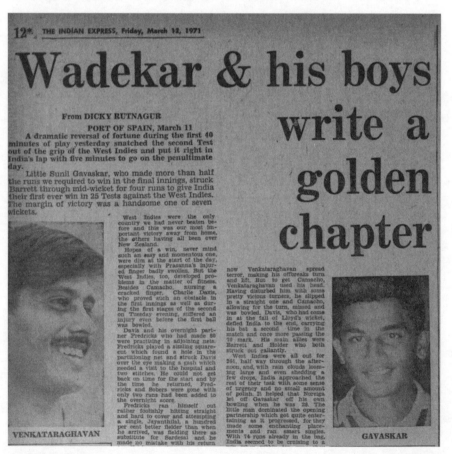

The Indian Express *was generous in its praise for Wadekar's team. (Used with permission from the New Indian Express Group)*

that Tiger did this because not only was Venkat honest, he was the only chap who could divide thousands by any number and arrive at the correct figure! This was no exaggeration as we were personally given a demonstration of this prowess by the off spinner. At the launch of our book *Mid-Wicket Tales*, Venkat had run into an old classmate from Guindy Engineering College. Turning to us he had said, 'Meet my friend Vasu, Roll No. 1331.' 'But how do you remember a 50-year-old number?' Venkat explained it simply, 'Easy man, 11 cubed is 1331.'

India had restricted West Indies in the second innings to 261 and so the target for a win was just 124 runs. India could see glory beckon. More than half of the fourth day's play still remained but rain clouds were gathering and there was even a smattering of rain. The spectators in the stands began to chant 'We shall overcome' and could not wait for the winning hit to arrive. Rutnagur commented that 'India approached the rest of their task with some sense of urgency and no small amount of polish'. Mankad and Gavaskar once again gave India a decent start and by the time Mankad departed, the target had been chopped down to just 50 runs. Sadly Durani failed again – Rutnagur called the shot, 'more agricultural than the plough itself' – and Sardesai snicked a cut off legspinner Barrett to the keeper. Abid, that honest cricketer, came in and was at the crease when Gavaskar hit Barrett to mid-wicket for the winning runs. Gavaskar has written that Abid took a single and generously allowed him to hit the winning boundary. The 15,000 spectators of Indian origin came surging on to the Queens Park Oval while the Blue Mountains shrouded in dark clouds provided a very pretty backdrop. Port-of-Spain seemed quite justifiably India's home away from home. There were tears of joy in the dressing room. 'India's first ever Test victory over W. Indies', said the simple headline on the sports page of *The Hindu*. It also carried photos of Venkat and Gavaskar, the heroes of the final day's play. The *Indian Express* was more effusive in its headline: 'Wadekar and his boys write a golden chapter'. In Trinidad, entire restaurant menus were written with the names of Indian cricketers while calypsos were composed extolling real and imagined virtues of the victorious visitors from India. The Indian High Commissioner at Trinidad threw a grand party to celebrate the win. The early morning news bulletins filtered into Indian homes over the radio announcing the grand win and the cricket-loving public hearing this, recognized it as the greatest cricketing achievement of the nation till that point of time. At schools, colleges and at office that morning, all the discussion was only about India's remarkable achievement; differences were forgotten, united as they all were by the happiness over India's finest victory till that time.

Test No. 683: Queen's Park Oval, Port-of-Spain, Trinidad, 6–10 March 1971: West Indies (Toss) 214 in 72.5 overs (Charlie Davis 71*, Rohan Kanhai 37; Erapalli Prasanna 4-54, Bishan Bedi 3-46) and 261 in 110.5 overs (Roy Fredericks 80, Davis 74*; S. Venkataraghavan 5-95, Salim Durani 2-21) lost to **India** 352 in 157.4 overs (Dilip Sardesai 112, Sunil Gavaskar 65; Jack Noreiga 9-95) and 125/3 in 49.4 overs (Gavaskar 67*, Ashok Mankad 29; Arthur Barrett 3-43) by seven wickets.

Captains: Ajit Wadekar (India) and Garry Sobers (West Indies)

7

Magical, Marvellous Chandra

India vs England, third Test, the Oval, London, 1971

The fifth day of the Oval Test, 24 August 1971, was a Tuesday but it was a holiday in India for Ganesh Chaturthi, the festival to celebrate the elephant-headed god. The match finished a little after lunch in England, so it would have been around 7 p.m. in India. Every cricket lover worth his salt was glued to the radio, listening to Brian Johnston, John Arlott and Trevor Bailey, that incomparable Test Match Special team bringing the ball-by-ball commentary from BBC. As Abid Ali cut the ball to the boundary for the winning runs, it was Johnston, his voice as fruity and sporting as ever, telling us that India had won. Everyone spent the next few hours in a trance. Younger Indians might recall a somewhat similar feeling when Kapil Dev's team defeated West Indies at Lord's on 25 June 1983 or when M.S. Dhoni's men won at Wankhede on 2 April 2011 – the same ecstasy, goofiness, hugging strangers, distributing sweets, dinner forgotten...

The key to the victory at the Oval lay in the first Test at Lord's. Just as India wrested the upper hand in the first match in West Indies to set the tempo for the series, Ajit Wadekar and his men took charge of Lord's. India held all the cards till the final hour of play. Three things epitomized the spirit of this Indian side of 1971 at Lord's. First,

Wadekar showed his intent when he came to the crease as John Snow steamed in to bowl. The first ball from Snow to Wadekar was a bouncer. Wadekar hooked him, in front of square. He then proceeded to hit a most compelling 85, an emphatic way of saying the Indians would not take a backward step. Second, by taking 17 wickets between them, India's spinners showed they had the firepower to bowl out England in English conditions. The third and most stirring indication of this side's feisty spirit was displayed on the final day, when India had to get 183 to win but more than the threat of English bowling it was the threat of rains that worried them. So they changed their batting order and sent the cavalier Engineer up the order to attack, and by the time he was out, India had reached 87 for 3 and India had less than a hundred to get. Rain was imminent but the batsmen plugged on. And soon the Indians lost Viswanath and Sardesai, too. By the time the rains came, India had lost eight wickets and were 38 runs short of the target. In his post-match interview, Wadekar, with that new-found confidence – arising from the West Indies series win plus his own batting form – was absolutely blasé and said the Indians took risks because they were going for a win racing against the rains. He said all this in his characteristic mumbling drawl and the reporters had to really lean and stretch to catch what this man from Bombay was saying. When a team was playing like that, even that drawl sounded cool!

The Oval, home to Surrey, venue of this third Test, has always been kind to spinners. It was also the second half of the English summer. The Indians would have loved to bat first but Wadekar lost the toss and Ray Illingworth batted first. Geoff Boycott, their safest opener, was injured and not available. The man who replaced Boycott was John Jameson, a tall, well-built, aggressive opener. Jameson had an Indian connection – he was born in 1941 in Bombay, where his father was a police officer. Jameson was also England's tactical response of throwing an aggressive opener to unsettle the Indians. India achieved an early breakthrough – as they had done in every England innings that summer – as Solkar dismissed Brian Luckhurst cheaply, caught in the slips by

Gavaskar with just five runs on the board. But for the next couple of hours, England was on top, with Jameson proving it was a good move to bring him into the team. Brisk and firm drives featured his robust approach. It was not until John Edrich, who had been watchful and dour, and had got his runs square off the wicket, fell to Bedi after making 41 that a mini collapse was triggered. Keith Fletcher pottered around and was consumed by Bedi; Jameson, who was on 82, was run out; immediately thereafter, Chandra dismissed Basil D'Oliveira for just 2. From the comfort of 111 for 1, England had descended to 143 for 5. After a brief resistance, Chandra clean bowled the England captain and the score now read a sorry 175 for 6.

It was here that England again took charge. Alan Knott, the world's best keeper during all his playing days, was also a very troublesome batsman, particularly for the Indian spinners. India prized his wicket the most throughout that tour. He had an unorthodox technique: he would play some outrageous shots and generally throw spinners off their stride. At the Oval, he was joined by a man with an illustrious lineage – Richard Hutton, son of Len Hutton. Richard had an unremarkable career and played only five Tests, all of them in that summer of 1971. But he played his best innings that day against India. While Knott attacked vigorously, Hutton bided his time. When Solkar returned to claim Knott for 90, England had reached 278 for 7. Now, with just the tail for company, Hutton unfurled his attacking shots. Snow deserted him quickly but Derek Underwood hung around, which gave Hutton time to leap ahead and gallop past 50, 60 and 70. Finally, Venkat dismissed the two of them, but England had reached 355. Looking back today, it is interesting to note that India bowled 108.4 overs in a day.

After the second day was washed out without a ball being bowled, on the third day, India sent out Gavaskar and Ashok Mankad, who too came from a proud cricketing lineage, the son of Vinoo Mankad, the legendary all-rounder. Ashok failed in all three Tests that tour, but India stayed with him as they played an unchanged team in all three Tests. He was a canny captain for Bombay in the domestic circuit, an astute strategist. In England, he remained sunny despite repeated failures. His singing and funny announcements in the dressing room were more valuable than the runs he scored. That morning, India began badly. Mankad left early, Gavaskar followed soon after and India were a sorry 21 for 2. Snow was at the time the best fast bowler in the world, but John Price, his new-ball partner, was perhaps among the fastest. He came off a long diagonal run, a tall man with a high action, and he made the ball fly off the pitch from a good length. He tested the Indians all through that summer. Once the two openers left, Wadekar and Sardesai, experienced and unflappable, weathered over 40 overs together. Then, much like England, India lost wickets in a heap. Sardesai had just crossed 50 and Wadekar was nearing his half-century when Ray Illingworth, the skipper, got Sardesai, Viswanath and Wadekar in a cluster with his off spinners. India slumped to 125 for 5. Once again, just as England did, India's lower order put up a fight. Engineer and Solkar got together for a 97-run partnership for the sixth wicket, with Engineer making 59 and Solkar compiling 44. At the end of day three, India were 234 for 7.

Just two days left, and not even two innings had been completed. On the fourth morning, after a rest day, Abid and Venkat fought back, adding 48 runs for the eighth wicket. The Indian innings ended at 284, conceding a lead of 71, but far less than what was feared when half the side had been dismissed for just 125. During this period in Indian cricket, Solkar and Abid were critical to the balance of the team. They were the archetypal utility cricketers whose contributions are buried under glorious exploits of the great batsmen and bowlers. Their figures are not outstanding, but in 1971–72, they regularly chipped in with bat and ball. In the eight Tests against West Indies and England in 1971, Solkar hit five fifties with a batting average of around 40 and took 12 wickets, while Abid Ali batted for an average of 26 and also took 16 wickets. They made sure India batted deep and had five bowlers at their disposal. To top it, Solkar at forward short-leg and Abid Ali at backward short-leg gave Indian spinners the best possible close-in catching support they could have asked for. Venkat, in a conversation with us on all-rounders, was emphatic that Kapil Dev's and Ian Botham's superior fielding and catching prowess must always be taken into account while comparing them with Imran Khan and Richard Hadlee, since one must be good in all three departments of the game to be called a great all-rounder. In the same vein, Abid's and Solkar's catching expertise must also be seen as part of what they brought as all-rounders.

England began their second innings shortly before lunch. Jameson and Luckhurst negotiated three overs each from Abid and Solkar without fuss and the lead stretched to 94 runs. Till this point on the fourth day it seemed like normal service, but as they say, it was just the calm before the storm. The tsunami hit the Oval, in the form of a tall, thin, long-haired, full-sleeved magical destroyer, with a name worthy of South Indian spinners: Bhagwat Subramanya Chandrasekhar. With lunch a few overs away, Wadekar called upon Chandra to bowl from the Vauxhall end. Those who had seen him bowl would know that Chandra loitered around fine-leg or third man, a bit lost in reverie until the captain summoned him. His field was set with minimum fuss. He would urgently, insistently, spin the ball from right hand to left many times before a delivery. He had a straight run-up, bounding in about ten paces and would bowl a mix of legspinners, top spinners and googlies that fizzed off the pitch. Sometimes he would lose control and bowl a rash of long hops. When walking around, he often held his right hand at the wrist with his left hand. Chandra fielded on the boundary and would throw with his left hand. His right hand, affected by polio in his childhood, was only for bowling magical legspinners, googlies and top spinners. Suresh Menon wrote touchingly about Chandra: 'We grew close after his playing days when I was starting out as a cricket writer and spent many evenings talking cricket either at a common friend's house or his own. Sometimes I slept over, and my respect for Chandra grew every time he took off his shirt to relax – something he never did in company. How could this man even hold a pencil with his right hand, let alone deliver a cricket ball with such venom?' Much in the same vein,

Bedi, his roommate on many occasions, has said that Chandra, even in private, would never be seen in a towel or with his upper body bared. Even on a masseur's table Chandra would be covered, for his right arm had been withered to the bone. There was only awe and admiration in Bedi that his comrade had overcome such a disadvantage to become one of the most feared bowlers in the world.

Chandra's tremendous love for the old Hindi film songs of Mukesh and K.L. Saigal is legendary. Once playing against Gavaskar in a Ranji fixture, he beat Gavaskar all ends up. Instead of exulting, he walked over to Gavaskar to ask, '*Suna kya?*' (Did you hear that), for wafting from a transistor radio in the stands was a song by Mukesh. Bedi said that Chandra did not understand the lyrics, but was captivated by the rhythm. The other story is perhaps not as well known. When the victorious team arrived at Santa Cruz airport and he was being given a hero's welcome, he wriggled away to pigeonhole Raju Bharatan and ask him if he had brought him the promised recording of Saigal's songs! Like many cricketers of his time from Bangalore and Mysore, Chandra was a product of tennis-ball cricket culture and it was the captain of Mysore state, V. Subramanya, who spotted his rare talent and catapulted him into the state Ranji team.

Chandra was a regular fixture in the Indian team after his debut in 1963–64 till he returned injured midway from a tour of Australia in 1967–68. The England series in 1971 was his comeback tour. In four innings thus far in the three Tests, Chandra had taken seven wickets for 341 runs. In those same four innings, Venkat had taken 11 for 306 and Bedi 10 for 324.

Now, when he came on to bowl, Luckhurst drove him back and Chandra touched it with his fingertips before it crashed into the stumps at the non-striker's end. Jameson, backing up, was short of his ground and India had got a breakthrough in a most fortuitous manner. The fun had begun. Chandra and Sardesai who liked to go to the races had backed a winner called Mildred on the rest day. So when Chandra was about to bowl to John Edrich, Sardesai shouted out 'Bowl him a

Mildred!' Chandra, on cue, delivered a devastating googly that pitched on middle and took the offstump, while Edrich was shaping to play the ball to the onside. So, 24 for 2 became 24 for 3, as Fletcher went first ball to an excellent diving catch at forward short-leg by Solkar. Lunch was taken at this stage and tremors were being felt in Illingworth's camp. Chandra could not wait to bowl as the Indian fielders walked back after lunch. At the pavilion end, Venkat came on to bowl. Wadekar had Venkat and Chandra wheeling away during the entire innings. The two spinners attacked D'Oliveira and Luckhurst, who defended desperately, until Venkat beat the former. As D'Oliveira came down to drive, the ball dropped in its flight and the mistimed lofted stroke was held in the country, that vast acreage around deep mid-wicket and long-on. Venkat told us, 'I might have got only two wickets in this innings, but I believe I bowled at my best right through the innings. I bowled unchanged from one end. I had a great tour, joint-highest of 13 wickets with Chandra in the Test series and 63 wickets in all the first-class matches the Indian team played, the highest by an Indian bowler. I took 9 for 93 in an innings against Hampshire.'

England's next wicket will qualify as one of the best catches at forward short-leg ever. Knott played Venkat's offbreak with a stretched forward defensive, and the ball hardly stayed in the air for a bit before looping to the left of the batsman. In a combination of unbelievable anticipation and incredible acrobatics, Solkar flung himself full stretch forward to catch it. England were now 54 for 5. From here, their innings went into a tailspin as Chandra cut through England like knife through butter. Illingworth was caught and bowled; Chandra rarely missed a catch off his own bowling and even when he held a return catch off a full toss, he made it seem as if he was expecting it. His next victim was Luckhurst, who had ploughed on to 36 when he fell to a blinder of a catch by Venkat standing at slip. If you look at the footage of this innings you will see that more of his teammates congregated around Venkat after this catch than when he claimed D'Oliveira or Knott. In fact, Chandra leapt in the air as Venkat caught the ball.

Almost immediately after, Chandra had his 'fiver' as Snow gave him a return catch and the scoreboard read 72 for 8. England's biggest partnership of 24 runs was for the ninth wicket between Underwood and Hutton. All this while Venkat and Chandra had bowled unchanged. Wadekar now brought on Bedi who promptly consumed Underwood, caught jubilantly by Mankad running in from backward square-leg. Wadekar asserts that during that entire series India did not drop a catch. That was no empty boast. When we ran some statistics for the mode of dismissals effected by India since they began playing Test cricket, we got some very interesting facts. Till the end of the 1960s, only around 40 per cent of the wickets taken by India were through catches by their fielders. But in the 1970s, this figure rose to 47 per cent. It dropped a bit again during the period 1981–2000 and then rose again in the golden decade of 2001–10, to almost touch the 1970s' level. This sharp increase in the catches ratio in the 1970s is a reaffirmation of the excellent close catching of those days.

After Venkat bowled the next over, the skipper immediately brought back Chandra. John Price, the No. 11 for England, was stuck on the crease as he missed a fizzing full-length ball from Chandra. Chandra's appeal and the umpire's raised finger were simultaneous. In one action Chandra whirred around to collect his sweater from the umpire. The job was done, England all out 101, Chandra 18.1 overs, 6 for 38. Undemonstrative as ever, just cradling his right wrist in his left hand, he accepted the congratulations offered by his teammates and then led the team back. Wadekar had his own cap pulled low as did many of the others so one could hardly see big grins or smiles as the team went back. It was just past 4 p.m. and India had the rest of that evening and the next day to score 173 runs to record their first win in England.

A fourth innings chase is tricky at all times, but more so if the bowling unit is strong. England had Snow and Price as fast bowlers, while Underwood and Illingworth would exploit the turn that the wearing wicket afforded. India got off to a terrible start, losing Gavaskar for zero, lbw, as he offered no stroke to one that came back. Mankad tried to stay, but with India's score on 37, he lost his wicket to the left-arm spin of Underwood. This was when Sardesai joined Wadekar. In a role reversal for both of them from the earlier series in West Indies, Wadekar, upbeat after finding his batting compass, batted fluently, while Sardesai was not fluent but hung in grimly. The experienced duo took India to 76 for 2, with Wadekar on a confident 45 at stumps. India needed 97 runs to win on the last day.

India got off to the worst possible start on the final day. Without a run being added to the overnight score, Wadekar was run out by D'Oliveira stationed at third man, as he responded to Sardesai's call for a sharp single. It would have been enough to shatter any captain but Wadekar in his book *My Cricketing Years* wrote that he was not 'unduly alarmed' as he was confident that the rest of the batsmen would do the job. He claimed to have promptly gone to sleep as soon as he reached the dressing room. Little Viswanath now joined Sardesai. A wicket at this stage would have spelt disaster but Viswanath came good, giving valuable company to Sardesai who was considered one of the best players of spin in his days. In *A History of Indian Cricket*, Mihir Bose wrote on this passage of play: 'In 105 minutes they put on 48. The tension was unbearable, every ball required careful watching...runs were not so much stroked as chiselled out of the hard, granite, English attack.' The score was 124 when Underwood dismissed Sardesai for 40 after Knott the keeper dove forward to take a catch right in front of the stumps off a defensive jab. The trusty veteran desperately wanted to be there till the end, but he later acknowledged Knott's catch was truly great. Knott himself ranked it among his five best catches. Shortly thereafter, Solkar fell, a rare failure for him, but at a very inconvenient time for India.

With half the side gone, India still needed 39 runs. It was reassuring to see Engineer stride out to the middle to join Viswanath. We now remember Engineer as a flamboyant, effervescent batsman; with his thick hair and large sideburns, the obvious choice for Brylcreem advertisements. According to Venkataraghavan, 'Engineer strengthened our team, coming back after missing the West Indies series. He played crucial knocks right through the England series.' His scores so far had been 28, 35, 22 and 59, and he continued from where he had left off. Engineer calmed the nerves of his colleagues and the millions glued to their transistors in India with three boundaries and some brisk running. Soon the target was just a boundary away. Illingworth, who had thrown in the towel, brought on Luckhurst to complete the formalities. Viswanath tried to end the match with a blow that would land the ball in Mysore, but instead lost his wicket. That gave Abid his second opportunity in six months to be in the middle when India won. As he promptly cut Luckhurst for the winning boundary, both Engineer and he tried to hare it down to the safe haven of the pavilion. Fat chance! Even before they were halfway, hordes of delirious Indian fans descended on the ground, and inexpertly and very uncomfortably, hoisted Engineer on their shoulders. That worthy, as we all know, was a large man and it was sheer good luck that the fans deposited him near the pavilion without damage.

As the Indian players came out to the balcony, the fans could not have enough of them. For each of them, it was probably the happiest moment of their lives. Sardesai recounted that John Arlott took him to the Oval long room where the members sat in glum silence, still shocked beyond words at the defeat and the loss of the series. Wadekar said, 'As I acknowledged the cheers of our supporters, I thought of those millions back home, who would share our joy and pride... The boys let themselves go and even Hemu (the stern manager) looked on indulgently...' Indian restaurants in England for the first time had occasion to celebrate an Indian victory, and came up with menus that included a Wadekar cutlet, a Gavaskar curry and a Chandra soup. Wadekar mischievously said that Chandra Soup was an apt one for the Englishmen had landed themselves in one the previous day!

Venkat remembered, 'It was Vinayaka Chaturthi day and when an elephant was brought from the zoo and strolled around the ground, the Indian team thought it was a great omen! It ended 26 matches without defeat for England and was Illingworth's first defeat in 20

Keith Miller, the great Australian all-rounder, called India's victory 'A historic triumph'.
(Used with permission from the New Indian Express Group)

matches.' Keith Miller, the great Australian all-rounder, in the *Indian Express*, called it 'A historic triumph'. Miller wrote that Abid Ali now had a story to tell his grandchildren over and over again. He declared, 'With that win over the West Indies earlier in the year and now the conquerors of England who trounced my own Australians, India are contenders for the best team in the world.'

Derek Underwood later wrote in his book *Beating the Bat*, 'Many other sides might well have cracked under the pressure, but [India] grafted as I have never seen Indian batsmen graft in inching their way along the path to a historic victory.' The entire British press acknowledged that a truly superior team had won. E.W. Swanton praised Chandra's bowling and Wadekar's 'cool shrewd handling on the field'. The *Daily Telegraph* ran an editorial saying that the Indian team had proved they were men for all seasons. John Woodcock who had earlier been totally captivated by the Indian spinners on their tour of the West Indies now wrote about the Oval win in *The Times*, 'Last Friday evening no one gave them the slightest chance of winning... But Chandrasekhar fooled us all and yesterday India kept their nerve where Pakistan and Australia have recently lost theirs.' Crawford White, in his column for the *Daily Express*, stated that once 'Chandrasekhar turned on that 6 for 38 bowling burst to paralyse England's innings for 101, this was their game'.

The Indian team came home to an unprecedented welcome. They were received like kings at Bombay's Santa Cruz airport, submerged in garlands of marigold, travelling in a cavalcade that took hours to cover a few miles because thousands of fans had come to greet them. The gratitude and happiness of a cricket-mad nation knew no bounds. For weeks after, cinema-goers in India were treated to visuals of this reception in the newsreel that preceded the screening of films. The audience in the cinema hall would spontaneously stand and clap as the cricketing heroes came up on the screen. It was an unforgettable time in India's cricket history.

Test No. 692: The Oval, London, 19–24 August 1971: England (Toss) 355 in 108.4 overs (Alan Knott 90, John Jameson 82; Eknath Solkar 3-28, S. Venkataraghavan 2-63) and 101 in 45.1 overs (Brian Luckhurst 33; Bhagwat Chandrasekhar 6-38, Venkataraghavan 2-44) lost to **India** 284 in 117.3 overs (Farokh Engineer 59, Dilip Sardesai 54; Ray Illingworth 5-70, John Snow 2-68) and 174/6 in 101 overs (Ajit Wadekar 45, Sardesai 40; Derek Underwood 3-72) by four wickets.

Captains: Ajit Wadekar (India) and Ray Illingworth (England)

8

Eden and Euphoria

India vs West Indies, third Test, Eden Gardens, Kolkata, 1974–75

From the heights of 1971, India fell to a disastrous low in their next tour to England in 1974. The Midas touch of Wadekar turned to ashes as India lost every Test that summer – 3-0 was the scoreline – but the tour was awful on more counts. There was bickering and bad blood in the team, a poorly handled case of alleged shoplifting against a player, and insult heaped for arriving late at the Indian High Commissioner's tea party. Gavaskar called it the worst tour of his career. Around the time India collapsed for 42 all out in the second innings of the second Test at Lord's, the Hollywood film *Summer of 42* was running in India. Reporters quickly dubbed this Indian tour 'Summer of 42'.

Although other teams have suffered similar fates – England were all out for 46 against Ambrose and company in West Indies in 1994; as recently as 2015, Australia were all out for 60 against England – the cricket-crazy nation treated the 42 all out as a national calamity. But there were more severe, pressing problems that year: a severe drought, the price rise and unemployment that had swept through the country. A major train strike had paralysed Indian Railways that summer and India's agitated youth were galvanized into a major democratic civil disobedience movement by the Gandhian socialist Jayaprakash Narayan.

Despite such turbulent times, defeat in what was ultimately only a sport caused extremely visceral and disproportionate reactions. Wadekar was summarily sacked and he retired from cricket. But it was difficult to find a successor. Venkat, his vice-captain, was not sure of his place in the team. Gavaskar was too young. No one was sure whether Engineer was the answer. Bedi was persona non grata with the board that had issued a show cause notice asking him why he appeared in interviews on television during that tour, and axed him from the first two games in the upcoming series against West Indies. So the selectors went back to Pataudi. Tiger would be leading a demoralized Indian team against Clive Lloyd's West Indians at a time when the latter too were in transition. Lloyd was leading for the first time, and his team had a number of debutant batsmen and an almost new bowling attack except Gibbs and Holder. But the Windies were a formidable side, and the first Test in Bangalore, at the newly constructed Karnataka State Cricket Association Stadium, later renamed M. Chinnaswamy Stadium, only confirmed these fears. Debutant Gordon Greenidge, skipper Lloyd and company pulverized India. To add to India's misery, Pataudi injured his hand while taking a catch and was ruled out of the next Test in Delhi. Gavaskar was announced captain for the Delhi game but he broke his thumb in a Ranji Trophy match and was ruled out of the next three Tests. In Delhi, the public was up in arms against the axing of Bedi and 'No Bedi no Test' banners were seen everywhere. The board climbed down at this protest and included Bedi in the team at the expense of Chandrasekhar.

On the morning of the Delhi Test, not even the players themselves knew who their captain would be until Venkat walked out for the toss with Lloyd. The match ended in an innings defeat. Pataudi was now fit to play and lead in the third Test in Kolkata; the Indian board, insensitive as ever, dropped Venkat from the XI. No wonder Bedi fumed that if there had been at least two more cricketers who had spoken their minds and stood up to the administrators at that time, things would have been different.

The series scoreline reading 0-2, Pataudi went out for the toss at Eden Gardens. India's opening pair was the experienced dasher Engineer and the very new Sudhir Naik. Its middle order was in a churn. The experiment to induct the plodding Kanitkar had failed and Brijesh Patel had shown his acute dislike for pace. Parthasarthi Sharma, the batsman from Rajasthan who made his debut in Delhi, would bat one-down. Desperate, India introduced a new middle-order batsman, the bespectacled Anshuman Gaekwad. Viswanath and Pataudi provided the experience in the middle order but neither seemed to provide any confidence. The former had made it a habit to get out after getting good starts while the latter was in the twilight of his career, his reflexes on the wane. India also dropped Abid Ali and Solkar and brought in a new pair of all-rounders – Madan Lal (a few Tests old) and Karsan Ghavri the left-arm seamer from Rajkot, making his debut.

Pearson Surita, in his rich baritone on radio, announced that India won the toss and would begin their innings 'with the impossible combination of Sudhir Naik and Engineer' but had no time to end that sentence because Sudhir Naik was dismissed off the first ball, caught by keeper Murray off Roberts. The second wicket fell shortly thereafter as Julien bowling left-arm over, swung the ball away from Parthasarthi Sharma and brought it back after pitching to shatter his stumps. Minutes later India lost Engineer caught by Lloyd off the express pace of Roberts. K.N. Prabhu described that acrobatic catch for the readers of the *Times of India*: 'Lloyd apparently polishes his shoes with some special jet propulsion for he is able to spring to any position in an instant.' Roberts at his fastest and best in that series, now set his sights on Viswanath and Pataudi. It was harrowing to watch the skipper play. Tiger was late on every ball, and it seemed like he was playing from memory. Soon a bouncer crashed into his jaw. Bleeding profusely, his gloves holding his gashed chin, Tiger walked off the ground. The 22-year-old debutant Gaekwad came out to join Viswanath. Gaekwad's strong suit was grit, guts and resilience, not attractive strokeplay. That is how he played throughout his career. Firm and brave, he calmed everyone's nerves. Viswanath was batting well as always and thankfully he did not give his wicket away. Together, they thwarted the West Indians for nearly two hours, adding 62 runs. Then the inexperience showed, as Gaekwad was foxed by the part-time Chinaman spin of Fredericks and lost his wicket. In came Madan Lal.

Everyone now remembers Madan for his ball in the 1983 World Cup that dismissed Richards, but he was more than that. Ghavri and he were useful medium pace bowling all-rounders who gave India some balance. Madan was modest but loved a fight. Had helmets been available early in his career, he might have done better as a batsman. At Eden Gardens, the score was 94 for 4 when he came to bat and he knew it would be a matter of time before a speedster got him. So when Roberts and Holder got a breather, he attacked the spinners with gusto, and like in the 'Wild West' stories, he wanted to get as many of them before they got him. He had ten boundaries in his 48, before Holder got him. The debutant Ghavri joined Viswanath, who had been batting serenely and crossed fifty, a milestone of significance as he had scored 28, 25, 29, 22, 32 and 39 in the last six innings, getting a start every time before being dismissed. Yet, here again, immediately after he reached his 50, he left, trapped leg before by Gibbs. The scoreboard now read 169 for 6.

A buzz went around the ground as the spectators saw the Indian skipper, his chin plastered, walking to the middle to resume his innings. Lloyd did the obvious – he brought on Roberts and Holder to bowl. But Pataudi had found his magic vein, and in a thrilling counter-attack, launched a cascade of four boundaries in one over from Holder. Tony Cozier was on the air at the time. Dazzled by the sheer courage and magnificence of this assault, Cozier in his mellifluous voice conveyed pleasure and admiration. The captain raced to 36 in no time before Roberts got him. As Pataudi walked back, the entire stadium rose, knowing they had watched the swansong of one of the bravest cricketers in the game's history. All one could hear on the radio for several minutes was the applause of those who were there to watch this brilliant phase of play.

Here, pause to consider that Pataudi played almost all his Test cricket with one eye after he lost his right eye in a car accident in England when he was just 21. To play after such a setback is itself amazing, but to then bat and field as Tiger did is unparalleled in cricket history. His century at Leeds in 1967 is one of the finest by an Indian in England, while his two stirring essays of 75 and 85 later that year at Melbourne were played not only with one eye but on one leg, as he had an injured hamstring. When he resumed Test cricket after losing his right eye, Gubby Allen, the English cricketer, asked him admiringly when he believed he could play Test cricket again. 'When I saw the English bowling,' replied Pataudi mischievously.

India finished at 233, leaving Fredericks and Greenidge to negotiate the few minutes before stumps on the first day. The next day India hit back; it was perhaps its best day in the series. It was not the spinners who did the damage but Madan Lal who ended up with the impressive figures of 4 for 22 runs from 16.1 overs. After his 48 on the first day, to follow up with this kind of bowling was brilliant. Some batsmen have, with wicked humour, wondered why he ran so many yards, arms whirling, to bowl at his pace. But Madan Lal kept surprising the batsmen, as he did the West Indians here. He got Greenidge and Kallicharran in twin strikes with the score at 42. West Indies were rattled further when Vivian Richards was run out for just 15. Lloyd did not stay long either, edging Bedi to Engineer after making 19, and West Indies had slipped to 115 for 4. Meanwhile, Fredericks continued to bat. His greatest innings was to come a year later in Perth but here he was doing a sterling job. Sharma dropped him when he was 15, but now he had crossed 50 and all he needed was a durable partner, which he found in Deryck Murray, the wicketkeeper-batsman with a luxuriant goatee. The Cambridge-educated Murray was a senior member in this side, someone whom Lloyd, new to his job, would consult regularly. This afternoon,

Murray and Fredericks added a valuable 74 runs. Fredericks completed his 100 and immediately gave his wicket to Madan Lal. Bernard Julien came out to replace him. Julien, whose batting reputation was based on a blazing century in England in 1973, hardly did anything of note thereafter. It was no different here. Bedi had him caught. Soon after, Murray was run out, and the West Indians were finally bowled out for 240, a lead of just seven runs.

Everything boiled down to the second innings. Anything less than 250 as a target for the Windies would not be adequate, but anything over 300 gave India a good chance because of their spin attack. Bedi, talking to us about that match in particular and those times in general, said, 'Yaar, we would ask the batsmen, give us something to bowl with. Give us 250 regularly, please. At Calcutta, they gave us more than that.' Midway through the Indian innings, 300 looked very unlikely. Opener Naik failed once again, falling to Roberts. Sharma arrived and it looked like it was a matter of time before he either ran Engineer or himself out. After hair-raising running on three occasions, he was sent on his way by a bullet throw from Lloyd at cover point. Prabhu wrote in the *Times of India*, 'Sharma ran like one demented.'

It was at this point that Viswanath joined Engineer. After his 52 in the first innings, he knew the team depended on him. Behram Contractor, famous for his cult column under the pseudonym Busybee, once wrote, 'When Viswanath scores thirty, Prabhu writes poetry.' His batting always had an ethereal beauty about it, and now he had found the magic key to ensure he did not fall in his thirties. Along with Engineer, who batted in his usual robust manner, a mixture of assurance and unpredictability, Viswanath stitched a stout-hearted partnership that took India to 120. Engineer was 37 years old, kept wickets and also opened the batting. That is a full plate even for a younger man. Engineer fell after an intense period of concentration against fast bowling after making a valuable 61. Once Engineer went, the frail middle order was exposed. Pataudi too was dismissed by left-arm spinner Willett. Gaekwad and Madan Lal failed this time, and the Indian innings at

192 for 6 was staring at an early demise. Ghavri, the debutant, came out to negotiate the remaining time that day and India ended at 210 for 6 when stumps were drawn. Viswanath remained unbeaten on 75, and Prabhu wrote, 'There is only one Viswanath. There is none like him.'

When the game resumed after rest day, the plot changed. Most people expected the Indian innings to fold up quickly, leaving West Indies a simple target. But Ghavri played the most significant innings of his career – just 27 runs, but he stayed for over two hours and helped Viswanath add 91 runs for the seventh wicket. Lloyd's tactics too were inexplicable that morning, as he took Roberts off after just three overs, during which he had Viswanath dropped in the slips and Ghavri in trouble. Raju Bharatan wrote witheringly, 'Not even a school boy captain would have committed such an elementary error.' Venkataraghavan told us Lloyd had been tactically poor in his first tour as captain; perhaps the blunders of Calcutta were on his mind when he said that.

The Calcutta crowd adored little Viswanath, as did crowds everywhere. That last day of 1974, he created an even more special place in their hearts. It was a most remarkable century, holding the innings together for more than a day while facing 263 balls; careful defence was leavened with 23 boundaries – every time he saw an opportunity to attack, he maximized the benefits. Prabhu in his dispatch on the fourth day's play averred, 'It was his best…and it contained all the wristy elegant strokes that mark Viswanath as an artist in a class above.' When he was finally bowled by a break back from Holder (the one bowler who troubled Viswanath in that series with his in-cutters) he had ensured Bedi and other bowlers would have more runs than they had asked for.

From this Test onwards, Viswanath was simply magnificent. He would come to the wicket, India cap on his head, sleeves rolled to the elbows, a small man, slim in those days, tap the pitch a few times and get going. Assured in defence, going back or forward, an innate ability to ride the bounce despite being a short man and then the ability to play an amazing array of cuts and square-drives that lacerated the fence between covers and third man. On the leg side, he had the gorgeous flick. Brian Johnston had, upon a brief examination of Viswanath in 1971, declared him 'a complete batsman'.

West Indies began their pursuit of 310 runs on the afternoon of the fourth day, with plenty of time for a team that boasted of Fredericks, Greenidge, Richards and Lloyd in its ranks. But there were two roadblocks: the condition of the pitch and the fact that no team is immune to the pressure of getting runs in the fourth innings. India got off to a dream start as Ghavri made a vital breakthrough, trapping Greenidge leg before for just 3. Alvin Kallicharran came one down. His century in the first Test in Bangalore against Prasanna, Venkat and Chandra proved he was the best West Indian batsmen against spin. Here, the stylish left-hander was into his groove straight away, making batting look easy. At the other end, Fredericks was bamboozled and bowled by Bedi. While Bedi was bowling well, Chandra was profligate and off the boil, and Prasanna seemed to lack penetration. In no time, West Indies had changed gears and the belligerent Richards and silken Kallicharran were surging ahead. From 41 for 2, the pair had quickly gone past 100 and more. Prabhu wrote: 'It was Richards who dispersed and discouraged the Indian attack... In 20 minutes after tea the complexion of the game had changed and the bowling looked deadbeat, the fielders footsore...'

Pataudi, realizing rather late that something desperate was needed, summoned Madan Lal. One can only use imagination to guess what went through Richards' mind as he saw Madan Lal ready to bowl. He had raced to 47, with his basic instinct to dominate bowlers ever present, and Lal's benign pace may have made him think, here comes fodder for my cannon. In his first over, Madan Lal delivered a good off-cutter on length, and in the words of Raju Bharatan, 'Richards, a trifle jazzily, played back instead of firmly forward and had his legstump knocked out of the ground.' Sport, in true reflection of human nature, sometimes throws up pleasant surprises. West Indies were now 126 for 3, with another 184 runs required for victory. The game had tilted once again and the day ended with Prasanna troubling Lloyd no end. Very perceptively, Prabhu wrote, 'There is enough room for the spinners to exploit this weakness in the early crucial hour tomorrow.'

Next morning, Pataudi started with Chandra, a bold move as the legspinner had not inspired confidence the previous day. The start was ominous as Lloyd belted three boundaries. But some instinct told Pataudi to continue with Chandra, and that is when the dam burst. A crowd of over 75,000 erupted as Chandra produced a lethal googly to clean bowl the left-handed Lloyd. The score: 163 for 4. Chandra's tail was up, the Eden Gardens crowd had their voice back, and soon Kallicharran too was gone, caught at slip playing across the line, succumbing to pressure. Chandra capped his morning with a third wicket on the reel, as Julien was nailed lbw. A friend who saw that match swears that Julien walked before the umpire gave him out, so plumb was he. At 186 for 6, only Murray and the tail remained. One of the most incisive descriptions of that morning came from Ron Hendricks, the legendary sports editor, in his report for the *Indian Express*: 'Wise-acres in the stands lamented, raved and ranted as Chandra was knocked about in his first three overs. What they did not know was that overnight dew had freshened the uncovered pitch and that it now gave Chandra the nip and bounce he required, and which he did not get yesterday afternoon… Chandra broke the backbone of the West Indies batting once he found his length and rhythm.'

Bedi got rid of Murray before West Indies crossed 200 and then wiped off the last two batsmen, Gibbs and Willett, as India romped home by 85 runs. Rajan Bala recounted how the previous night Pataudi barely pecked at his food as he worried over who should open India's bowling on the final day. As his teammates were dispersing after dinner, Pataudi told them, 'I have decided to leave it in the hands of Chandra. He will either win the match or lose it.' Prasanna described playing under Pataudi's captaincy thus: 'When West Indies batted, I saw Tiger's genius as captain. On a slow pitch he had medium pacer Madan Lal and Ghavri bowling to them. His hustling tactics paid off… Tiger gambled like a crazy punter. His daredevil tactics paid

'Chandra broke the backbone of the West Indies batting once he found his length and rhythm.'
(Used with permission from the New Indian Express Group)

off. The crowd worshipped him. Tiger got the best out of everybody.'
For a humorous dousing of romantic narrations, one must read what
Suresh Menon wrote: 'It was a practical decision as the other bowlers
needed some time to catch their breath in the New Year.' Apparently,

the other bowlers had wined rather generously at the New Year's Eve party the previous night!

The year could not have begun on a better note. Less than a fortnight later, India drew level beating the Windies in Madras. We watched the magnificent Viswanath play the finest-ever 'non-100' innings in Indian cricket at Chepauk. Many people believe his 97 not out is among the greatest ever innings by a cricketer but Viswanath ranks his innings at Eden Gardens higher. The innings in Madras only followed what had begun in Calcutta, where Viswanath crossed the Rubicon.

Test No. 750: Eden Gardens, Calcutta, 27 December 1974– 1 January 1975: India (Toss) 233 in 80.3 overs (Gundappa Viswanath 52, Madan Lal 48; Andy Roberts 5-50, Vanburn Holder 2-48) and 316 in 143.2 overs (Viswanath 139, Farokh Engineer 61; Holder 3-61, Roberts 3-88) beat **West Indies** 240 in 81.1 overs (Roy Fredericks 100, Deryck Murray 24; Madan 4-22, Bishan Singh Bedi 2-68) and 224 in 84.2 overs (Alvin Kallicharran 57, Vivian Richards 47; Bedi 4-52, Bhagwat Chandrasekhar 3-66) by 85 runs.

Captains: M.A.K. Pataudi (India) and Clive Lloyd (West Indies)

9

Emulating the Invincibles

India vs West Indies, third Test, Queen's Park Oval,
Port-of-Spain, Trinidad, 1976

An air of resignation had set in among Indian cricket fans, as Lloyd set India 404 to win in the late afternoon of the fourth day. Even after Gavaskar, Gaekwad and Mohinder had steered India to 134 for 1 at the end of the day, there was despondency among our friends as they discussed the fate that awaited India on the final day. They required 279 runs to reach a summit that had been scaled only once before, and that too by the invincible Australian team of 1948. One of our friends said defeat was such a foregone conclusion that he would shave off half his moustache and roam around the metropolis if India achieved a miracle of a win. Contrast his pessimism with the faith and optimism of thousands of East Indians in Trinidad who poured into Queens Park Oval on the final day: dressed colourfully, accompanied by their music, their humour and wit effervescent as ever and their belief in the Indian team complete. As their hearts sang for a faraway motherland that perhaps even their fathers or grandfathers had never seen, the Trinidadians of Indian descent never stopped cheering and spurring on the Indian batsmen for even a minute, the entire day. They ran every run with the Indians on that fairy-tale final day and when it was over they ran on to the ground in unbounded joy.

Till this game, the one occasion when a target of 400 was breached had been achieved by Bradman's all-time great Australian team of 1948, when they scored 404 for 3 to beat England at Leeds. It is now 40 years since Bishan Singh Bedi's team scored 406 for 4 to defeat Lloyd's team at Port-of-Spain, but so rare is the feat that only twice since then has more than 400 been scored in a winning cause. This puts into perspective how historic a feat this was.

The 1976 tour was a two-leg tour for India – first to New Zealand for three Tests and then to the Caribbean Islands for four Tests. By the time India played the third Test against West Indies in Port-of-Spain, they had been living out of suitcases for three months. Bedi, with a guffaw recalled, 'We must have travelled for 75 hours going from India to New Zealand to West Indies! Only we could do such crazy twin tours.' The Indians had left their shores in early January 1976 to play three Test matches in New Zealand, which they drew 1-1. They played the first game of the four-match series against the Windies in March at Kensington Oval, Bridgetown, Barbados. Crushed by an innings and 97 runs, Indian batsmen were blown away in both innings. Only Viswanath had a fifty to show as consolation.

The second Test was played in Port-of-Spain in the last week of March. After Kensington Oval, the Queen's Park Oval seemed like a home ground, with enough spectators of Indian descent to keep India's spirits up; it was also where India had their first-ever victory against the West Indians back in 1971. The ground would prove lucky for India once again. With the first day washed off, it became a four-day affair, and Bedi put the West Indians in to bat and dismissed them for just 241. In turn, as Gavaskar scored his customary century (Port-of-Spain was Gavaskar's favourite ground) and Brijesh Patel too hit a ton, the Indians put up an imposing 402. The West Indians escaped with a draw, finishing at 215 for 8. Venkataraghavan remembered the game vividly: 'We could have won... In their second innings, Lloyd top-edged me and Solkar and Brijesh, then our two best fielders, collided and the catch went to ground. Lloyd went on to score 70 and helped the Windies save the game.'

The next match was at the Bourda Oval, Guyana – a batting paradise. Bedi recalled his first-ever helicopter ride in Guyana under bizarre circumstances. Madan Lal and Bedi were trying to kill time near a large open space where an ancient helicopter stood. The pilot was a big-built fellow and Bedi riled him by asking him whether that thing could fly. The gigantic pilot came menacingly to Bedi and asked him if he wanted to check it out. The two looked at each other, shrugged their shoulders and said, 'Sure.' Whereupon, the helicopter took off and after some time the pilot landed right in the middle of the Bourda Oval! The story does not end there; Bedi added with a smile that it was the only time they saw the Bourda on that tour, as it rained so much that the ground became a lake. The third Test was then shifted back to Queen's Park Oval. For India, it was divine providence – the ground they liked the most was going to give them another chance. The West Indians sweetened things further by resting Andy Roberts for the last two Tests.

Due to the difference in time zones between India and the Caribbean Islands, Indian newspapers could only give lunchtime scores in their morning editions. The reports and scorecards of a day's play would reach readers a full day later. K.N. Prabhu of the *Times of India*, Kishore Bhimani of the *Statesman*, and Tony Cozier and Dicky Rutnagur with their special columns were all read with that frustrating gap between the actual time of action and the printing of the newspaper. Luckily, All India Radio decided to cover the Test matches from West Indies for the first time ever that year. Suresh Saraiya in English and Ravi Chaturvedi in Hindi provided ball-by-ball commentary, and avid followers in India happily stayed awake to listen to the action. Every few overs, listeners would be reminded that it was the munificence of the tyre giant Dunlop that had enabled all this: 'Ting ting. This commentary is brought to you courtesy Dunlop. Dunlop leads the way, all the way. Ting ting.' At around 2 a.m. India time, the commentary would go off air and then return a few hours later with the recording for the subsequent period of play.

Nothing in the first four days gave any clue about the fairy-tale ending that was to come. Unlike the second Test, where India had a vice-like grip from the first ball, West Indies called the shots in the third Test. They won the toss and batted first to put up 359, on the back of a mammoth 177 by the peerless Viv Richards. Bedi, Chandra and Venkat did almost all the bowling; Bedi had 4 for 73, Chandra had 6 for 120 and the luckless Venkat went wicket less as a couple of catches went down off his bowling. When it was India's turn to bat, none of their batsmen stayed to convert their starts into substantial scores. Gavaskar, Amarnath, Brijesh Patel made twenties while Viswanath and Madan could not go beyond the forties. Holding, aged just 22, was already on his way to becoming one of the most feared fast bowlers. He destroyed India with 6 for 65. By mid-morning on the third day, West Indies had bundled India out for 228 and gained a significant lead of 131. Their batsmen could now go after the bowling and give Lloyd a massive lead, and still have enough time for their bowlers to dismiss India a second time.

It would have been easy for India to throw in the towel, but it was here that their bowlers put in a lion-hearted performance. Madan Lal and Amarnath bowled their medium pace thriftily and gave no easy runs. Then the three spinners bowled tirelessly and with great skill for nearly 85 overs between them. Venkat had 3 for 65 off 30 overs and led the attack. A most skilful century by Kallicharran and some lusty blows towards the end by Holding wrested back the initiative and took West Indies to the eventual 271 for 6 when Lloyd declared, setting India a target that had never been touched before in the history of the game: 403 runs. He had Holding and Julien for pace and the spin of Raphick Jumadeen, Albert Padmore and Imtiaz Ali to exploit a spin-friendly track on the last two days. West Indies seemed to hold all the aces, and Bedi at breakfast admitted as much to some of his friends in the Indian press contingent.

Gavaskar walked out to the middle, accompanied by Gaekwad, who was playing as an opener for the first time, with more than a day and a half left in the game. It was imperative that India should not lose an early wicket. Gavaskar in his *Sunny Days* wrote, 'I was confident that we could save the game as the wicket was still good, but the thought of winning never entered my mind.'

Bedi recalled, 'Polly Kaka (Umrigar) was a good man. He and I had a long conversation and the only thing we were clear about was that when the West Indies claimed the second new ball, we must not be more than three down and our No. 4 or 5 should face the second new ball. If we succeeded in doing this, we had a chance. If not, we would lose. Polly Kaka gave the batsmen practice by soaking the ball in water and chucking it at the batsmen on concrete pitches. He had begun this exercise as soon as the Barbados Test was lost, but this practice was important.'

Gavaskar was quite positive against Holding and Julien while Gaekwad defended solidly. Finally, it was spin that created the breach. Gaekwad, whose weakness against left-arm spin has been mentioned earlier, fell to Jumadeen with the score at 69. There still remained time to play out on the fourth evening, and in came Amarnath to join the original Little Master, who had shown great form and fierce intent. In each of the preceding five innings on this tour, Amarnath had looked technically compact and courageous, but had not managed to cross the twenties. Here was an opportunity to make amends. Those who have watched him bat will recollect that while he faced pace with utmost courage and skill, he was also masterly against spin. Light on his feet and decisive in movement, when he played those gorgeous inside-out shots or the lofted straight hits, one saw a master at work.

When Gavaskar and Amarnath batted together, there was always great calm and confidence in the dressing room. Bedi, for all his disagreements with Gavaskar, was clear that he had not seen a better opener than the Mumbaikar. As for Amarnath, Bedi remained fond of him and full of admiration. Bedi told us, 'Jimmy was all substance

– calm, focused and ready to fight on the ground till the last breath.'

However, Bedi felt the father Lala was more showman than substance. To spice that comment, Bedi narrated: 'Once when Mushtaq Mohammad, Lala and I were talking, Lala said, "In our days we could do 30,000 skippings with a rope in thirty minutes.' To which, Mushtaq replied, "Sir, please first count 10,000 in thirty minutes and then we will think of doing 30,000 skippings in thirty minutes.'" All this was related in earthy Punjabi that made the narration even more mischievous.

That evening, Gavaskar and Amarnath safely negotiated the play till stumps. India was 134 for 1, Gavaskar brilliant on his way to 86 not out. Prabhu wrote with great prescience, 'There are 279 runs ahead. A great deal depends on how far Gavaskar will go. It is too great a burden for one man alone to bear. But there are others who are willing to share part of it. Mohinder…not for a moment in the 101 minutes he batted did he falter against pace or spin. This is the sort of cricket that wins matches…'

Play on the fifth day commenced with the hosts needing nine wickets and the Indians requiring 270 runs. B.R. Jones, the West Indian correspondent for *The Hindu*, wrote, 'Energised by Gavaskar's sterling performance yesterday, the vast population of East Indians here began their trek to the Oval from almost the break of dawn. They came from the south and central areas of the country, trendily attired and long before the Indian players arrived at the ground.' Gavaskar could not capture the scintillating fluency of the previous day but completed his century. He left immediately thereafter with the score at 177. Lunch was taken with India at 197 for 2 after surviving two scares – a missed run-out with Amarnath yards out of his crease and a huge appeal for lbw against Viswanath that was turned down.

After lunch, Amarnath played anchor while Viswanath turned up in his best form. Tony Cozier, commentator and sports scribe, wrote in his column for the *Indian Express*, 'The vital point was that they had lost no further wickets and this allowed them to accelerate through the brilliance of Viswanath, exactly when it was needed.'

At 223 for 2, as Lloyd called for the new ball, Viswanath unleashed some gorgeous batting. Jones wrote, 'Viswanath held a mid-pitch conference with his colleague and then proceeded to hit two of the most graceful cover-drives in this match.' The two put on 159 runs in 220 minutes, of which Viswanath's contribution was 112. As Viswanath hit Holding for three to reach his century, Jones noted, 'A six-year-old kid ran on to the field to congratulate Viswanath while the crowd roared.' India had achieved the vital objective that Bedi and Umrigar had wanted – India's Nos. 3 and 4 were there to take care of the second new ball. Venkat recalled, 'Mohinder was magnificent in this innings and the match really turned when they took the new ball and Vishy went berserk!'

Viswanath finally got out in the only way he could have that day, which was a run-out. Out came Brijesh Patel. Those who have seen Patel walk to the middle will remember that he had a slouch, communicating his diffidence to the opposition, to his own mates and to the crowd. Yet, he was a bold strokeplayer. With India needing just 63 to win in the last 20 mandatory overs, Patel sprang to life. It was reassuring to hear the commentary that while Amarnath was all care, Patel cut lose hitting 48 in a flurry of boundaries. Amarnath finally got out with India needing just 11 for a win, and trudged off most disconsolately. Tony Cozier wrote, 'It would have been fitting for Mohinder to have been at the wicket when the winning run was scored, for his was a job most maturely done. For seven hours and 20 minutes, the young all-rounder had defied the West Indies, ensuring no wicket fell at the other end as Gavaskar and Viswanath fulfilled their roles.' Cozier had spoken for all of India. Gavaskar was so impressed by Amarnath's development on this tour that he wrote, 'He is without doubt the most technically accomplished batsman in the side today.'

Everyone remembers that on the 1983 tour to the Windies, Amarnath came back the next day after being struck by a Malcolm Marshall bouncer to play a brilliant innings that resumed with a hooked six. But there is more to Amarnath than just such vignettes. On India's most difficult tours of Pakistan and West Indies in 1982–83, he was, apart from Gavaskar, the only Indian batsman to put up a valiant fight. It should surprise no one that he is among only four Indians who have a batting average of over 50 in overseas Tests.

The winning hit duly came with a few overs left. Jones reported, '…shouts of the crowd must have been heard halfway around the Caribbean', while Prabhu wrote, 'When Patel pulled Jumadeen to bring up the victory with six overs remaining, the crowd came racing to the pavilion, and the cheers of the Indian supporters echoed from the Northern Hills which towered over the skyline. Among the cheerleaders was veteran writer Phil Thomson who had been at that Leeds match (1948) too. It was a moment to savour, for cricket history had been made.' After the match, Ravi Chaturvedi invited Bedi to the radio box, but made him wait while he went on an inane spiel on air praising Indira Gandhi and the 20-point programme (the 'bees sutri karyakram') of her government – this was the time of the Emergency, and we weren't allowed to forget Indira Gandhi or her programmes even during sports commentaries.

The next day, The Hindu's headline said 'India registers historic win' while the Times of India headline was emphatic saying 'India's feat rates higher than that of Bradman's team'. Congratulatory messages and telegrams poured in from everywhere. One of the first messages Bedi received was a telegram from Indira Gandhi, saying, 'Congratulations to you and your team on an exciting and well-earned victory.' Two years later, when Indira Gandhi won a by-election from Chikmagalur in 1978 (after the Janata Party under Jayaprakash Narayan swept to power in a thundering rejection of the Emergency), Bedi insisted on sending her a congratulatory cable from Pakistan where the Indian team was playing. Many tried to dissuade him but his logic was clear. She had been among the first to wish him when the team won in Port-of-Spain, now it was his turn to congratulate her. Prime Minister Morarji Desai was apparently quite peeved by Bedi's action. Bedi's large heart is well known but we had a first-hand experience. When the floods hit Chennai in December 2015, Bedi, desperate about the well-being of his friends, phoned us to inquire if Venks (Venkataraghavan), Woorkeri (W.V. Raman) and a few other Chennai-based cricketers were safe. We had to reassure him that we would do our best to contact them. When he got a copy of our first book, he called us the same day, to tell us how much he enjoyed the book but in typical Bedi candour, said we were not forthright enough when we discussed suspect bowling actions.

Back to Port-of Spain 1976. For the West Indians, the defeat was impossible to swallow. They had lost 5-1 to Australia a few months ago, and to now lose to a weaker side like India at home was akin to salt on a raw wound. Lloyd was livid, and decided he would never depend on spin again; ferocious fast bowling would be his only suit. That strategy was implemented with immediate effect. For the fourth Test at Sabina Park in Kingston, the West Indians prepared a fast pitch. It also apparently had a ridge from which the ball flew. They brought in Wayne Daniel and Vanburn Holder to join Holding and Julien. That summer, their pace attack terrified the wits out of England. Outraged by Tony Greig's crass 'we will make them grovel' pre-tour sledge, the West Indians thrashed England. They never looked back. Soon Malcolm Marshall, Joel Garner and Colin Craft came into the side, and for the next 15 years West Indies ruled the cricketing world as their fearsome fast bowlers pulverized the batsmen of the opposing teams without mercy. In an ironic way, was India's historic win at the Queen's Park Oval responsible for the rise of a formidable West Indies?

Oh, that Cassandra among our friends was forced to shave half his moustache and everyone – neighbour, friend, family and stranger – asked him about it. He ate crow many times till his moustache grew back.

Test No. 775: Queen's Park Oval, Port-of-Spain, Trinidad, 7–12 April 1976: West Indies (Toss) 359 in 109.2 overs (Vivian Richards 177, Clive Lloyd 68; Bhagwat Chandrasekhar 6-120, Bishan Singh Bedi 4-73) and 271/6 dec in 104.3 overs (Alvin Kallicharran 103*, Lloyd 36; . Venkataraghavan 3-65, Chandrasekhar 2-88) lost to **India** 228 in 102.4 overs (Madan Lal 42, Gundappa Viswanath 41; Michael Holding 6-65, Imtiaz Ali 2-37) and 406/4 in 147 overs (Viswanath 112, Sunil Gavaskar 102; Raphick Jumadeen 2-70) by six wickets.

Captains: Bishan Singh Bedi (India) and Clive Lloyd (West Indies)

10

That Monumental Chase

India vs England, fourth Test, the Oval, London, 1979

Another story, another magnificent chase. At tea on the final day, as the Oval was bathed in sunshine, India had reached 304 for 1, with only 134 more runs needed, and enough overs and time in hand. The dressing room was agog with anticipation. Journalist Rajan Bala, privy to the dressing room atmosphere, revealed, 'Victory was what was being discussed in the dressing room throughout the day. By teatime everybody was tense. The time had come to strike.' The captain of the Indian team, Venkataraghavan remembers every minute of that day. He told us, 'When the fourth innings started, we weren't thinking victory but when the first wicket put on 200, we knew there was a chance. What had seemed impossible appeared real. We were so well placed at tea.' Word had spread that India was set to make history and the crowd had swelled in anticipation. Glory beckoned.

But not every tale of valour ends happily. This is one such story – a famous game between India and England at the Oval between 30 August and 4 September 1979. It was the fourth and final Test of the series with England leading 1-0. India's charge at a mammoth target of 438 at the Oval was heroic but in the final overs India stumbled and drew a match that they had almost won against all odds. They could not square the four-Test series, despite one of the grandest finest fourth innings ever, leaving all Indians disconsolate, none more so than captain Venkataraghavan.

India had never won a Test in England after 1971, but this time, Venkat had shepherded his team well – with masterly batting by Viswanath and Vengsarkar at Lord's while the weather had rendered Leeds irrelevant – to ensure India could square the series if they beat England at the Oval. The day before the Oval test, Rohan Kanhai, the West Indian legend, told Venkat, 'You've got to win, maan.' Venkat had earlier told journalist Rajan Bala, after India had drawn the second and third Test matches, that 'The Titanic has been saved'. Bala, much pleased with that imagery, promptly quoted Venkat in his column to convey the optimism of the captain.

The Test was played in sunshine. Martin Williamson, recalls, 'At the end of what had been a wet and cold summer, the sun shone throughout the match.' India's team had a forced change. Amarnath, who had been hit on the head in a county match, was ruled out. India chose to replace him with a batsman, Yajurvindra Singh instead of spinner Chandrasekhar. So the bowling was in the hands of Kapil Dev, Ghavri, Bedi and Venkat. The batting line-up comprised Gavaskar, Chauhan, Vengsarkar, Viswanath, Yashpal Sharma and Yajurvindra Singh. Bharath Reddy was the keeper as Kirmani had been dropped for this series. Mike Brearley won the toss and batted first. The dour and defensive Boycott had a debutant opening partner, left-handed Alan Butcher. Together they invested the first morning with such exaggerated defence and caution that England crawled to 57 by lunch. They lost Butcher to Venkat, who, Rajan Bala in his report for *The Hindu* noted, was bowling again at his best after quite some time. Later that evening, when Botham was threatening to take charge, Venkat deceived him with drift and flight to have him stumped. Bala remarked, 'It was good for Venkataraghavan and the team that he produced the finest delivery of the day to get rid of Botham.' England finished the day at 245 for 5, Graham Gooch holding things together with an adhesive unbeaten

79. The other contributions were a fine innings of 52 by Peter Willey (like Venkat he was to also become an ICC umpire) and a brisk 38 by Botham.

On the second morning of the Test, the bowlers polished off England's last five batsmen for just 60 runs, with Gooch failing to add to his overnight tally. However, by the end of the day, India had surrendered the advantage back to England. They lost Chauhan, Vengsarkar and Gavaskar for just 47 runs to the pace duo of Bob Willis and Ian Botham. Chauhan edged an outswinger from Willis to Botham in the slips. Then Vengsarkar, trying to deflect a ball from Willis, edged it to the debutant wicketkeeper David Bairstow, who juggled and spilled the ball on to his boot, before an agile Botham swooped to catch the rebound off Bairstow's boot. In his summary of the day's highlights, Richie Benaud described that wicked ball as 'a perfect legbreak' bowled at speed. Botham then completed a purple patch by getting Gavaskar with a perfect outswinger. India tried to get out of this difficult situation with Viswanath and Yashpal looking secure, but immediately after tea, the latter was beaten by the extra pace of Willis, who trapped him lbw for 27 with a ball that Rajan Bala called the fastest of the day. Meanwhile, Yajurvindra Singh joined Viswanath, who batted beautifully, until he got out at the worst possible time, just before stumps, as Botham tempted him with a wide outswinger. Viswanath, who had earlier helped himself to delectable boundaries through square-cuts and off-drives, could only edge it to the slips this time. Terry Cooper wrote, 'Viswanath had played exquisitely for almost three hours.' With his departure, India had descended to 137 for 5. In hindsight, it is interesting to read the concluding line of Bala's dispatch that day: 'India's tail was exposed with the arrival of Kapil Dev…' At the start of what would prove to be a glorious career as an all-rounder, Kapil was being referred to as a tail-ender by one of India's most respected journalists.

The next day, the Test went inexorably further into England's grasp. After a brief flourish from Kapil and Bharath Reddy, England wrapped up the last five wickets for merely 41 runs. Mike Hendrick took three

Enterprising Indians brought a baby elephant to the Oval on the fifth day of the 1971 Test. It was the festival day of Vinayaka Chaturthi and Indian players thought it was a good omen. (Courtesy Getty Images)

Bishan Singh Bedi's picture-perfect dismissal of Andy Roberts in the 1975 Test against West Indies. (Courtesy Kasturi & Sons)

Kapil Dev burst on the scene in 1978 and changed the face of Indian pace bowling. His ring of fielders on the first morning of the 1979 Test against Pakistan says it all. (Courtesy Kasturi & Sons)

Indian spectators could not get enough of Ajit Wadekar and his team at the Oval in 1971 after India's first-ever victory on English soil. (Courtesy Getty Images)

The Indian cricketers came home to a rapturous welcome after the series win in England in 1971. The motor cavalcade took hours to travel a few miles. (Courtesy Nandini Sardesai)

This catch by Eknath Solkar in the 1971 Test exemplifies the quality of India's close-in catching during this era. (Courtesy Getty Images)

Indian spectators crossing over to Lahore to watch the 1978 series. For many of them it was a deeply personal visit to the place they had left after Partition. (Courtesy Getty Images)

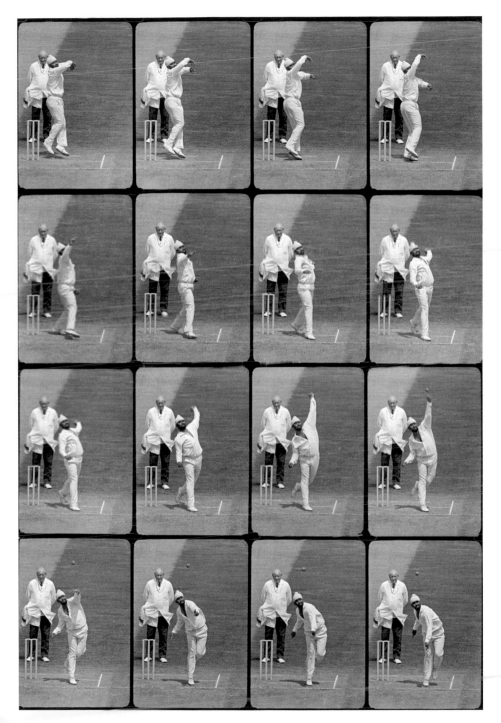

'Paradise is watching Bedi bowl all day at one end,' said Jim Laker, the great off spinner, about one of the greatest left-arm spinners in history. (Courtesy Getty Images)

Vengsarkar reserved his best for Lord's. He is the only non-English batsman to score three centuries at the ground. (Courtesy Getty Images)

The fourth-innings scorecard of the historic tied Test in possession of the Tamil Nadu Cricket Association, and signed off by none other than Sunil Gavaskar. (Courtesy Tamil Nadu Cricket Association)

Dean Jones's monumental double-century in the tied Test was scored in the killing humidity of Chennai. He blacked out after returning to the pavilion and was rushed to hospital. (Courtesy Kasturi & Sons)

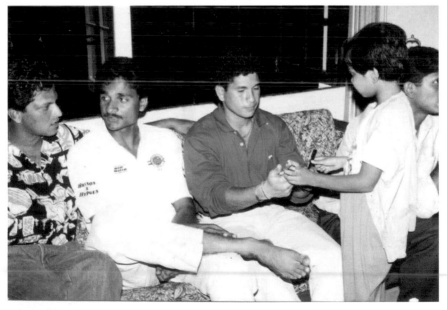

Javagal Srinath and Sachin Tendulkar, in the early days of what turned out to be a glorious career. (Courtesy R. Mohan)

Chepauk gave a standing ovation to the Pakistan team after a heartbreaking defeat in 1999, and will be remembered forever for its generosity. (Courtesy Kasturi & Sons)

Sachin Tendulkar and Shane Warne: fierce contestants on the pitch, but buddies outside. (Courtesy Getty Images)

while Yajurvindra Singh playing soundly was left unbeaten on 43. A lead of 103 gives any side a great sense of security, and Boycott relished the situation. With plenty of time left in the match, India bowled 65 overs and Venkat employed defensive fields. England also played the waiting game, and Boycott was the best person for this. At the end of the day England had a lead of 280 runs with seven wickets in hand; Boycott had pitched tent with his unbeaten 83.

On day four, England was expected to do all the running, but that was not the way it began. On the one hand was 'Boycott's sloth' – the words of a cricket correspondent sorely tried by that opener's slow batting – and on the other were a clutch of three English wickets that dragged England to 215 for 6. Botham was one of the three, and Terry Cooper's report had an interesting line on his dismissal: 'Botham was run out, neglecting to ascertain Boycott's intentions as he charged up the pitch.' One could sense an oblique reference to the run out being Boycott's revenge on being deliberately run-out by Botham the previous year in Christchurch against New Zealand. Twenty-one runs later, Venkat sent Brearley back, and at this stage, Bairstow, father of Jonny Bairstow who now plays for England, joined Boycott, who eventually completed his ton. The two took England to a position from where Brearley could declare, setting India a target of 438 to get in 500 minutes. Martin Williamson recalled, 'Few believed an Indian side that had only passed 300 seven times in 15 tour matches had a chance of chasing down what would have been a record target.' Gavaskar and Chauhan negotiated the last session of day four very well. 'The pitch, now much slower in pace than on the first three days, had nothing to offer the quicker bowlers, wrote Rajan Bala, while the Reuters' report acknowledged 'both the openers are alive to their responsibility and put their heads down to the Herculean task'. India ended the day at 76 for no loss, with Gavaskar playing so well that cricket scribes felt a century was certain. In their assessment of India's chances, however, journalists were more circumspect. Bala wrote, 'It is likely that they will hold out to save the match and win a lot of respect by such a performance. Victory is another matter altogether…' The Reuters correspondent said, 'India would have to give a repeat of their Lord's performance in order to avoid defeat at the Oval.'

Resuming the fight on the fifth morning, Gavaskar looked fluent and confident while Chauhan, steadfast and solid in his defence, looked as though he would have to be evicted from the pitch. Brearley set attacking fields but slowly India's openers forced the captain to disperse them one by one. Gavaskar drove left-arm spinner Edmonds for a boundary to reach his fifty, and Chauhan slashed Hendrick high to get one for himself. Gavaskar reached his ton well before lunch with a lovely off-drive off Willey, with India going to lunch at 192 for no loss.

The two broke the record set by Merchant and Mushtaq Ali for the highest opening partnership against England, and the first wicket finally fell at 213 when Chauhan slashed a catch to Botham off Willis. In walked Vengsarkar; he had already made a mark in that series with a fine century at Lord's – the start of his love affair with that ground. That day, his task was to stay with Gavaskar. He did that, and more. Gavaskar was playing the innings of his life – not one false stroke, not beaten once, breathtaking drives and delectable shots off his legs in the arc between mid-on and square-leg. Vengsarkar did not lag behind. He was a tall, upright, elegant batsman and the majestic cover-drive off Willis and scintillating on-drive off Botham were outstanding.

And so at tea, the Indian dressing room was in a marvellous mood; they needed just 134 runs with nine wickets in hand. Word had spread that India was set to make history and the crowd at the Oval had swelled in anticipation. Martin Williamson wrote of the effect that India's stirring batting was having on the crowd: 'One recollection I have is of a slightly surreal atmosphere among those, like me, who would usually have been steadfastly hoping for a clatter of wickets. Even the England fans started quietly hoping that India might pull off a sensational win. It could just have been a combination of sun and beer.'

Gavaskar and Vengsarkar resumed after tea. Brearley slowed the game drastically. In the next 30 minutes, England bowled just six overs to defensive field placements, even while Gavaskar completed a magnificent double-century. Then, with just 72 to get in 12 overs, the first stumble occurred. Williamson wrote of this moment: 'The thrust and counter-thrust of cricket often offer a twist just when the outcome seems decided. At the Oval it came when Vengsarkar timidly drove Edmonds to Botham for 52.' India were 366 for 2, and Venkat promoted Kapil Dev, expecting him to hit a few lusty ones to help reduce the run rate. Just 20 and callow, not knowing that one can take a few balls to get his eye in before attacking, Kapil holed out for zero, caught by Gooch off Willey. Norman Preston, then in his last year as editor of *Wisden*, was unforgiving of Venkat's decision to promote Kapil and delay Viswanath's entry, although he was factually wrong in saying Viswanath came five-down at 410. Viswanath went in at the fall of the fourth wicket at 389.

Then Gavaskar, on 221, took a drink break, which gave Brearley time to organize things with Botham. The first ball after the break, Gavaskar, perhaps his concentration broken, chipped Botham into David Gower's hands at mid-wicket. At 389 for 4, Viswanath came out to join Yashpal to try and get things on keel, but that was not to be. Adjudged caught at covers off Willey, Viswanath, who always walked before the umpire could give him out, stood unbelieving at the wicket this time. Yajurvindra Singh came and went immediately, after a dubious lbw to Botham, who was now controlling the fate of the match. In the last few overs, he had taken a catch, grabbed two wickets and would take Yashpal too in the next over, again lbw. Venkat promoted himself above Ghavri, but was run out by who else but Botham. The Indian captain believed he was not out, but the umpire said otherwise; Venkat trudged off, his pullover smeared with mud after his dive to get in the crease. In fact, it was in this match that Botham achieved the fastest double of 1,000 runs and 100 wickets.

The Indian dream had crumbled; from 366 for 1, India had subsided to 423 for 8, losing 7 wickets for 58 runs and the match was called off with nine required off the last ball. Rajan Bala criticized the umpiring in *Sportstar*: 'Yashpal and Yajurvindra Singh got doubtful lbw decisions, while Venkataraghavan, given run-out, thought that he was in.' Yajurvindra later said that the umpiring that afternoon was as though to prevent an Indian win, calling out the decisions against Viswanath (a bump ball catch), his own lbw (off his thigh pad) and Yashpal's lbw dubious. Thirty-six years later, Venkat told us that the two lbws and his run-out by umpire Constant were terrible decisions and this incident had some bearing on his own resolve to become a top-class international umpire.

By 1979, India started getting TV highlights but these 90-minute capsules would be telecast a day later. So it was a remarkable evening the day after the match ended, as thousands of cricket lovers sat glued to their TVs watching Gavaskar's epochal double century in a match that had already ended 24 hours ago. Even today, one of the more popular YouTube searches is Gavaskar's innings. Rajan Bala on behalf of millions of Indians wrote, 'Gavaskar, writer of cricket history through his deeds, added another glorious chapter by leading India on what was accepted unanimously as an impossible chase… there could have been no better display of the art and science of batsmanship. If there can ever be absolute perfection in batting then this was it.' Geoff Boycott, who fielded during every ball of that innings, wrote in his book *The Best XI* that Gavaskar 'played one of the most remarkable innings I've seen'. He added, 'there's a bloody-mindedness and if he makes his mind up there's no shifting him'.

Should Venkat have sent Kapil at the fall of the second wicket? Dicky Rutnagur, most dispassionate among cricket correspondents of that era, simply said, 'Kapil Dev was sent up the order to give a decisive spurt but was not equal to the occasion.' But after the experiment to promote Kapil up the order bombed, why did the captain not revert to the regular batting order for the rest of the innings? He sent Viswanath at No. 6 and promoted himself ahead of Ghavri when the sixth wicket fell. Brearley, the England captain, wrote in his book *The Art of Captaincy* that Venkat had erred and the team exposed its panic. How ironic that

Venkat, whom Prasanna in *One More Over* described as 'a sound but not imaginative leader', should have made an adventurous move that was fraught with risk, even though Bedi called his spin comrade a fine strategist. Venkat even today is insistent: 'Sending Kapil at No. 4 was a good move – just three or four hits from him would have settled the issue.'

At the end of the day, luck had played a role. 'What if' questions in hindsight are mostly useless. The game, ultimately the master, can sometimes bestow great kindness and at other times be cruelly unpredictable. For Gavaskar, the hero of this Test, more glory beckoned. For Venkat, to come within a handshake of a famous win and then lose the way, it was bitterly disappointing. The Indian board in a barbaric handling of change announced Venkat's sacking even as the team was on the flight back to India. To make matters worse, the pilot insensitively announced his dismissal and the appointment of Gavaskar as the new captain on the aircraft's PA system. As the announcement was made, Venkat, his face impassive, closed his eyes. We could not resist asking Venkat about this, but he smiled and said, 'The game has given me so much, I have no regrets, nor do I dwell on unpleasant things. My overall memories are positive. I am happy I played for India.'

Test No. 854: The Oval, London, 30 August–3 September 1979: England (Toss) 305 in 124.5 overs (Graham Gooch 79, Peter Willey 52; S. Venkataraghavan 3-59, Kapil Dev 3-83) and 334/8 dec in 116.5 overs (Geoffrey Boycott 125, David Bairstow 59; Karsan Ghavri 3-76, Kapil 2-89) drew with **India** 202 in 79.3 overs (Gundappa Viswanath 62, Yajurvindra Singh 43*; Ian Botham 4-65, Mike Hendrick 3-38, Bob Willis 3-53) and 429/8 in 150.5 overs (Sunil Gavaskar 221, Chetan Chauhan 80; Ian Botham 3-97, Peter Willey 2-96). **MotM**: Sunil Gavaskar

Captains: S. Venkataraghavan (India) and Mike Brearley (England)

11

Fiercer than the Ashes

India vs Pakistan, second Test, Feroz Shah Kotla, Delhi, 1979

On the morning of 4 December 1979, we were at the breakfast table at Oberoi Maidens in Delhi when we saw Zaheer Abbas, Majid Khan, Wasim Bari, Sadiq Mohammad and Asif Iqbal hurriedly downing their food at the adjoining tables. Other Pakistani cricketers were rushing about calling out loudly to each other. They were already in their whites and the whole room was throbbing with the excitement of the Test that was about to begin at Kotla. We wistfully looked at them, wishing we could just leave aside our business meetings and instead go watch the game. At precisely that moment, the lobby manager came up and asked us to attend a phone call. The person on the other end said, 'We are extremely sorry, sir, but your appointment for the day has been cancelled as the R&D manager has taken ill.' We nearly yelled in delight. Twenty minutes later, we were at the ground.

India and Pakistan had earlier played a series in 1978 after a break of 17 years. The two countries had fought two wars in the intervening years – in 1965 and 1971. Indira Gandhi and the Congress had been swept out of power in 1977, an indictment of her imposition of the Emergency. The Janata Party won a thumping majority and formed the government. Across the border, a few months after Morarji Desai was sworn in, Zulfiqar Ali Bhutto, the Prime Minister of Pakistan, was deposed in a military coup and General Zia-ul-Haq assumed command of that country. A year later, the leaders of the two countries embarked upon a few initiatives to improve bilateral relations. Resumption of cricket ties was one of them.

Since Pakistan had toured India in 1961, India toured Pakistan in September 1978 for a three-Test series and three one-day matches in a series touted as a 'Friendship Series', which India lost 2-0. The Indian government had told captain Bedi and manager Fatehsinh Rao Gaekwad that the spirit of friendship must be preserved at all times, but the series was anything but. Pakistani fielders incessantly sledged Indians. Even a rookie like Mudassar Nazar was disrespectful to someone like Gavaskar. Many years later, Mudassar admitted that senior players had goaded youngsters like him to be nasty and aggressive while they would pretend to be sober statesmen. Indians copped more than just rough decisions; the umpiring, always contentious between the two teams, was also biased. To top it, Zaheer Abbas and Majid Khan feasted on an ageing spin attack and virtually brought about the demise of the famed quartet.

Now, in the winter of 1979, Pakistan was paying the return visit and it would be a six-Test series. By this time, Bhutto had been tried and hanged, while in India, as a result of wrangling in the Janata Party, Morarji Desai had quit as Prime Minister. The cricket captaincy had also changed hands, with Gavaskar now leading India and Asif Iqbal, Pakistan. Iqbal had migrated in 1960 at the age of 17 to Pakistan from Hyderabad (India). He was the nephew of Ghulam Ahmed, the Indian off spinner of the 1940s and 1950s.

The first Test in Bangalore was a cautious draw, and the caravan moved to Delhi for the second Test. After Pakistan won the toss, Majid Khan and Mudassar Nazar came out to face Kapil and Ghavri. We were seeing Kapil bowl, 'live on the ground', for the first time and it was a joy to behold: his smooth run-up, the perfectly side-on delivery where he almost showed his left shoulder blade to the batsman, the brisk pace and the appreciable movement off a consistently fine line and length. He reduced Pakistan to 36 for 3 within 90 minutes of play. No doubt the pitch was helpful to seam, but Kapil exploited the conditions fully, getting the first two wickets in the most emphatic manner – clean bowling first Majid Khan and then Zaheer Abbas. Majid lost his offstump, failing to read one that went straight and inside his bat swing. It became 13 for 2 with Zaheer's dismissal. R. Mohan wrote, 'With the first ball of his seventh over, Kapil Dev pitched one right up and the ball ducked under Zaheer's intended cover-drive and seamed just that shade to knock back the offstump. Zaheer was so thoroughly disgusted with himself that he drew the stump out and laid it on the ground before beginning his trek back to the pavilion.'

In the stands, an animated discussion began when Gavaskar elaborately placed Chauhan at leg-slip for Mudassar. It turned out to be a well-thought-out strategy that was also executed perfectly. Mudassar had the habit of moving across his stumps and flicking to the leg side. Kapil came around the wicket, Mudassar edged an intended flick and Chauhan did not have to move to take a good catch. The *Times of India* had the luxury of two senior scribes reporting on the game. K.N. Prabhu wrote, 'It's many a long day since I saw an Indian pace bowler strike as Kapil did in his early spell this morning. Kotla has never seen anything like this, not since Khan Mohammad got Pankaj Roy and Vinoo Mankad.' Sriman was even more nostalgic: 'Not since C.R. Rangachari had electrified a Delhi crowd with sustained pace bowling some 30 years ago had Delhi seen anything so thrilling.'

Except for one further success, these wickets were India's brightest spots that day. Javed Miandad, pugnacious as ever, and the likeable bearded left-hander Wasim Raja first put together a half-century partnership before Miandad fell to Ghavri. The pitch had begun to play easier; spinners Doshi and Shivlal Yadav could not provide the tight support that would have helped their pacers. Iqbal joined Raja, who was playing fluently and would ultimately prove to be Pakistan's best batsman in this tour. That day, we saw Raja at his best. At stumps – play ended a bit early because of lengthening shadows – he had reached 94, with Iqbal on 63. The two had put on 127 runs. As the day wore on without success, the crowd turned irritable and began to boo the team. Sitting on the grassy steps, the crowd seemed to raise the tempo of their 'Hai hai' chants when they spotted Ram Prakash Mehra, the Delhi cricket boss. We thought it was a harmless diversion but Prabhu, in his report of the day's play said, 'Kotla, without a trace of concrete, is an idyllic setting for cricket – if only the larrikins in the crowd who made a din during the afternoon will remember that this is so.'

The second day began joyfully for India but ended in gloom. In the very first over of the day, Ghavri had Asif caught by Vengsarkar. Kapil, in the next over, dealt a body blow to Pakistan, claiming Raja lbw, who tragically missed his century. After a brief period of play, Kapil bowled Wasim Bari, the wicketkeeper, even as Imran Khan was batting confidently. Gavaskar brought Binny from the Delhi Gate end, and he struck immediately as Abdul Qadir played a careless shot and was bowled. Binny, who had made his debut in the previous game on his home ground, had now claimed his first Test wicket. His joy was doubled immediately as his dipping full toss struck Imran on his pads right in front of the stumps. Shortly thereafter, the tenth-wicket pair had a mix-up and Pakistan was dismissed for 273. India had done well to take six wickets that morning for just 56 runs. R. Mohan made the interesting observation that 'Three pacemen brought about one of those rare occasions in Indian Test cricket history when they bagged all the wickets of an innings.'

The rest of the day belonged to a young pencil-slim fast bowler named Sikander Bakht. Pakistan's premier fast bowler Imran Khan had to go off the field with a hip injury after bowling just 7.3 overs, but Bakht did not let Pakistan feel his absence as he sensationally ripped through the Indian batting to bring them to 126 for 9 by end of the day, taking eight wickets by himself. In fact, Bakht was the first pacer to claim eight wickets in a single innings in India. Chauhan and Vengsarkar were dismissed playing at outswingers but worse was to follow. Gavaskar drove Bakht back uppishly, and the bowler diving to his right to catch it, ended up deflecting the ball on to the stumps at the non-striker's end. Viswanath, backing up, was caught out of his crease. A short while later, Bakht delivered the mortal blow with a brute of a delivery that reared up and took the shoulder off Gavaskar's bat. Even as the ball was dying in front of Majid Khan at first slip, Wasim Bari – the best Pakistani keeper ever – dived to his right and completed an excellent catch. The innings came apart after that. Binny was out lbw, then Bakht clean bowled Kirmani as India buckled to 70 for 6. Kapil tried to attack his way out but was bowled after a brisk 15. As Ghavri and Yadav also fell to Bakht, India were on the mat at 94 for 9. Doshi joined Yashpal and the pair put on 32 – the highest partnership of the innings – before the second day ended a few minutes early. A stunned crowd made its way out of the stadium. R. Mohan praised Bakht for perfectly sticking to the cardinal principle of bowling length on this Kotla pitch and added: 'His ability to swing the ball a shade late in the air as well as his propensity to seam it away when the shine was on, brought out the worst in India's batsmen.'

Pakistan was truly in the driver's seat. After Iqbal disposed of Doshi first thing in the morning, Pakistan began their second innings with a lead of 147. Mudassar Nazar left for just 12, caught behind off Kapil. Majid Khan began to discover some form and progressed to 40 when he snicked an outswinger from Binny to Kirmani. 68 for 2 became 68 for 3 when Miandad pushed the ball to cover and set off for an impossible single that Zaheer quite rightly refused. Miandad could not beat Gavaskar's throw to the keeper. Raja came out to join Zaheer, who then began to play his strokes, dispiriting the Indian bowling. Kapil was listless and only Binny bowled well, maintaining length and swinging the ball. After adding 75 runs, Zaheer reached his 50 and then succumbed to Binny, again a wicket from an outswinger on the right length and line. By the end of the day, Pakistan had progressed to 197 for 4, a lead of 344. The newspapers were harsh on the Indian bowlers and feared the worst. 'Indian bowlers fall short of expectations,' was *The Hindu*'s headline while the *Times of India* said, 'Pakistan in a commanding position'. Next day was rest day; Pakistan would have enjoyed it, but the Indian team must have been worried, thinking of what needed to be done over the next two days to salvage the game. *The Hindu* ran a piece, 'Difficult but not impossible task ahead for Indian batsmen', perhaps trying to cheer up its despondent readers. The fourth innings on the fourth and fifth days would under any circumstances be daunting.

But a most determined Indian team took the field on the fourth morning and captured the remaining six wickets, giving away just 45 runs. Kapil turned up in good form and consumed Iqbal without any addition to his overnight score. At the other end, Doshi proved to be a good foil, getting the prize wicket of Raja who, after lofting him for a boundary, lashed out at him once more. Kapil Dev at mid-wicket spotted the ball late but lunged forward and took the catch with both hands. Like Keith Miller, Garfield Sobers and Ian Botham, the other great all-rounders, Kapil too was the most natural athlete. Doshi then dismissed Imran, who swung against the spin and was caught by Chauhan. He had bowled a most valuable spell of 6-2-15-2, with his two wickets, the first wickets for a spinner in the Test. Abdul Qadir and Wasim Bari tried to defend their way out, but Gavaskar called for the second new ball and Kapil and Ghavri polished off the last three wickets. Pakistan was bowled out for 242. All the talk on the rest day about when Asif should declare had become irrelevant.

India now had a target of 390 runs, and they were in a far happier mood now. Mohan reminded his readers, 'Thrice in the recent past India has scored 400-plus in the fourth innings of Tests – once to win at Port-of-Spain, once to go down narrowly at Adelaide and the last time to draw at the Oval.' India's mood was lifted higher when Imran held his hip in pain and went off the ground after bowling just one over. Bakht once again had to shoulder the burden, but he could not capture his dominance of the first innings. Still, he got rid of Gavaskar, even though the maestro had smashed him for three fours in a bid to hit him out of the attack. Going after another outswinger, he feathered it to keeper Bari. A determined Vengsarkar joined Chauhan, and the two looked secure at the wicket. But with the score on 92, Chauhan was trapped in front by a rank shooter from Bakht from the pavilion end. Most wickets had fallen from this end, so in the press box a witty scribe had rechristened the Delhi Gate end as the Deadly Gate end. By end of day's play, India were 117 for 2; Vengsarkar on 32 and Viswanath on 13.

The equation for the final day's play was straightforward: 270 minutes plus 20 mandatory overs to either score 273 runs or capture the remaining eight wickets. The pitch was showing signs of wear, and the pavilion end would be dicey for the occasional ball would keep low. Pakistan was going to be dependent on Bakht and to a lesser extent on left-arm spinner Iqbal Qasim. Viswanath and Vengsarkar ensured there were no shocks in the critical first hour. Mohan wrote, 'Runs were being gathered only if they could be obtained without any risk and if some balls went unpunished, it just could not be helped. Vengsarkar and Viswanath were serving India's larger interests.' Just before lunch, Viswanath was defeated by a fine ball from the spinner, a faster one that bowled him. India were 154 for 3.

The most stirring phase of the match would begin soon. As Yashpal joined Vengsarkar, the partnership blossomed. As the threat of defeat lessened with each passing over, the batsmen raised their tempo. Sriman wrote about Vengsarkar's well-planned innings: 'It had all the virtues of grim determination and discipline in the beginning when the task on hand was only to survive and a sense of urgency and the willingness to meet a challenge when victory seemed possible.' His partner Yashpal also played some rousing drives and cuts. Although he could not match the elegance of Vengsarkar, Yashpal's positive spirit was priceless, and he ran like a terrier between wickets. By tea, India had moved to 251 for 3, with Yashpal completing his fifty while Vengsarkar was in his eighties.

India needed another 139 runs in the 30 minutes and 20 mandatory overs after tea. Iqbal slowed the game down with frequent stoppages as Pakistan repeatedly complained about the ball to the umpires. Iqbal Qasim was asked to bowl from over the wicket outside legstump to a six-man leg side field. These were legitimate tactics, but they conveyed that the hunter had now become the hunted. Yashpal, visibly fretting at these tactics, lost his wicket at 276, Bakht getting him with a great diving return catch. Out came Kapil Dev, with India needing 114 runs in the 20 remaining overs. Vengsarkar was in 'attack mode' and Kapil, capable of big hitting, got into the act straight away. The Indian crowd then experienced for the first time the thrill of what is today a familiar 'slog overs charge' in a limited-overs game. The crowd, in the pavilion stands and on the grassy stands square of the wicket, was on its feet, yelling encouragement at fever pitch. The adrenaline surging in his veins, Kapil smashed a run-a-ball 21 before Mudassar trapped him leg before. India now needed 82 runs from 14 overs.

But that was the final charge. India sorely missed another big hitter. Binny struggled to hit shots and the asking rate climbed. With four overs to go, India needed 34 runs, but once Asif bowled a maiden, everyone knew that the match would be drawn. After the 19th mandatory over, with India at 364 for 6 – 26 short of the target – both teams called it off. Vengsarkar came back to a standing ovation for his 146 not out, having batted magnificently for 522 minutes. It was such a blemishless knock that Mohan later commented he had edged or missed not more than 10 deliveries of the 370 balls he faced.

Historian Ramachandra Guha was delighted when we told him we would include this game in our list of greatest Tests. In his book *The States of Indian Cricket* he says, 'In his retirement Vengsarkar must look back with satisfaction on a playing career of considerable achievement: including a record at the home of cricket unmatched by any other Test batsman (the three centuries at Lord's), and his six Test centuries against the West Indies. As he looks out from his balcony at the monsoon winds coming over the Arabian Sea, dare say that memories of that long vigil at the Feroz Shah Kotla must give him as much pleasure as any other innings he played for India.'

Had India pulled this off, it would have ranked as one of their finest wins. Yet, even in a draw they had scored a moral victory and went into the rest of the series high on self-belief. Pakistan, on the other hand, went downhill. They lost the next Test in Bombay. We were in the stands at Chepauk as India beat them by ten wickets in the fifth Test. Gavaskar ground out 166 and then Kapil Dev demolished their second innings with a haul of seven wickets to finish with eleven wickets in the match. The Indian team had erased the bitter memories of their defeat in Pakistan the previous year. For the Indian cricketer and the Indian cricket fan, it was a period of happiness. For Iqbal, the Pakistan captain, the loss of the series meant the end of his fine career.

Test No. 863: Feroz Shah Kotla, Delhi, 4–9 December 1979: Pakistan (Toss) 273 in 91.5 overs (Wasim Raja 97, Asif Iqbal 64; Kapil Dev 5-58, Roger Binny 2-32) and 242 in 80.5 overs (Raja 61, Zaheer Abbas 50; Kapil 4-63, Dilip Doshi 2-31) drew with **India** 126 in 41.5 overs (Sunil Gavaskar 31, Yashpal Sharma 28*; Sikander Bakht 8-69) and 364/6 in 131 overs (Dilip Vengsarkar 146*, Yashpal 60; Bakht 3-121).

Captains: Sunil Gavaskar (India) and Asif Iqbal (Pakistan)

PART 3

1981 to 2000

Everyone's Game

From the laid-back 1970s, we now move to the glamour, glitz and high-decibel game that cricket became during the 1980s and 1990s; both cricketing and socio-economic reasons making us consider these two decades as a single phase. However, even within this continuum, there is a distinct difference between the 1980s, when one-day cricket burst upon India and changed the landscape forever, and the 1990s, when commerce truly took hold of the game.

This is the period when one saw the impact of limited-overs cricket on fielding and running between wickets in particular. The impact of India's success in the one-day game was starkly seen in the increased pressure and public expectations on Indian cricketers. This is also when the game's economics changed dramatically, with Kerry Packer beginning the trend with his World Series cricket in 1977, players getting professional remunerations, and TV and technology leap-frogging the game into a dazzling spectacle. In 1991, India underwent economic reforms and liberalization, which changed the fabric of Indian society. Consumerism hit a new high; privatization opened up transport, goods, services and the media. Cricket embraced this as well, with TV telecasts, accompanying advertisements and endorsements following very quickly.

By the time the 1980s began, the spin quartet had gone, and India's bowling was in transition. Kapil had arrived and India had a pace attack for the first time in its cricket history, with the fast bowler leading its bowling. India went to the 1983 World Cup as 'no hopers' and stunned the world instead. Kapil's 1,000-watt smile as he lifted the Prudential

Cup is now a defining image of the times. Mihir Bose in *The Magic of Indian Cricket* wrote, 'The triumph of 1983, delightful as it was, was also something of a trap. It made Indians think they ought to win every match.' In February 1985, India won another memorable limited-overs tournament, the Benson & Hedges Cup in Australia. A tournament in which India won every match, it's now remembered as the one where Ravi Shastri won an Audi as the Man of the Series.

That was it. From then on, limited-overs cricket became India's favourite sport. Globalization, liberalization, the riches and huge endorsement deals were still years away, but the first indications of change were clear, not just in the way the game was played, but more importantly, in the way spectators were responding and reacting to the game. Whether in Melbourne or Madras, Indian crowds, high on their team's one-day performances, expected their team to also win Tests every time it stepped on the ground. Quite often the results were in stark contrast to the expectations of a country whose appetite had been whetted by the 'World Champions' tag. Lloyd's team visited India in 1983–84 after having lost the World Cup, and pulverized India into submission in the Test series. The year after, England under David Gower handed India a hiding at home. The two of us watched England outplay India in every session of the match at Chepauk.

In Indian cricket, the bridge between the old-world amateur and the modern professional cricketer was the cricketer who played in the 1980s. We thus had Shastri, Srikkanth, Maninder Singh, Navjyot Sidhu and Sanjay Manjrekar joining hands with Gavaskar, Kapil, Amarnath and Vengsarkar to form a good team. Sandeep Patil thrilled the crowds with his swashbuckling strokeplay while Binny and Madan Lal provided honest support to Kapil. Spin was the weakness, though. Dilip Doshi did well in the brief period between 1979 and 1983, but he was already 33 years old when he made his debut. Shastri and Maninder did service for much of that decade but were not the kinds who bowled innings-destroying spells. Laxman Sivaramakrishnan, the legspinner, showed great promise but faded away within a couple of seasons. Shivlal Yadav, the off spinner, was inconsistent. This weakness in spin – after the era of the spin quartet – was a key chink in what otherwise was a pretty strong team.

A clear influence of one-day cricket was the improvement in out-fielding, though. The close-in catching in the 1970s was world-class, but it was the 1980s that saw a surge in the quality of out-fielding. Madan Lal, Maninder Singh, Srikkanth, Kapil and Binny were very good while Mohammad Azharuddin was a truly brilliant all-round fielder, marvellous in the slips, at silly-point and in the outfield. The days of the physical trainer had only just begun and the drills and methods were pretty basic, with dives in the outfield not in vogue in the 1980s. Indian cricket grounds had not yet acquired their billiards table quality that would later match any of the best grounds in the world. Venkataraghavan said of this improvement, 'In the years of Mankad and Gupte, they had no fielding support, only Umrigar could catch. Then from our times, we got excellent close-in fielders. The out-fielding was still weak, only Surti and Pataudi (could field). Then came Kapil and Azhar. Today, most of our fielders are as good as any in the world.'

The captaincy during the 1980s was largely in the hands of either Kapil or Gavaskar. For Gavaskar, his captaincy may have soured after India were soundly beaten by Pakistan in 1982–83, but the problems had begun earlier. To the average Indian fan, Gavaskar's approach had a bloody-minded defensiveness. But Gavaskar also departed in style, with the Benson & Hedges triumph in 1985, when India played its most flawless one-day cricket ever. Gavaskar's captaincy that fortnight was inspired. A man with an impeccable sense of timing, he gave up the captaincy at the pinnacle of this achievement in Melbourne. Kapil had the reins again. When India lost the 1987 World Cup semifinals to England at the Wankhede, it signalled the exit of Kapil from captaincy. Vengsarkar, the seniormost cricketer then, captained India in a couple of home series and on a difficult tour to West Indies. R. Mohan, who covered every Test between 1981 and 1999, was clear that while Kapil was an attacking, instinctive captain, Gavaskar became defensive because he did not believe India's bowling could penetrate the batsmen after Kapil's opening spell.

Then in 1989, a boy who ought to have been preparing for his Class X examinations and whose voice had not yet broken, stormed into the Indian team. No one could have known that when Sachin Tendulkar would finally say 'Enough', he would have notched up a 100 international centuries and over 30,000 runs in all forms of the game.

India's contests with Pakistan during the 1980s were nerve-racking and demanding for both players and spectators. A significant difference exists in the way England and Australia play the Ashes and the manner in which India and Pakistan compete in sports. With stark political and historical overtones omnipresent, the two countries only resumed cricketing ties in 1978 after a break of 17 years. Then in the 1980s, in an attempt to improve bilateral relations, they played against each other frequently: in 1979–80, 1982–83, 1984, 1986–87 and 1989. These matches were fiercely fought with crowds at fever pitch.

This was also the time the Sharjah circus came into being. Yet, playing on dead pitches in front of polarized crowds and in a hostile environment was hardly the best way to foster good cricketing relations. Players put up pretences of being good friends off the ground but if they could scrap, swear and sledge on it, how could they recover to share a drink or a meal in the evening? Sharjah was perhaps the worst thing to happen to cricket. The match-fixing and bookie–player/administrator nexus that ruined the game towards the late 1990s were perhaps learnt and honed during those days of Sharjah cricket, and left an indelible mark on the game.

Another sign of changing times was that cricketers began to be treated as 'superstars'. Indian cinema had coined the phrase for actors like Rajesh Khanna and Amitabh Bachchan in the 1970s and cricket now followed suit. Pataudi, Jaisimha and Durani might have had a glamorous following in the earlier days but it was only in the 1980s that Gavaskar and Kapil were 'anointed' superstars. The game has never been the same again. Even if these two superstars could have coexisted happily, the public and the media would not let them be. When Kapil was captain, people had doubts whether he could lead a superstar like Gavaskar. Later, when Gavaskar became captain and Kapil had a few ordinary games, Kapil's commitment was most unfairly questioned. Mohan, as cricket correspondent of *The Hindu* at the time, had a ringside view and said that the rivalry between Gavaskar and Kapil was debilitating. Rajan Bala too did not pull his punches in his book, adding that the seeds of this discord were sown during the time Gavaskar and Bedi were at loggerheads. The North versus West games, he said, 'degenerated into a Bedi versus Gavaskar' battle. Camps in the team were inevitable and 'the boys from the South were not sure who to side with and preferred to remain as neutral as possible'. The Gavaskar–Kapil feud became embarrassing enough for then BCCI President N.K.P. Salve to summon both of them and ask them to bury their differences. The feeling was that Gavaskar never forgot or forgave anyone who crossed him.

India played 78 Tests in the 1980s, evenly distributed, home and away. To choose India's finest Tests among these, the easy one to begin with is the 'tied Test' against Australia in Chennai in September 1986 – just the second instance of a match ending in a tie, and an unforgettable one. Another easy pick is India's come-from-behind win in Melbourne in February 1981, when Greg Chappell's team was ambushed by Kapil, Ghavri and Dilip Doshi – a match of high drama and acrimony that is also unforgettable for Sunil Gavaskar's near walkout! The third Test on our list is a fine victory at Lord's in 1986, when Kapil's men riding on the shoulders of a magnificent Dilip Vengsarkar completely outplayed England. One match that tempted us was Gavaskar's last Test in Bangalore in March 1987 against Pakistan where he played one of his most heroic innings. On a minefield of a pitch, India lost by 16 runs, but apart from Gavaskar's valiant 96, the rest of the team disappointed so we let this one go.

In the period 1990–2000, India played 75 Tests; of the 41 Tests it played away from home India lost 16 and won just two, against Sri

Lanka and Bangladesh. Azharuddin captained India in 47 of these games. In fact, he had two stints that sandwiched Tendulkar's unhappy two tenures that comprised 25 Tests. Azhar's team began the decade with disappointing visits to New Zealand, England, Australia and South Africa, losing all four series. It was the manner of those defeats that was deflating – in none of these overseas tours did India remotely look like winning. R. Mohan, chatting to us, was severe in his indictment, saying that Azhar's captaincy was regressive and he should never have been made captain. Tendulkar as a captain was passionate, but the stress he brought upon himself was unbearable. His teammates too would be consumed by guilt if they did not fulfil Tendulkar's expectations. According to Mohan, Tendulkar had burning passion but it was coupled with strategic inadequacies.

The Indian team in the 1990s were tigers at home and lambs overseas. On spinning tracks at home, Kumble was formidable, and combined with Venkatapathy Raju and Rajesh Chauhan to deliver comprehensive wins for India. India won 18 matches and lost only seven. On home pitches, all the Indian batsmen came to the party. Abroad, despite Tendulkar, there would invariably be a collective collapse every odd Test, and India did not have the resources to take 20 wickets. Although Kumble was India's best bowler, he was yet to be greatly effective. Kapil, well past his prime, huffed and puffed till 1994, and though Srinath had arrived in 1991 – even as a raw 22-year-old he was a handful in Perth on his first tour – he hardly got games. It was only in 1996 that Srinath and Venkatesh Prasad joined hands to form a good opening attack that could test the opposition in the pace-friendly conditions in England, Australia or South Africa. Unfortunately, when India toured South Africa and West Indies in 1997–98, Srinath was unavailable as he had to undergo surgery to his right shoulder, and thus Sachin did not have this potent combination when he needed it the most.

Not surprisingly, we could not pick even one game from India's overseas Tests in the 1990s, and had to exclusively choose from India's home games: the first Test against Pakistan in Chennai in 1999, immortal for Tendulkar's most heroic knock-in-vain, with the 'Kumble ten wickets' Test in the same series at Kotla; and the victories against strong sides from South Africa and Australia in 1996 and 1998. The win against South Africa in 1996, memorable for Srinath's spectacular match-winning burst; and the win against Australia in 1998 at Chepauk, remembered for Tendulkar's domination of Warne.

Towards the latter half of the decade, the Fabulous Four formed the core of India's batting (barring Laxman, who had not yet found his feet), Srinath became a worthy successor to Kapil and Kumble's exploits were starting to leave others far behind. Yet the period, while rich in individual brilliance, somehow did not translate into overseas glory. Dileep Premachandran, editor-in-chief of *Wisden India*, thought it took these legendary players a few years before they matured as a group around the same time. Another drawback was that India did not have a settled opening pair, and Navjot Sidhu did duty for much of the decade without a stable partner. This meant that India regularly lost early wickets abroad, putting tremendous pressure on the middle order. The 1990s also had their share of wasted talent: Vinod Kambli began gloriously but messed it up and faded away. Pravin Amre, a compact player whose century on debut in South Africa oozed class, never received support and India lost him.

In an epochal event in 1994, Tendulkar grabbed the opener's role in one-day cricket and dominated the world stage from that day. By 1996, he was at his peak, a position he occupied almost till retirement. Ganguly and Dravid made memorable debuts at Lord's in 1996 and announced themselves as future stars for India. A high point of the decade was Kumble's ten wickets in an innings at Kotla in 1999 – a feat that had only been achieved by Jim Laker and one that is as rare as a tied Test. The busy junction between St. Mark's Road and Mahatma Gandhi Road in his home town Bengaluru is now named 'Anil Kumble Circle', serving as a permanent reminder of this marvellous individual achievement.

India's performances in the premier one-day tournament were also a fair indication of the kind of mania that had gripped the nation. India failed to qualify for the semifinals of the World Cup in Australia in 1992 as well as in England in 1999 and the millions of fans tried to find solace in the fact that at least they had beaten Pakistan. When the World Cup was hosted in India in 1996, India reached the semifinal but none wanted to accept anything less than an appearance in the final. But in the semifinal, Azharuddin chose to bowl first after winning the toss on a horribly underprepared track at Eden Gardens. By the time India batted, the pitch had deteriorated. As India was crumbling to defeat, the spectators unable to stomach a sporting debacle exploded into destructive behaviour. The game was called off and awarded to Sri Lanka. This match typified the changing expectations and make-up of the crowds, so partisan that they were unable to bear reverses to the home team.

One of the changes one saw in the 1990s – as a result of the superstardom frenzy – was that India's cricket-watching public now worshipped individual feats. That Tendulkar was the world's best batsman, even though India was not winning Test matches abroad, seemed to give us greater joy. The gulf in the attitude of the Indian public and the Australian or South African public was stark. For Australia and South Africa, team performance was the only barometer. Individual feats were recognized but accorded little importance if the team did not fare well. This preoccupation with individual glory and individual records created a frenzy that was fanned by media in the post-liberalization age. As TV channels started competing for eyeballs, the jingoistic hype and thunder reached insane proportions. Once this frenzy caught on, it never let up. Years later, one TV channel ran a prime-time programme every evening of a game titled 'Match ka mujrim kaun?' which translated in English would be 'Who is the criminal in the match?' The all-pervasive crassness reduced Indian cricket to the status of a C-grade movie, but who cared, the TRPs were going through the roof.

Consider these numbers: Cricketers were paid around ₹400 per Test match in the 1960s and ₹700 in the 1970s. When cricketers began to get ₹7,500 for a Test in the 1980s, it seemed a good jump. The prize money for the World Cup in 1975 was £4,000 and went up to £66,200 in 1983. If that looked good, it hardly prepared us for the mind-boggling numbers that were to follow after the media and TV explosion. Colour TV was introduced in India when the country hosted the 1982 Asian Games. Those were the days when BCCI had to pay Doordarshan to telecast Test matches live! All this changed when Prime Minister Narasimha Rao's government launched the 1991 economic reforms. With liberalization, private and foreign broadcasters could engage in limited operations in India, and the business of cricket broadcasts turned upside down. BCCI, which had earlier paid Doordarshan, now invited bids from TV channels involving huge sums for the right to telecast matches. With extremely lucrative telecasting rights and the accompanying advertising revenue, the coffers were overflowing. Every cricketer was handsomely endorsing a number of products; many of them had managers to help with their contracts. TV brought them every day into our homes, and they would be coaxing us to try out sundry products even when there was no cricket.

In 1995, TV in India covered more than 70 million homes through more than 100 channels. By 2004, there were 130 channels. The cricketers' remuneration followed a similar graph. From ₹7,500 per match in the 1980s they began to get ₹300,000 per Test and along with the income from advertising endorsements and Test cricketers were now truly well-paid professionals. The match fees have taken more than a couple of leaps in the new millennium. It is good that the first-class cricketer too is benefited. A Ranji Trophy cricketer, if he were playing for a good side, could make over ₹1.5 million in a season. With its rising financial clout, Indian cricket could no longer be pushed around by England or Australia. Soon India would dwarf them in terms of financial muscle to the extent that the Indian board would subsidize cricket in other countries. By a strange but appropriate coincidence, we wrote these lines just a day before the passing away of Jagmohan Dalmiya who presided over BCCI during these times of change.

By the mid-1990s, India had grounds and stadiums as good as any in the world. The Mohali stadium had facilities that outdid the best in the world. A number of new venues came up while first-class cricket went to small towns. Grounds all over India were now manicured and maintained impeccably. Cricketers came from various small towns and not just from metropolitan middle-class homes. The MRF Pace Foundation in Chennai was an important addition and Dennis Lillee coached there till Glenn McGrath replaced him recently. R. Mohan asked us to add another important element: 'You must note that we got our first professional cricket consultant in the late 1990s, Bob Simpson. He introduced planning and strategy, focus on running between wickets and fielding drills. If we did well after 2001, we may also need to acknowledge Simpson's contribution.'

While India was embracing the changes that were sweeping cricket, Australia and England never lost sight of history and tradition or the primacy of Test cricket. The Ashes series remains the marquee event in their cricket calendar. The Boxing Day Test is a sacrosanct event in Melbourne in Australia and Durban in South Africa while England ensures regular five-Test series in their summer. The crowds for Tests in these countries never flagged and they seemed to reiterate that long-form cricket was ultimate. In India, the crowds, however, seemed primed to enjoy only one-day cricket. They came with less enthusiasm for Test matches, while domestic cricket was played in front of empty stands. With year-round cricket, Indian cricketers are often unavailable for Ranji Trophy and Duleep Trophy matches. However, their Australian and English counterparts play Sheffield Shield and county cricket almost without fail.

Finally, for us and the spectator, what ultimately remains etched in our memories as the 1990s came to a close was the desecration of a sport. The scandal of match-fixing exploded in our faces as the decade came to an end, with South African captain Hansie Cronje admitting that he had accepted bribes from Indian bookies. One saw the unravelling of sordid episodes – of disreputable bookies and their henchmen trying to entice morally weak cricketers into corruption. The Indian players who were in the net of match-fixing investigations never accepted any hanky-panky but the banning of Azharuddin, Ajay Jadeja and Ajay Sharma told its own tale. Sleaze had now besmirched the sport. Suspicion and cynicism corroded the pure pleasure of enjoying a sport. A run-out, a missed catch, a poor stroke, a no ball, a wide or a juicy full toss – each of these was no longer a natural error that invariably occurs in any game.

If it was a feeling of betrayal for the spectator, it was even more so for the honest player. The dressing room atmosphere was vitiated. It is no secret that the honest players shunned those who they believed were not clean. Their revulsion was apparent. Rajan Bala in *The Covers Are Off* wrote, 'Was one of the reasons for Tendulkar quitting as captain the fact that he did not want anything to do with people who had brought discredit to the game?' Faithful fans swore off the game. It was clear that they had been deeply hurt.

Our frustration is not with the rampant commercialization, but with the lack of accompanying governance. With mega bucks and mega power involved in the sport, poor governance can only be catastrophic. The hubris and non-accountability of the board became all too evident when money started pouring in. Looking the other way when things were probably happening under one's nose – this was the darkest period of Indian cricket. We have still not learnt our lessons. The skulduggery has only become more sophisticated. One learnt new terms like spot-fixing: with pre-arranged signals, a no ball, a wide or a maiden over could all be done for a price. All the skeletons tumbling out of the Indian Premier League (IPL) cupboard twelve years later only showed that for Indian cricket administrators, good governance, probity and accountability to the cricket fan was farthest from their minds till the Supreme Court came down hard and made sure they would not have any escape routes, but the full extent of the clean-up remains to be seen.

12

Fury and Ecstasy

India vs Australia, third Test, Melbourne Cricket Ground,
Melbourne, 1981

On Tuesday, 10 February 1981, a Test match was just a yard from being forfeited in fury by a captain, who blew his top after an atrocious decision against him by an incompetent umpire and a mouthful from a triumphant bowler. An incensed Sunil Gavaskar dragged his opening partner Chetan Chauhan off the Melbourne Cricket Ground (MCG). The fuse was actually waiting to blow all summer. When it finally did that Tuesday morning, MCG became a seething cauldron. Had Chauhan taken the two or three steps to cross the ropes, the match would have been forfeited. It could have become one of the lowest points in Indian cricket and might have had far-reaching repercussions on Indo-Australian ties and even on international cricket. However, the manager of the Indian team, Wing Commander Durani, alert and calm, told Chauhan to wait inside the ground, and escorted one-down batsman Vengsarkar to the boundary and waited till he entered the ground. The match would now go on. In fairy-tale fashion, this game is now remembered as one of India's greatest fightbacks ever.

The Melbourne Test was the third in a long tour that comprised an ODI tri-series (Australia, New Zealand India) followed by three Tests against the Aussies. The Indians did nothing much in the ODIs and bowed out. They were trounced in the first Test in Sydney and escaped with a draw in the second Test in Adelaide. Gavaskar, Viswanath and Vengsarkar had all failed to fire, and the only highlight of the tour so far had been the incandescent 174 by Sandeep Patil in Adelaide.

The series, though, had been played in the background of events that were not in the spirit of the game. Greg Chappell, the Australian captain, had been pilloried after his infamous order to younger brother Trevor to bowl underarm and prevent New Zealand from winning the one-day final a week ago. Posters with the slogan 'Greg's underarm stinks' had come up all over Melbourne. Benaud called it the most disgraceful thing he had seen on a cricket field. Even the Prime Minister of New Zealand, Robert Muldoon, stepped in and described the ball as 'the most disgusting incident I can recall in the history of cricket'.

The umpiring was also poor right through the season and it was not just the New Zealanders and Indians who said so. Even the much-respected Australian commentator Alan McGilvray called it shameful. This was not new in a tour to Australia; Borde, even 46 years later, remembered that back in 1968, India's bid for victory in Brisbane was derailed by a couple of shocking decisions. During the 1977–78 tour under Bedi, it was difficult to get lbw verdicts while catches that bounced a whole foot in front of fielders were claimed and given. In 1981, Rex Whitehead, umpiring in his first series, showed himself to be quite incompetent.

The Melbourne pitch had been substandard for a few seasons now, and this trend continued into this match. Greg Chappell felt it had never been worse before the match, while Gavaskar predicted a low and uneven bounce. Yet, upon winning the toss, Chappell decided to field, what Australian newspapers called an unnecessary risk. K.N. Prabhu's column had the prescient headline 'Melbourne wicket could help India level series'.

Yet, after three days of cricket, Greg Chappell held all the aces. India was dismissed for just 237 on the first day, with Dennis Lillee and his partner, the strong and energetic Len Pascoe, all over India. If Lillee bowled aggressively with surgical precision, then Pascoe bowled with pace and hostility. India made a woeful start once again, with Chauhan getting out for zero, fending a snorter to short square-leg. Vengsarkar, for whom this tour was forgettable, edged Pascoe to slip. Gavaskar left soon after and India was an unhealthy 47 for 3. If India reached 237 it owed it to Viswanath. A deeply worried Viswanath (so worried by his poor form that he even forswore his favourite tipple of beer) had been struggling all through the tour and just as people were saying that he was over the hill, the stylist responded with one of his finest centuries. While all other batsmen were fending off balls from their face, Viswanath seemed to be playing on a different pitch altogether. Much like his other great knocks, this century in Melbourne too was under the most adversarial circumstances – when the pitch was at its worst, the bowling most hostile, and the rest of the batting had caved in.

Viswanath was superbly gifted and we were fortunate to have watched many of his knocks from the stands. For instance, his immortal 97 not out against a most hostile West Indies attack at Chepauk in 1975, his ton against West Indies in 1979 on a spiteful pitch again at Chepauk and his century at Brabourne Stadium in 1973 against Tony Lewis's England. As he reached the landmark in this last game – breaking the hoodoo of Indian debut century makers not scoring another – Tony Greig lifted the tiny man and cradled him in his arms, to the merriment of an adoring audience. Even shorter than Gavaskar, Viswanath, rather than getting behind, preferred to play beside the rising ball, to stroke it gracefully to point or glide it to square-leg. The amazing thing was that he seemed to have so much time to play the ball even when other batsmen were jumping around hurriedly, as though barefoot on a hot-tin roof. On each of these occasions, the master showed how it was done, with extra time to play, and graceful strokes to keep the runs coming. None of his centuries have been in a losing cause. Vishy was elegance personified and never did anything that was not graceful at the crease. A sportsman to the core, he always walked when he nicked the ball. Among Indian players of his era, he was by far the one whom the crowds loved the most.

On a pitch where Lillee and Pascoe were running amok, Viswanath had the class and temperament to construct a lovely century. Serene and imperturbable, he was canny too, maximizing the plunder off spinners Bruce Yardley and Jim Higgs while keeping the pacers at bay. Sandeep Patil briefly entertained with a flurry of lovely drives before miscuing a hook off Lillee. Yashpal and Kapil could not survive for long and it was left to Kirmani – for the umpteenth time in his career – to provide that crucial support in the lower order. That inspired Shivlal Yadav to stay at the wicket for nearly 80 minutes, and it was in his company that Viswanath completed his century. Yadav paid a big price for his doughtiness though; a yorker from Pascoe crashed into his toe, and though he stuck on in great pain, later that evening, a visit to the hospital showed he had fractured his toe. India were all out that evening and the Australian openers Dyson and Graeme Wood safely played out a couple of overs from Kapil Dev and Ghavri before stumps.

On the second day, Kapil and Ghavri dismissed Wood and Dyson early. Although Kim Hughes used his feet beautifully to the spinners and made 24, Yadav defeated him to put Australia at 81 for 3. There was little joy for India thereafter. Chappell and Allan Border put up a century stand, with the captain classical and elegant as always, and the latter resolute in the beginning and then opening out as the Indian bowling flagged. Chappell's dismissal for 78 brought no respite as Doug Walters joined Border. By the end of the day, Australia had reached a healthy 272 for 4. Border was five away from a ton and Walters, coming towards the end of a fine career, was playing on 36. The Indian bowling that was competitive to begin with had become flat. Kapil picked up an injury and had to go off, so Gavaskar could only call for the second new ball late. Yadav was courageous, bowling with a fractured toe, despite finding it difficult to even run a few steps. He would field in the slips and bowl, with painkiller injections every two hours. Prabhu, on the eve of the match, happy that Yadav had joined Doshi in a spinning partnership, had written, 'Yadav's inclusion has been an encouragement to Doshi – as the presence of a sapper is to a miner.'

On the third day, as Australia continued to prosper, Border duly completed his century and Walters went on to make 78. They finished with a potentially match-winning first-innings lead of 182 runs. It was at this moment that the Indians stood up and mounted their best partnership of the series. Gavaskar slowly recovered his touch and Chauhan, always a fighting, loyal partner, played his part. The day ended with India salvaging some lost ground as the openers put on 108 runs when stumps were drawn. Gavaskar, whose highest score in the series thus far had been 23, was unbeaten on 59.

The next day, the cricketing world was rocked by a quake of some magnitude. After Gavaskar and Chauhan added 57 untroubled runs to take the score to 165, Lillee cut one back into Gavaskar. The ball hit Gavaskar's pads and a ferocious appeal went up. As Whitehead raised his finger, Gavaskar was stunned (he later said he had not merely edged the ball but 'played' the ball on to his pads). Gavaskar began to remonstrate while walking away, and Lillee pointed to his pad and gave him an unpalatable mouthful. At that point Gavaskar snapped. A stunned audience watched Gavaskar in a blind rage suddenly go across to Chauhan and ask him to walk out, clearly with the intention of forfeiting the match. Chauhan most unhappily dragged himself off even as his captain pushed him on with a couple of nudges. He was a yard from the boundary ropes – had he crossed the boundary, the match would have been forfeited – when the manager of the Indian team, Wing Commander Durani, literally accompanied Vengsarkar right to the pavilion gate and urged him on to the ground. An unprecedented crisis had been averted, and though the cricket resumed, all discussion was only about Gavaskar's dismissal, Lillee's provocation and Gavaskar's furious response.

Lillee maintained that it was Gavaskar's frustration on not having played him well on the tour that finally snapped him. Seething with fury, Gavaskar admitted that 'smoke was coming out of (his) ears' and his reaction was that of a wronged man in rage. Mohan wrote in *The Hindu* that this incident could have been 'a permanent blight on Indian cricket'. Once you accept that Gavaskar had erred, one is also left with the issue of abysmal umpiring. It was Rex Whitehead's *tenth* howler of the series, most of them against India. This lbw was the proverbial last straw, and Lillee's crude send-off blew Gavaskar's top. And it was not just Indians who were irate; minutes after the incident, Australian spectators put up posters all over the ground: 'Blind or biased?' asked one, while another read, 'Quickest draw this side of the West'. The third poster simply said, 'Rex is the Hex'. *Sportstar* quoted the Australian commentator Alan McGilvray expressing disgust at the quality of umpiring. McGilvray, in his 200th Test as commentator, had prepared a chart of umpiring decisions that season to show how substandard the umpiring was, and said, 'This has been a most unpleasant season for me.' Gavaskar felt that Australians had no right to complain about umpiring when they came to India because they themselves offered such shoddy umpiring. R. Mohan told us Ian Chappell, who had been in the commentary box then, suggested immediately that neutral umpires were needed.

When the innings resumed, Chauhan's concentration had cracked, and after playing so well for his 85, he gave it away with a slashed catch to point. Apart from Patil, Chauhan was the only other Indian who had a substantial score in the series, with 97 in Adelaide. Within his limited abilities, Chauhan always played doggedly but was destined never to hit a century in Tests. Viswanath, hero of the first innings, joined Vengsarkar, who was playing better than at any other time in the series. Both batsmen seemed to be in little trouble and added 67, with the score moving to 243 – a lead of 61. It seemed like India could perhaps set Australia a challenging fourth-innings task. Chappell called for the new ball and the game swung their way immediately. First, Lillee broke through Viswanath with pace and then Pascoe bowled a perfect outswinger, which Vengsarkar snicked to keeper Rodney

Marsh. Yashpal did not have the wherewithal to survive for long and was bowled by Pascoe. At 260 for 5, India was just 78 runs ahead with only five wickets in hand.

As the wicketkeeper Kirmani joined him, Patil played a cameo, belting 36 at better than run-a-ball. Patil was always grand to watch – what crunching drives he would play – and it is an abiding regret that we did not get enough of him on the world stage. We were in Bombay during the early 1980s, and always tried to catch a match featuring Bombay or West Zone for the sheer pleasure of watching him bat. Patil's strokes had a special ring to them. After his 174 at Adelaide, Benaud on TV called Patil's strokes 'pearls around the ground'. In demanding conditions in England against Willis and Botham as well as against the pace of Lillee and Pascoe, Patil had centuries. His 'away Tests' average is over 47, fifth highest among all Indian batsmen. One shot he played (we were seated behind the bowler) was an unforgettable bowler's back-drive: he 'crunched' it on the rise, it bounced once on the pitch and then before you could even react, it had skimmed along to hit the sight screen. More than 52 per cent of his Test runs came in boundaries, which puts him in the company of the game's finest strokeplayers.

Patil left at 296 and Kapil, who came out with a runner, went first ball, playing an awful slog at Yardley, the spinner. The innings was in terminal decline, with Yadav unfit to bat, and India wound up for 324. All hopes of a challenging target had evaporated. Australia needed just 143 to win, and even with the vagaries of the pitch, they were expected to wrap it up quickly.

Yet, it was in the fourth innings that India truly came to the game, even as its bowling unit was in tatters. As Dyson and Wood opened, Kapil couldn't bowl as he was off with a leg injury, and Yadav too was out of the match. An injury that Doshi had suffered on his instep during an earlier tour match now caught up with him and he began to limp. Ghavri, among all the walking wounded, seemed to be the only able-bodied bowler. There was no option but to ask Sandeep Patil to share new-ball duty with him, even if as a formality for a few overs.

Australia were 11 for no loss when the drama began. Kirmani caught Dyson off Ghavri, a dubious decision as the ball seemed to go off thigh pad rather than the bat. But on the very next delivery, Ghavri bowled the ball of his career. It was not a brilliant ball; on the contrary, it was one of his poorer offerings, a half-tracker that pitched, had little pace and kept low. Yet, one of the best batsmen at the time somehow missed it completely. The ball nearly bounced a second time before it hit the stumps. 11 for 2, Chappell out first ball. Mohan wrote, 'It was a rank long hop but it helped change a whole series.'

The glimmer of hope had arrived for the Indians. The ball was turning, and the pitch was definitely inconsistent. Wood, the other opener, stepped out to flick Doshi, missed and was stumped in a flash by Kirmani. Australia ended the day on 24 for 3. A story that has gone around is that at the end of the fourth day, Lillee was heard telling folks to put money on an Indian victory. His reasoning was that Australia were too dependent on Chappell and since he was gone, Australia would not survive.

Overnight, the masseurs worked on Kapil's hamstring and got him in some shape to bowl. Pumped up on painkillers, his thigh heavily strapped, Kapil took the field. Doshi limped along beside him. Between them, they scripted history. For the rest of the innings, which was to last 33 overs, the two injured warriors bowled unchanged. It was a wonder that Kapil managed to run up and bowl. On that dubious pitch, he knew he had to just pitch it on the spot, and he was unerringly accurate throughout. Doshi, for his part, knew there was turn and uncertain bounce for him. Prabhu wrote, 'The least bit of help and one can see Doshi's spectacles glistening as deadly as a laser beam.'

India got an early breakthrough the next day as Hughes played an ill-advised cut to a ball from Doshi that drifted in and straightened to hit the stumps. With Australia on 50, nightwatchman Yardley departed, his stumps shattered by a Kapil delivery that kept low and homed in like a torpedo. Kapil then struck thrice in a row. His next victim Border would count himself unlucky, because it was not clear whether he had edged the ball to Kirmani or missed it – one more victim of poor umpiring. But Kapil's next two victims were clean-bowled. Marsh's stumps were uprooted by a sharp low leg-cutter while Lillee was bowled by another accurate ball that swung into him in the air. The Australian innings was in a shambles at 69 for 8. Doshi, relentless from the other end, was in the words of Mohan, 'keeping the pressure at boiling point'. The close-in fielders were all over the batsmen. Walters alone seemed untroubled, playing safely and picking his runs. The Indians had found it impossible to dislodge Walters throughout the series, and he ended up with an average of 72 without scoring a century. Australia faced a small target, and had even one batsman strung a partnership with Walters, the pressure would have quickly come back on India. Moreover, given their physical conditions, Kapil and Doshi would not have had much left in their tank. But it was too late. As Pascoe, flustered by an appeal, stepped out of his crease, Vengsarkar from silly-point broke the stumps. Soon, Australia's misery came to an end as Kapil claimed Higgs leg before. Australia had been bundled out for 83, their second lowest score in the last 40 years. Kapil and Doshi – one-legged warriors – had scripted an amazing victory, with the former claiming 5 for 28 in an unbroken spell of 16.4 overs, bowled on one leg, painkiller injections and pure adrenaline.

Even seasoned Indian reporters were not unaffected by the dramatic events of the final day. When the last wicket had fallen, none of them held back. Prabhu in a column headlined 'India's epic win', wrote, 'As I type this dispatch, the Indians return to the pavilion with the tricolour borne aloft… and in my mind's eye, for my own eyes were misted over with joy, I could visualise stout trenchermen merrily sitting down to breakfast at home. Rejoice my beloved country.' Mohan wrote, 'It was the greatest, unparalleled and most effective coup d'état staged by an Indian team in the history of Test cricket.' Newspaper headlines screamed 'Tornado Kapil hits Australia'. Even shorn of all the hyperbole, this game will rank right up among the greatest comebacks in Indian cricket. The win also meant it was the first series India had not lost in

Australia, for they had lost every prior assignment, even the one against Simpson's depleted team in 1977–78. To level a series against a full-strength Australian team, and to do so after a morale-sapping quality of umpiring through the summer and with three injured bowlers must rank among the bravest victories by an Indian team. Imagine, if indeed Gavaskar had forfeited the game, Indian cricket history would have been denied one of its finest moments.

Test No. 895: Melbourne Cricket Ground, 7–11 February 1981: **India** 237 in 84 overs (Gundappa Viswanath 114, Syed Kirmani 25; Dennis Lillee 4-65, Len Pascoe 3-29) and 324 in 109.1 overs (Chetan Chauhan 85, Sunil Gavaskar 70; Lillee 4-104, Bruce Yardley 2-65) beat **Australia** (Toss) 419 in 156.3 overs (Allan Border 124, Doug Walters 78; Dilip Doshi 3-109, Sandeep Patil 2-28) and 83 in 48.4 overs (Kapil Dev 5-28, Karsan Ghavri 2-10) by 59 runs. **MotM:** Gundappa Viswanath.

Captains: Sunil Gavaskar (India) and Greg Chappell (Australia)

13

Lords of Lord's

India vs England, first Test, Lord's, London, 1986

Touring England in the first half of their summer is the biggest disadvantage for a team like India. The weather, often damp and cold in the early summer, is alien to those who come from a hot, tropical country; the pitches do not help the spinners and the visiting batsmen find it difficult to cope with the seaming tracks and swinging conditions. The convention is for India to visit England in the first half of the summer on alternate tours. Since Gavaskar's team had visited England in the first half of the summer in 1982, one would have expected the 1986 tour to take place in the latter half – the drier half – of the season, which would suit the Indians better. However, the BCCI, due to compulsions of its domestic cricket calendar, sent its team in the first half, and the first Test was being played in early June. Graeme Wright, editor of *Wisden*, wrote that this decision of the Indian board 'condemned Kapil Dev's team to the colder, more unsettled half of the English season'. India had won only once in England before – Oval 1971 – in 54 years of its Test history, and when the two teams had played in India in 1984, Gower's England had comprehensively beaten them.

The dice and history seemed loaded against India. However, England too had a couple of its own problems. David Gower was under severe pressure after losing 5–0 in the Caribbean Islands. Peter May, chairman of selectors, did not help by nominating Gower captain for just the first two Tests. Ian Botham was in the dock for writing that he smoked cannabis, and had been dropped for the series. Derek Pringle – Botham's replacement – was going to bat at No. 6, and Steven Pye, recounting the match in an article for the *Guardian*, wrote, 'Quite why England chose to go into the Lord's Test with just five specialist batsmen is baffling. Surely a team of such brittle confidence needed the reassurance of six batsmen.'

India, on the other hand, was on an upswing, and their tour to Australia in 1985–86, while drawn, had been positive. Kapil in his second stint as captain was a more assured leader now, and though the game was being played in early June, India's pace combination of Kapil, Chetan Sharma and Binny was capable of using the conditions as well as England. Complementing this pace trio was the left-arm spin of Shastri and Maninder Singh. The batting was strong and it did not really have a tail, as its bowling all-rounders batted deep. This Indian team had good balance.

On a dark and gloomy day, Kapil won the toss and inserted England in to bat at Lord's. Although it was a positive move given that he had a decent pace attack, the pitch was lifeless – Mohan in *The Hindu* called it the slowest ever that England might have played on – and there was no movement for the pacers. But Chetan Sharma was spirited, and bowled tirelessly throughout the day, using the Lord's slope well. With his whippy action he ceaselessly attacked the batsmen, as Kapil Dev, Binny and the spinners played second fiddle. Graham Gooch was thoroughly safe, intent on caution and scoring only when absolutely certain. Tim Robinson, his opening partner, not in the same class but keen on getting a move, scored 35 before giving Azharuddin a catch as he played across the line to Maninder. Gower joined Gooch and England went to lunch at 83 for 1.

The match sparked to life after lunch when Kapil took off the spinners and brought back pace. Chetan Sharma broke the middle-order in a terrific burst. He first got Gower caught behind off an intended pull, and then beat Mike Gatting with sharp pace and inswing to shatter his stumps. Shortly after, he beat Allan Lamb again with pace, and the batsman could only inner-edge a catch to short-leg. At 98 for 4, Kapil's decision to bowl seemed to have worked. However, from there on, England recovered on the back of Gooch's day-long vigil. He was now the accomplished accumulator, taking over three hours to reach his fifty but raising his tempo later in the day and reaching his century by that evening. Pringle, who came to bat under enormous pressure – the thought that he was filling Botham's boots must have sounded more silly than daunting to him – was subjected to a series of short balls from Chetan Sharma. He batted well and in his moderate Test career, this was one of his better knocks. Pringle and Gooch put on 147 runs before Sharma bowled Gooch off the last ball of the day.

The second day – darker and gloomier than the first day – would perhaps have been among the slowest and most boring periods of play in that entire season. England played to occupy the crease, while India bowled accurately without ever taking off the pressure. Chetan Sharma, bowling faster than the previous day, and Kapil troubled the batsmen frequently but without success. After an hour of dour batting, India broke through with Kapil getting Emburey. The score had crawled to 264. Binny, who was introduced late into the attack, finally got India the wicket of Pringle by bringing a ball back into him. Sharma consumed Paul Downton the keeper. At 294, the innings was done, with England batting for half the day and scoring just 49 runs. Chetan Sharma had a five-wicket haul, a reward for sustained hostility.

When India's turn to bat came, Srikkanth gave it his customary start with a flurry of four boundaries. A female topless streaker ran on to the ground to protest the exclusion of Botham and created a stir all around. As soon as normalcy returned, Srikkanth was out. Everyone said he had been distracted by the streaker, and we forgot to ask him if that indeed was the case when we spoke to him about this Test. After

Amarnath joined Gavaskar, India was secure at 83 for 1 when the day ended. Just 132 runs had been scored in a full day.

The third day belonged to Vengsarkar. He came early to the crease at 90 for 2 as Gavaskar unexpectedly played a poor shot off Graham Dilley. Amarnath raised the tempo with some lovely batting against the quick bowlers. He was not averse to hooking and played some handsome drives to cover and down the ground. Vengsarkar settled in quickly in the most assured manner. The two added 71 runs before Amarnath, in two minds whether to loft Edmonds over his head or check his stroke, mistimed a catch to mid-on. Azharuddin, the wristy stylist, added 71 runs with Vengsarkar. Gower took the new ball, and the Indians accelerated with a series of boundaries, with Azhar playing delightful shots. However, after a couple of lovely drives off front and back foot to Dilley, he hit a catch back to the bowler, much against the run of play.

Azharuddin's departure marked the start of a sudden slump. From 232 for 3, India collapsed to 264 for 8 as Shastri, Binny, Kapil and Chetan Sharma were dismissed by England's pace bowlers one after another. Vengsarkar, meanwhile, was batting beautifully – tall, upright and elegant. Vengsarkar's fifty was the fastest of the match. At 264 for 8, Vengsarkar received valuable support from the debutant Kiran More, who played a useful hand of 25. They raised 39 runs before More left and the last man Maninder walked in, with Vengsarkar five short of his century. He kept his tryst with history by hitting a boundary and running a sharp single to reach the landmark of three centuries at Lord's, a feat that not even all-time great batsmen like Bradman, Viv Richards, Chappell or Sobers have achieved. Calling his batting, 'breath-taking', Mohan wrote, 'There were any number of shots to admire in Vengsarkar's unbeaten 126 – placements into square third man off the back foot, square-drives off either foot, elegant drives into mid-wicket and the occasional cut.' Robin Marlar, the former Sussex cricketer who for many years contributed to *The Hindu* and *Sportstar*, said that

Vengsarkar 'became not only the truly historic figure of the game but of the tour'. Vengsarkar served Indian cricket for 17 years, playing 116 matches and scoring 6,868 runs at an average over 42 with 17 centuries.

We saw Vengsarkar play for the first time in January 1979, against West Indies, completely at sea on a dicey Chepauk pitch, not only technically but temperamentally unhappy. Then in 1983, we had the privilege of watching the same Vengsarkar in full pomp and at his elegant best, stroking a top-class century against a fearsome West Indian attack at Bombay. If he had not been asked to open the innings at the beginning of his Test career, he would have found his bearings as a classy middle-order batsman much earlier. At his best, Vengsarkar combined majesty and serenity, attack and defence, marvellously. He was a most elegant batsman when at peace and between 1985 and 1988 had such a golden run that he was considered one of the best batsmen in the world.

On the fourth evening, India's last wicket pair put on 38 runs and when Maninder was dismissed, India had a lead of 47 runs. England played out the remaining few overs that Saturday evening and were 8 for no loss. Next day, Sunday, was rest day. When play resumed on Monday, it belonged to the Indian captain. A match that would have chugged along to a draw was stirred to life by a superb spell of fast bowling. The conditions might have been helpful but Kapil was at his best. Bowling up the slope from the pavilion end, Kapil consumed the top three for just one run off 19 balls and reduced England to 35 for 3. They had still not wiped off the small lead that India had. Kapil got Robinson with one that climbed from just short of length to hit the shoulder off his bat. Marlar called it a 'killer ball'. This was a planned dismissal against a batsman who was committed to the front foot. Then Kapil brought one back sharply into Gooch, beating him comprehensively and trapping him lbw. Next, an artfully concealed ball that held its line beat left-handed Gower as the England captain played for the inswing. It was a match-winning spell.

Lamb and Gatting tried to retrieve the situation with a 73-run partnership against the bowling of Binny and Sharma, but just after England crossed 100, India broke through. Lamb went for a cut against the accurate Shastri and edged to wicketkeeper More. A few runs later, Chetan bowled Gatting for the second time in the match, and once again with a sharp off-cutter. Graeme Wright, editor of *Wisden*, called Sharma 'a pocket battleship of a fast-medium bowler' in his tour summary and added, 'Aggressive and volatile, he nonetheless bowled with great control, and the ball that came back from outside offstump found more than one open gate.' Chetan Sharma unfortunately never recaptured the magic of this tour and faded away after playing 23 Tests. Ironically, he was just 23 when he played his last Test match.

When Kapil brought himself on, he bowled a leg-cutter that was too good for Pringle who edged to the keeper. England were now 121 for 6, effectively only 74 runs ahead. At this stage, Downton and Richard Ellison put up an obdurate defence. For over two hours the two kept India at bay. Finally, when the score was 164 – the two had added only 43 in 31 overs – Downton swept Maninder. Shastri caught the ball at square-leg. 'As though it were a precious pearl,' said *The Hindu* correspondent. Often when a partnership is broken, another wicket follows quickly. So it was here, as Ellison fell to Binny with the score at 170. The innings folded up for 180, and that was the end of the day's play too. India's bowlers had turned the match upside down. Captivated by Kapil's bowling, Marlar wrote, 'The Indian captain bowled straight, straighter than the English bowlers. He made the ball move both ways and varied his pace. He produced a killer ball for his first wicket... This was quite simply match-winning bowling...'

On the last day, India needed 134 to win – an achievable target, but they had a few hiccups. Srikkanth left when the score was 10. Gavaskar for the second time in the match got out after having made a start, edging Dilley to the keeper, who dove like a goalkeeper in front of first slip to catch it. India needed 103 to win at that stage, with Amarnath uncharacteristically batting nervously at his end. The arrival of Vengsarkar – again batting with great certainty – helped him compose himself, and he began to defend solidly while Vengsarkar did the bulk of the scoring. The two added 45, but when India was still over 50 runs from victory, both fell. Pringle dismissed Amarnath and Vengsarkar followed, bowled by Phil Edmonds, the left-arm spinner. Azharuddin and Shastri now took up the task of taking India past the line, with Shastri in particular hitting some sparkling boundaries. At 110 for 4, with 24 needed for a win, Azharuddin was run out going for a third run. Fittingly, out came the captain to finish the match. Kapil hit the remaining runs by smashing four boundaries and a six over mid-wicket. India had won by five wickets. Gower was summarily sacked by the English selectors and Robin Marlar dramatically wrote, 'The head of the present incumbent David Gower was chopped off and all but held up dripping with blood for the populace to seek like that of Medusa, the Gorgon in old Greek mythology.'

It was the 18th instance of India asking the opposition to bat after winning the toss, but on almost all the earlier occasions, it was a defensive ploy to avoid batting first on a pace-friendly pitch. Here at Lord's, it was not a defensive option and it was the first time ever that India had won after putting the opposition in. In that sense too, Lord's was a watershed win. Ted Dexter adjudicated Kapil 'man of the match' ahead of Vengsarkar. The tour proved to be marvellous for India. In the next match at Leeds, India thumped England (captained by Mike Gatting) by 279 runs, with England dismissed for just 102 and 128 runs in its two innings, sealing an emphatic series win.

When we asked Srikkanth about the match, he said, '[This match] gave us the belief that the English could be beaten... Vengsarkar was brilliant and he had a two-year golden run when he scored in practically every match... that spell Kapil bowled was truly terrific. Kapil was super talented, a marvellously gifted player. With Vengsarkar and Mohinder we had a strong batting line-up supported by good all-rounders. Another significant aspect was that Chetan and Roger were very good in this series and gave Kapil excellent support.'

Graeme Wright wrote, '...the real strength of India's batting was its depth. In the Test matches there was no tail to speak of.' Most observantly, he added, 'A winning team is usually a happy one, but it was greatly to India's advantage, and to the credit of the players concerned, that during the Indians' tour of Australia, Kapil Dev and Gavaskar had formed a bond of friendship, the outcome of which was to be India's most successful tour of England.'

Kapil and Lord's, Vengsarkar and Lord's – the connections will always be special. Kapil and his team gave Indian cricket its happiest moment at Lord's in June 1983 when they lifted the World Cup. Now in June 1986, he had captained India to their first-ever Test win at Lord's. Vengsarkar has said he would like to take the Lord's pitch wherever he went – on his first visit here in 1979, he hit a match-saving century; in 1982 he repeated the feat; and in June 1986, he scored a match-winning ton on his third visit, a feat no overseas batsman has ever equalled.

Test No. 1046: Lord's, London, 5–10 June 1986: England 294 in 128.2 overs (Graham Gooch 114, Derek Pringle 63; Chetan Sharma 5-64, Roger Binny 3-55) and 180 in 96.4 overs (Mike Gatting 40, Allan Lamb 39; Kapil Dev 4-52, Maninder Singh 3-9) lost to **India** (Toss) 341 in 137 overs (Dilip Vengsarkar 126*, Mohinder Amarnath 69; Graham Dilley 4-146, Pringle 3-58) and 136/5 in 42 overs (Vengsarkar 33, Kapil 23*; Dilley 2-28) by five wickets. **MotM:** Kapil Dev.

Captains: Kapil Dev (India) and David Gower (England)

14

It's a Tie!

*India vs Australia, first Test, M.A. Chidambaram Stadium,
Chepauk, Chennai, 1986*

Kapil announced after this match, 'I felt like going to the beach, stand on the sand facing the sea and scream and scream till I got it out of the system.' Half of Madras's cricket-crazy public, and most newspaper editors in the country, were kicking themselves; they had assumed the last day would be a boring final day and had missed the game of their life. The editors had pulled out their staff photographers from the ground, assuming the game was dead, and deployed them elsewhere. The only person to take a quality photograph of the game as it finished in a heart-stopping tie was an amateur photographer, Mala Mukherjee.

Australian cricket had had a turbulent few years after the fading away of greats like Lillee, Chappell and Marsh. Kim Hughes had proved incapable of leading Australia and tearfully gave up the captaincy midway through the 1984–85 home series against West Indies. A weeping Hughes in his farewell press conference said, 'The constant criticism, speculation and innuendo by former players and a section of the media over the past four or five years have finally taken their toll.' The Australian selectors asked Allan Border to lead. He too found the job equally difficult and hopeless as the team continued to perform poorly. Soon after Border took over, a group of players who had been selected for the 1985 Ashes tour withdrew and instead chose to be part of a rebel tour to South Africa. This was a clear violation of the Gleneagles agreement signed by Commonwealth nations in 1977 that specifically forbids contact and competition between their sportsmen and any organization or team from apartheid South Africa. Border saw this not only as a betrayal of Australian cricket but a blow to the fight against racism.

Although Border's team was trounced in the Ashes series, worse followed. When India toured Australia in 1985–86, Border's team would have lost once again, but were rescued by rain. New Zealand, who had never beaten Australia in a home series, beat them later that year. Border's patience had worn thin by then and he threatened to quit if the team did not improve. It was at this juncture that the Australian board brought in Bobby Simpson as the coach. Border and Simpson formed an amazing partnership from the moment they came together, and in just over a year's time, they held aloft the World Cup. The Aussies never looked back after that. Except for a few blips – like the early elimination from the 1992 World Cup and defeats at the hands of a very strong West Indies – they surged forward. They proceeded to dominate world cricket over the next 15 years, and the roles of Border and Simpson in this resurgence can never be forgotten. The beginnings of their journey were to be found in the tied Test in Madras in September 1986, played against an India fresh from their victory over England that summer.

While the Indian team looked well settled, Border's team, in contrast, was inexperienced and had seen no success. Geoff Marsh was playing only his seventh Test and was just beginning a partnership with David Boon at the top of the order. The one-down strokemaker, playing his third Test, was a fresh-faced Victorian named Dean Jones. He would be among the main heroes of this fabled Test, but as the match began, his only concern was that he should not let his captain down. Steve Waugh, just 21, was playing only his sixth Test; no one at the time knew he would be an all-time legend by the time he retired. Wicketkeeper Tim Zoehrer was a sledging, scrapping personality. Their fast bowlers were Craig McDermott – who would be their best fast bowler between the times of Dennis Lillee and Glenn McGrath – and the very tall Bruce Reid. For spin, they had the pedestrian left-armer Ray Bright and – in the words of *Wisden* editor Mathew Engels – the 'idiosyncratic Greg Matthews'. Amidst this rather inexperienced group was Border, their marvellous shepherd.

Chennai at any time other than December and January is oppressively humid, with sweat pouring down within a few minutes of play. But Chepauk is a blessed ground and has been the venue of many thrilling contests with its sporting pitch that has something for both fast and slow bowlers as well as for batsmen. Some of India's greatest players like Kapil, Viswanath and Tendulkar reserved their best for Chennai. The sporting crowd in Chennai too deserved the best, for they are good-humoured, knowledgeable and capable of appreciating an opponent's prowess with generosity. One of the best things about Chidambaram Stadium was that the league cricketers were provided tickets for the best view – right behind the bowler – in the 'D' stand opposite the pavilion. We were lucky to watch this match from this stand on the first, third and the fourth days. Yet, we were unlucky too, for on the fifth day, instead of being at the ground, we were at work in north Madras. However, by 3 p.m. we both knew that the match was heading for a humdinger finish and sneaked off to the factory manager's residence to watch the last 30 overs of an amazing final day.

Those of us in the stands wanted a drink every few minutes, and it was many times worse out there in the middle. Border won an important toss and batted first, his first task – to secure the Test. In what Mohan wrote as being 'a soporific day's play', Australia made just 211 for 2, with Boon playing the whole day in self-denial – he was out just before stumps – and making a century. No bowler seemed to extract anything from the pitch. India too suffered in the heat and lost More within the first hour to food poisoning. Luckily, they had Chandrakant Pandit in the team and he was a proper keeper.

The second day belonged to Jones for his monumental double-century. He resumed at 56 not out and then played for much of the day. His scoring was a lot brisker too and his century arrived smoothly. Once his captain joined him, the young Victorian and Border batted together for the next four hours, all through the hottest time of the day. Jones was dehydrating, tottering and vomiting frequently, unable to hold the liquids that he was taking. Yet, his tougher-than-nails captain remained unmoved. Even as Jones was on the verge of a blackout, Border told him that he was a softie and perhaps a Queenslander would be better than a Victorian for the task on hand. Jones grit his teeth and carried on, and finally had the vicarious satisfaction of seeing his captain go first, though Border made a century.

Jones was finally out for 210, having batted and run between wickets for 502 minutes – an extraordinary figure considering the sapping humidity and his own debilitation. So far gone was he that he was rushed straight to the hospital for saline drips. Jones recalls that towards the end of his innings he was urinating in his pants. He has no recall of being taken to the hospital. All he remembers is returning to the pavilion. 'Jones comes of age as Test batsman,' declared *The Hindu*; Mohan wrote, 'There was not a shot in the book that Jones did not play… His stirring shots against Kapil told the whole tale.' By end of day two, Australia were 556 for 6.

After thirty minutes on the third day, Border declared at 570 for 7. The match was secure, there could only be one winner from here and it was in this mood that McDermott and Reid took the new ball. Opening for India were the impregnable Gavaskar and the mercurial Srikkanth. The latter was at his best around this time, and his daredevilry made him a favourite with spectators. Chepauk was his home ground and with a twirl of the bat, a look at the sun, and a sniffle, the man was off to a blazing start. Gavaskar was still in single digits when Srikkanth had raced to fifty. Then disaster struck thrice. Matthews, the quirky off spinner, after being hammered for 15 runs in an over by Srikkanth, got Gavaskar caught and bowled. Then, backing up for a non-existent run, Amarnath was run out. Srikkanth being Srikkanth, even after two wickets had fallen, went after Matthews, and gave a catch to Greg Ritchie. From 62 for none, India were 65 for 3 and in big trouble. The trusted firm of Azharuddin and Shastri tried to repair the situation. Both played their strokes freely but neither could convert their fifties into something substantial. Azharuddin left first, caught and bowled by Ray Bright. Pandit batted well and just as Shastri and Pandit had compiled a 50-run partnership, Matthews dismissed Shastri. At 206 for 5, Kapil came out. Within a few minutes he saw Pandit go – once again a batsman had given his wicket away after a sound start. Kiran More, indisposed, was out soon after. Kapil now had only the tail and with India 300 runs behind Australia, a follow-on seemed certain. Kapil guided Chetan Sharma safely through to stumps, but 270 for 7 was a sombre end to the day; as *The Hindu* wrote, 'Misplaced batting priorities put India in a spot.'

Next morning, Kapil turned on his magic. The effortless strokeplay, the smooth driving, and the enviable control in his methods – all these were wonderful to watch. There was a natural grace in Kapil's batting and one knew one was watching the most enchanting period of batting in this match. He did not take any risks, but marvellously seized every opportunity, going at virtually run-a-ball. His off-drives left the fielders standing while his onside shots were powerful and decisive. When Sharma got out with the score at 330, the follow-on had still not been averted. But Shivlal Yadav stayed with Kapil and his 47-run association was vital; India avoided the follow-on and Kapil completed his century. When India were finally dismissed for 397, Kapil, the last man out, had made a fabulous 119 at a strike rate of 86.23.

It was already the afternoon of the fourth day and only two innings had been completed. The rest of the day was anticlimactic. Australia scored 170 runs in the 49 overs that India bowled, and the five wickets it lost were all to the left-arm spin of Shastri and Maninder. As we went home, all talk was about Kapil's knock and the match finishing in a draw in all likelihood.

To everyone's surprise, Border declared on the fifth morning on the overnight score. Mohinder Amarnath told us that Border's declaration caught everyone in the Indian team offguard. 'That final day, we did not expect Border to come and tell us he had declared on the overnight score. It was such a challenging declaration – 348 to get in an entire day, at four runs an over. An Indian captain would not have declared.' Srikkanth, typical of the man, even 30 years later believed India ought to have won. 'It was a very sporting declaration and yes, we were surprised. But we knew we had a great chance. We began well and all the top batsmen made runs. At tea we were sitting pretty.' For his part, Srikkanth made a brisk 39 off just 49 balls with six boundaries and India were off to a flying start. At 55, Srikkanth was dismissed and that brought Jimmy to the crease. In many ways the antithesis of Srikkanth, Amarnath had his own memories of the match: 'I remember this long partnership with Sunny. We did not have any specific goal. We played and assessed the game from time to time and then at one stage it became clear we had an excellent chance. Srikkanth gave us the start in his usual way. You know him, he is happy-go-lucky and we left him to his own ways. He gave us flying starts in both innings.' Mohan told us that he distinctly remembered Srikkanth's dismissal. 'It was crucial. Border knew he would loft the ball if given the bait and deliberately left long-off vacant. Matthews flighted, Srikkanth took the bait and Steve Waugh running across from mid-on brought off a wonderful catch.' Thirty years later, Srikkanth is still the same fidgety, impatient person. While conversing with us about this game, he was juggling calls on his phone and assorted office work and answering our questions without breaking stride, and bringing the same edginess to everything!

Amarnath and Gavaskar put on a century partnership before the former was dismissed just after he completed his half-century. Azhar came out to join Gavaskar. India were going serenely, not at the required rate but reasonably within hauling distance. At tea, India were 190 for 2, still needing another 158 to win. At 204, India lost their third wicket, Gavaskar falling ten short of a century. It was Gavaskar's 100th consecutive Test, the first player to achieve this feat. The inexperienced Pandit, in only his second Test, gave the innings its momentum by playing a stroke-filled innings full of positive intent. India required just 118 with seven wickets in hand when the mandatory 20 overs began. Just when they seemed to be on top, India suffered twin blows. Azhar, on 42, charged Bright and was caught by Ritchie at cover. Matthews got rid of Kapil for one. India were now 253 for 5, the target 100 runs away and only Shastri among the top order remained. After a brisk 39 from just 37 balls, Pandit was dismissed, bowled by Matthews, his concentration upset by Zoehrer's sledging.

At 293 for 6, Shastri only had Sharma and Shivlal Yadav to help him, because he knew Maninder would not count. Shastri continued to bat beautifully and Chetan once again batted well to help add 40 runs. Shastri, undisturbed by whatever the Australians did, was taking India closer to the target with every stroke. Jimmy told us, 'Ravi Shastri was superb…brave and aggressive. Despite the boundary fielders he would go for attacking shots. He was beautifully steering us to victory and if Yadav or someone else had stayed we could have won because of Ravi's efforts.'

Only 18 were needed off the last five overs when Chetan Sharma cracked and lost his wicket after another war of words with Zoehrer and Co. The next ball clean bowled More. India were 331 for 8 and the match had now swung Australia's way. Yadav came to the pitch, immune to neither the pressure nor the snapping comments of a pumped up close-in field. One mighty blow went over long-on for six and India were only a boundary from victory. But Yadav still pumped up and overcharged, rashly attempted a sweep the next ball and was bowled. India now needed four runs to win, while Australia needed the last wicket. Amarnath was full of praise for the way Border marshalled his team that day. 'Full credit to Border. He was very shrewd. He managed to get his players – the wicketkeeper and others – to irritate our younger players, you know the language they use on the ground. So Pandit, Chetan Sharma, Yadav, they all got out because of this.'

The crowd was going nuts while the dressing rooms were jangling with nerves. Some friends who worked in the vicinity of Mount Road had rushed to the ground as the mandatory overs began. To this day they believe they have not seen a more exciting finale in any game of cricket. As the pendulum swung crazily one way and the other, neither team was holding back; a friend described it as the equivalent of a boxing bout that goes on till one of the pugilists is knocked out.

In Shastri, India had the coolest head in the middle. As Matthews bowled the final over of the match – the 87th over of the innings – Shastri took two off a mistimed stroke and then calmly crossed over for a single that tied the scores. He had done the most important thing – levelled the scores to rule out defeat. Matthews' fifth ball rapped Maninder Singh on the pad, and umpire Vikram Raju raised his right hand index finger high into the sky. Mohan wrote that the decision 'was a testament to the integrity of Indian umpires', but Shastri has not forgiven Raju to this day, convinced that Maninder had edged the ball on to his pads. As soon as the umpire raised his finger, the Australian players jumped on each other and celebrated as though they had won. Shastri accompanied Maninder on the long walk back to the pavilion. He had batted superbly, hitting 48 runs off just 40 balls with two sixes. Srikkanth, recollecting the scene in India's dressing room, told us, 'We were very disappointed not to win, we were not at all thrilled about the tie. At tea we were sitting pretty but we lost wickets unnecessarily and made Matthews such a hero!'

India had scored at four an over and at no point did they call off the hunt, but Border and his men were magnificent; particularly Matthews and Bright who bowled intelligently and heroically right through the day. Matthews bowled 38.5 overs without a break. Wearing the baggy green even while bowling, the full-sleeved quirky off spinner bowled an excellent line outside the offstump through the match. He never

The suspense beats a Hitchcock thriller

Sportstar magazine was profuse in its praise – and for no simple reason. This was only the second time in cricket history a Test had been tied. (Used with permission from Kasturi & Sons)

had such a match again. As for Bright, he played two more Tests and his moderate international career was over.

The tie had far-reaching benefits for Border's team. They found the wellspring of self-belief and recaptured the Australian ability to fight at all times. Dean Jones, a hero of this match, told Andrew Miller, the UK editor of Cricinfo, 'I think the tied Test marked the renaissance of Australian cricket.' There have been only two 'tied Tests' in 140 years of Test cricket, two out of 2,200 Tests so far. When the first tied Test happened in 1960 in Brisbane, the entire cricketing world was captivated by an unprecedented occurrence. At the Gabba, Australia and West Indies scored 737 runs while 40 wickets fell. At Chepauk, India and Australia scored 744 runs while 32 wickets fell. Brisbane was a see-saw game. In Madras, Australia were on top for four days and it was Border's bold declaration and India's spirited response that enabled the drama of the final day.

After the Brisbane tie, Jack Fingleton wrote that the final minutes were so exciting that he put his typewriter away and completely forgot his job as a reporter. Now after the Madras tie, in a similar vein, Mohan wrote, 'We never believed we would actually live to see a tied Test... Those with weak hearts may not have borne easily the drama of that last over.' Mike Coward, who has written of Australia's visits to the subcontinent with a deep understanding, wrote that while Brisbane was played in great sporting spirit between two teams who respected and admired each other, Madras was played between teams with no warmth for each other. 'Sadly, no such mateship and understanding exists between the teams under the leadership of Allan Border and Kapil Dev. Indeed, it is difficult to recall a more acrimonious Test than this one.' Border swore at umpire Dotiwala, while Tim Zoehrer's crude gesture after an appeal was turned down was most distasteful. At one point Pandit had to be led away when things looked like they were going to get physical. The Aussies believed it was the heat, humidity and the tension of the final day that led to such controversies. Mohan, however, reminded readers that bad blood had existed from earlier encounters: 'Let it not be forgotten it was Allan Border who refused a glass of water to Kapil Dev when the latter had been rendered distraught after a stroke of his had killed a seagull in the Adelaide Test.'

Test No. 1052: MA Chidambaram Stadium, Chepauk, Chennai, 18–22 September 1986: Australia (Toss) 574/7 dec in 170.5 overs (Dean Jones 210, David Boon 122, Allan Border 106; Shivlal Yadav 4-142) and 170/5 dec in 49 overs (Boon 49, Greg Ritchie 28; Maninder Singh 3-60, Ravi Shastri 2-50) tied with **India** 397 in 94.2 overs (Kapil Dev 119, R. Shastri 62; Greg Matthews 5-103, Ray Bright 2-88) and 347 in 86.5 overs (Sunil Gavaskar 90, Mohinder Amarnath 51; Bright 5-94, Matthews 5-146). **MotM:** Dean Jones and Kapil Dev.

Captains: Kapil Dev (India) and Allan Border (Australia)

15

Pace, the Trump Card

India vs South Africa, first Test, Sardar Patel Stadium, Motera,
Ahmedabad, 1996

We move forward a full ten years from the tied Test in 1986 to select the next of India's greatest Tests, a reaffirmation of our opinion that in the 1990s, there were only a few memorable Tests played by India and they were all at home.

South Africa had been readmitted into international cricket in 1991 after the lifting of apartheid and the formation of a democratic government under Nelson Mandela. In what was a masterstroke, Ali Bacher, chief of South African cricket, got them to play their first series after readmission against India, a country closely associated with the anti-apartheid struggle since Mahatma Gandhi's early years in that country. India then visited South Africa to play a Test series in 1992. In 1996, South Africa were paying a return visit, with three tests in Ahmedabad, Kolkata and Kanpur.

India's Sachin Tendulkar had two difficult stints at captaincy – 17 Tests in the period 1996–97 and 8 Tests in 1999–2000 – before giving up the post entirely. He began well nonetheless, winning his first match, a strangely organized one-off Test against Australia at Kotla in August 1996 (the first time the two teams competed for the Border–Gavaskar trophy), and three months later, led India in a three-Test home series against a strong South Africa, led by Hansie Cronje, in his second series as captain. This game was Sachin's second Test as captain.

There were some exciting players in the Indian camp: a stylish left-hander called Ganguly and a technically perfect right-hander called Dravid had just announced their arrival in style over the summer in England, and in Ahmedabad, a soft-spoken Hyderabadi by the name of V.V.S. Laxman would make his debut. Little did we know that in a few years, these three along with their captain would be known as the 'Fab Four', one of the finest middle orders in cricket history. As for the bowling, Venkatesh Prasad had joined Javagal Srinath, his mate from Karnataka, as the new-ball partner; India had not had such a combination for a long time. Left-arm spinner and useful lower-order batsman Sunil Joshi, from the small town of Gadag in Karnataka, had forced his way into the Indian team. Then there was Kumble, leader of the attack.

In a throwback to the early years of Indian cricket, when the majority of players would be Marathi speaking, in 1996, the mother tongue of the bowling unit was Kannada, with Prasad and Srinath often discussing their bowling in their mother tongue. Sunil Joshi, who hides a terrific sense of humour behind a straight face, narrated to us more than a few conversations that took place between these bowlers during that period: Sachin would demand from him the exact plan for the dismissal of a batsman, and he would be tongue-tied. Srinath would then prod him in Kannada to say something and escape for that moment. Then there was the time Kumble loudly asked Srinath why he was standing at the top of his bowling mark and not bowling; to which Srinath replied in Kannada, how can I bowl when Sachin is standing in front of me like Nandi, the bull, asking me how exactly I would get the batsman out with the next ball.

It was a young team, with only Manjrekar, Woorkeri Raman and Azharuddin over 30 years in age. In a curtain raiser for *The Hindu*, R. Mohan wrote, 'This is going to be a great Test series then. The South

Africans, unbeaten in a Test series in the five years since their return from wilderness, versus the Indians, unbeaten in a Test series at home for ten years. As the unstoppable force takes on the immovable object, the prospect of absorbing cricket over the next five days at Motera is very high.' The South Africans were taken on a visit to Gandhiji's Sabarmati Ashram, where they were made welcome. But a visit to the ground at Motera brought them back to earth. One look at the brown strip and coach Bob Woolmer told the press, 'I think the top of the pitch is crusty and soft underneath. It will turn definitely. And it might be difficult to bat on.'

Tendulkar won the toss and immediately decided to bat, which meant South Africa would have to bat last on a dangerous pitch. Though Cronje had a reputation for losing the toss regularly, he was one of the best captains in the world at the time. He marshalled the South Africans astutely on the first day and his bowlers and fielders backed him fully. The South Africans bowled well on the first day, wresting the initiative from India by forcing errors from the batsmen. Allan Donald was superb and Fanie de Villiers supported him well. Nayan Mongia left early to a dicey lbw. Manjrekar, the other opener, played well till the Chinaman bowler Paul Adams got him on 34. The bowling was tight and the fielding as one expected of the South Africans brilliant. Jonty Rhodes was spectacular, dealing crushing blows to the Indian batting with a brilliant catch first at short mid-wicket to get rid of Tendulkar and then a lightning pick and direct hit to run out Azhar. Both batsmen had been felled when they were on the verge of building substantial scores. Tendulkar had hit a brisk 42 off 64 balls. He played a straight-drive, a cover-drive and a square-drive off Fanie de Villiers, each of them exquisite and then cover-drove Adams to the fence twice. It was India's first look at the unorthodox Adams, who bowled in a whirl of arms and seemed to be looking at his shoes as he delivered the ball.

One of the less satisfactory features of the match, however, was the quality of umpiring. Bansal and George Sharp had built a reputation of being trigger happy, so much so that journalist G. Viswanath cheekily predicted before the match began that it would not end in a draw, simply because the two umpires would be raising their finger quite regularly! And true to their reputations, they gave a couple of dubious decisions on the first day. In a spirit of even-handedness, they dished out ropey decisions to South Africa, too. The dusty desolate Gujarat Stadium also did not have the ambience and atmosphere to start off a potentially exciting series, neither did it have amenities for the public. There were just 10,000 folks in a stadium with a capacity of 55,000.

By the end of day one, India were 215 for 8, consumed by umpires, Rhodes's electrifying fielding, and by Allan Donald, who struck hard even on a brown flat track. Experts predicted the game was well poised, and they were proved right on the second day. South Africa ended at 205 for 8, as dead-heat a situation as one could imagine after two well-contested days. The Indian spinners bowled very well, with Kumble and Narendra Hirwani offering the full spectrum of legspin – fast and accurate at one end, with a slow and tantalizing mix of spin and googly from the other. The most successful bowler that day was left-armer Joshi. Among his victims was Rhodes, foxed by a ball that pitched and turned from offstump for a catch in the slips. Poor umpiring brought the wickets of Cronje off a dubious decision, and Darryl Cullinan, who was batting beautifully on 43, slaughtered by a shocker. Indian scribes did not hesitate to castigate Bansal for the howlers: 'On both occasions, it was embarrassing to see Bansal's finger go up. The injustice meted out to Cullinan was an inequity perpetrated against the match itself. It ruined the game as a spectacle...'

Reduced to 119 for 7, Pat Symcox and Fanie de Villiers resisted the Indian spinners in a 63-run partnership that ensured South Africa were merely 21 runs behind India at stumps. On a pitch where the Proteas would bat fourth, a lead in the first innings was precious, which they achieved the next morning. Tendulkar, with perhaps his only error in the game, delayed the new ball and by the time Srinath claimed the last two wickets, de Villiers had reached 67 not out and helped South Africa take a lead of 21.

When India batted again, Donald in his opening burst removed Manjrekar and Mongia. By the day's end, South Africa had dismissed seven Indian batsmen for 172, and India had a lead of only 149 with Laxman the lone recognized batsman at the crease. While the senior batsmen faltered, the young and inexperienced duo of Laxman and Dravid showed good technique, resolve and unflagging concentration. Dravid made 34 watchful runs in 150 minutes before he fell leg before to Symcox. Laxman, who came to the crease at 82 for 4, was unbeaten on 50 when stumps were drawn. His batting bore resemblance to fellow Hyderabadi Azhar, and many pointed out even the similarity in his top-hand grip with that of the latter. In the years to come, Laxman would prove to be India's finest second-innings player, an expert at batting with the tail and magical when it came to shepherding India to victories chasing tricky targets. Prasad told us that Laxman is 'a lovely gentle person, soft-natured and polite, but when it came to battling at the crease, he is the toughest steel'. Laxman's career was not a neat linear graph of growth and achievement. Early in his career, he was forced to open the innings, the only position available. As an opener, he did moderately, if one excludes the incandescent 167 in a lost cause in Sydney in January 2000. It was only in Kolkata 2001 that we discovered the true Laxman.

Just as one was feeling thankful that the third day was not being marred by poor umpiring, the lumpen element in the crowd threw an egg-sized stone at Paul Adams, who was fielding on the boundary. Unlike earlier visiting captains like Mark Taylor, who did not bother about such insane behaviour, Cronje took his team off the ground. Mohan wrote, 'The fault actually lies with our country because the response to defeat or impending defeat as in Calcutta in the World Cup, in Bangalore during the Titan Cup and here has not exactly been sporting.' Even Gopal Gandhi, India's High Commissioner to South Africa, issued a statement in Durban, expressing regret on behalf of the millions of cricket lovers in India, saying it was a disgraceful act which had besmirched India's cricketing culture and hospitality.

That evening, Laxman told reporters, 'The skipper has told me to stay at the crease. I have to continue the task tomorrow.' As luck would have it, he got out as soon as the fourth day's play began. In a matter of a couple of overs, Prasad and Hirwani were dismissed and India were all out for 190, setting South Africa just 170 to win. It certainly seemed like it would be the last day of the Test.

For Tendulkar, the die was cast. Even though the pitch was showing wear and tear and he had Kumble, Joshi and Hirwani, the small target gave him no breathing room. Cronje too knew India would come hard with their spinners, and so he and his batsmen were preparing themselves mentally and in the nets for a searching examination by spin. Tendulkar, enjoying his early days of captaincy, was keen and willing to experiment and make things happen. He decided to surprise the South Africans with the pace of Srinath. It was a masterstroke.

Srinath's spell in this match ranks among the finest spells of fast bowling by an Indian. The crowd at Motera will of course never forget it, neither will those who watched on television. Srinath was accurate and hostile. Four of his victims were either bowled or lbw while the other two were caught behind by Mongia. Srinath himself would later acknowledge that he had never bowled with such sustained pace, accuracy and venom before this. He dealt blows in clutches of two wickets each off successive balls on three occasions, and South Africa were decimated in 38.5 overs.

The procession began with a marginal lbw decision against Hudson when the ball might have missed the legstump. Cullinan was caught behind off the next ball, a beauty. Unlike his stock inswinger, Srinath straightened this one from a perfect length and line to force the edge. Left-handed Gary Kirsten – who later coached India – and Cronje, batting beautifully, seemed to stem the tide for a while as Srinath rested. When the score was 40, Joshi bowled a wicked ball to Kirsten that beat him completely and trapped him lbw. Kumble accounted for McMillan, and then it was over to Srinath. He got wicketkeeper Richardson – the current International Cricket Council (ICC) CEO – caught behind, attempting an unwise cut shot and with the next ball trapped Jonty Rhodes plumb in front. Rhodes, playing with a strained hamstring, was hampered in his movement and could not come fully forward. At 96 for 6, Kumble proved too good for Symcox and de Villiers. All that was left was for Srinath to do his two wickets in two balls trick – he bowled Donald off his pads for a duck, as the fiery South African retreated from the pace of his opposite number, and then bowled Paul Adams first ball. India had bundled out the visitors for 105 to emerge winners by a large margin of 64 runs.

Reminiscing on this move, Tendulkar wrote in his autobiography, 'The South Africans would undoubtedly expect me to attack them with spinners on a crumbling pitch. Instead, I decided to use Javagal Srinath, because Sri, with his extra pace, could also get the ball to reverse-swing. Swing at a good pace is very difficult to deal with and in no time Srinath had given us a dream start, reducing the South Africans to 0–2. He was bowling beautifully and had the batsmen in all sorts of trouble. I put Sunil Joshi on at the other end to keep the batsmen in check and not concede too many runs.'

This was also more or less along the lines of what he said at the press conference after the match-winning spell: 'It was one of the best spells from Srinath. I have seen him bowl fast in Cape Town, in Australia and against the West Indies in Mumbai. The South African batsmen were sweeping and padding all the time and settled to a particular frame of mind. That's the reason I brought back Srinath. I think this change, in particular, was very crucial. He got a fantastic rhythm and he ran through the side.'

Some months ago, we caught up with Venkatesh Prasad over coffee to talk about this match. Prasad is known to recollect and paint pictures of old stories as though they occurred yesterday. As he spoke to us, he was in full flow, interrupted only by friends and acquaintances who stopped to exchange greetings with him. His coffee went cold as he remembered Srinath's spell. In the process, he also analysed Srinath the bowler. After all, he was Srinath's new-ball partner for a fair period of time. Prasad said, 'Sri was the best Indian fast bowler I have seen, perhaps the best fast bowler India has produced. He had skill, guile and pace. He made life miserable for Cronje and the others. He was essentially an inswing bowler, and he bowled back of length, so even if the batsmen were beaten, the ball would go over the stumps. In those days we did not have a truly professional coaching staff, any special mental conditioning – all that only came with John Wright's tenure – otherwise Srinath would have done even better. With experience, he bowled a little fuller and developed the one that straightened. In fact, he got his first five-for in this match. I had already got five wickets in an innings earlier at Lord's and he would joke saying he had to slog for his five-wicket feat while I got it just like that! We had a friendly competitive side to our partnership, we helped each other and we spurred each other on. In the next match in Kolkata I got six South African wickets. He helped me a lot. He was one of the most humorous guys in the team.'

Tendulkar did not hesitate to bask in the happiness of this achievement. He wrote in his autobiography, 'It was the high point of my captaincy; the plan to use Srinath from one end had worked really well. Hansie Cronje walked up to me after the game and confessed that he had been caught off guard. He had expected me to employ spinners and had a strategy in place to negotiate the turning ball on a wearing pitch. He did not have a plan for Srinath, and by the time he had come to terms with our tactics the match was over.'

Cronje, dour as ever, after paying the customary compliments to the victor, added, 'It was not the best pitch in the world. In fact, it was probably the worst I have played a Test on. Practice facilities were non-existent. The crowd was very volatile.' Mohan, whose reportage was objective and unbiased, had the last word: 'A remarkable result in an extraordinary match, perhaps the best win by India at home in a long time.'

Test No. 1338: Gujarat Stadium, Motera, Ahmedabad, 20–23 November 1996: India (Toss) 223 in 99 overs (Sachin Tendulkar 42, Sanjay Manjrekar 34; Allan Donald 4-37, Pat Symcox 2-48) and 190 in 79.2 overs (V.V.S. Laxman 51, Rahul Dravid 34; Paul Adams 3-30, Donald 3-32) beat **South Africa** 244 in 98.1 overs (Fanie de Villiers 67*, Daryll Cullinan 43; Sunil Joshi 4-43, Narendra Hirwani 2-38) and 105 in 38.5 overs (Hansie Cronje 48*, Gary Kirsten 20; Javagal Srinath 6-21, Anil Kumble 3-34) by 64 runs. **MotM:** Javagal Srinath.

Captains: Sachin Tendulkar (India) and Hansie Cronje (South Africa)

Ganguly cuddling his first two champagne bottles after two centuries in his first two Tests. Five years later he would lead India to unscaled heights. (Courtesy Getty Images)

The two men who breathed new life into Indian cricket with their partnership. Laxman and Dravid during their historic partnership in 2001 against Australia. (Courtesy Getty Images)

The portrait of a happy team: Indian players go into a celebratory huddle after winning the series in Pakistan in 2004. (Courtesy Getty Images)

Venkatesh Prasad's cherished mementos: The ball with which he took five wickets for no runs against Pakistan in Chennai and the one with which he took five wickets on debut at Lord's. (Courtesy Venkatesh Prasad)

Kumble's 600th wicket was Andrew Symonds – a bizarre coincidence after the incidents of Monkeygate in the previous Test at Sydney. (Courtesy Getty Images)

Kumble: statesman and captain. The respect his teammates had for him was unbelievable. Here he playfully poses after his 600th wicket. (Courtesy Sunandan Lele)

How many classic knocks has Rahul Dravid played in the toughest conditions! Seen here in the course of a masterly ton at Leeds on a green-top, which was a turning point in India's cricket history. (Courtesy Getty Images)

Respect! Unnoticed, Steve Waugh went all the way to the boundary, retrieved the ball from the gutter, walked back to Dravid and gave it to him as a cherished memento. (Courtesy Getty Images)

Boisterous celebrations in the Indian dressing room at the Wanderers in 2006 after the win against South Africa. (Courtesy Sunandan Lele)

An endearing photo of Rahul Dravid with his wife Vijeeta and son Samit after another overseas Test victory, this time against West Indies in 2006. (Courtesy Sunandan Lele)

The scoreboard says it all as Yuvraj lifts Sachin in a bear hug after a famous chase at Chepauk in December 2008. (Courtesy Getty Images)

Miracle at Mohali: At the end of another magical match-winning act by Laxman. Ojha, Raina and Laxman embrace in joy. (Courtesy Getty Images)

India became the No.1 Test side in December 2009. On 18 February 2010, India beat South Africa to retain their ranking. That evening, Dhoni gifted his match jersey to Colonel Vembu Shankar, a decorated army hero and winner of the Shaurya Chakra, India's third highest gallantry award. (Courtesy Col. Vembu Shankar)

16

Clash of the Titans

India vs Australia, first Test, M.A. Chidambaram Stadium,
Chepauk, Chennai, 1998

This is the only occasion in the book that we refer to a game between two nations in terms of an individual contest between two players, but with good reason. If ever there was a head-on contest between two legends that decided the outcome of a game poised on knife's edge, this was such a game. Champion versus Champion. Tendulkar versus Warne in Chennai has been told and retold by the thousands who were there at the ground and by many more who claim to have been there that day. A few weeks later, Tendulkar versus Warne occurred twice in two days in a 50-overs tournament in Sharjah where amidst a swirling dust storm, Tendulkar unleashed his own gale force on Warne and the Australians. It was an unforgettable season.

When Australia played India in Chennai in March 1998, it was the 59th Test of 25-year-old Tendulkar's career and the 64th Test of 28-year-old Warne's career. From January 1993 to February 1998 (just before this game), Tendulkar had scored 3,021 runs, including ten centuries, with a batting average of 60.42. Warne, during the same period, had taken 291 wickets at 23.07. To say that Warne and Tendulkar were both at their peak around 1998 will be limiting, for both were magnificently consistent right through their long and illustrious careers. Their averages for their entire careers – Tendulkar, 53.78 (batting) and Warne, 25.41 (bowling) – are proof of this and if at times they dropped briefly from such peaks that was due to injuries or other circumstances. Having said this, Tendulkar was at his destructive best in the years 1993–99 and then rediscovered that magic during 2008–10. These two were already on the path to becoming all-time cricketing greats; the Indian ended up being deified as the 'god of cricket' in his country while the Australian is hailed as the best legspinner in cricket history.

This Test was the first time the two were facing off against each other since the legspinner's debut at home in January 1992. Australia under Mark Taylor – one of the best captains in Australian cricket history – were coming to India on the back of five consecutive series wins over England, South Africa and New Zealand, but both Glenn McGrath and Jason Gillespie, their premier fast bowlers, were injured. India, on the other hand, were coming off a winless run of 12 matches stretching back 18 months. The captaincy had gone back to the unimaginative and laid-back Azharuddin after Tendulkar's unhappy stint as skipper.

Before the Test, the Australians had played a warm-up match against Ranji Trophy champions Mumbai; rarely has a warm-up game had such a decisive impact on the series. Tendulkar, captaining Mumbai, decided it was important to establish a psychological ascendancy over Australia in the warm-up game itself, and told his batsmen to attack Warne at any cost to prevent him from settling into a rhythm. The strategy was hugely successful, as Warne went for over 100 runs in 16 overs, while Tendulkar hit a blazing double-century. Interestingly, it was Tendulkar's first double-century in first-class cricket. The Australians collapsed in their second innings and Mumbai handed them a crushing 10-wicket defeat.

Tendulkar's preparation for this series was more meticulous than ever, if such a thing were possible. He had identified Warne as the main (and perhaps only) threat and had prepared elaborately. In one of the more interesting chapters in his autobiography, Tendulkar discusses the fascinating technical adjustments he made. Warne's strength lay in the marvellous drift he got in the air from off to leg, which lands the ball in the 'blind' side of the batsman. Tendulkar decided that instead of being side-on, he would open up his stance, stand a little outside legstump, not step out of the crease and instead, from the crease, slog him to mid-wicket periodically. Warne on his part kept his powder dry – despite the hammering against Mumbai, not once did he go round the wicket. But Tendulkar knew Warne would bowl round the wicket in Chennai. So for a week in Mumbai and then in Chennai before the match, he practised against former Indian legspinner Sivaramakrishnan, asking him to bowl into the scuffed-up area outside the legstump. When the Chennai Test began, he was well prepared. Tendulkar was by nature a batsman who dominated bowlers. Warne by nature was a crafty, attacking bowler. There could not have been a better duel in Test cricket in those times.

India won the toss and batted first, with three spinners – Kumble, Venkatapathy Raju and Rajesh Chauhan – to exploit a turning wicket in the fourth innings. Opener Sidhu had a makeshift but capable partner in Nayan Mongia. Michael Kasprowicz and Paul Reiffel, the Aussie pace bowlers, held no terror. When the spinners came on, Sidhu took to them and looked good after clouting them for two sixes. The openers put on 100 runs for the first wicket and just when it seemed India would pile on a big score, Mongia was caught behind off Kasprowicz for 58 with the score at 122. At 126, Sidhu was run out – a big setback, given how well Sidhu was dismantling the spinners.

Out came Tendulkar, and the noise as he came out to bat was deafening. He was facing Warne and immediately smashed a four down the ground. The crowd went bonkers. The next ball was flighted and spinning. Tendulkar went after it, aiming another powerful drive into the offside. But the cunning ball was already curling away and it took the edge and flew fast, high and to the right of Mark Taylor at slip. Taylor, one of the best slip fielders ever, stretched to his right and took it with utter nonchalance. Tendulkar: caught Taylor bowled Warne 4.

A deathly silence fell over the stadium, and Tendulkar knew he had thrown away his hand in overeagerness.

From that point, the innings could not take off. The fact that Kumble came at No. 7 meant India had a long tail. He stuck on and helped Dravid take India to 232 for 5 when the day ended. Next day, once Kumble was removed, the Aussies were into the tail and India folded up. Dravid got a 50, but there were no substantial partnerships in the innings and India were all out for 257. Warne had come back strongly to take four wickets, but the surprise was a new young off spinner, Gavin Robertson, who stuck to a good line outside off, made the ball turn in and got four scalps.

On day two, India fought back. Kumble came on early and got rid of Michael Slater. The debutant seamer Harvinder Singh sent back Taylor when the score was just 44. Then at 57, Kumble bowled Steve Waugh. Australia laboured through the rest of the day against Kumble and left-arm spinner Raju. At 95, Raju had Ricky Ponting caught behind, and then off spinner Chauhan got rid of Greg Blewett. Raju claimed Mark Waugh, the stylish bat who had played very well for four hours. At 173, Australia lost Reiffel as Dravid took his second smart catch at slip off Kumble. Warne and Healy saw Australia through to 193 for 7. The pitch had little for the pace bowlers but it had turn and bounce for the spinners. Mongia, who had a faultless match behind the stumps, wore a helmet while keeping to them, and while it is a common sight now, he was among the first stumpers to do so.

Healy took charge on the third morning. He got unexpected support from tail-ender and debutant Robertson. From 201 for 8, they took Australia to 297 before Healy fell for 90. Healy was an important member of that strong Australian team – an outstanding keeper and a valuable lower middle order bat. At Chepauk, he played his customary battling innings, spending over four hours in the middle. Robertson got a maiden fifty and Australia wrested a crucial 71-run lead.

When India batted again, Sidhu and Mongia wiped off 43 runs before part-time bowler Blewett got Mongia. That brought Dravid to the crease and the second-wicket pair took India to 100 for 1, a lead of 29, when stumps were drawn. Sidhu crossed fifty for the second time in the match. Sidhu was successful throughout that series, giving India a start every time and taking on the spinners too, providing an important platform for the other batsmen. Tendulkar in his autobiography acknowledged the role played by Sidhu: 'He had attacked Warne from the start of our second innings and had set the game up for the other batsmen.'

On the fourth day, Sidhu was dismissed early by off spinner Robertson and Tendulkar came out to join Dravid with India 44 runs ahead. The match had now entered a critical phase. Tendulkar settled in nicely, with a tuck to leg for two and a back cut for four when Warne pitched slightly short. After smashing a half-tracker from Warne off the back foot to extra-cover for four, he turned his attention to Robertson. Using the full depth of the crease, he moved back to pull the off spinner for a four and then picked him from outside offstump and hoisted him over mid-wicket for six. He treated the crowd to a sumptuous square-cut off Reiffel. The score had bounded along beyond 200 and Tendulkar had raced to 50.

Now, Warne bowled round the wicket to Tendulkar, as he knew he would. All his pre-match preparation was coming to fruition. Here it is in Tendulkar's words: 'I started out watchfully and was soon into my groove. As expected, Shane Warne started to bowl round the wicket and I instantly took the attack to him and hit him over mid-wicket. From an individual perspective it was a defining moment in the game.' Tendulkar combined his attacking instincts with sound judgement and it made for a thrilling spectacle.

There was no stopping him. He was taking Warne to the cleaners by pulling him off the back foot and clubbing him off the front foot. Then he stepped down and lofted Robertson into the crowd beyond the extra-cover boundary. Dravid stayed with him to add 113 runs before getting out to Warne, his sole victim in India's second innings. Azhar joined Tendulkar, who was peppering the boundary and also hitting sixes into the rapturous stands. Tendulkar reached his hundred off just 123 balls as he turned Kasprowicz to fine-leg for four. With Azhar too on attack, the scoring rate was well over four runs an over. When the latter was out for 64, India had already reached 355, but the pounding continued for Australia. Ganguly came and had his share of the fun too.

When Azhar finally called a halt to the innings, Tendulkar had hit 155 not out off 191 balls with 14 fours and four sixes. The Indians had scored 313 runs that day in 72 overs. *Wisden* in its match report said, 'Tendulkar's belligerence was awesome and his shot-placement enthralling.' Azhar had set Australia a target of 348 runs in 105 overs, so his bowlers could have a go at the batsmen that evening. What a coincidence that it was exactly the same target Border had set the Indians at the same ground in 1986 in the tied Test! Like Border's declaration, this too was a challenging one, but the Australians had been thoroughly demoralized by Tendulkar's assault on their top bowler. They had also spent an entire day chasing leather in very hot and humid conditions, and even a spirited captain like Taylor could not remain unaffected.

The Australians' misery was complete in the final hour of play, as India knocked out three batsmen for just 31 runs on the board. Srinath bowled Slater, who failed in his attempt to counter the pressure with aggression. Kumble dismissed Blewett to a catch by Dravid at silly-point. Paul Reiffel came as nightwatchman but to Australia's dismay, it was their captain Taylor who was dismissed off the last ball of the day by Kumble. A match that had perhaps slightly tilted Australia's way until the third evening had completely swung India's way. Venkataraghavan, the former India captain and one of the umpires for this game, had told Tendulkar the previous evening that it would be difficult for India to force a win from the position they were in. Tendulkar, however, was confident they could do it and turned in a virtuoso performance on day four.

On the fifth day, the Australians resisted for a while as India's spinners pegged away, probing for the mistake that could come any time.

Finally, Kumble broke through after 12 overs, getting Mark Waugh. Australia's score stood at 54 for 4. The nightwatchman Reiffel finally went, caught by Azhar off Raju, after defending stubbornly for 100 minutes. The left-arm spinner then immediately trapped Ponting lbw and Australia were 92 for 6. If there was one country where Ponting was never at his best, it was India. Not just on this tour but on his subsequent visits, too. Six overs after Ponting's departure, Raju claimed Steve Waugh as Dravid took his third catch of the innings. Healy played defiantly in a lost cause. Warne hit 35 but Chauhan dismissed him and Robertson off consecutive balls. The annihilation was completed by mid-afternoon, as Australia were bundled out for 168 in 67.5 overs. Kumble had eight wickets in the match and Raju six. Chauhan had chipped in with three. India had beaten Australia by 179 runs.

On a pitch affording turn, with a clutch of close-in fielders and a large animated crowd, the umpires were under enormous pressure. A couple of decisions that morning were marginal while one was certainly unfortunate. The Chennai crowd was sporting as always. *Wisden* did not forget to mention this, saying the crowd was exuberant but well behaved, adding, 'The conspicuous camaraderie between the locals and a substantial group of visiting Australian supporters was most heart-warming.'

In his essay titled 'Tendulkar outwits Warne', Ian Chappell wrote, 'It's rare enough that in the middle of the fourth day a Test match is evenly poised. To then have one team's champion facing his opposite number with the game hanging by a thread is heaven for a cricket fan.' *Wisden* in a summary of the three-Test series, which India won 2–1, wrote, 'The 446 runs Tendulkar scored in the series, at a strike-rate of 80.65 per hundred balls received and a Bradmanesque average 111.50, were the product of sheer genius.'

Amidst all the admiration for the maestro's genius and his technical preparation, it is illuminating to read what Tendulkar wrote about his meticulous physical preparation to counter the oppressively humid conditions in Chennai: 'Having played a lot of cricket in Chennai, I knew that the physical preparation in the lead-up to a Chennai Test has to be different from normal. You have to prepare your body for the heat and humidity well in advance and I always did so at least 36 hours before the match by drinking a lot more water than normal. The extra water intake was particularly important, because you lose so much fluid during matches at the Chidambaram Stadium.'

The two could not be more different in their personalities, but their genuine friendship is based on immense mutual respect. Tendulkar has always acknowledged the genius of Warne and in his autobiography said, 'A true great, Warne would not let you relax for a single delivery.' Warne on his part has publicly declared without a trace of inhibition that Tendulkar gave him nightmares. Gideon Haigh's wonderfully non-judgemental biography *On Warne* provides us rich insights into the generosity of the Aussie legend whose fan following in India only grew even greater when he led a modest Rajasthan Royals to victory in the IPL.

Test No. 1,405: M.A. Chidambaram Stadium, Chepauk, Chennai, 6–10 March 1998: India 257 in 104.2 overs (N.S. Sidhu 62, Nayan Mongia 58; Gavin Robertson 4-72, Shane Warne 4-85) and 418/4 dec in 107 overs (Sachin Tendulkar 155*, Mohammad Azharuddin 64, Sidhu 64) beat **Australia** 328 in 130.3 overs (Ian Healy 90, Mark Waugh 66; Anil Kumble 4-103, Venkatapathy Raju 3-54) and 168 in 67.5 overs (Warne 35, Healy 32*; Kumble 4-46, Raju 3-31) by 179 runs. **MotM:** Sachin Tendulkar.

Captains: Mohammad Azharuddin (India) and Mark Taylor (Australia)

17

A Hero's Heartbreak

India vs Pakistan, first Test, Chepauk, Chennai, 1999

The tension between India and Pakistan is omnipresent, and cricket, despite all the platitudes, only seems to expose the edginess; who can deny that any World Cup match between India and Pakistan is no mere sporting contest but invested with illogically huge emotions by the public in both countries? The strain on the few Indian cricketers we spoke to who played in the 1980s, especially in those crass one-day tournaments in Sharjah, cannot be described. One pitied them. In such circumstances, many have questioned whether sporting ties have any significant role to play in building relations. And yet, governments periodically on both sides at various times in the last 40 years have tried to get the bilateral cricket series going from time to time.

And so, after nine long years, India and Pakistan were once again playing a Test series in 1999. This tour, a two-Test series, was one more attempt to build relations through sport and had materialized after Prime Minister Atal Behari Vajpayee went to Pakistan in 1998 in an act of statesmanship. The series had stirred up tension and drama even before the Pakistan team arrived. Shiv Sena protesters, enraged that bilateral cricketing ties with Pakistan were being revived, vandalized Delhi's Feroz Shah Kotla, the venue for the second Test.

In this heightened atmosphere, security at Chepauk for the first Test was unprecedented. More than 3,000 policemen were deployed at the ground. The Cricinfo correspondent's report began thus: 'On reaching Gate No. 13 of the "G" stand by 0730 hrs, I found to my horror that the Tamil Nadu police, for some esoteric reason were not allowing black bags inside. I had to make a frantic search to jettison my Cricinfo bag somewhere...'

This was a battle between two formidable teams. Wasim Akram's Pakistan and Azharuddin's India were well matched. Akram and Waqar Younis formed one of the world's best fast bowling combinations, while Saqlain was a top-class off spinner whose doosra was causing great consternation among batsmen all over the world. Pakistan's batting, which had the great Inzamam-ul-Haq, Saleem Malik and Saeed Anwar, was good but not in the same league as its bowling. India on paper was the stronger batting side: Tendulkar was at his peak, Azharuddin on his day could be brilliant, and Dravid and Ganguly had established themselves as excellent batsmen. The bowling comprising Srinath, Prasad, Kumble and Joshi was capable but did not have the lethal edge that the Pakistani combination had. The series would be showcased as a battle between Pakistani bowling and Indian batting.

At Chepauk, Pakistan won the toss and batted first. Srinath opened the bowling with an attacking field and was accurate and hostile, though Prasad was taken for a few boundaries. Anwar was dropped by Azharuddin – one can count such instances on the digits of one hand– but Srinath got his reward soon after, first getting Afridi caught low at first slip by Ganguly and then trapping Anwar leg before, offering no shot to one that came in. This early breach was enough for Kumble to set about the Pakistani batting. He first caught and bowled Inzamam off a full toss that dipped on him and then nailed Ijaz Ahmed leg before right in front of the stumps. Pakistan were stumbling at 66 for 4. India continued to make breakthroughs after lunch. Srinath – with an outstanding spell of sustained line and length – beat Saleem Malik's prod and bowled him. That brought the wicketkeeper Moin

Khan to the wicket. Wicketkeeper-batsmen who come in at five or six down are always mettlesome. They can irritate, they can turn the match, and they are invariably of a mould – street-smart, canny and combative.

That afternoon, Moin first helped Yousuf Youhana (later after converting to Islam from Christianity, he came to be known as Mohammed Yousuf) put up a 63-run partnership that was broken by Tendulkar. Since the man bowled all sorts of deliveries, one needs to mention it was a legbreak that stayed in line with the stumps and trapped him leg before. Moin then stitched a partnership of 60 with skipper Akram and helped Pakistan to 214, before being dismissed by Kumble who then knocked off the last three wickets. Pakistan were all out for 238 and Kumble had taken 6 for 70, the first among half a dozen excellent feats in the match. There was still time for Akram and Younis to test the new Indian opening pair of Sadagopan Ramesh and V.V.S. Laxman. Ramesh, the elegant left-hander, showed temperament and style on debut, as he clipped 38 runs nonchalantly. Clearly, it was India's day.

By the end of the second day, however, India had lost the advantage. Although the match looked 'arithmetically' even, India had failed to take a sizeable lead, something that was vital, since they would have to bat last. Akram got both openers early and Saqlain, at the peak of his prowess, imposed himself on the middle order to take five wickets. Tendulkar, trying to dominate Saqlain as soon as he came in, lost out, reminiscent of the way he came to grief while attacking Warne the previous year. Qamar Ahmed in *The Hindu* succinctly summarized the day: 'Once Wasim Akram had opened the gate with some superb exhibition of fast bowling the men of experience and substance were foxed out by the uncanny ability and talent of Saqlain Mushtaq, the off spinner.' Shahid Afridi polished off the tail as his fast-skidding wrist spin killed the Indian innings. India, like Pakistan, had a couple of dogged fifties from Dravid and Ganguly, but they lost wickets regularly. Only a 25 not out from Sunil Joshi at the end helped India take a notional 16-run lead. Pakistan wiped that off in the evening but India could feel happy they were rid of Anwar.

However, Afridi was waiting for them. Once Ijaz was out to Kumble very early on the third day, for the next three hours and more, it was all Afridi. It was only the second Test of his career but his one-day exploits had announced the damage that Afridi could inflict. He chose Chennai for an exhibition. Inzamam, his partner in the third-wicket stand, was also in an attacking mood as they added 97. When Inzamam left for 51, Yousuf Youhana also came in a belligerent mood, and hit 26 in quick time. With Afridi plundering fours and sixes at will, India wilted. He was so dominant that he even helped the out-of-form Saleem Malik stay with him and the two stitched a century stand before Joshi got Malik.

It was a hot and unhappy afternoon for the Indians. Pakistan had scored at four runs an over and had already reached 275 for 5. Afridi, well past his century, seemed set for more carnage. Then came one of the most sensational sessions in the match. Bookended between the great feats by Saqlain, Kumble, Afridi and Tendulkar, Prasad bowled a remarkable spell, where he took five wickets for no runs and reduced Pakistan from 275 for 5 to 286 all out. It was this spell that ensured Pakistan did not set India an impossible target but a gettable 271 runs. Next morning, every correspondent criticized Azhar for not bowling Prasad earlier.

We asked Prasad about this spell. Candid as ever, he said: 'At that time I was at my peak. My rhythm was good, my mindset was positive. I bowled with the confidence that I could get a wicket any time and yet I was not getting wickets…at Chepauk too, I was bowling well but not getting returns. And then…in the second innings, Azhar did not bowl me. For three to four hours it was Srinath and Kumble mostly with Joshi and even Tendulkar but not me. Fielding at fine-leg, I could not bear it and I wanted a break. I went back to the pavilion and put my face in my hands. I think my eyes were wet with tears of frustration. Gaekwad, the manager, came over to ask if I was all right and I just waved him away. I gathered myself, saying I can only put in my efforts;

the results are not in my hands. I went back to the ground and Azhar gave me the ball just to give Srinath a change of bowling ends! But now I had the ball in my hand and it took me only two deliveries to realize it was reversing. I mixed conventional and reverse swing on a perfect length, bowling with complete focus. Afridi thought he would attack me and hit me into cow corner. I uprooted his offstump with one that moved from leg to off. My only feeling at that time was to thank God. In no time I wiped out the rest of the batsmen. One of them, at the non-striker's end, thought he was clever by signalling to the batsman which way the ball will reverse by seeing the shiny side in my palm. He did not know that I had already seen him and mid-stride I changed my grip. The batsman thought it would be an inswinger, but the ball swung out and the keeper took the catch. People talk of the "mental aspect" of the game, they talk of tactics, but I have two phrases that I keep telling my wards. One is, "understand the ball". Each ball behaves differently. You are not scientists but if you try, you can quickly realize how it is behaving and then apply your skill. The second phrase is "be aware". At all times be aware of your surroundings, observe keenly. That is how I caught the Pakistani non-striker signalling to his partner and employed the double bluff.' Prasad rued that there was no computer or video analysis during his time. Everything depended on the bowler memorizing what he observed and literally drawing images of field placements in his notebook.

The pitch, drier with every passing day, would definitely help Saqlain but also aid the reverse swing of Wasim and Waqar. In those days, the duo put enormous pressure on even the most experienced openers. That evening at Chennai, Waqar rattled India by getting rid of Ramesh and Laxman in his second and third overs. Tendulkar came out at 6 for 2 with an hour's play left and announced his intentions with three beautiful boundaries. Dravid gave him grim company. India needed 231 to win with eight wickets in hand, and every newspaper said the game was headed for an exciting finish. *The Hindu* simply said, 'A thrilling climax in the offing'.

It was a packed and expectant Sunday house on the fourth day, but by lunch, the crowd had been deflated. Soon after play began, Akram conjured up the kind of beauty only the best can bowl. With his deceptive whippy action, a ball on perfect length, a tad shorter than previous deliveries. It might have come slightly in the air, but upon pitching it moved away to beat Dravid's defensive push to take the off bail. In the knowledgeable 'D' stand, many of the spectators, league cricketers themselves, felt it was the best ball they had seen in a long time. In a recently televised conversation with Akram, Laxman too called it the best ball Akram had bowled. Dravid's dismissal was followed by two poor decisions against the home team that broke India's back. If the lbw against Azhar was dubious – to Azhar's credit he walked away without fuss – the second decision was called 'absurd' by the *Sportstar* correspondent and 'bizarre' by others. Ganguly's edge went to silly-point, hit the ground and bounced a foot in front of keeper Moin who claimed the catch. Steve Dunne, who was never a great umpire, lifted his finger. G. Viswanath wrote, 'His nerves seemed to have cracked on a crucial day of the Test.' India scored only 46 runs and lost three top batsmen by lunch.

Now, Mongia joined forces with Tendulkar. Akram, knowing Saqlain was the key, backed him with attacking fields even as the target came down to less than 160 runs. In his autobiography, Tendulkar wrote, 'I was fully focused on the job at hand and had gone into a zone where I was praying before each ball was bowled. Even when Nayan was on strike I was rehearsing in my mind how I'd have played the balls bowled to him. In effect, I was trying to bat at both ends.' Mongia was a capable batsman who was not afraid to play strokes even while he could defend soundly. The afternoon session was classic. Neither side yielded; India scored only 60 runs off 29 overs but importantly Pakistan could not break through. At tea, India were 148 for 5, needing 123 runs.

Sometime before tea, Tendulkar's back began to hurt and every little movement was excruciatingly painful for the maestro. The batsmen changed gears after tea. Tendulkar attacked Saqlain with a sudden fury, smashing four stunning boundaries in one over. There were pulls, cover-drives and sweeps as he moved into the nineties. Mongia also opened up, swinging Saqlain over mid-wicket for a six. Akram was forced to take the new ball in the 80th over but the runs continued to flow. India were going at more than a run a minute. Tendulkar reached his century to a rapturous reception and the partnership too was well past 100. Then came the first of two match-turning events. With India on 218 for 5, needing only 53 runs for victory, Mongia finally played a bad shot. He had batted so well for his 52 but when he was dismissed caught at mid-off by Waqar, it was to a senseless wild hoick against Akram.

The next man in, Sunil Joshi had won a place in the team after years of toil and hard work. His job here was to stay with Tendulkar while that man went for victory. Together, they added 36 exhilarating runs in six overs, Tendulkar was in full flow, driving, pulling and lofting boundaries, but his back was gone. He did not want a runner; never in his entire career did he want a runner. Akram kept Saqlain going at one end. The off spinner too never flagged; when you get hit by the maestro off perfectly good balls, you just take it on the chin and plug away.

Finally, with India needing just 17 runs, Saqlain broke through. Tendulkar came down the track as Saqlain drifted one into him. It was the doosra that upon pitching turned to off and bounced. Tendulkar's mistimed lofted drive speared up high over mid-off. Wasim Akram, running back and circling, was never going to drop the ball. One of the finest innings in Indian cricket had come to an end. Tendulkar walked off to a standing ovation, lasting many minutes, from an adoring audience.

Almost immediately, it was all over as India collapsed from 254 for 7 to 258 all out. Kumble all at sea, lbw Akram. Sunil Joshi, caught and bowled off a leading edge by Saqlain. After Prasad played a clueless over, Saqlain bowled Srinath. The off spinner had bowled long spells through the day for figures of 32.2-8-93-5. The Pakistanis were celebrating. The crowd was gutted but somehow found within it the generosity to sportingly applaud the victors who ran round the ground in a lap of honour.

Meanwhile, Tendulkar was in tears in the dressing room. He was adjudicated Man of the Match, but this was no consolation and he was emotionally in no condition to come out and receive the award. 'My world seemed to collapse around me and I just couldn't hold back the tears.' What cruel fate is it that a day of one of your finest achievements is also a day of such great sorrow? In one of the finest essays on Tendulkar, Rohit Brijnath wrote, 'When Tendulkar plays, India stills, it quietens, till it is almost possible to hear a collective exhalation with every shot. In a land where governments stutter, the economy stagnates and life itself is an enduring struggle against failure, he is deliverance...' Brijnath referred to the charge that Tendulkar could not help India over the line by saying, 'It suggests that his beauty is often ineffectual, painting masterpieces in isolation, and that he is apt to leave more of a memory than an impact... To indict him for getting out for 136... is to disregard the fact that the rest of the team contributed 86 runs.'

It was only fair that there were happier times and great team successes ahead for Tendulkar, culminating with the World Cup triumph on his home ground in 2011. Many years later, when Tendulkar was on the verge of his 100th international ton, Gideon Haigh wrote, 'He has constructed a career along the lines of one of Europe's great gothic cathedrals, built to last, to serve future generations, full of splendour, grandeur, romance.'

When a team collapses and cannot make 17 runs with three wickets in hand, how can such a match qualify as one of its finest? True, it was a most thrilling contest that was decided only in the final overs of the game. There were centuries on both sides and if one side had a bowler with a haul of ten wickets, the other side had two bowlers who took six wickets in an innings each. Of course it had one of the greatest centuries ever in a losing cause. But what put this match's greatness beyond debate was the fantastic and generous response of the spectators that showed how sports and sportsmen should be treated. The spectators found within themselves a great magnanimity when they would have been heart-broken by the loss to an arch-rival. Ramachandra Guha in *A Corner of a Foreign Field* tries to explain that the innate gentility and sportsmanship of the Chennai crowd should not come as a surprise because 'it had no ancient memories of Moghul rule or modern memories of Pakistan'.

This series turned out to be special. After losing this splendid edge-of-the-seat thriller at Chennai, India bounced back to beat Pakistan at Kotla. Kumble earned an exalted position in cricket's hall of fame by capturing all ten wickets in Pakistan's second innings, becoming only the second cricketer to ever perform this feat. As Laxman caught Wasim Akram at short-leg off Kumble, the entire nation rejoiced. It was no little balm to Tendulkar.

Test No. 1442: M.A. Chidambaram Stadium, Chepauk, Chennai, 28–31 January 1999: Pakistan (Toss) 238 in 79.5 overs (Moin Khan 60, Yousuf Youhana 53; Anil Kumble 6-70, Javagal Srinath 3-63) and 286 in 71.2 overs (Shahid Afridi 141, Inzamam-ul-Haq 51; Venkatesh Prasad 6-33, Sachin Tendulkar 2-35) beat **India** 254 in 81.1 overs (Sourav Ganguly 54, Rahul Dravid 53; Saqlain Mushtaq 5-94, Afridi 3-31) and 258 in 95.2 overs (Sachin Tendulkar 136, Nayan Mongia 52; Saqlain 5-93, Wasim Akram 3-80) by 12 runs. **MotM:** Sachin Tendulkar.

Captains: Mohammad Azharuddin (India) and Wasim Akram (Pakistan)

PART 4

2001 to 2010

The Rise to the Top

As the new millennium dawned, Indian cricket was in its depths. The game felt desecrated. Those who knew we loved the sport mocked us for our passion for something that was so obviously corrupt. Newspapers and magazines kept putting out sordid details. Nobody was spared. Manoj Prabhakar accused Kapil of match-fixing, and the legendary cricketer wept on live television, hurt beyond endurance by the unsubstantiated abuse. In South Africa, Cronje hung his head in shame after being found guilty of accepting money from Indian bookies. Azharuddin, Ajay Jadeja and Ajay Sharma too were barred from cricket. Everything and everyone looked suspicious. All kinds of unsavoury people seemed to have had easy access to the cricketers. And like Nero, the administration fiddled away. While Warne and Mark Waugh in Australia and Cronje admitted to their indiscretions and guilt, none of the Indian players admitted anything.

The scandal claimed its victims in various ways. The simple trusting fans lost their innocence. The journalist who followed Indian cricket and cricketers with an emotional bond became cynical. The Indian dressing room was destroyed. Even though we never heard a word in public of any player condemning another, those who were privy to the dressing room knew that tainted players had been shunned. Free conversations in the dressing room shrivelled as a watchful eye was always cast on the players under a cloud. Those few years were the most miserable in Indian cricket.

Who could have imagined that Indian cricket's brightest period was about to begin after its darkest hour? Sometimes, wisdom and intuition come together to create destiny. When Tendulkar gave up the captaincy, India's selectors chose Ganguly as the new skipper. Passionate about playing for the country and doing whatever was required to forge a capable and competitive team, Ganguly had the good fortune of having the finest colleagues to help him. Tendulkar, Kumble, Dravid and Laxman were already among the best players in the world, but they now closed ranks with Ganguly and formed a formidable phalanx. Utterly incorruptible, team and country above all, they knew that destiny had given them the unique opportunity to help India go to the top. In these players, India also had the finest ambassadors of the game and the country: thorough professionals who excelled in their sport, took pride in their performance and were men of impeccable behaviour.

The board – heeding Dravid's recommendation – brought John Wright as the coach. Sharda Ugra, who knows this period of cricket intimately and was co-author of John Wright's *Indian Summers*, told us, 'The Ganguly–Wright combination was to produce much magic.' They had one common goal – to make the Indian team successful. John Wright wrote in his memoir, 'One of the keys to our progress was the fact that there were two distinct generations within the team. The older generation led; the younger generation sparked. VVS Laxman was the bridge between the generations…the youngsters loved and respected him.' Wright often speaks admiringly of the integrity and commitment of Dravid, Tendulkar, Kumble, Srinath and Laxman. He wrote, 'There were many times when I marvelled at their qualities and was humbled by their maturity and wisdom.' Ram Guha in a tribute to Sachin when he won the '*Wisden* Cricketer of the year' in 2010 wrote, 'Indian cricket was long marked by personal rivalries and parochial jealousies; if that seems now to be behind us, this is the handiwork of a generation of gifted and selfless cricketers, among them Dravid, Laxman, Ganguly and Anil Kumble, but perhaps Tendulkar most.'

Ganguly provided the visible emotion and vivid expression. He was unabashedly demonstrative (as his famous bare-torso shirt waving display at Lord's showed); he wore his emotions on his sleeve; riled up the opposition; did not care for criticism from opposing teams; and was accountable and answerable only to his band of cricketers. For Ganguly, merit would be the sole criterion for selection. It did not matter where the players came from. He ensured that younger players with spunk became an integral part of his team. He had the uncanny knack of spotting the 'match winner' among these youngsters. Thus the blithe spirit of Sehwag, the in-your-face Yuvraj Singh, the moody but match-winning Harbhajan and the emotional but crafty Zaheer came together in the journey towards glory.

Many years later, at an event for our earlier book, Srinath recounted how, when he came into the Indian team, there was an overpowering culture of deference to seniors. His contribution during those early years of the Ganguly period was to help reduce this distance between the young and the old. Ganguly insisted youngsters could speak their minds freely. The youngsters in turn revered Sachin and the other elders. They addressed Sachin as 'Paaji' (elder brother) and felt blessed to share the dressing room with him, but at the same time they could joke, pull his leg and talk cricket openly and incessantly with the Little Master without awe.

In modern times, the coach has become important. India knows only too well how its fortunes have risen, fallen and risen uncannily with different coaches at the helm. We had the unobtrusive, behind-the-scenes coaches like Wright and Gary Kirsten, when India played at their best, and the technically brilliant but insensitive Greg Chappell, when the players were at their unhappiest. Prasad was wistful as he told us how much players of his time missed a coach like Wright: 'no computers, no mental conditioning, and no professional thinking' (Prasad's catch-all phrase).

In the pre-Wright times, the 1990s, the Indian team suffered from a fear of failure; some fielders would not attempt a catch because if dropped, that would count against them. Bowlers were under greater pressure than batsmen. All this changed when Wright took over. Ganguly as captain combined well with Wright and both had a clear vision and road map. A week after we spoke to Prasad, we met R. Mohan who added, 'Ganguly along with Wright was the most effective combination. See the results. Ganguly was truly the most open, backing whoever he thought was talented. Of course he was opinionated and not particularly democratic but he was also least parochial – even better than Pataudi in this respect.'

After Wright, the Chappell era was a problem. Ugra says that intellectually, he and Dravid might have been on the same plane but the team missed out. 'Kumble's time was again a fine period. He was hugely respected and liked by the players for his fairness; he treated everyone the same and his expectations were stated clearly and simply. It instilled faith in everyone.' Ugra thought that if Kumble had been made captain earlier, perhaps he could have managed Chappell better and kept him out of his players' hair.

Getting Kirsten after the fiasco with Chappell was a great stroke. Kirsten was different from Wright, gentler with the senior players and giving them space and responsibility. With Dhoni, he formed a good combination. Kirsten brought with him his friend and mental conditioning expert Paddy Upton. Mohan praised the Kirsten–Paddy Upton duo for caring about the personal life of the players and ensuring they achieved a balance between work and life. The South African cricket philosophy was that wives should accompany players to ensure a stable married life as cricket schedules could kill a marriage. Mohan added, 'A lot of analysis with computer guys like Ramki helped coach and captain plan strategy, bowling lengths and so on. One of the key things Kirsten visualized in the fitness strategy was that fast bowlers should be able to bowl a fourth spell at 4.30 p.m. as quickly as the first spell at 10 a.m.' Team spirit and team ethic did not mean agreement at all times; it meant every thought, argument and action would be absorbed in the interest of the team. Whatever the issues, they remained within the dressing room. Win, lose or draw, the Indian team earned enormous respect from everyone. It never became an unbeatable team like Australia but it became a team that other countries feared.

One of the reasons India did so well in this period was Virender Sehwag. The fabulous middle order was helped immeasurably by the wonderful starts Sehwag gave India. How many other openers have over 8,500 runs and an average of around 50? A handful. However, no other opener has over 8,500 runs in Tests, an average of 50 and a mind-boggling strike rate of over 80. Before Sehwag came on the scene, opposing captains could set India targets of around 350 with 120 overs to try to force a win. After Sehwag, no captain dared give India an asking rate of less than four runs an over.

It can be unequivocally argued that there has never been an opener like Sehwag. The closest to him in modern times is David Warner, and the only other may have been Victor Trumper, who played a hundred years ago. Sehwag represented the confident, street-smart, modern Indian cricketer; those who came from the small towns of India had a 'can do' spirit emblazoned on their shirts: Zaheer from Shrirampur in rural Maharashtra, Harbhajan from Jalandhar in Punjab and Dhoni from Ranchi. They blended seamlessly with the erudite and urbane Dravid and Kumble, and the gentle Laxman. The captaincy changed hands during this decade but each succeeding leader carried forward the good work. The stewardship of the team was always with men worthy of that responsibility and who fulfilled that with grace and decorum.

Dileep Premachandran, editor-in-chief of *Wisden India*, talked us through the four different captains during this phase: 'Ganguly was sheer will and force of personality rather than any tactical genius. He was an extrovert, provocative on purpose. Dravid was perhaps tactically the best among them all and a fine strategist. But he carried the burden of the Chappell association – guilt by association – and he led a side that had become a bit complacent towards the end of Ganguly's tenure. Kumble, just for the way he led India in Australia, was marvellous. No one crossed Kumble; he commanded respect and was a strong personality. He played the stop-gap but was the essential bridge between Ganguly and Dhoni. Dhoni should be viewed in two phases: 2008–10 and post 2011. In the first phase he had the resources, a solid team at its peak, and he was very good. Post 2011, the Fab Four, Zaheer, Harbhajan and Sehwag were on the wane, so, his resources had dwindled. He was undemonstrative and even when he was winding up the opposition he was so subtle, they would not even know.'

India also had its most successful opening pair during this period. Gautam Gambhir and Virender Sehwag shared 87 partnerships and scored 4,412 runs between them with 11 three-figure stands. Gambhir was gritty. Quick to temper, he could even recklessly get physical with a Shane Watson, someone 30 kg heavier than him! Left-handed and right-handed, grouchy and blithe-spirited, together they provided India solidity and momentum at the top. If the Indian teams in earlier eras performed below their potential, do not be too harsh on them. The middle order of those days never had an assured opening pair like Gambhir and Sehwag, and would invariably be exposed to the new ball very early. Gavaskar alone was magnificent; however, opening is not a solo task but a partnership.

India's bowling remained relatively weaker. One might find this observation questionable as Kumble, Zaheer and Harbhajan were at their prime. These three were the principal match-winning bowlers and captured over 1,300 wickets between them, around 40 per cent more than the spin quartet. But we use 'relatively weaker' only in comparison to the 'once in a lifetime' batting line-up, which was, quite simply, the best in the world. Other leading countries had sharper bowling attacks – Glenn McGrath, Brett Lee, Jason Gillespie and Shane Warne for Australia; Allan Donald, Shaun Pollock, Morne Morkel, Makhaya Ntini and Dale Steyn for South Africa; James Anderson, Andrew Flintoff, Matthew Hoggard, Stuart Broad and Graeme Swann for England. For India, Zaheer Khan had Ajit Agarkar, Ashish Nehra, Ishant Sharma, Sreesanth at various times as his pace bowling colleagues.

India also played a sole spinner abroad on most occasions, either Kumble or Harbhajan. Only at home would both spinners play. During this entire period, India mostly played four bowlers, with Tendulkar and Ganguly as part-time change bowlers. But what had changed was that unlike the spin quartet of the 1970s or any of the bowling attacks in earlier years, for the first time, Indian bowlers had the benefit of a bank of runs to bowl with. Even when the opposition scored 500, India's batsmen outscored them to set up opportunities for the bowlers. With the advantage of a good score behind them, the mindset of bowlers changed – they had the freedom to employ attacking fields and were not afraid to try out variations.

In India, batting has always been the star and bowling just the bridesmaid. Pace bowling was even lower on the totem pole. Even when Kapil was leading the bowling, he could not build a bowling community. It was Srinath who began the change. He spoke to Ganguly and Tendulkar on behalf of the bowling unit, ensuring a self-respecting space for the bowlers, and he passed on his wisdom and experience to the newcomers. Srinath and Ganguly might have their arguments but even when Srinath was all but retired from cricket, Ganguly could still pick up the phone and tell him, 'Sri, your tickets to South Africa for the 2003 World Cup are ready, just come to Sri Lanka and get some practice.' John Wright, in his memoir, wrote Srinath was 'the heart and soul of the team, a leader who looked after the young fast bowlers and cheered us up'. Zaheer continued this wonderful and generous tradition. Indian cricket is all the better for this. This period owes a special debt to Srinath and Zaheer.

Anand Vasu, Premachandran's colleague at *Wisden India*, made this perceptive analysis: '2002 Leeds was a turning point. On a seamers' wicket, where we usually collapse in the first innings, we chose to bat first, put up a good start and the heavyweights scored hundreds. Then we used the seaming English conditions to take 20 wickets. Subsequently, we won matches overseas on the back of seam bowling – Zaheer supported by Ashish Nehra, Irfan Pathan, R.P. Singh, S. Sreesanth or Ajit Agarkar. The opposition was now scared to prepare a fast or seaming track because India were able to exploit conditions as well as them and also had superior batting strength. Our batting superiority was not just the fab four but the explosive Sehwag and in New Zealand, his partner Gambhir as well.'

How good was this team? If one had attempted to create an all-time India XI in 1995 and then repeated the exercise in 2010, one would have replaced at least half a dozen of the old stalwarts with the cricketers who played between 2001 and 2010. Sehwag, Dravid, Tendulkar, Kumble, Dhoni and Laxman would inevitably force their way in. This batch of cricketers ticks every box better than any of the previous eras. They won in every country, and around four of every ten matches they played abroad.

As Wright said, 'They became a true team.'

One of the telling features of this team was their resilience. They took pride in their performance and hurt when they lost. In earlier years, the Indian team would either capitulate or even miss a winning opportunity. Not this team; in fact, they were at their most dangerous when against the wall. None exemplified this spirit better than Laxman. Every game that India won from a most difficult position would invariably find Laxman playing a heroic role in them. Who says nice men do not finish first? Peter Roebuck explained this combination of silk and steel thus: 'Laxman is a warrior by instinct and a man of peace by manner... His genius is peculiar and requires the most particular conditions. His greatness lies in the fact that those conditions are the toughest, not the easiest.'

One holiday afternoon – it was Gandhi Jayanti – Mohinder Amarnath, in that calm gentle tone of his, told us, 'Sehwag and Laxman have not been given due credit for their role. They added the crucial difference to the team. For example, you look at our victories and in 80 per cent of them you will find Laxman. He will outshine any other player in our wins. And of course, Sehwag. These two are somewhat like Sangakkara, who is easily among the best ever but is in the shadows of other great names. In our bowling, Zaheer was both hard-working and clever. He had the advantage of being a left-armer and he was a fine thinker. And there is a tradition of senior players helping the younger players, Zaheer did that perfectly.'

This fine team's record could have been better but for a few blemishes. They needlessly lost a match at Sabina Park against Lara's men and the series in West Indies in 2002. They squandered the lead they had taken in Adelaide by losing in Melbourne in 2003–04. In South Africa, after the win at the Wanderers in 2006, they lost the next two Tests. Wright says that after the win against Pakistan in 2004, complacency crept in among the younger members. These were the aberrations in an otherwise fine period.

We asked Premachandran to dissect the 10 years for us: 'For the last 12 to 15 months of the Wright–Ganguly period, there was a bit of unhappiness behind the scenes [after] Laxman [was] dropped from the 2003 World Cup and Kumble [had] to sit out matches and some insecurity [started creeping] in Ganguly as his form started dipping. Chappell was at a different level as a thinker of the game, but he had less than half the people skills [of Wright] and trusted and spoke to the wrong people. In the Kirsten–Dhoni period, the happiness quotient in the team was highest. The seniors had a last purple patch, and we had a settled opening pair in Gambhir and Sehwag. Paddy Upton had a big role in helping the team [remain] positive and focused. Both Kirsten and Wright were happy to be in the background, not seeking limelight or credit. When the team did well, they let the players take the credit but if the team struggled they came forward to defend them – even if they might have given the players a bollocking in private.'

It was a remarkable ascent to the top that began with Kolkata 2001, one of the greatest wins in cricket history. Towards the end of 2008, India was close to being anointed the No. 1 Test team in the world, which they achieved by December 2009. During this period (March 2001 to January 2011), the team won 46 matches, and we picked 11 of them to complete our list. Unlike in the earlier sections, here we do not feature any draws or defeats. Most are shoo-in selections.

Playing at your best abroad is the hallmark of a good team. Among these 11 matches, eight were won abroad, spanning virtually every major cricketing venue. What could possibly be a more compelling way to conclude this essay?

18

The Greatest Game Ever

India vs Australia, second Test, Eden Gardens, Kolkata, 2001

'On the second night…I sat in room 214 of the Taj Bengal with what I felt like my only friends: four cans of Heineken and five cigarettes. Australia had made 445, despite a Harbhajan hat-trick, the first by an Indian in a Test and we were 128 for 8…this was one of the loneliest, most desolate nights of my life.' – Indian Summers, *John Wright*

In 2001, Steve Waugh and his team had the swagger of an all-conquering army. Australia had won 15 Tests on a reel, and the only country where they had not won a series since 1969 was India. Waugh called the Indian tour the 'last frontier'. On the other hand, India was on the floor, still recovering from the match-fixing shake-up. In 14 Tests in two years, they had lost seven; they won only against Zimbabwe and New Zealand at home and against Bangladesh at Dhaka. Tendulkar had resigned from the captaincy in 2000, after a loss to South Africa, and some suggested it was a protest against bringing the 'tainted' Azharuddin and Mongia back into the side. Now they had a new captain in Ganguly, just three Tests into the job, untried and untested. A new coach, imported from New Zealand, was being resented by former Indian coaches Kapil and Anshuman Gaekwad. The Australians were enjoying this chaos. Their talk was a deliberate mix of claims, potshots and jibes, all part of their strategy that Waugh famously called 'mental disintegration'. Like always, the Aussies' focus was on the rival captain: throw him off balance and the rest of the side will be cooked. They did not know what they were getting into. To be honest, not many knew Ganguly, and the steel he was made of.

Before the series, the Indians were put through the wringer by John Wright at a well-planned camp. It was only for fit men, from 7 a.m. to 7 p.m. on the ground, and team meetings and strategy at night. India had already lost Kumble for the series, his arm in a sling after a shoulder surgery. Wright felt his absence 'was the main reason why Australia would go in as favourites'. With Kumble unavailable, a number of spinners were at the camp as Ganguly and Wright tried to spot the key to their woes.

At the camp, Ganguly insisted Wright see a young, lanky Sikh bowl. Harbhajan Singh was said to be temperamental, his action had been called suspect, and he had taken only 21 wickets in eight Tests before he lost his place two years ago. But Ganguly wanted Wright to take a second look. Now, what Wright saw was a competitive man, getting lots of spin and terrific bounce. Captain and coach made their punt for the series: Harbhajan was selected, and Wright and Kumble, the teachers, worked with him. They drew a box, 20 cm wide and 60 cm long on good length outside offstump, and when Harbhajan bowled there, he would hit the top of offstump every time. Wright's plan was to bat straight against the Aussies, bowl outside off, set restricting fields and try and catch everything. Only if all these four things happened would India be able to compete.

Yet, when the series began in Mumbai, it seemed most of the things planned at the camp could not be executed. Waugh won the toss and put India in. McGrath and Warne skittled India out for 176 and apart from Tendulkar's 76, they had little to show. When Australia batted, Harbhajan and debutant left-arm spinner Rahul Sanghvi reduced

Australia to 99 for 5 but the formidable duo of Adam Gilchrist and Matthew Hayden took the game away in a whirlwind partnership of nearly 200 runs in just 32 overs. Both hit tons, Gilchrist hitting four sixes in a punishing 122 made from just 112 balls. The wind taken out of their sails, India folded up for just 219 runs in their second knock, giving away wickets to the part-time off spin of Mark Waugh. The only substantial knock was again by Tendulkar. Australia won by 10 wickets. Ganguly failed in both innings and the Australians, including the gentler Gilchrist, were taunting him. The ugly side of Aussie cricket too was on display when Slater ranted and argued with umpire Venkataraghavan and batsman Dravid when he had evidently not taken a clean catch. He was not even slapped on the wrist. Anyone else would have copped a suspension for such behaviour. Slater is now a commentator; and the irony is that he will perhaps tell listeners about the virtues of playing the game well.

It was now over to Kolkata. Australia, who had won 16 Tests in a row, were up 1–0, and their confidence levels were never higher. India, meanwhile, had lost Srinath to injury, so they would now play without their two main bowlers. Three changes were made – Zaheer, Raju and Prasad for Agarkar, Sanghvi and the injured Srinath. Australia replaced Damien Fleming with Kasprowicz.

At Eden Gardens, Ganguly showed he had his own methods of getting under the opposition's skin – he simply made Steve Waugh wait for the toss. Once Waugh called correctly, the Aussies were given a great start by Hayden and Slater who put on 103 before Zaheer had Slater caught behind. Justin Langer joined Hayden; after the two had put on 90, Hayden was just three short of his second century in the series when he lost his wicket to Harbhajan, the beginning to what would be the young off spinner's finest day.

After Zaheer dismissed Langer for 58, Mark Waugh left, caught behind off Harbhajan, for 22 with the score at 236. Now it was time for high drama at Eden Gardens. When the score moved to 252, Ponting left for just 6, out lbw. The next ball, Eden Gardens erupted as the dangerous Gilchrist went, lbw, trapped on the crease by Harbhajan. Perhaps the ball pitched outside leg but Bansal raised his fast-as-a-trigger forefinger. The very next ball, Warne received a full delivery that he dug to short-leg, where Ramesh came up with a reflex catch. Ramesh recalls the incessant buzz around the ground after Harbhajan had taken two off two as though it were yesterday. The crowd was on its feet while he was crouched at short-leg, anticipating the inside-edge to him. That anticipation was the reason he could swiftly go low to his right and take the catch neatly off the next ball. Eden Gardens went up in a crescendo that shook the stands. Bansal asked for TV replays to convince himself that the catch was clean. Harbhajan had taken India's first-ever hat-trick in Tests and with a five-wicket haul, he had pulled India right back into the game. Australia were now 252 for 7, Kasprowicz fell to Ganguly before stumps and Australia ended the day at 291 for 8.

But Steve Waugh, the warrior, was still at the crease. He made it count on day two, as India were totally frustrated. Gillespie and Waugh put on 133 runs for the ninth wicket before Gillespie fell for 46. Australia were now past 400. McGrath, last man in, provided unexpected support to Waugh and helped him reach his century. The innings was finally done at 445 when Waugh was out for 122. Anand Vasu, doffing his hat to Waugh, wrote, 'When his troops fail him, Waugh steps up to the war front himself.'

The Indians had bowled 131.5 overs and were leg weary after more than four sessions in humid conditions. When they came out to bat, they demonstrated the meaning of the cliché 'a batting procession'. Ramesh fell to Jason Gillespie before India had scored, and soon it became 34 for 2 as S.S. Das was caught behind off a ball from McGrath. McGrath then went on to trap Tendulkar at the score of 48. No recovery was possible because between the score of 88 and 113, India lost five more wickets. Dravid battled to 25 in almost two hours of self-denial. Ganguly hit

23. India ended the day at 128 for 8, with Laxman batting on 26 and Raju for company. Vasu wrote with rare harshness, 'Collapses happen in Test cricket. But when a team limps off the ground like an errant pet dog whipped by its master, tail between its legs, there is no grandeur in the defeat... An emotionally drained crowd poured out of the Eden Gardens with the words "let down" on their minds.'

That night, Wright contemplated an early and inglorious exit as coach. The players must have been equally miserable. Prasad told us that some of them got together to reignite their own self-belief. Harsha Bhogle had been invited to talk to the players before the series began. He told them that, though young, they carried the huge responsibility of making their countrymen happy. One sentence from his talk now stuck in the players' minds – many of our countrymen lived desperately hard lives and went to bed happy if India played well.

On the morning of day three, Prasad promised Laxman he would defend his wicket like a precious pearl. He did so for 47 minutes before Laxman was out for 59, adjudged caught by umpire Willey when the ball had gone off his forearm. His knock had 12 boundaries, the best strokes of the innings, and full of positive intent and self-confidence. When Laxman came back – India, behind by 274 runs, had been asked to follow-on – he was told to keep his pads on and bat at three. Wright recalls, 'Laxman just beamed.' Both Ganguly and Wright wanted an attacking strokeplayer to bat one-drop. They saw Laxman as the man for that role and asked Dravid to move down the order.

India began their second innings better and the openers put on 52 before Ramesh was out for 30 to a clever piece of bowling by Warne. Laxman came one-drop, and immediately hit McGrath for a four. Sometimes one might like to reflect on the import of a particular shot to a game, a series or even an entire career. Perhaps that off-drive was the moment the golden period for Indian cricket began.

Right then, however, a match had to be saved. At 97, Das was out for 39 as he trod on his wicket, going too far back to play Gillespie to leg. Tendulkar came and went, caught Gilchrist, bowled Gillespie for 10, India 115 for 3. All of India groaned in frustration and Anand Vasu reported that 'his dismissal caused a good many dejected fans to troop out of the stadium'.

Ganguly walked in to a searching examination by McGrath and sledging from everyone fielding close. He batted sensibly, took the singles and let Laxman stamp his authority. The two added over 100 runs, before Ganguly perished late that evening for 48. After exchanging hot words with McGrath, he was caught behind. India were 215 for 4. The shadows were lengthening as Dravid walked in. After his first year in Test cricket in 1996, when he went in at No. 6 or 7, Dravid had never batted this low. He had made the one-down position his own. Today, he had been asked to go at six, not only because Ganguly and Wright believed Laxman was better suited but also because of a feeling that he struggled against Australia. Dravid, if he was seething inside, would not let even his closest friends know. Playing for India and doing what was best for the team was all that mattered to him.

Laxman, meanwhile, made the day his own. Pace and spin came alike to him. There were no half-measures. If served a boundary ball, Laxman did not hesitate, he sent it to the fence. Wright observed that Laxman had found the way to harness talent and self-belief. He played at No. 3 the way Ian Chappell always believed one ought to play. Anand Vasu called it a thoroughly polished innings, which in retrospect seems restrained praise, but he wrote his copy with India still trailing by 20 runs and only six wickets in hand. Vasu analysing Laxman's century, wrote, 'Getting so comfortable against Shane Warne, Laxman would dance down the wicket at will and play smart on-drives. Using his wrists, the Hyderabadi stylist would send the ball anywhere between mid-on and square-leg.' There were pulls, flicks, on-drives and cover-drives of supreme grace. Here was a batsman toying with the Australians. Vasu concluded his dispatch with these sobering words: 'Even at 109 not out (246 balls, 19 fours) Laxman's work has just begun.'

Day four was, without exaggeration, an epochal day in Indian cricket: 335 runs were scored at around four runs an over, without a single wicket falling. By the end of day, Laxman and Dravid had an unbroken partnership of 357 runs, and had broken many records. Confidently and with increasing tempo, Laxman and Dravid, session by session, took the game away, first securing it and then magically preparing a challenging fourth-innings target for Australia. Umpire Peter Willey recalled, 'I don't think I had an appeal at my end the whole of day four... Easily they were two of the best innings you will ever see in cricket, in the context of the game. As much as Laxman's double century was great, I reckon Dravid's 180 was equally great.' If Eden Gardens was despondent the previous day, they were deliriously happy that day. Sample the youth and vibrancy of Anand Vasu's reporting as he says, 'Today was one of those days when every pressman in the Eden Gardens felt like abandoning his seat and rushing out to join the chanting, hooting, yelling crowds.'

~

India reached lunch at 376 for 4, with Dravid completing his fifty while Laxman had raced to 170. In the 29 overs between lunch and tea, they added 115 runs. India now had a lead of 217. Laxman had motored past 225 while Dravid had completed a marvellous ton. Dravid celebrated the milestone with vehemence – perhaps the only time in his career – pointing his bat at the commentary box. That evening he explained the gesture saying, 'This is a team that is fighting against the best team in the world and we have been quite distressed at some of the scathing criticism in recent times.'

The final session saw the Aussies on a leather hunt. India finished at 581 for 4, Laxman not out 275 and Dravid unbeaten on 155. The lead was 307. At the end of that day, one recalls receiving at least four to five phone calls from friends and colleagues who had seen an unbelievable day's play at Eden Gardens. One of them spoke in a voice literally quivering with uncontained joy and wonderment. Neither Dravid nor Laxman played a false stroke the entire day. It was no exaggeration. We knew with every passing hour that we were watching one of the finest partnerships of all time. From then on, for the rest of his career, whenever Laxman batted, we both always watched him with a great sense of anticipation. All we can say is, after Viswanath, he was the Indian batsman who moved us the most.

Wright recalled that Laxman returned smiling and 'fresh as a daisy' after every session while Dravid would need heaps of iced handkerchiefs to keep his dehydration under control. Laxman's 281 is rated fifth among the 100 greatest Test innings by *Wisden* and as the greatest performance in the last 50 years by a distinguished panel for *Cricket Monthly*. Wright said, 'He produced batsmanship that was beyond the imagination, let alone the capability of most players. Quite simply the greatest innings I've ever seen.' What is amazing is that Laxman almost did not play this game because of a back problem. Wright with wry humour writes that Laxman's back and shoulders were out of alignment (called listing) and he would be straightened at every break by physio Andrew Leipus and sent out to bat. Andrew Leipus in admiration said, 'Through it all his smile never disappeared... It was just a surreal experience to be there and watch him first-hand, just go, go, go to overcome the pain, the heat, the exhaustion, the dehydration, the cramping, the opposition, the pressure.' Zaheer Khan, his roommate, said that at night Laxman slept on the floor because of his backache. That this gentle smiling hero batted from the evening of the second day to the morning of the fifth day with such physical conditions makes this effort even more remarkable. Laxman's treatment of Warne was special. Warne saluted Laxman, saying, 'We gave them everything. I was bowling in the footmarks and Laxman was hitting the same ball through cover or whipping it through mid-wicket.'

Rahul Bhattacharya wrote one of the finest tributes to the Dravid–

Laxman partnership in the *Wisden Almanack 2013*, calling them 'Two southern gentlemen': '...Laxman curling the ball through imperceptible gaps, Dravid regaining lost form through pure unblinking will, Laxman now flick-pulling the fast bowlers as if tossing Frisbees, now driving them on the rise, sinuous jabs that raced improbably across the big green outfield, Dravid now blocking, now shouldering arms, now leaning back to cut, the old sureness slowly redeveloping, Laxman inside-outing Warne miraculously from far outside legstump, now whipping him against the turn, Dravid, fully restored, emboldened to come down the track himself and wrist Warne across his break, all of this in the huge sound and growing belief of a hundred thousand in Eden Gardens, an energy that must be experienced to be understood...'

Coming back to day five of the match: the question on everyone's lips was, when would Ganguly declare? If someone had asked this even in jest two days previously, he would have been called insane. Wright and Ganguly had a ticklish issue on hand – they could not give Australia a chance to win, but they could not declare so late that a draw was the only option. Finally, when Ganguly declared with a lead of 385, and with only 75 overs left to bowl, we both felt the declaration had come too late and condemned the game to a draw. However, the best insight into the timing of this declaration came from none other than Wright himself: 'I was strongly of the view that the Aussies didn't like being played out of a game to the point that all they could do was hang on for a draw, so we delayed the declaration until just before lunch.'

Slater and Hayden took Australia to lunch at 24 for no loss off 12 overs. After lunch the two carried Australia to 74 before Slater was consumed by Harbhajan. Langer and Hayden took Australia past 100 by the 28th over, at which point Langer was caught close-in by Ramesh off Harbhajan. A snaky arm ball from Raju trapped Mark Waugh leg before. With the score at 116 for 3, there were 44 overs left. Steve Waugh joined Hayden and for almost an hour they played untroubled cricket, although Ganguly dropped Waugh. Then Harbhajan broke through, as substitute Hemang Badani, an agile fielder, took a sharp catch to his left at leg-slip to dismiss Waugh.

That dismissal burst open the dam gates. In India, and especially in Kolkata, on the fifth day, the pressure on visiting teams can be unbearable. Eden Gardens with over 80,000 excited spectators roaring as their spinners preyed on visiting batsmen has been one of the most gladiatorial sights in world cricket. On that fifth evening, Australia's middle order experienced their most intimidating batting environment, and wilted. From 166 for 3 in the 46th over, Australia collapsed to 174 for 8 by the 51st over. Once Waugh got out, Ponting too went, caught close-in by Shivsundar Das, 166 for 5. He had a poor tour, his pinched expression throughout that series the only memory for Indians until his aggressive behaviour in Sydney in 2008. Some Australians like Benaud, Harvey, Gilchrist, Steve Waugh and Warne are remembered with affection by Indians of a certain generation, some like Ponting unfortunately are not.

At the other end, in an inspired move, Ganguly brought on Tendulkar, and in three consecutive overs after Harbhajan's twin strikes, Tendulkar landed three crushing blows. He claimed the oak-like Hayden first and the dangerous Gilchrist in his next over, both lbw. Then in the 51st over of the innings, Tendulkar disposed of Warne with a googly for zero. His ability to land and turn his legbreak, googly and offbreak sent the crowd into raptures. John Wright wrote: 'The crowd and the Indian players feed off one another...wickets tend to fall in clusters... delirium reigns and the stands literally shake.'

With 25 overs to go, just two wickets remained. The crowd was on edge and could not wait, expecting the next ball to deal the blow. But Kasprowicz and Gillespie defended and with every passing over, the oohs and aahs got more pronounced. Then in the 60th over of the innings, Gillespie succumbed to the combination of Harbhajan and short-leg catcher Das. The 80,000 people collectively held their breath and exhaled with every ball for the next nine overs. The light would fade soon. Then Harbhajan bowled the ball that sealed it – not full, not short, McGrath put his front foot out but offered no stroke. The ball rapped him on the pads, umpire Bansal raised his finger and the stadium erupted. The players raced towards each other to embrace and celebrate. The crowd sent up the biggest roar of the day. 'The greatest win ever' was the headline of a column that Australian Malcolm Conn wrote for *Sportstar*. Vijay Lokapally wrote in *The Hindu*, 'Whipped by critics, and ridiculed by some former players, this band of young performers silenced one and all with a fabulous achievement against the best team in the world.'

This Test was the making of Laxman and Harbhajan, but more importantly, it kick-started a glorious decade for Indian cricket. Till this game, Laxman had played 20 Tests for an average of 27. For the rest of his career, Laxman scored 7,915 runs in 114 matches, at an average of around 50 with 17 centuries and 51 fifties. He proved to be a fabulous match-winner. Harbhajan too had come from nowhere to become India's bowling hero, with a match haul of 13 for 196 that included India's first-ever hat-trick. In Chennai, he won the next Test and the series for India. The incredible 32 wickets in this three-Test series earned him the sobriquet 'Turbanator'. Over the next nine years, in 84 Tests, Harbhajan would take 340 wickets. Still active in the circuit at the time of writing, he is the tenth highest wicket-taker in Test cricket with 417 scalps.

Looking back, one can easily argue this game perhaps had the greatest impact on Indian Test cricket. Not merely because it was one of the greatest fightbacks in history, but because it came at a juncture when Indian cricket was beleaguered, and needed it the most. It gave the billions for whom cricket is a religion hope, belief and conviction. If Indian cricket goes through any vicissitude in the future, it can always go back to Kolkata: Kolkata will always be the wellspring.

'When India wins at Eden Gardens, the spectators light up their newspapers like torches. I hoped they were the editions in which we'd been written off... I'd played 80-odd Tests and seen a lot of cricket, but nothing to compare with that game. It was a privilege to be in the Indian dressing room that evening,' Wright wrote nostalgically, in the chapter aptly titled 'The greatest comeback since Lazarus.'

Test No. 1535: Eden Gardens, Kolkata, 11–15 March 2001: Australia (Toss) 445 in 131.5 overs (Steve Waugh 110, Matthew Hayden 97; Harbhajan Singh 7-123, Zaheer Khan 2-89) and 212 in 68.3 overs (Hayden 67, Michael Slater 43; Harbhajan 6-73, Sachin Tendulkar 3-31) lost to **India** 171 in 58.1 overs (V.V.S. Laxman 59, Rahul Dravid 25; Glenn McGrath 4-18, Michael Kasprowicz 2-39) and 657/7 dec in 178 overs (f/o) (Laxman 281, Dravid 180; McGrath 3-103) by 171 runs. **MotM:** V.V.S. Laxman.

Captains: Sourav Ganguly (India) and Steve Waugh (Australia)

19

The Ascent Begins

India vs England, third Test, Headingley, Leeds, 2002

If we were to choose one Test that was a decisive inflection point in India's ascent to the top, it would be Headingley 2002. On a green top, in conditions tailor-made for the home team's seam bowlers, India batted first, put up a great total and then took 20 wickets using the same conditions better than their opponents. It was not just a win. It was a statement that India could overcome opponents even in the most difficult circumstances. From Headingley onwards, India began to win abroad regularly, almost four out of ten tests in the next eight years. Thirteen years after this Test, Kumble said, 'We were able to prove people wrong. Sourav decided to bat first in Headingley under conditions not helpful for batting. It was a bold move and the players responded to the challenge by beating England. It ignited a spark in us that we could perform away from home.'

The lead up to Headingley was not rosy. On the cricketing front, after its thrilling NatWest Trophy triumph, the team had lost the Lord's Test and was trailing 0-1 in the four-match series as it headed to Headingley for the third Test after drawing at Trent Bridge. Meanwhile, the players were also embroiled in a dispute as ICC World Cup rules prohibited individual advertising contracts and they were vehemently opposing these restrictions. Jagmohan Dalmiya, the BCCI boss, was threatening to send a second-string team to the ICC Champions Trophy if a solution was not found. Wright tried to get the team to focus on the cricket, telling them that a strong performance on the ground would help their cause more than anything else.

Coach and captain made some bold moves that summer. None bolder than their decision to move Sehwag up as opener. In hindsight, it was perhaps the most important decision during the Wright–Ganguly period. Sehwag announced himself with blazing knocks of 84 and 106 at Lord's and Trent Bridge and never looked back, only to become the most attacking opener in Test history. The Indians also decided to play two spinners, a serious shift as India had of late played Harbhajan as first/sole-choice spinner with Kumble as the backup. At Headingley, they dropped left-arm fast bowler Ashish Nehra to accommodate both spinners, and in a tactically sound move to balance the team, they brought in Sanjay Bangar as opener in place of Wasim Jaffer. They also overlooked S.S. Das, who had scored a 250 against Essex in a tour game before the Test. This gave them the flexibility of using Bangar as the backup third seamer in conditions where his sensible swing bowling would be useful.

At Headingley, overcast, leaden skies and a damp, greenish pitch, as if tailor-made for English seamers, greeted them. But the team had, in Kumble's oft-repeated words, decided to 'take the conditions out of the equation'. Wright wrote Dravid 'was sick of us putting teams in on-green wickets and not being able to roll them; he argued that with our spin attack, we'd always have a chance if we could make the other side chase 200 in the fourth innings'. Ganguly, Kumble, Dravid and Wright had made up their minds to play two spinners, bat first even in seam-friendly conditions, put up a score and beat England with spin in the fourth innings. Ganguly's confidence stemmed from having the strongest batting side in the world, as he himself said later. Before the game, the team visited Geoff Boycott's home and while Mrs Boycott

served them a Yorkshire lunch, Boycott gave them sound advice for
the game at Headingley.

Next morning, Botham at the toss interview could not believe
Ganguly had chosen to bat. 'You are batting first?' he asked to make
sure he had heard correctly. 'Yes, we are playing two spinners and
want to bowl last.' 'You need luck' was all that Botham could manage
before going over to interview Nasser Hussain. Within a few overs,
Sehwag was dismissed and Dravid strode out to join Bangar. Matthew
Hoggard was bowling downhill and Andrew Caddick in the channel
outside off with a cordon of close-in catchers to grab the edge when it
came. In such tough conditions, Bangar and Dravid had to be brave,
concentrate fiercely, take blows on fingers, chest and shoulder and ensure
India did not lose another wicket soon. The *Wisden Almanack* recorded
that 'Dravid was immaculate from the start, watching each ball like
a seamstress and ignoring the ones which thudded into his shoulder,
helmet or chest. Bangar was an admirable sidekick.' Anand Vasu wrote,
'It all began, as it so often does in Indian cricket, with Dravid showing
his bat-maker's label to every ball bowled at him and setting up the
kind of platform his freer-stroking colleagues could exploit maximally.
With the obdurate patience of a Trappist monk, Dravid saw off the early
movement on a rain-soaked day at Headingley, defied the gloom that
shrouded Leeds in the guise of a thick blanket of clouds, and showed
his colleagues what was possible with a little application.'

The fifty came up only a few minutes before lunch but the Indians
had negotiated the first session with character. As the two Indian
batsmen prepared to resume battle, Wright sought out Dravid who he
had marked as most crucial to India's first-day effort. 'Trying to plant
a positive thought, I told Dravid at lunch time that a hundred in those
conditions would probably be his best.' Dravid knew better than anyone
else that the post-lunch period would be no easier. Ralph Dellor in his
dispatch on the first day noted, 'Every over was a test of patience and,
even when the sun came out, the ball still swung and the batsmen were
still happy to concentrate on survival.'

The sensible, courageous role of Bangar in this Test has often been overlooked, and his maturity and fortitude understated as he gave durable company to his illustrious partner. His fifty was even slower than Dravid's and he survived a catch to Andrew Flintoff in the slips after crossing the landmark. He added 170 with Dravid and his vigil lasted almost five hours before he was caught off a lifter from Flintoff, bowling from the Kirkstall Lane end. 'A splendid study in concentration,' said Ralph Dellor in praise of Bangar. He had surpassed Ganguly's expectations by miles.

Tendulkar was playing his 99th Test and walked out to huge cheers, and with the comfort that India had already played out the most demanding phase of the match. The scoreboard read a healthy 185 for 2. A few minutes later, Dravid flicked to leg and brought up one of his most satisfying centuries. G. Viswanath's report for *The Hindu* was appropriately titled, 'A priceless effort by Dravid'. Towards the end of the day, as the bowlers flagged, runs were easier to come and Dravid had handsome hits to cover, straight down the ground and the leg side too. In the *Guardian*, David Hopps wrote, 'Even his finest cover-drives, or clinical clips through square-leg, encouraged appreciation rather than excitement.'

This was the kind of innings that defined Dravid – steely of purpose and resolve, fierce concentration and courage and application of the highest skill in the most testing conditions. Dravid told us: 'I was born with a good temperament and concentration came naturally to me as a kid. I had an ingrained value for my wicket. I was my school's best batsman and therefore right from those days you know how important your wicket is for the team. I was born with some talent for the game; it is a God-given gift. And to make the most of it, I practised for long hours to help me focus ball by ball. I am by nature an analytical person and think about my game a lot. But in time, I also recognized not to overdo it and realized one has to trust oneself and one's game. Experience teaches you and it is critical that one is watching and learning all the time. And what is important is also to recognize that there will be some areas which you will never crack and be comfortable.'

The next day, Tendulkar and Dravid unfurled attacking strokes to every part of the ground, rattling along at over four runs an over. All the watchfulness and self-denial of the previous day was now being cashed in with interest. When Dravid finally departed, he had made 148 of the finest runs and India had reached an imposing 335 for 3. Boycott recalled that when the Indian team got on to their bus at the end of the day his wife catching Dravid's eye, called out, 'Well played, Rahul,' to which Dravid replied with a smile, 'It was your lunch that did it, Mrs Boycott.'

The Prince of Kolkata came out to replace Dravid, swinging his bat in his left hand and not merely because Ashley Giles was bowling – left-arm spin was favourite fodder for his bat – but because he now had England on the ropes. Tendulkar was past fifty when Ganguly joined him. David Hopps observed, 'Tendulkar has been charmed by his first Test appearance at Headingley. Yorkshire have named a hospitality box after him in their new East Stand, in celebration of his season here a decade ago as the county's first overseas player, a historic breakthrough that as a Bombay broth of a boy he never entirely recognized. He has what might be a unique effect upon even the most brusque of Yorkshiremen: he makes them sound like old softies... There was a serene, even cheery, air to his innings...'

He made the day memorable for himself and his countrymen as he overtook Bradman with his thirtieth century. Even as Hussain and Giles tried to chain him with left-arm over-the-wicket, Tendulkar responded with his best batting of the summer. The real entertainment came in the last session of the day. As the light deteriorated, Ganguly refused the umpires' offer to stop play and instead decided to rub the advantage in. He reached his hundred and then smashed two consecutive sixes. An elderly gentleman in the stands was struck on the head by one of these hits and was led away bleeding. Luckily, he did not suffer serious damage. The gloom dispelled as Ganguly and Tendulkar hit the third new ball for 96 at nine an over. Their 249-run partnership was India's best-ever fourth-wicket stand against England.

Hopps wrote of the carnage that evening, 'The Prince of Bengal, to his delight, had reduced England's bowlers to servility. His attacking shots, until the final assault, were sometimes as flawed as Tendulkar's were unblemished but he proceeded throughout as if the flagging bowlers were servants in his employ. He did not much care for running, ambling along as if a sedan chair was awaiting him a few yards down the road.' The day ended with Ganguly's dismissal for 128 off just 167 balls and India on a mammoth 584 for 4. India had added 348 runs in 83 overs on day two, including the blitzkrieg against the third new ball. Vasu wrote, 'It was an all-out assault that dismantled every tactic Hussain could conjure up, bruised every carefully cultivated bowler's ego, and thrilled the fans.'

Next morning, Tendulkar could not complete a double-century and Ganguly declared at 628 for 8. Vic Marks, the former English player, in his column for the *Guardian* said, 'This is not a batsman's paradise, but for most of the match the batsmen have prevailed. To be more precise, Indian batsmen have prevailed; their golden middle-order triumvirate of Rahul Dravid, Sachin Tendulkar and Sourav Ganguly all played sublime innings that ultimately humiliated mechanical English bowlers.'

Hussain's openers began well. Robert Key and Michael Vaughan took England to lunch at 61 without loss, but the breakthroughs came after lunch. Key was caught off Zaheer, his mode of dismissal prompting English scribes to write him off from the Ashes tour that winter. Kumble had Vaughan palpably leg before but was denied by umpire Orchard. Vic Marks did not hesitate to lash out at this error, saying, 'How he failed to give Michael Vaughan out lbw to Kumble when England's most fluent batsman was on 52 is beyond me.' A short while later, Orchard raised his finger to send Mark Butcher on his way, upholding an appeal from Kumble, as England became 109 for 2. Skipper Hussain joined Vaughan and was patently uncomfortable, taking knocks on his fingers as Ajit Agarkar, bowling a splendid spell

of eight overs, tested him. Vaughan survived a dropped catch behind
the stumps but off the next ball, Sehwag caught him at cover for the
score to become 130 for 3. The rains came down and interrupted the
afternoon's game. When play resumed, Hussain and John Crawley
tried to fight back but the pressure told, as Zaheer trapped Hussain
leg before for 25. If it was Kumble who troubled England before the
rain break, it was Harbhajan who brought them to a skidding halt
with twin strikes after the interruption. At 164, he got Crawley caught
by Laxman and off his next ball he had the prized wicket of Flintoff,
winning a raucous but marginal lbw from umpire Orchard. At 164 for
6, the follow-on target of 428 looked as far away as the next planet.
Amidst all this, Alec Stewart was fighting hard. He enjoyed a life off
the first ball he faced from Zaheer but after that, seemed least troubled
by either the two spinners or the pace of Zaheer and Agarkar. At 185
for 7, he found a willing partner in the doughty Ashley Giles and the
two stitched a 70-run partnership before Giles fell for 25. A little later
Harbhajan claimed Caddick and England ended the day on a sorry 264
for 9, more than 350 runs adrift. As Vic Marks noted in his dispatch,
'England knew they would be hard-pressed to save this game if the
rain stays away.' On the fourth morning, Kumble quickly knocked over
Hoggard – the two spinners had bowled 51 overs between them for
six wickets and the pacemen Zaheer and Agarkar had chipped in with
four wickets bowling 34 overs between them, in what was a wonderful
team bowling effort.

With England trailing by 355, it was enough for Ganguly to ask
Hussain to bat again. When they came out to bat again, Agarkar was
in full form and got the priceless wicket of Vaughan cheaply. The
Yorkshireman was trapped leg before when England had just 28 on
the board. Vic Marks with kindly humour said, 'Agarkar has had a
half-decent summer but he still celebrates every wicket as if he cannot
quite believe it.' Mark Butcher, more famous for his resolute heroics
in Ashes contests against Australia, now joined Key and attempted
to import that same dogged determination to help England survive.

Key, under pressure, tried to focus on his batting. A few good drives interspersed his defence, but better men than him have been transfixed on the crease by Kumble's quicker ball. India's champion spinner nailed him on the back foot. That brought Hussain to the crease, jaws clenched in determination.

Butcher had fought well for his 42 in two hours of watchful batting when he fell to a lapse in concentration against the gentle swing of Bangar. Suddenly India's fifth bowling option had given them a break when their front-line bowlers had come to a halt. A little later Bangar again provided a breakthrough as he got John Crawley for his second failure of the match, a victim of indifferent bounce as his drive ended up in the hands of a jubilant Sehwag. At 148 for 4, the old firm of Stewart and Hussain set up repair shop. In contrasting style, the two veterans proceeded to battle for the next three hours. Tea came and went. Hussain did not hesitate to play attacking shots, taking the odd risk or two with aerial hits. Stewart, not as fluent or confident as in his first innings, hung on and denied the Indian bowlers for nearly 40 overs as the Englishmen ended the day at 239 for 4. The pair had put on 93 runs in an unbroken partnership; Hussain was just ten runs away from a fine century. Indian spirits were droopy and Marks made the telling observation that 'it was India's captain Sourav Ganguly who was a listless figure by the close. In the early-evening shadows, when Hussain drove one ball past him at mid-on, Ganguly failed to pursue it, allowing Hussain to run four while a none-too-impressed Sachin Tendulkar raced across from mid-off to retrieve the ball'. In the same essay, Marks showered praise on Hussain's fighting qualities: 'He closed the fourth day 10 runs short of what would rank among his finest Test centuries, four hours' unyielding effort that conquered his own exhaustion… It is too early to talk of Michael Atherton, and his epic captain's resistance over 10 hours in the Johannesburg Test seven years ago, but Hussain's aim will be to emulate it.' England had fought hard and kept the Indians at bay in the final session.

Unfortunately, the fight was snuffed out rather quickly on the final day. India required just 25 overs to capture the remaining six wickets. The Madras-born Hussain was not to be denied his century. He and Stewart took England to 265 before Hussain edged Kumble to Sehwag at short-leg. It was ironic that the more secure Hussain lost his wicket even as the struggling Stewart had survived. Within minutes Flintoff collected a pair as Zaheer Khan had him caught in the slips by Dravid, a continuance of his horrendous record at Headingley. This was his fourth straight duck in four appearances at the ground. At the same score, Stewart now fell, this time Kumble getting him caught off a legbreak that took the edge.

Kumble had delivered twin blows with top-class deliveries. He was getting the ball to turn and rear up from a difficult length. With seven gone, there seemed little to play for as Giles and Alex Tudor put up a semblance of resistance, which ended with a misunderstanding between the two of them over a single. The last two wickets – Tudor and Caddick – were shared by Kumble and Harbhajan and the Indians celebrated with abandon as the last English pair walked off disconsolately. They were beaten by an innings and 46 runs in their own backyard, in conditions that were meant to overwhelmingly favour them. Hussain was gracious in defeat, saying, 'We've been thoroughly outplayed from the first morning to this afternoon. All credit to the Indians. They handled the conditions much better than we did.'

What is remarkable is that India won virtually every session in the match. First, when they batted in conditions that favoured the bowlers the Indians demonstrated the virtues of concentration, determination and confidence in their technique. When it was their turn to bowl, they showed a much greater awareness of length and line as well as the benefits of a balanced attack that bowled with unflagging concentration. Every player contributed; the big century makers, the pace bowlers and the spinners and the unsung hero Bangar. What escapes the radar in such flawless wins is the kind of thinking, planning, preparation and execution. Ganguly said: 'It was a big decision to bat first and the way we batted then was important to us. Kumble's a great bowler. Both he and Harbhajan bowled very well together in tandem but it was a very good team effort. We've played well overseas for the past year and we are a good unit. We stick together.'

This was the game where self-belief propelled the Indian team towards glory. They did not choose an easy option; they chose the harder one and they knew that if they succeeded, such a victory would have far-reaching benefits for the team. Wright, noting that it was India's first Test win in England since 1986, called it India's best overseas win ever. No wonder either that Kumble, one of the heroes of this Test, rated the win as one of India's most crucial achievements in cricket.

Test No. 1613: Headingley, Leeds, 22–26 August 2002: India (Toss) 628/8 dec in 180.1 overs (Sachin Tendulkar 193, Rahul Dravid 148, Sourav Ganguly 128; Andrew Caddick 3-150, Alex Tudor 2-146) beat **England** 273 in 89 overs (Alec Stewart 78*, Michael Vaughan 61; Harbhajan Singh 3-40, Anil Kumble 3-93) and 309 in 110.5 overs (f/o) (Nasser Hussain 110, Stewart 47; Kumble 4-66, Sanjay Bangar 2-54) by an innings and 46 runs. **MotM:** Rahul Dravid.

Captains: Sourav Ganguly (India) and Nasser Hussain (England)

20

Only the Second Time in History

India vs Australia, second Test, Adelaide Oval, 2003

A subtle but noticeable shift had begun to be noticed in world cricket since 2001. One of the significant indicators of this shift was that Australia, the leading Test team, now considered its Tests against India as the biggest challenge. India seemed to bring out its best when playing against the Aussies. The last time the two met in India, Ganguly's team had stunned Australia with the epic comeback at Eden Gardens and followed it up with a victory at Chennai to claim the series. Steve Waugh's famous 'final frontier' remained unconquered.

Now, in 2003–04, the Indian tour to Australia was avidly awaited. It was special for another reason: it would be Steve Waugh's final international series, and Australia had invested a lot of time and emotion on this 'farewell tour' for their great captain. John Wright wrote that the Aussies also brought their psychological gamesmanship to the hilt, shooting off disparaging remarks against every Indian player. Of course he knew Ganguly's team could look after themselves.

India did its cause no harm by playing a superb draw in the first Test in Brisbane. Even the best touring teams are daunted and often defeated in the opening match at the Gabba, where the pitch and conditions hit visiting teams even before they are fully settled. Not this Indian team.

They might have played poorly on the opening day but Zaheer bowled a destructive spell on day two to restrict Australia. When India batted, the skipper decided to uncork his best innings ever to stamp India's authority on the tour. The irony behind Ganguly's glorious century was that the Indian skipper had sought out Greg Chappell himself in November 2003 for advice on his batting and then proceeded to play so wonderfully that Chappell in the commentary box was full of praise. When the latter became India coach, everyone knew the fractious relationship they shared. The Brisbane match ended in an honourable draw, the skipper had led from the front and the Indians had not yielded.

For the second Test, the venue moved to the Adelaide Oval, one of the prettiest grounds in the world, with the river Torrens flowing close by and the lovely St Peter's Cathedral looking down. India lost Harbhajan before the game began with an injured finger that required surgery. Kumble replaced him. It was always stressful for Ganguly to choose between Harbhajan and Kumble when India played only one spinner, but the mutual trust between Ganguly and Kumble helped them tide over such difficult situations. Kumble now had his chance. Irfan Pathan made his debut in the Test after Zaheer too was ruled out due to injury.

The coin frowned on Ganguly; Australia decided to bat first and sent the hapless Indians on a leather hunt. The only time they smiled that day was when Pathan took his first Test wicket in the third over, when he got Matthew Hayden. In came Ponting – at the time, there was no one more dominating and authoritative than him in the world at one-down. No one sized up a scoring opportunity faster and made bowlers wilt the way he did. There was a ruthless inevitability about Ponting in his pomp. That morning, he put on a century stand at five an over with Langer, and added a brisk 65 with the stylish Damien Martyn. Steve Waugh made 30 before Nehra got him. At 252 for 4, it did seem a breakthrough of sorts but Australia were already going at five an over and now Simon Katich came to frustrate the Indians. When a stylish player takes a bowler apart, it is bearable, but if an ungainly batsman bats implacably, the levels of frustration are much higher. Invariably these workmanlike batsmen also steal singles. Katich added 138 runs with his partner and was dismissed only towards close. Ponting put up one heck of an exhibition, going at a strike rate of close to 70. He peppered the short-square boundaries at the Adelaide Oval at will and even when Ganguly set a 7–2 offside field he pierced it with utmost ease. When play ended, Ponting was unbeaten on 176 and Australia at 400 for 5, had won all three sessions of day one.

But this Indian team was resilient, and had a stubborn streak in them. Ganguly kept that streak suitably raw and exposed at all times, while Kumble never believed in giving up and in fact toiled harder when the odds were stacked. India hung on and chipped away. It was not like Zaheer's magic in Brisbane; this was harder, more sustained but relentless. At 426, Agarkar made the crucial breakthrough to get Gilchrist. At 473, Kumble dismissed Andy Bichel. Gillespie frustrated India and as Ponting went well past 200, the pair took Australia to 556 for 7. This was when Kumble turned on his magic; in five balls, he polished off the last three wickets. First, Ponting fell for a colossal 242 and then the tail-enders Williams and MacGill were out for blobs. A score of 556 all out was huge but a sight better than what India feared at start of day.

The Indian innings began with fireworks from Sehwag, and in less than an hour India had scored 60. Sehwag galloped to 40 at less than a run a minute. But Andy Bichel bowled a spell that hit India right in the bows, with Aakash Chopra caught and bowled first, then Sehwag fell. The fireworks had been too brief. Within a few balls, the blow that the Indians feared most came: Tendulkar's second straight failure in the series, caught behind attempting a force into the offside. Then, as though to doom India, its captain, never the surest of runners, threw it away with a run-out. From a heady 60 for no loss in 11 overs, India were 85 for 4 before the 21st had ended. Dravid looked forlorn amongst the celebrating Aussies in the middle, but joining him was his old comrade Laxman.

Laxman's stride to the middle was always brisk, often with a knotted kerchief at his neck in the well-known Hyderabadi style. As Laxman and Dravid came together, their aim was to remain unseparated that evening. This first and immediate milestone was achieved, and by end of day, Laxman had crossed 50 and the two had put on close to a hundred; there had been no risks but no slavish defence either. India were still 176 runs away from making Australia bat again but that was something to worry about on the morrow.

Next morning, Wright met the two batsmen before they went out and told them that while Kolkata 2001 was a miracle, Adelaide 2003 would be another. Neither said anything in response as they walked out. They didn't need to, for their bats did the talking. In their long and illustrious careers, Dravid and Laxman had 86 partnerships for 4,065 runs at an average of 51. They had 12 hundred stands, but the two everyone wants to relive over and over would be Kolkata 2001 and Adelaide 2003. While the former lasted nearly five sessions and 376 runs, the latter lasted over three sessions for 303 runs.

The two treated the spectators to a symphony of splendid strokes on the third day. If one played the pull, the cover-drive and the straight-drive, the other would play gorgeous flicks and square-drives. India went to lunch at 252 for 4 with both batsmen in their eighties, and after lunch, Dravid reached his century with a soaring six into the stands at square-leg, a pull that had a hint of top edge. In the 31 overs in the second session, the two batsmen added 136 at over four an over. Laxman took the partnership past 300 off the first ball of the last over before tea, with a magnificent cover-drive that had the commentators in raptures. The very next ball, Laxman was caught behind and that was tea with India at 388 for 5.

The two batsmen returned to the pavilion to a generous ovation, with Dravid unbeaten on 158 and Laxman out for a sublime 148. By day's end, India had progressed to 477 for 7, Dravid tantalizingly at 199 not out. Later that evening, Laxman said, 'We just concentrated on the present, and playing the ball according to its merit. [We] never thought about Eden Gardens. During the lunch break, the teammates kept saying we must repeat the Kolkata performance but in the middle we did not discuss it at all.' Chloe Saltau, writing in the *Age*, put into words the fears of the Australians, '...by summoning the spirits of Eden Gardens and letting them loose at the Adelaide Oval with a 303-run stand for the fifth wicket, Dravid and Laxman brought India eye-to-eye with Australia in a Test series that so many expected would be hopelessly unequal'.

Next morning, Dravid shepherded the tail and helped India add 135 more runs before he was last man out. He had batted a monumental nine hours and fifty-four minutes to make 233 runs off 446 balls. Except for 12 overs in the Indian first innings and 15 overs in the second, Dravid was on the Adelaide Oval for every minute of the Test match, either fielding or batting. Sambit Bal called it 'the finest performance by an Indian batsman in an overseas Test'. Dravid himself ranked this amongst his greatest knocks but even then qualified it by adding, 'Only centuries that help win Tests count.' That is the essence of Dravid.

In over 130 years of Test history, only seven pairs have put two or more triple-century partnerships. Prior to Dravid and Laxman, only Don Bradman and Bill Ponsford and openers Graeme Smith and Herschelle Gibbs had achieved this feat. Since then, Hashim Amla and Jacques Kallis, Jayawardene and Sangakkara, and Ponting and Michael Clarke have joined them. Yet, unlike all these pairs who batted next to each other in the batting order, the uniqueness of Laxman and Dravid was that their triple-century stands came when one of them batted at No. 3 and the other at No. 6, in other words at two ends of the middle order. Both these efforts came after the middle order collapsed and defeat was a real threat.

The study of such partners is fascinating. Observing them at their game to catch the 'X factor' is something only the best of sports writers are blessed with. One of them, Rahul Bhattacharya, in his article 'Two southern gentlemen', wrote: '...Dravid, given to over-intensity, honed relaxation into a fine art. Before matches, he willed himself away from self-torture through video analysis and training sessions, to long lunches, long sleep, and slow living. Waiting to bat, he watched the game only briefly. He was no contest, it is true, for Laxman, who was fond of showering when the man before him went in, and thereafter might be found lying under a table listening to music on headphones... For all that, they could give off very different impressions: Dravid seemed to care a little too much, Laxman not enough. This may be because Dravid perspired heavily and tended to grimace, whereas Laxman looked always a serene stroller in pleasant climes. It may be because Dravid committed himself to sincere footwork, whereas Laxman (against pace) trusted his hands and the curvy abstractions of what he once told me was his "bat flow"... Dravid was the spine and Laxman the nerve.' Ayaz Memon in the *Times of India* wrote what all of India would readily resonate with: 'If Ramesh Sippy were to make *Sholay* today, he would be tempted to name his two leading protagonists Dravid and Laxman instead of Viru and Jai as the epitome of friendship and partnership in fighting a common cause.'

On the fourth morning, a little before lunch, with a small lead of 33, Langer and Hayden came out for the second knock, which seemed prosaic after the heroics of Laxman and Dravid. The game was coiling itself up to serve us a whirling vortex of excitement over the next four sessions. It chose Ajit Agarkar as its hero. On a previous tour to Australia, Agarkar could not score a run to save his life; his scores read like a metropolitan pin code and earned him the moniker of 'Bombay Duck'. His bowling too had never been an epitome of consistency. He had promising pace and good outswing but the net output was invariably disappointing. The number of chances Agarkar received often vexed the ordinary cricket fan, but if one talked to his colleagues, one would be surprised to hear the thought he put into his game.

The fourth day was one of those days: bowling a sustained length and line, Agarkar got the ball to move both ways. He prised open the innings by getting Langer and Ponting before lunch and then polished off the last four wickets to wrap up the innings. Agarkar finished with 6 for 41 off 16.2 overs, and Australia had lasted just 56.2 overs. They were bowled out for under 200 in four hours. Wright had this theory that Australia were always vulnerable in situations where there was little scope for them to dominate, at which times the urge to dominate would get the better of them. He combined with Ganguly to set clever fields that denied them value for their big drives. Some experts offer this chafing at the leash as the reason for the Aussies self-destructing that December afternoon. Sambit Bal called it out as 'a combination of weariness, tight bowling and a fatal urge to dominate the bowlers'.

Briefly in the middle, Waugh and Martyn looked like putting up something substantial, which is when Ganguly called upon Tendulkar to do his bit of magic. Sure enough, the Little Master obliged with perfect, curling legbreaks that spun enough to beat the bat and take the outside edges. Martyn was caught superbly by Dravid for 38 and the score read 109 for 4. Waugh left soon after, caught by Dravid for 42, this one a straightforward catch, amidst much jubilation among the Indian fielders. Then followed some worry, as Gilchrist, capitalizing on a life given by Parthiv Patel behind the stumps, raced to a run-a-ball 40 and Australia motored to 183 for 5. But the worried frowns dissolved as Kumble bowled Gilchrist round his legs with a perfectly pitched googly for 43. Then, in a matter of just six overs and 13 runs, Agarkar finished off the innings with four in a row. One of those dismissals was a miscued hook by Katich that went so high to long-leg that Boycott, on TV, had time to say 'catch it' five times before Nehra took the catch. Australia were dismissed for 196 and India had to get 230 to win. Peter Roebuck made an interesting observation that reflected the spirit in the Indian team: 'Both Kumble and Tendulkar found themselves chasing balls to the boundary. Both senior players dived full length in a desperate attempt to save a single run. No wonder the youngsters responded. With every ounce of strength in its body the Indian team wants to win.'

In the ten overs left that day – a fourth-innings target of 230 can be tricky – India knocked off 37 runs thanks to the belligerent Sehwag, whose value to the Indian team of those years can never be stated enough. India could sleep more calmly that night, with less than 200 to get and all wickets intact.

On the final day, India did have its quota of worries, not alarming but vexing. Chopra got out first but Dravid joined Sehwag who continued to belt boundaries. The score had moved to 79 when Sehwag saw the legspinner MacGill being introduced. Eyes lighting up, he gave him the charge. A swish and miss and Gilchrist whipped the bails off. Wright has a plaintive paragraph about this sacrificial dismissal in his book: 'The trouble with Viru is that he doesn't think spinners can bowl or should be allowed to bowl.' As Sehwag returned after committing hara-kiri, Wright wrote, 'This time I did not wait for Sehwag. I vacated the dressing room and went for a walk around the ground.'

Tendulkar joined Dravid and proceeded to play his first substantive innings of the tour. It was not a big knock, just 37, but it was vital, putting up a partnership of 70 and soothing the nerves in the dressing room. When Ganguly fell with the score at 170, India needed 60. In walked Laxman, and straightaway he began to toy with MacGill, picking him from his stumps and from outside off to whip him to mid-wicket, or playing him inside out to the cover boundary. Dravid, meanwhile, was going on and on. He was now batting in his cap – the helmet had been discarded – as only MacGill and Chinaman bowler Katich were operating. Waugh had thrown in the towel. With just nine to get, Katich removed Laxman for 32 and Parthiv Patel, too. Almost in poetic recognition of his heroic contribution, Agarkar was at the non-striker's end as Dravid latched on to a half-track long hop from MacGill, smote it to cover boundary and let go a fierce yell with all the pent-up emotions of the game. Dravid embraced his comrade at the other end as the Indian dressing room went berserk. Quietly, unnoticed, the Australian skipper went all the way to the cover boundary, retrieved the ball from the gutter, walked back to Dravid and gave it to him as a cherished memento. Waugh thinks the world of Dravid, as does Dravid of Waugh. In sport, the greater the adversaries, the greater their mutual respect and admiration. When Waugh wrote his autobiography he sought out Dravid to write the foreword.

Thus ended one of the grandest comeback victories in cricketing history. After all, how many teams have won after the opposition made over 550 runs in the first innings? Only one. England in 1894–95. Australian newspaper headlines the next day reflected their huge respect for the spirit of the Indian team: one said, 'United they stand', while the other said, 'Courage under fire'. The *Times of India* devoted an entire editorial called 'Shining India' extolling the win.

Peter Roebuck, always supportive of Indian aspirations, wrote, "This was a mighty effort by a team that refused to be beaten, a team whose whole is greater than its parts, a team for a contemporary and confident country... India did not tiptoe into Australia. Ganguly's team came ready for a fight. Australians are adept at sensing and exploiting weakness. Give them the proverbial inch and they will take a yard. Between them, Ganguly and Sandy Gordon, the team psychologist, realised the need to get on to the front foot. Ganguly said the Australians were vulnerable and his team believed him.' Years later, in confirmation of Roebuck's assessment, Ganguly said, 'What is important is what you do before the Tests begin, not what you do after.'

Test No. 1673: Adelaide Oval, 12–16 December 2003: Australia (Toss) 556 in 127 overs (Ricky Ponting 242, Simon Katich 75; Anil Kumble 5-154, Ashish Nehra 2-115) and 196 in 56.2 overs (Adam Gilchrist 43, Steve Waugh 42; Ajit Agarkar 6-41, Sachin Tendulkar 2-36) lost to **India** 523 in 161.5 overs (Rahul Dravid 233, V.V.S. Laxman 148; Andy Bichel 4-118, Katich 2-59) and 233/6 in 72.4 overs (Dravid 72*, Virender Sehwag 47; Katich 2-22) by four wickets. **MotM:** Rahul Dravid.

Captains: Sourav Ganguly (India) and Steve Waugh (Australia)

21

The Nawab of Multan

India vs Pakistan, first Test, Multan Cricket Stadium, 2004

It took 72 years for India to record their first individual triple-century, and 52 years to record their first series victory in Pakistan. Both events are part of India's fairy-tale tour of 2004 where they first won the ODI series and then the Test series against Inzamam-ul-Haq's Pakistan. Neither of these events ought to have surprised us. This Indian team forged over the past three years under Ganguly was unrecognizable from the teams that had visited Pakistan earlier. They had a confidence that bordered on cockiness, having won a Test on every overseas tour in the last few years, and had just returned from Australia where they retained the Border–Gavaskar Trophy, very nearly wresting the series, too.

In keeping with the spirit of a new India, the man who hit a triple-century was perhaps the most aggressive opener in cricket history. He came from a unique mould; there had been none like Sehwag before and there is unlikely to be one like him again in our lifetime. A country that had been brought up on tales of a careful and correct Merchant and Gavaskar as the epitome of opening batsmanship could rejoice in the irony of it all: the opener who took the most audacious risks had lasted five sessions and 375 balls to reach an untouched summit.

Mihir Bose wrote, '72 years after India's Test debut, an Indian did score 300 in a Test innings and it is in keeping with the remarkable Indian cricket story that it was the most unlikely Indian who achieved it, not at home but in the heart of India's greatest cricket rival'. A mistaken illusion exists about Sehwag being reckless and inadequate in technique but John Wright forever dispelled such notions: 'His technique is remarkably good. He's beautifully balanced, with a very still head and no sideways movement. That minimal movement gives him extra time to play his shots, which he does with the full face of the bat, and his balance and hand speed enables him to hit the ball incredibly hard... the way he made the transition from the middle order to opening is nothing short of genius...' Sehwag remains the only Indian to have a hit a triple-hundred; in fact, he hit two and just missed out on a third.

This Test against Pakistan was played in the last week of March in Multan. Multan was like a furnace but that does not adequately describe the combination of heat and dust that put Multan at an unparalleled plane of oppression. As the game began, the crowd at the venue was barely a thousand. Heat, dust, flat wicket and a desolate stadium. Osman Samiuddin, lamenting the poor crowds, in his article, 'Ghost stadiums', said, 'If a Test match against India cannot bring more than 5,000 people in a city of 1.5 million people, then nothing can save it – except, perhaps, an Inzy triple-century and a nail-biting last-day finish...'

While India was on a clear upswing, Pakistan was rebuilding and its recent track record did not inspire much confidence. Their best years were behind them, when they had Wasim Akram, Waqar Younis and Saqlain Mushtaq to bowl them to winning positions. This new generation of Pakistan cricketers had the calm Inzamam-ul-Haq to lead them. Pakistan's batting fortunes would rest on his big broad back and on the undoubted talent of Yousuf Youhana.

India, however, began with a setback as their captain had not recovered from a strained back. All the desperate physiotherapy to get him right in time had failed, so Dravid would lead. Ganguly's batting slot went to Yuvraj Singh, a man after Ganguly's heart. Harbhajan was out for many months now – the finger surgery forced upon him during the earlier tour to Australia had still not healed – and Kumble was back as India's main spinner and leader of the bowling unit. Two young fast bowlers, Irfan Pathan and L. Balaji, had made such strides in recent times that they would share the new ball with Zaheer Khan. Opener Aakash Chopra was a dependable counterfoil to the mercurial Sehwag while adding value as an expert catcher at short-leg.

Dravid won the toss and sent his openers to do battle against Shoaib Akhtar and Mohammad Sami in a hot, dusty, empty Multan stadium. Sami was fast and skiddy but Shoaib was meant to be terror. With a long run-up from the boundary, heels almost touching his buttocks with every stride, there was an evident narcissism to his bowling. His menace was also at odds with his gentle, liquid eyes, while his temper was so uneven that he could fulminate against his captain at one minute and glower at the opposing batsman the next. He was capable of bowling at 150 kmph consistently – who would not want a weapon like that to shake up your favourite foe? The pitch that had been baking in the heat drew the fangs out of even Shoaib. While Chopra preserved his wicket, even if it meant scoring 15 off 60 balls in the first session, Sehwag had hit six boundaries and was, as always, going at a run-a-ball.

In recent times, one of the finest chronicles of a cricket tour is *Pundits in Pakistan* by Rahul Bhattacharya, a book rich in social commentary, wit, wisdom and cricketing insights. Writing about the Multan Test, Bhattacharya described the difference in the character of the two openers in a delightfully witty interlude. Requesting his maverick partner to wait and not dash for a single, Chopra is said to have told Sehwag, '*Nahin! Rukiye, vahin rukiye!*' thus informing readers in four words about the extraordinarily genteel Chopra. In the hot afternoon, Shoaib tried to needle Sehwag, failed, and ended up losing his own cool. India's buccaneer batsman apparently asked the speedster, 'Are you bowling or are you begging?' in such earthy lingo that even the Pakistani fielders laughed at their fast bowler's discomfiture. Chopra is a fine, erudite cricket writer today, and Sehwag, one feels, may not write about his exploits. Yet, whenever he does, he will speak his mind for sure – without hesitation, without inhibition, completely naturally.

Well before lunch, Sehwag had launched his first six off Shabbir, the third fast bowler. The hot still air of Multan was not helping the bowlers at all and Sehwag's stand-and-deliver drives and cuts drove them to helpless distraction. Sehwag crossed 50 in 60 balls and Inzamam introduced Saqlain shortly after the first drinks break. If Pakistan had a chance, it was with Saqlain. Sehwag, as Wright had noted, would take outrageous risks against even the craftiest spinners. True to form, Sehwag clobbered Saqlain for 14 runs including a mighty six to mid-wicket. The hit, however, gave hope to Saqlain and he had Sami posted at mid-wicket in case Sehwag overreached himself. Which he did, for in Saqlain's next over, Sehwag mistimed a swing, but Sami dropped a catch that came straight to his midriff. Bhattacharya wrote, '… something died inside Saqlain at that moment. He played hereafter in sorrow.' The moment had been lost and Sehwag went to lunch, 76 not out. Chopra was still with him, 25 not out.

Sehwag reached his century shortly after lunch off 104 balls with four sixes and 14 fours. Eighty per cent of his runs were through boundary hits, so one can say Chopra's '*Rukiye, vahin rukiye*' was interpreted by Sehwag to mean, no running, only smashes to the fence. Chopra left a little later for an honest but anonymous 42. Greg Chappell in his column announced that Chopra and Sehwag formed a perfect pair. Stand-in skipper Dravid had a rare failure and left for just six, with India at 173 for 2. By tea, India had reached 228 for 2 and Sehwag had crossed 150. The few spectators in the stands were curling up in whatever shade they could find while Sehwag rained blows from his flashing blade. Sehwag, believe it or not, slowed down in his 190s. He had thrown it away in Melbourne after scoring 195, hitting a full toss down deep mid-wicket's throat trying to reach a double-century with a six. So at Multan, when Tendulkar told him '*Shot khelo lekin shot banao mat*' (Play your shots but don't manufacture them), Sehwag heeded the words. He ran two runs to sedately reach 200. By end of day, his hero had reached 60 not out, while he had blithely gone to 228 and the bedraggled Pakistani team contemplated another day of merciless hiding that would inevitably follow.

Sadly for Pakistan, it did. India reached 467 for 2 on the second day at lunch, and Sehwag and Tendulkar had added 112 in 28 overs, exactly four an over. Tendulkar reached his 33rd hundred, serene as ever. Two events took centre stage that afternoon. The first, of course, was Sehwag's triple-century, the first Indian to reach it, which he did with a mighty swing off Saqlain that landed the ball with a thump many rows back into the empty stands. The helmet came off, the spotted bandana on the head made him look more pirate-like than ever, while Tendulkar embraced him for a feat he himself may have dreamed of but was achieved by a man he enjoyed watching.

There are things beyond cricket that give you precious insight into the cricketer as a person. In the NatWest series in 2002, Sehwag had exasperated Wright beyond endurance with another casual dismissal. As he walked into the dressing room, Wright, in white fury, had grabbed him by the collar to ask how dare he play like that and then walk into the room as though nothing had happened. Things could have soured forever between the two. Both knew they had erred, Sehwag for the way he played and Wright for blowing his top in that manner. They managed to talk it out because coach, captain and player knew whatever they were doing together was to make the team successful. No rancour remained. Two years later, in Multan, after Sehwag made his triple century, all photographers were seeking keepsake snaps. As the cameras focused on Sehwag, that wonderful man pulled away and sought out Wright, dragging him by his hand and insisting that he too be photographed along with him. He wanted to communicate to the world that Wright too shared his success.

The brainwave to promote Sehwag to open the batting in 2002 must surely be one of the most significant events in Indian cricket. Ever since Sehwag began opening, India's batting took on a swagger that was hitherto unknown. When Sehwag was at the crease, India galloped at over four runs an over, irrespective of the pitch or other conditions. Sehwag's record in the first innings is phenomenal: he averaged over 62 with 22 centuries, most of them big hundreds and invariably India would wrest the advantage on the back of his swashbuckling batting. Sehwag thus created winning opportunities in the most unique manner. His second-innings record may suffer in comparison but he had created enough fear in the opposition that they never or only very rarely set India a target that was less than four runs an over. If today India's young Turks bat fearlessly irrespective of the target, it is largely because of the confidence and fearless mindset that Sehwag has helped create.

When Sehwag retired, Laxman wrote a wonderful tribute to him: 'For all his batting style, he [Sehwag] is totally devoid of flash and bling and flamboyance as a human being. He is extremely helpful to older cricketers, peers and youngsters alike. He goes out of his way to help them out, and he does so quietly and without fuss or publicity. It is impossible not to be drawn to him for his simplicity and for the goodness of his heart – a heart of gold, caring and giving, even if bowlers around the world may not see it in the same light.'

Now, on to the second event which kicked up a huge storm. With Tendulkar not out on 194, and around 18 overs left in the day, Dravid declared India's innings closed. It was a huge moment in Indian cricket. That evening in a press conference, Tendulkar said he was disappointed about the declaration, which was enough for every journalist to hound out and ferret stories, to look for real and imagined conspiracies. In an Indian team in a different period, it could have caused permanent damage. But the team of the 2000s was different. Yes, it was an avoidable event, and there may have been residual anger and disappointment, and fences would probably have to be mended but the glue and adhesive for all this to happen was the bedrock of mutual respect and a shared mission to make India the best team in the world. The players closed ranks, and not one word emerged from Tendulkar, Dravid, Ganguly, Kumble or Wright after this. There were no favourites to whom a juicy titbit was fed. Sometimes a recovery from a crisis makes the team stronger. The Tendulkar declaration was one such event. Even today, Tendulkar may not like that Dravid declared, but he knows Dravid did what he believed was right for the team. Wright had a rare insight: 'There was fault all around. I should have convinced Dravid to declare earlier and he should have grasped it is one thing to declare when a batsman is 170 or 180, quite another when he's 194... As soon as I heard that Sachin had publicly expressed disappointment, I knew we had a hot potato on our hands. I talked to Rahul, who agreed to have a chat with Sachin before things got out of hand. That combination of steel and serenity, so evident in Dravid's batting, is the mark of the man... he can stand back and put the issue in perspective... he [Sachin] and Rahul talked it through and resolved the matter and we focused on winning the Test match.'

This is one episode about which Tendulkar is frank and open in his autobiography. Let him therefore put the lid on it for us: 'Despite this incident, I am glad to say Rahul and I remain good friends, and even on the field our camaraderie remained intact until the end of our careers. We continued to have some good partnerships and neither our cricket nor our friendship was affected.'

Next morning, the match resumed with Pakistan 42 for no loss and on a flat pitch in hot and dusty conditions, a draw seemed most likely. But India was tenacious. Kumble would not let the ball go out of his hands, in effect telling Dravid he would look after one end while Dravid could rotate the seamers from the other end. There would be long barren periods, but Kumble would plug away. The young Indian pace bowlers got them the breakthroughs. Dravid caught Taufeeq Umar, a left-hander with a perennially bemused look, at slip off Pathan, while Balaji trapped Imran Farhat, noticeably more pugnacious, leg before. Balaji has only a guest appearance in Multan; his best exploits were to come in Rawalpindi in the series-deciding win, though he had already endeared himself to Pakistani fans through the ODI series, who sang '*Balaji zara dheere chalo*' while the Tamilian with little knowledge of that hugely popular song grinned incessantly and innocently.

Yasir Hameed and Inzamam now put together a substantive show. Inzamam, always classy, had time to play his shots, reading Kumble well, and flicking him to mid-wicket off a googly he spotted early or going back to play the stock ball into offside for graceful boundaries. Bulky, ponderous, and despite being a poor runner between the wickets, he was among the best with bat in hand. That afternoon, Multan's most famous son took Pakistan to a most comfortable 233 – a partnership of 160 he shared with Yasir – and a century seemed to be his for the asking, when Kumble, bowling forever, got him caught by Chopra at short-leg. Replays showed the world's best umpire Simon Taufel had made a mistake. Mike Marqusee wrote for *The Hindu*, 'Inzamam walked from the crease at a pace so funereal that one wondered if he would ever reach the dressing room.' It had taken India 68 overs to take three wickets; Kumble had bowled 23 overs before Taufel favoured him.

From there on, it was a story of resolutely sticking to their bowling plan to prise out 17 more wickets. Young Irfan Pathan planned Yasir's dismissal by bowling over the wicket, wider and wider outside off, until the bait was taken and the edge went to Parthiv Patel. From 243 for 4, Pakistan again stitched a partnership, this time between Yousuf Youhana and Abdul Razzak. Razzak's bowling had fallen away but his batting was still useful. He played steadfastly and helped add 78 with Youhana. Zaheer Khan broke the partnership with a not-so-great ball that drifted down the leg side. As Youhana flicked, Taufel felt it had taken bat or glove on its way to Patel. With half the side gone, Pakistan were still 340 runs adrift.

Moin Khan, always the scourge of India – most notably in Kolkata in 1999 – joined Razzak and it seemed they would see Pakistan through for the day. Almost to reaffirm to the public that all was well, Dravid and Tendulkar had frequently conferred on bowling changes and field placements through the day. Now, Dravid asked Tendulkar to bowl the last over of the day. Licking his fingers, Tendulkar, bowler of everything, bowled a googly on his last ball. Moin, mentally locked on survival, was transfixed, could not read it and squared up. With bat describing a despairing arc, he allowed the googly, in slow motion horror, to go between his legs and hit the wicket. Replays showed that the ball had brushed his left thigh before bowling him.

Memory is a strange thing – it can be very precise while recalling certain events. Moin's dismissal was one such. We were a group of colleagues, closeted in a guest house in the small town of Bagalkot, preparing for a teachers' workshop the next day. Till Moin's dismissal, we had been working smoothly while watching the match on TV. As soon as the ball went between Moin's legs, all work stopped. For the rest of the evening, young as well as portly middle-aged academics forgot their assignments and incessantly mimed Moin's dismissal, sometimes opening their legs so exaggeratedly that a football could have passed through!

Moin Khan was shattered beyond just the loss of his wicket, for he played only one more Test after that. The day ended with Pakistan at 364 for 6, and the Indians went whooping all the way back to the pavilion. Bhattacharya's last sentence about the day's play read, 'Whichever way, this was a moment of genius and it signified closure to much more than the day's play.'

India dominated every session from start to finish the next day; it was as though Pakistan's will had been broken from the very first ball of the day, when Irfan Pathan, bowling like a tiger, unleashed a perfect bouncer that Razzak could only fend off glove to the wicketkeeper. Within no time Pakistan had lost their eighth and ninth wickets. A small but meaningless partnership ensued between Sami and Shabbir before Kumble bowled Sami. Pakistan were all out for 407 and were asked to follow-on, 268 runs behind.

Though India had bowled 126 overs in the Multan heat and had by now lost the services of Zaheer, Dravid felt his bowling had enough in the tank, especially since he had Kumble to take care of one end. What a champion this man was – he carried the bowling on his shoulders, and did not let his spirits droop even when wickets were not coming. Over after over, he would hitch up his trousers and bowl on, glowering at fielders if they slacked, applauding them when they put in effort.

Irfan Pathan partnered him from the other end, sensible, mature beyond his years, focused and fully understanding his role. Kumble struck the first two blows as Imran Farhat was caught behind and in the next over consumed the other opener, Taufeeq, nailed lbw as he offered no shot, frozen with indecision. Then India dealt Pakistan the mortal blow. Yasir played to wide mid-on and called Inzamam for a sharp single, something the great batsman would not attempt even in a tight one-day game. The ball went to India's swiftest fielder Yuvraj Singh, who in balletic motion, swooped on the ball and from a low, knee-high position whipped a natural left-handed athlete's throw that hit the bullseye at the striker's end. Bhattacharya describes this delightfully as 'the turning point in the match, not as in turning point, the point at which the tide turns, but the point from where the tide can no longer turn...inevitability entered the game'.

Yasir fell after that, dispiritedly sweeping part-time left-armer Yuvraj into Sehwag's hands. A little after tea, Pakistan, just past 100, lost Razzak, snapped up at short-leg by Chopra off Kumble. It was a well-timed flick but India's specialist close-in catcher made it look absurdly easy as he pulled off a one-handed stunner. Moin fell leg before to Irfan, 113 for 6, when the innings was not even 50 overs old. Youhana, who had crossed his half-century when Moin was out, was waging a lone battle on the other end. Forlorn, he watched Kumble take India another step closer to victory as he trapped Sami leg before. Saqlain then played his last innings for Pakistan and was out for zero. Multan was a sad farewell for this fine player. His was the eighth wicket to fall at 136, and Pakistan were on the verge of defeat.

The next hour and 14 overs belonged to Youhana, not in hope but in doomed valour, as he lashed out. As Shoaib gave him quiet company, Youhana went for broke. His 100 came off just 145 balls before Kumble dismissed Shoaib. India could not finish off the innings that evening even though Dravid claimed the extra half-hour to wrap up things. They duly came back the next day and delivered the final blow in front of empty stands, winning by an innings and 52 runs. Kumble in a lion-hearted effort had taken 6 for 72 off 30 overs. In all, he bowled 69.3 overs for eight wickets across two innings in the toiling heat of Multan, the warrior who epitomized the Indian spirit.

India had beaten Pakistan comprehensively by an innings and 52 runs. The members of this team would have been too young to have seen or heard of the hurting losses of 1978 and 1982, but for the elders, this victory brought a kind of peace and closure. Sehwag was of course the toast of all India. People now recognized his genius for only a man uniquely endowed could ever bat like him. Sehwag, on his part, always spoke of the hard work in his growing-up years, lugging his kit 40 kilometres every day from Najafgarh in Haryana to Delhi on buses and rickety two-wheelers for training with his first coach, A.N. Sharma.

The Hindu in its editorial said, 'Sport is also a test of character and a great part of the battle is played and won in the mind. And Indian cricket, in recent times, seems to have acquired a quality that has made all the difference: mental toughness.' Sambit Bal, summarizing the game for *Wisden Almanack*, wrote, 'This is an Indian team that is beginning to live out the collective fantasy of an irrationally cricket-crazy nation. Countries who haven't known the misery of barrenness might find it hard to comprehend the fuss over one Test win, but 50 years is a long wait, and even though Test cricket can no longer compete with one-day cricket in the passion stakes, India will savour and celebrate this win with fervour.'

Test No. 1693: Multan Cricket Stadium, Multan, 28 March–1 April 2004: India (Toss) 675/5 dec in 161.5 overs (Virender Sehwag 309, Sachin Tendulkar 194*; Mohammad Sami 2-110) beat **Pakistan** 407 in 126.3 overs (Yasir Hameed 91, Inzamam-ul-Haq 77; Irfan Pathan 4-100, Tendulkar 2-36) and 216 in 77 overs (f/o) (Yousuf Youhana 112, Imran Farhat 24; Anil Kumble 6-72, Irfan 2-26) by an innings and 52 runs. **MotM:** Virender Sehwag

Captains: Rahul Dravid (India) and Inzamam-ul-Haq (Pakistan)

22

Beating Them in the Bullring

India vs South Africa, first Test, Wanderers, Johannesburg, 2006

Between the Wright–Ganguly and Kirsten–Dhoni period were the troubled times when Greg Chappell was India's coach. Chappell took over just as the gloss was coming off towards the end of Wright's tenure. Wright timed his departure perfectly. After the Indian team had recorded some fabulous wins between 2001 and 2004 (especially the series victory in Pakistan), it was the start of a period of complacence. The seniors had their feet on the ground but some of the youngsters were carried away by the success. Ganguly's form too fell away and he was beset with insecurities. It was around this time that Wright chose to leave, and Chappell came with his own set of ideas and sound theories but accompanying them were his poor people management skills. As much as Wright ensured things remained in the dressing room, Chappell brought everything to the public gaze. Harbhajan, Zaheer, Sehwag, certainly Ganguly and even Tendulkar endured their most unhappy times during his tenure. Dravid understood Chappell's tactical and strategic priorities well but was sandwiched between unhappy teammates and a coach who had no sense of the train wreck he was causing.

India was on its fourth tour to the country, but hadn't won a single

Test here yet and if there was one country where they had not performed well it was South Africa. It seemed to be no different this time. The tour hadn't gone well thus far. They had been convincingly beaten in four ODIs, with the first game abandoned. India had won the inaugural T20 game, but that was the only bright spot.

This was the background leading up to the first Test, to be played at the Wanderers in Johannesburg. The Bullring, as that ground is known, can be intimidating for visiting teams. With its design of tier-upon-tier stands, visiting teams believe they are entering a gladiatorial arena. Despite the unconvincing build-up to the first Test, it was clear that Dravid would lead from the front. Though his fractured finger had not healed properly, he had declared he would play. His captaincy tenure was marked by his bold tactics and a bustling positive approach. For the first Test, Sehwag would open with Wasim Jaffer, so there was no place for Gambhir. India brought Ganguly into the XI, indicating they valued his experience and combative nature. Kumble was the sole spinner; Harbhajan was excluded. Zaheer would have Sreesanth and V.R.V. Singh as his fast bowling comrades. The evening before the first Test, Dravid made light of his injury and then for good measure added, 'I look around in the dressing room and I see quality players. It would be a dangerous thing to write us off.'

In a weird occurrence, the Wanderers pitch had received an inadvertent overdose of watering overnight. S. Dinakar, reporting for *The Hindu*, wrote, 'The Test series was off to a bizarre beginning, with the match starting 90 minutes late due to some wet areas on the pitch. Host association Gauteng Cricket Board said curator Chris Scott, concerned about the cracks on the pitch widening by the third or fourth day due to the intense heat, had applied wet hessian on the track and then covered it. This, combined with the sweating under the covers, left some portions of the pitch moist.'

As a captain, Dravid believed that batting first was the most positive way to play (remember how he insisted India bat first in their famous Headingley 2002 win?). Despite the damp pitch, he had no fears about batting first after winning the toss, a decision called 'recklessly brave' by South African cricket correspondent Neil Manthorp. Typical of the man, Dravid owned full responsibility, saying, 'It was my call.' He did not get the beginning he expected of the team. Both openers were back in the pavilion very soon. Jaffer was dismissed in the tenth over, leg before to Makhaya Ntini and barely had Dravid arrived at the crease, when Shaun Pollock, in the very next over, consumed Sehwag, caught by keeper Mark Boucher.

India now had Dravid and Tendulkar together at the wicket, and there could not have been a more accomplished pair they could have wished for. Dravid was holding a bat after almost a month; his finger had not healed; the pitch was difficult and he was peppered with blows to the body by Ntini, Steyn and Pollock. He weathered all this, showing impeccable judgement of what to play and what to leave. He was in effect conveying two messages – one to South Africa to say we will fight and the other to his teammates saying nothing is easy. Meanwhile, Tendulkar was in good form and played exquisite drives off the pacemen. Just when it seemed Dravid and Tendulkar had weathered the best that South Africa could throw at them on a pitch with a lot of seam and bounce, both succumbed to Kallis. After 42 overs of hard work, India were reduced to 110 for 4.

Laxman arrived and was fluent as always; the pitch's conditions have never fettered the stylist. Ganguly was clearly emotional – that it meant so much to him to be back in the squad showed and he wanted to prove he belonged. Graeme Smith welcomed him with bouncers, but they didn't faze him. He later said, 'I had been here before. I had a picture in my mind about the kind of surfaces here, about how they would bowl at me and the technical adjustments I had to make.' When play ended on a truncated day, India were 156 for 5, Ganguly returning unbeaten on 14. India would have been a lot happier if the fluent Laxman had not been ousted just minutes before close, the ball from Ntini swinging away to take the edge.

The pitch continued to favour fast bowlers on the second day with pronounced movement and bounce. Ganguly fought well and even as he avoided bouncers, when he did get a ball that was pitched up, he smote it to mid-wicket for six. He also played his gorgeous square-drives when provided the opportunity. But he remained the sole warrior: Dhoni departed when the score had moved to 167, Kumble at 188, and then Zaheer and Sreesanth at 205. V.R.V. Singh, a young 22-year-old paceman from Punjab playing just his third Test, now provided Ganguly the most unexpected company. Even as Ganguly was preparing to take as many runs as he could before the innings closed, Singh provided entertainment with his own brand of No. 11 batting. Attempted pulls would elude mid-off and he would sheepishly grin as he collected a bonus boundary.

Ganguly at the other end did not smile; he grit his teeth and collected the runs. The two were exasperating Smith and his fast bowlers. The South Africans could have bowled better but they focused on bowling short. Before they knew it, India's last wicket had added 44 runs in 5.5 overs – bringing great cheer to the Indian dressing room but frowns and gnashing teeth for Smith's men. A total of 249 on that Wanderers pitch was worth a lot more. Knowledgeable pundits of the game, who knew the Bullring and the pitch, said that Ganguly, Tendulkar and Dravid's efforts were worth twice the runs they had scored.

When South Africa batted, it became clear that the experts were not exaggerating. The pitch assisted good bowling; the Indians bowled a far better length as compared to their more renowned counterparts and the Kookaburra ball, so long as its seam was pronounced, did its work with deadly effect. Even in their wildest nightmares the confident South Africans would never have expected themselves to be reduced to 21 for 4 three balls after lunch and brought down to 45 for 7 in just 17.1 overs. It was the maverick Sreesanth who in one unbroken spell of top-class seam bowling decimated South Africa. His analysis read 10-3-40-5, one of the best displays of seam bowling by an Indian in recent times across all conditions and formats.

While Zaheer Khan maintained the pressure from the other end and chipped in with the early wicket of Herschelle Gibbs and later A.B. de Villiers, Sreesanth in a spell that was only interrupted by the lunch break, grabbed the wickets of Smith, Amla, Kallis, Boucher and Pollock. He was deadly accurate, and got his wickets through leg before, caught in the slips cordon and bowled. Neil Manthorp described India's match-winning eccentric bowler in *Wisden* thus: 'Their hero was Sreesanth, the wild and wacky seamer from Kerala playing only his sixth Test, who started South Africa's collapse for 84 in their first innings with a maiden five-for. There was no eccentricity in Sreesanth's actual delivery, which arrived with pace, aggression and a vertical seam.'

Dravid's captaincy had brought out the best in India's bowlers. Since he could not field in the slips because of his fractured finger, Dravid was either at mid-off or mid-on, constantly having a word with or placing an encouraging arm around the shoulders of his young pacemen. He did not have a deep point or deep square-leg for he expected them to pitch the ball up and not offer any width for batsmen to cut or pull. We watched the entire innings on a giant TV screen at a pub in central Bangalore. What one saw was the remarkable precision with which Sreesanth bowled. The seam had rarely been presented better, the length could not have been improved by an inch while the movement generated was so perfect it induced the edge or beat the bat coming down in defence. Such was the riveting quality of the bowling that even the revelry inside the pub was muted as the tipplers realized they were watching a precious session of play.

There was little left in South Africa's innings. Left-handed Ashwell Prince and tail-ender Andre Nel added a few before Kumble came and closed out the innings, getting Prince caught behind and then clean-bowling last man Ntini. South Africa had unbelievably collapsed for 84, in less than 26 overs, their lowest score at home since 1956–57. Conceding what under the circumstances was a gigantic lead of 165 runs, they had dug a huge hole for themselves. Next morning, *The*

Hindu's sports page carried the headline 'India gives South Africa a taste of its own medicine'.

Only a bowling feat of the kind that India had delivered could now hope to extricate the hosts. But that was not to be. South Africa's bowlers, barring Shaun Pollock, again bowled a length inferior to Indian bowlers; only Pollock hit the right lengths consistently and produced the perfect ball to get rid of Dravid. They got Sehwag before he could do any damage and dismissed Tendulkar cheaply. Even after these blows, at 61 for 4, India were comfortably placed, for they were effectively 226 for 4. They had Laxman and the rejuvenated Ganguly at the crease. Ganguly seemed to carry on from the first innings and constructed a useful partnership of 58 with Laxman. When he left at 119 for 5, he had contributed 25. India ended the day at 146 for 5, with Laxman, at 42 not out, in the process of stitching another one of his precious second-innings knocks.

Sure enough, Laxman continued in the same vein next morning. Though Dhoni and Kumble were dismissed as soon as the third day's play began, Laxman found a staunch ally in Zaheer Khan. Taking his batting more seriously than he is wont to, Zaheer batted for nearly two hours as he helped Laxman put on 70 and India's lead moved close to 375. When Laxman's vigil ended after he was caught off Ntini, he had done his job and more. Manthorp wrote, 'Laxman displayed the temperament of a scholar, ignoring the inevitable snorters which still came his way. Quietly grateful when these missed his bat or the stumps, he tucked singles away on the leg side and regarded each of his dozen fours as a great bonus in an innings of 73 as valuable as many centuries.'

India's innings ended shortly thereafter for 236, but not before Sreesanth had twirled and danced after hitting Nel for a six. If his antics were merely quirky, people would have enjoyed him as a 'character'; what grated was that he showed unnecessary vehemence and fury when he celebrated his victims. It soon became clear that here was a man of unbridled and unwarranted aggression who must be giving hell to his own mates as to the opposition. Nevertheless, it was this man who had bowled India to a winning position on the second day. Before the third day finished, he would contribute even more to India's cause.

With an impossible target of 401 given the batting conditions at the Wanderers, South Africa approached their second innings with an air of fatality. The Indians once again bowled with lovely presentation of seam, and on the right lengths and the right line. Within 12 overs, the back of South Africa's second innings had been broken: Gibbs went for zero, drawn by a ball that angled away from him as Zaheer bowled left-arm over. Smith then slashed at a ball that Sreesanth took away from the left-hander and Sehwag at deep gully pouched a sharp catch. With the score at 32, Hashim Amla succumbed to Sreesanth, caught behind by Dhoni as he feathered a perfectly bowled outswinger. The demented celebrations from Sreesanth earned him a fine. Then de Villiers completed a poor match by getting run out. Only a marathon from Kallis could have thwarted India, but that was not to be.

By end of day's play, South Africa had lost half their side for 167. Three of the five wickets were taken by Sreesanth, who had eight in the match. It had been a day when India had worked hard to strengthen their hold. Bobilli Vijay Kumar of the *Times of India*, wrote, 'The day might have been slow but, just like an art film, it was gripping and eye-opening.'

Next morning, Boucher fell to Zaheer as soon as play began, but Prince and Pollock frustrated the Indians for an hour, scoring nearly 70 runs in that time. However, India now had Kumble bowling probingly on a fourth-day pitch. Soon he breached Pollock's defence in a well-planned manner by bowling him two flighted legbreaks followed by a quick full ball that Pollock missed completely. This breakthrough hastened the end. A little later, Kumble nailed Nel on the crease with a quick one and then bowled Prince round his legs with a full-pitched googly. Prince had battled hard for over five hours and was unlucky to miss a hundred, even though it would have been a distinction in a lost cause. Ntini was the last wicket to fall; the South Africans had lost their last five wickets before lunch on day four. India had taken 20 South

African wickets for just 362 runs and beaten them comprehensively by 123 runs.

For South Africa, it was a pity that Shaun Pollock achieved the landmark of 400 Test wickets in a match they lost. He had been one of South Africa's most loyal servants and would soon bring down the curtain on an illustrious career. His effortless loose-jointed action was a joy to behold while his precision was of a quality that only few in the history of the game have equalled.

While India had been under the pump for some time, in his own studious manner Dravid had reminded everyone they had won their previous series in the West Indies and that the criticism was premature. No one paid heed then, but everyone now acknowledged this feat. The Wanderers win even received praise in Parliament when the Speaker of the Lok Sabha, Somnath Chatterjee, congratulated the team. *The Hindu* called it a 'sensational win' while some former players called it India's finest overseas win ever. Former captain Ganguly graciously praised Dravid's captaincy, saying, 'His field placements were brilliant. This forced the bowlers to bowl a particular length, which was the right length.'

That evening, the Indians celebrated this win, harder and wilder than any of their earlier wins. In their unrestrained overexuberance, they spilled champagne and caused sufficient damage to the property in the changing rooms; BCCI ended up compensating the Wanderers Club. The win itself was emotionally draining, and the Indians did not have anything left in the tank for the next two matches. Dravid himself endured a relatively lean run in his next four innings as did Tendulkar. India lost the second Test in Durban; then, despite scoring 417 in the first innings in Cape Town, they collapsed in the second innings to lose the third Test and the series. Wanderers was the sole bright spot on that tour to South Africa, an achievement that came in the midst of a tough period when the team was at a low ebb. It was India's first win in South Africa and was achieved when all the odds were stacked in favour of the home team.

Test No. 1823: New Wanderers Stadium, Johannesburg, 15–18 December 2006: India (Toss) 249 in 79.5 overs (Sourav Ganguly 51*, Sachin Tendulkar 44; Shaun Pollock 4-39, Makhaya Ntini 3-57) and 236 in 64.4 overs (V.V.S. Laxman 73, Zaheer Khan 37; Pollock 3-33, Andre Nel 3-58, M. Ntini 3-77) beat **South Africa** 84 in 25.1 overs (Ashwell Prince 24, Nel 21; S. Sreesanth 5-40, Anil Kumble 2-2) and 278 in 86.5 overs (Prince 97, Pollock 40; Kumble 3-54, Sreesanth 3-59, Zaheer 3-79) by 123 runs. **MotM:** S Sreesanth.

Captains: Rahul Dravid (India) and Graeme Smith (South Africa)

23

Steel, Not Jelly

India vs England, second Test, Trent Bridge, Nottingham, 2007

The 2007 World Cup was perhaps the biggest blow of the decade for India; after losing to Bangladesh and Sri Lanka, they were knocked out in the group stages itself, and as India exited the World Cup, the last visuals of Dravid brushing a tear away in the dressing room haunted Indian fans across the world. The failed campaign was only the culmination of an unhappy period when Greg Chappell was the coach. Chappell might have brought genuinely good ideas and plans but he wrecked the team with his ill-judged execution. Players felt exposed and insecure; they felt alienated and unjustly compromised. To people observing from a distance with an impartial eye, it was evident that Chappell had handled things poorly. What made it worse was that he did not even want to recognize his mistakes. Dravid, during his two years as captain, suffered from the burden of association with Chappell as coach. The early ouster from the World Cup 2007 was the last straw. As the unhappiness of the cricketers with Chappell became public, he resigned. The players felt liberated and the cricket-crazy nation waited for the next lease of life.

BCCI, very careful with who the next coach would be, were in no hurry to decide. For the tour to England in the summer of 2007, they sent an interim staff of manager Chandu Borde and an all-Indian contingent of homespun coaches Lalchand Rajput, Venkatesh Prasad and Robin Singh. This arrangement was to last till BCCI appointed Gary Kirsten in 2008.

Despite this troubled background, India went to England as a team that now regularly won abroad. Since 2000, they had been winning a Test on every overseas tour barring New Zealand. They were no longer poor tourists and as Dravid memorably said, the team would 'do more than just be part of the summer'. And they showed this outlook from the very first Test at Lord's, which they saved by the skin of their teeth. The last wicket pair of Dhoni and Sreesanth held on for six overs as Vaughan's England desperately tried to wrap up the game. For once, India could thank their bête noire, umpire Steve Bucknor (who had given dubious decisions against India earlier and would give some more in the infamous Sydney Test later). Bucknor ruled Sreesanth not out when he seemed lbw to Monty Panesar. Rain came at the most opportune moment and India got out of jail. Most importantly, India had never lost a series after emerging unscathed from the first Test of a tour.

The teams moved to Trent Bridge, one of the warmer and friendlier grounds in England. Ram Mahesh, the young correspondent of *The Hindu*, wrote that the 'lichen-layered, chipped-tile roofs, the Grandfather clock and the modest rafters' created this homely welcoming atmosphere. That summer, heavy clouds favoured swing and seam and bowlers from both sides tested the skills of the batsmen to the fullest.

The game started four hours late after overnight rain. Not every ground has excellent drainage systems and Trent Bridge was modest in this respect. Dravid (who believed in batting first most times) decided to bowl after winning the toss, seeing the overcast conditions and greenish pitch. His bowling attack was made of the rejuvenated Zaheer Khan, the mercurial Sreesanth and the young left-arm pacer R.P. Singh, with spin in the hands of the ever-reliable Kumble. This team was also without

Sehwag and Harbhajan, both of whom had lost form and motivation under Chappell. They had in fact also lost Zaheer after India's tour to Pakistan in 2006, but he had worked his way back with wisdom and willpower, spending the 2006 summer playing for Worcestershire in county cricket, bowling many overs to not only recover form but also to emerge an even more complete bowler. In the batting department, the openers were unfancied: the tall and stately Wasim Jaffer, the busy, bustling Dinesh Karthik, who bent low to play unorthodox and innovative strokes. The middle order was of course the 'Fabulous Four'.

Having put England in, Dravid needed the bowlers to back him. They did not let him down. They stuck to their task; there was both industry and intelligence in their work. In his second over, Zaheer induced Andrew Strauss to play a drive at an outgoing ball, only to be caught in the slips by Tendulkar. A few overs later the Zaheer–Tendulkar combination struck again, this time getting rid of Michael Vaughan who could not negotiate the round-the-wicket attack by Zaheer. England were floundering at 24 for 2 in the ninth over of the match. R.P. Singh then struck the third blow getting Kevin Pietersen leg before. Ravi Shastri wrote in his report for the *Wisden Almanack*, 'Throughout the game, left-armers Zaheer and R.P. Singh showed tremendous control from over and round the wicket, and they swung the ball both ways: conventional swing most of the time after all the rain, reversing it only when the ball was really old… The right-handers in particular did not seem to know which way the ball was going to swing.'

England tried to recover through a partnership between Paul Collingwood and Alastair Cook, the latter showing the virtue of playing late. The pair had taken the score to 101 when Collingwood aimed a loose drive off Sreesanth and edged the ball onto his stumps. India then had a slice of luck as a marginal lbw decision went in its favour. Change bowler Ganguly – useful medium pacer in those conditions – struck Cook on his pads and even though the batsman was well forward, the umpire sent him on his way. India had again gained the upper hand. By the time a shortened day's play ended, India had two more successes.

Kumble had Matt Prior caught at slip and a few overs before close, the relentless Zaheer trapped Ian Bell leg before. Zaheer was bowling splendidly on his return, continuously challenging every batsman with his length, line, variations in angle and swing. Venkatesh Prasad, who was India's bowling coach on that tour, rubbed his hands in glee recollecting the moisture in the Trent Bridge wicket that morning. He was delighted that India had inserted England and said his bowlers did a perfect job in those conditions. As always, Prasad was grinning and telling us all this as though it happened yesterday.

Next morning, Kumble and Zaheer ensured the tail would not wag. Kumble bowled Tremlett for 20, while Zaheer got his fourth wicket in Panesar. Kumble closed out the England first innings for 198, bowling the clueless Jimmy Anderson. England had lasted less than 66 overs and surrendered the advantage to India.

The question now was, would India drive home this advantage? And India's replacement openers now proved their weight in gold, negotiating the tricky hour before lunch, preserving their wickets and consolidating their position after lunch. Karthik and Jaffer then posted the first-century stand for the first wicket by India in England since the stand between Gavaskar and Chauhan in the famous Oval Test of 1979. Mike Brearley writing for the *Guardian* complimented them handsomely: 'India's less highly-rated openers did marvellously well, each repeating their half-centuries at Lord's. They had a fair share of luck against excellent bowling by James Anderson, Ryan Sidebottom and Chris Tremlett, but despite being beaten quite frequently they had the confidence to keep playing attacking strokes, so the score kept ticking over.'

Making close to 150 in three hours, the two openers blunted England's fast bowlers in seam-friendly conditions. Both left within minutes of each other, though, on either side of the tea break, but they had laid the platform to reach an impregnable position. At 149 for 2, the celebrated duo of Dravid and Tendulkar came together. Untroubled till Dravid fell just before close, the pair put on nearly 100 as India ended day two ahead by 56 runs and seven wickets in hand. Tendulkar had crossed fifty and seemed set for a ton. It was a day totally dominated by India but Brearley questioned Vaughan's field placing. He found Vaughan's field placings like short mid-on, short mid-wicket and short extra-cover unnecessarily cute, when the conditions and bowlers' lengths called for orthodox fields. Brearley was also unhappy that Vaughan did not have a short-leg and wrote that this ruled out 'being caught off an inside edge... Sidebottom bowled without a short-leg for most of the time, yet it must be one of his main methods of dismissal when the ball swings.'

On day three, Tendulkar and Ganguly resumed in conditions where left-arm seamer Sidebottom in particular posed searching questions to Tendulkar. Tendulkar brought all his skill and determination to the battle. Sambit Bal in *Cricinfo* wrote, 'Tendulkar's battle against Sidebottom...will soon be the stuff of folklore. Had Tendulkar perished then, it was conceivable that India would have collapsed.' Tendulkar and Ganguly constructed an invaluable partnership, taking India to 342 before Tendulkar was given out by Taufel, erroneously adjudging him lbw while offering no shot to Collingwood, even when the ball was missing the stumps. Tendulkar fell agonizingly short of a hundred, though he will have happy memories of Trent Bridge for he crossed 11,000 Test runs in the course of that innings. Laxman now joined Ganguly and the two took India past 400 when Taufel contentiously ruled Ganguly caught down the leg side. Taufel later told the press that while he regretted giving Tendulkar out, he would give Ganguly out every time on the evidence he had. Ganguly had fought well to make 79 that included a defiantly hooked six against the hot pace of Tremlett.

Dhoni went quickly but Kumble, who would eventually finish as the only Indian batsman with a century in the series, showed determination and helped Laxman add exactly 50 before Laxman fell for 54. In walked Zaheer. It was the post-tea session, India's lead had crossed 250, England had bowled over 155 overs; the fielders were dispirited and they now played a juvenile prank. As Zaheer prepared himself to bat, he saw a couple of sticky Jelly Beans strewn on the pitch. As he tossed them away, a few more found themselves on the pitch again. Zaheer found it insulting and ridiculous. The close-in fielders, Cook or Bell, were probably the culprits, but Zaheer thought it was Pietersen and yelled at him. 'You got the wrong man,' responded Pietersen. Suddenly, tempers were frayed and relations between the two teams, never great, now threatened to overcome the game.

India batted on till they were all out for 481. England had 16 overs to negotiate that evening but more importantly, they faced a riled-up Zaheer Khan. Luckily, Cook and Strauss saw through the day without damage. That evening, apart from the dubious dismissals of Tendulkar and Ganguly, all the attention was on the 'Jelly Beans incident'. Both captains tried to defuse things, Collingwood tried to make light of it while Zaheer was calm but fuming at what he thought was childish and disrespectful behaviour.

The episode was big enough for Nasser Hussain to devote a couple of paragraphs in his report for the *Wisden Almanack*: 'Trent Bridge also saw both teams crossing the line of acceptable behaviour... The bad behaviour was taken one step further when one of the England players put Jelly Beans on the pitch before Zaheer went out to bat. The issue of who did it was irrelevant (Sky had no television evidence but Ian Bell was named by several newspapers). Players should respect the opposition: let them know they are in a battle, but don't be childish or juvenile. They would not have done it to Tendulkar, so why Zaheer... by winding up Zaheer, England made a major mistake.'

Next morning, Zaheer took no time to remove Cook leg before to one that he shaped into the left-hander. Michael Vaughan came out and along with Strauss, mounted a rearguard action that demonstrated skill and determination, with neither hesitating to play shots. Prasad recalled watching his bowlers with some frustration. There was help in the pitch but the bowlers were all over the place, trying too many things. As they came in for lunch, Prasad told Tendulkar, 'Sach, what is happening, the guys are not bowling in the right areas.' Tendulkar immediately called

Dravid into the discussion and together asked Prasad to have a chat with the bowlers. Prasad told the three fast bowlers that the pitch had enough juice, and they did not need to try too many things but just focus on the length and line. Prasad was so animated narrating the incident that one can imagine how passionately he must have spoken to the bowlers at Nottingham. He added, 'Zaheer is different. He has so much talent, fine wrist, seam position and control, that he can try a number of things on the ground. But the others get lost if they try and experiment like him. With the others, it is best to stick to one consistent approach or line of attack.'

After lunch, the Indian bowlers found their second wind and achieved two key breakthroughs. Within minutes of resumption, Zaheer got Strauss caught behind by Dhoni. Ten overs later, R.P. Singh outfoxed Kevin Pietersen with one that he could not read and offered no shot. As the ball rapped him on the pads, Pietersen walked, knowing instantly he was gone. When Collingwood joined Vaughan, the captain was already batting on 60, looking most assured. A century was certain. Zaheer, despite his smouldering anger, was focused on bowling at his best. Sreesanth on the other hand was behaving poorly. He had already bowled a terrible beamer to Pietersen that might have felled him, and yet did not seem genuinely apologetic. Then he bowled a bouncer from a no ball to Collingwood, where he was a brazen foot or three beyond the bowling crease. Dravid, disgusted, promptly removed him from the attack. Sreesanth was also fined 50 per cent of his match fees. If Jelly Beans was juvenile, Sreesanth was brainlessly boorish.

Just as Nasser Hussain had made a gallant rearguard century at Leeds in 2002, here at Trent Bridge, Vaughan crafted one of his finest centuries as captain. It was a comeback series for Vaughan after a knee operation and his batting oozed class. Vaughan completed a wonderful ton, batting with unwavering concentration. Collingwood and Vaughan stitched a century partnership together and the huge deficit was cleared.

Vaughan was finally out on 124, after batting elegantly for five hours, in the only way possible – through a stroke of bad luck. Even now one can recollect the dismissal as it happened in fatal slow motion. Vaughan attempted to play Zaheer to the leg side, but the ball hit his thigh pad. It could have bounced away anywhere, but instead it chose to flop down and trickle on to disturb the stumps. Irrespective of whom you supported, you had to feel for the distraught England captain. The match turned in a matter of minutes. Of the last ball of the same over, Ian Bell was sent on his way, leg before to a Zaheer special for zero. A little later, R.P. Singh served up another beauty from round the wicket to clean bowl Matt Prior. Finally, with England's score on 324, Collingwood too departed, caught behind off Zaheer. The second new ball had proved decisive. Kumble now polished off the tail in a spell of four overs. England, from a relatively sturdy 287 for 3, had lost their last seven wickets for 58 runs.

Mike Selvey wrote in the *Guardian*, 'Zaheer Khan, with nothing more than a tilt of the wrist and malevolent intent, bowled India to the verge of victory with five stunning wickets as he snaked the ball mesmerically from around the wicket, first one way and then the other in the spirit of the great Wasim Akram... Such practitioners are the aerobatic equivalent of the wrist spinners with their legbreaks and googlies.'

An impressive pattern was emerging. India's away wins were not merely on the back of heroic individual performances but were the result of a most effective bowling attack that had the right mix of pace and spin for the first time in their Test history. In the 1970s, the spin quartet created the few overseas wins with little help from the pacemen, but it was in this decade that India consistently won abroad – the batsmen gave the bowlers enough to bowl with while the combination of pace and spin worked perfectly. In overseas Tests in these ten years, 60 per cent of the wickets came from the Indian pacemen and 40 per cent from spinners. Whether at home or abroad, India's bowlers on an average took 15 wickets in a match, far superior to anything Indian bowlers had achieved earlier.

Pause to also consider another facet of Indian cricket's growth. Five years back at Leeds, on a green top in swinging conditions, India batted first to make a statement that they had the best batting in the world, and won. Here at Nottingham, they sent England in, because they believed they had the attack to knock England out in those conditions, and won. This was the difference. Earlier, when India inserted the opposition, it was to avoid batting first against pace bowling. Now they sent the opposition in because they believed their pace bowlers were as good, or when they decided to bat first, they did so because they knew they had the best batting line-up. No wonder games like Leeds 2002 or Nottingham 2007 are milestones in Indian cricket history.

Vaughan was sorely disappointed. He had nursed hopes that England would challenge India with a tricky target of around 150 runs. Instead, the target was now merely 73 runs. Although India lost three wickets on the fifth morning, they cantered home. They had dominated every session except when Vaughan and Collingwood were at the crease. There could be no claimant other than the magnificent Zaheer Khan for Man of the Match. Dravid was elated. He said, 'Zaheer showed what a leading bowler must do. Whenever we asked questions of him, he stood up and got it done. When the game was in the balance...he grabbed it by the scruff and did what match-winners do. The second new ball was critical, I knew it had to count. I just asked our bowlers not to get excited, to put it in the right areas, and they responded magnificently.'

Amidst all the praise for Zaheer, Ram Mahesh reminded readers of *The Hindu* that 'R.P. Singh produced absolute purlers. The deliveries to get rid of Kevin Pietersen and Matt Prior in the second innings were straight from Wasim Akram's handbook – snaking inswingers to the right-hander from well outside offstump.'

It was a happy tour, with no Chappell looming in the dressing room and the players not having to look over their shoulder. After India drew the next match at Oval, they finally won a Test series in England after 21 years. Dravid stepped down as captain at the end of the tour with the satisfaction of a victorious show. The pain of the World Cup elimination had dulled. The man who would take over from him was

Anil Kumble, one of India's most respected cricketers, a man who could well have been captain much earlier. Indian cricket, after a brief period of unhappiness, was again resurgent. They would only grow stronger in the course of the next few years.

Test No. 1841: Trent Bridge, Nottingham, 27–31 July 2007: **England** (Toss) 198 in 65.3 overs (Alastair Cook 43, Ian Bell 31; Zaheer Khan 4-59, Anil Kumble 3-32) and 355 in 104 overs (Michael Vaughan 124, Paul Collingwood 63; Zaheer 5-75, Kumble 3-104) lost to **India** 481 in 158.5 overs (Sachin Tendulkar 91, Sourav Ganguly 79; Monty Panesar 4-101, Chris Tremlett 3-80) and 73/3 in 24.1 overs (Wasim Jaffer 22, Dinesh Karthik 22; Tremlett 3-12) by seven wickets. **MotM:** Zaheer Khan.

Captains: Rahul Dravid (India) and Michael Vaughan (England)

24

Poetic Justice

India vs Australia, third Test, WACA, Perth, 2008

When we asked seasoned cricket writers to choose four of India's greatest victories, each one of them chose Perth 2008, for two inseparable reasons – Australia had been conquered in their bastion at the fast and bouncy WACA; and the victory was further remarkable because it came after a terrible week of controversies in the previous game in Sydney. Unbidden, they also spoke of the magnificent role played by the captain Anil Kumble, who combined statesmanship with brilliant powers of execution in handling the explosive situation in Sydney and then getting his team focused on Perth. Kumble was past 37, and captained India in 14 Tests in what was his last year of international cricket. This was the period after the previous coach Greg Chappell had been sent on his way, and before Kirsten took over.

Kumble had a simple but committed team of Indian coaching staff. He knew he was a stop-gap captain before a younger, long-term captain took over. Seven years later, delivering the Dilip Sardesai Memorial Lecture, Kumble said, 'The modern captain faces more challenges than his predecessors did. Issues arise, especially when a team is on tour that requires a statesmanlike approach. Captains must keep the bigger

picture in mind. It is important to carry the team on these occasions.'
So he did, during this series, which brought out the best in him.

While India had been trounced in the first Test in Melbourne by
337 runs, the second Test in Sydney was completely different. India
batted magnificently, on the back of a 154 not out by Tendulkar, to score
530 and take a 69-run lead in the first innings. Australia then batted
very well in its second innings but it seemed Ponting had delayed his
declaration because he gave his bowlers just over two and a half sessions
to bowl India out. On a mad fifth day – full of acrimony, poor behaviour
and awful umpiring – India were dismissed just minutes before stumps
and Australia won by 122 runs. India had competed as much as the
umpires had allowed them to.

But Sydney had already been shaken up by the 'Monkeygate
controversy' on the third day. Batting with Tendulkar, Harbhajan
Singh was accused of racial abuse against Andrew Symonds. Hayden
and Clarke complained and later deposed before Mike Proctor, the
inquiry commissioner, that Harbhajan had called Symonds a 'monkey'.
Harbhajan denied this and his batting partner Tendulkar, who was
within earshot at the pitch, flatly refuted the Aussie accusations. It
finally emerged that Harbhajan had said '*maa ki*' in Hindi. The two teams
closed ranks over their respective dramatis personae, Harbhajan Singh
and Symonds. Bitterness boiled over. The Indian board backed its team,
flexed its muscles in the inquiry over Monkeygate and even threatened
to call off the tour. As Laxman recalled, at the end of the Sydney Test,
the team stayed put in their bus for over three hours not knowing if they
would drive to Canberra (if the tour continued) or would drive to the
airport (if the tour was aborted). Such was the heat generated. The final
day's events only added fuel to the fire; a combination of unnecessary
aggro and poor sportsmanship from the Aussies, notably Ponting, and
very incompetent umpiring by Steve Bucknor and Mark Benson. Greg
Baum in his review for *Wisden* wrote, 'Questionable sportsmanship,
poor umpiring and alleged racism set the second Test at Sydney on a
daily more precipitous edge, and tipped it over as Australia pursued a

record-equalling sixteenth successive win on the last day in typically relentless fashion. They did snatch improbable victory from the jaws of stalemate, but it seemed to be made Pyrrhic in its moment by the engulfing firestorm.' Peter English in his column asked Ricky Ponting to open his eyes and see the damage he had done by the way he and his team conducted themselves on the ground. Peter Roebuck, even more forthright in his column for *Sydney Morning Herald*, asked Australia to sack Ponting. He wrote, '…the hosts had forgotten themselves; had forgotten about sport and sportsmanship in a desperate pursuit of victory. It was the lack of manners that stuck in the craw.' Bucknor was dropped from the umpiring panel and not a single Indian anywhere in the world was unhappy. The Australian team was not unaffected by all this, though Ponting put up an unnecessary, unrepentant defence.

Kumble, meanwhile, shepherded his team in Canberra. There, instead of brooding over Monkeygate or over the incompetent umpiring decisions of Benson and Bucknor against India, the captain got his team to focus on Perth. India was 0-2 down, the series could at best be drawn, but Perth was the most difficult of grounds. No Asian team had won in Perth; in fact, no country had beaten Australia in Perth since 1997.

Kumble made a couple of key changes too. Dynamic opener Sehwag was brought back and Dravid, the stop-gap opener for the first two Tests, went back to his one-drop position. Yuvraj Singh, who had done little of note so far, was dropped. Harbhajan was unfit and Irfan Pathan was drafted in. The new ball would be in the hands of left-armers R.P. Singh and Pathan, and the rookie Ishant Sharma. By playing Pathan as the third seamer, Kumble also strengthened the batting. India's line-up read: Wasim Jaffer, Sehwag, Dravid, Tendulkar, Ganguly, Laxman, Dhoni, Pathan, Kumble, Ishant Sharma and R.P. Singh. Australia were playing a four-man, all-pace attack that included Shaun Tait who was making noises for clocking the fastest ball. With a slinging action reminiscent of Jeff Thomson, who might have bowled the fastest ball ever (those were the days when there were no speed guns), Tait in fact broke the 100-mile barrier a few years after the Perth Test.

Kumble won the toss and batted first. Before the match, his message to the team was to not get worked up about the WACA pitch and 'take the pitch and conditions out of the equation'. Jaffer and Sehwag opened against Brett Lee and Mitchell Johnson. Sehwag indulged himself with six quick boundaries and in less than ten overs, the openers had put on 50. Greg Baum wrote that Ponting was confused enough by a south-easterly wind to bowl Lee and Johnson from the wrong ends! India lost both openers after drinks. That brought Dravid and Tendulkar together, and thus began an exhibition by two of India's finest batsmen ever. Premachandran told us he rated this innings by Dravid very highly. He had not been in great form, he had also opened without success in the previous two matches, but here he showed character, combining technique, grace and resolve in the best manner possible. One of his strokes was a mesmeric cover-drive. Ram Mahesh wrote, 'Always an index of his batting health, the stroke stood apart, for it came off a ball that was very nearly 150 kmph. Crucially, Dravid found his touch through the leg side.'

Tendulkar was in sublime form at the other end and another century was his for the asking when he was out to a marginal lbw decision for 71. The two had put on 139 at over 3.5 runs an over, and when Tendulkar left, India were a healthy 198 for 3. Ganguly did not stay long, but Laxman and Dravid did well to add 64 runs. Both got out at the same time, Dravid missing his ton by seven runs and Laxman after making 27. Dhoni and Pathan stayed till close of play and India had scored almost 300 runs for six wickets on the first day. Next morning, the two added a few useful runs but the last few wickets fell for nothing, including one that Roebuck called 'a ropey decision'. Australia could feel they had done well to dismiss India for 330.

When the Australians came to bat, India's seamers showed they could use the conditions better than their more famous counterparts. Pathan and R.P. Singh bowled better lengths, seaming and swinging the ball better and testing the batsmen more frequently. The results were staggering. By the 19th over the Australian innings was in a shambles, with half the side gone for 61. In his column for the *Age*, Baum wrote, 'In the sort of baking heat that deters even dogs from barking, a hush had fallen on the WACA Ground.'

The damage had begun early, with Pathan consuming both openers, Chris Rogers (playing because Hayden was injured) and Phil Jaques. Soon after, R.P. Singh got left-hander Mike Hussey caught behind for a duck, the first duck of his career. Ishant now came on and delivered two crushing blows with leg-cutters. He got Ponting to edge to Dravid at first slip and then had Michael Clarke caught by Dhoni. Ram Mahesh, proclaimed in *The Hindu*, 'On a stewing-hot second day, the third Test burst into flames.' Gilchrist joined Symonds, who had already enjoyed a life, and the two played some attacking cricket to add 102 runs at nearly six an over. Both completed fifties at around a run-a-ball before Symonds edged Kumble and the ball ricocheted off Dhoni's gloves to Dravid. It was Kumble's 600th wicket and the clock at the WACA showed 4.49 p.m. *The Hindu* saluted this achievement on its front page, and in a tribute in the same newspaper, Roebuck wrote, 'Cricket will look back and marvel at his achievements. India will look back and wonder at its slowness in appreciating him.'

There was no further resistance from the Aussies. R.P. Singh came back for a superb spell in which he got Gilchrist, Lee and Stuart Clarke all caught behind by Dhoni. The ball to Gilchrist was a beauty, kicking off a length, as it moved away to take the edge. Kumble caught and bowled Tait. In just 50 overs, the Indian bowlers had rolled Australia over for 212 runs, its lowest total in 24 Tests at home. Ram Mahesh cheekily wrote, '…the parched sea-gulls were the only Australians making any noise'. India now had a lead of 118 runs and with Sehwag opening, nothing else but a flying start to its second innings could be expected! At five runs an over, India finished the day at 52 for 1. They could not have hoped to be better placed at the end of a day that belonged to their bowlers.

Pathan, who had come one-drop the previous evening as nightwatchman, frustrated Australia on the third morning. Though they bowled better – they got the dangerous Sehwag for just 43 and then prised out Dravid, Tendulkar and Ganguly – they could not breach Pathan's defence. When he finally went for 46, the scoreboard read 160 for 6. Ian Chappell praised him, saying his resurgence was pleasing. A lead of 278 at this stage was not adequate. A savvy Dhoni then joined Laxman at the crease. The scoring rate dropped as both played carefully. Baum described Laxman's innings as 'a pragmatic, battling 79' and indeed his innings and his partnership first with Dhoni, who made 38 and then with R.P. Singh, who unexpectedly made 30, effectively took the match away from Australia. When Laxman was last man out, India had scored 294 in their second innings and had set Australia a target of 413, something they had never achieved before.

Australia's opening pair was a weak link and given the form that Pathan was in, it was a matter of time before he consumed them in the second innings. Rogers was caught behind and Jaques was caught in the cordon. Ponting and Hussey played out the rest of the day as Australia ended at 65 for 2. Despite this grim position, Alex Brown in his column 'Test of history awaits' for the *Age* was looking at possible scenarios of an Australian win, however improbable that might be. If nothing else, the column helps us understand that correspondents everywhere, not just in India, look at the picture from their own country's perspective.

The next day is known in cricketing lore as a David-and-Goliath battle between the 19-year-old rookie Ishant and batting legend Ponting. Had Ishant swiftly dismissed Ponting, nobody would have remembered but he tormented Ponting over after over, repeatedly beating him, knocking him on glove and abdomen, rapping him on the pads, turning him square before finally claiming him. After a long spell of seven overs, it seemed the moment had passed, and Ponting had managed to survive everything including a most confident appeal for leg before. One could see R.P. Singh come running up to replace Ishant. Seeing an imminent bowling change, Sehwag rushed up to Kumble and on the stump mike everybody could hear him urge the captain to give Ishant another over. 'Ponting is batting, and Sharma bowls longer spells for Delhi.' Kumble then turned to Ishant and asked him, '*Ek aur daalega kya?*' (Will you bowl one more over?). The first ball of that new over, Ishant bowled a perfect leg-cutter that took the edge of Ponting's bat and nestled in Dravid's hands at first slip.

Prasad told us he had not seen such a fine spell for a long, long time. Premachandran wrote, 'Ishant's nine-over spell was as good as any from a visiting bowler in Perth over the past decade... Starting with an edge off Hussey that didn't quite carry to second slip, he tested both batsmen with lively pace and steep bounce while maintaining great seam position. His height was the most significant factor, with even length deliveries causing problems.'

With twenty minutes to go for lunch, and the score reading 114, India had broken through. It was the only wicket Ishant took in the innings, but he had the most profound impact on that day's game. No wonder Sambit Bal wrote, '...scorecards don't often tell the story. It was a day when Ishant Sharma shook up Ricky Ponting and set up a famous win'.

R.P. Singh dismissed Hussey after lunch, as poor a leg before decision as the one against Tendulkar, and in both cases, it seemed umpire Asad Rauf had not accounted for the bounce in Perth while sending the batsmen on their way. Within three overs India struck again as Kumble nailed Symonds, rooted at the crease, with a quick ripper that crashed into his pads. Billy Bowden's finger went up quickly even before Symonds – who never walked when he was out and often looked querulous when given out – could show his bat to the umpire. Premachandran in delightful prose wrote, 'Having drunk from a reservoir of luck in Sydney, Symonds found the well bone-dry across the continent in Perth.'

At 179 for 5, Gilchrist joined Clarke, who had been batting beautifully. The bowling then began to wilt as Gilchrist and Clarke added 50 in quick time. Though Clarke was doing most of the scoring, things could change completely if Gilchrist got going. Gilchrist, as dangerous in the middle as Sehwag was at the top, had taken many a match away in an hour of batting. Yet, in an inspired move, Kumble brought on part-timer Sehwag, the only off spin option he had. Kumble always believed that the full-pitched googly or offbreak outside legstump was the best way to get Gilchrist, as he might miss the sweep and be bowled.

Sehwag, underrated but a canny bowler, showed his golden arm. From over the wicket an offbreak pitched full outside leg on the rough and as Gilchrist missed the sweep, it turned and bowled him round his legs. It was a mortal blow.

In his next over, Sehwag dismissed Lee for a duck, caught by Laxman. With the team tottering on 229 for 7 and the target as far as the next planet, Johnson joined Clarke who was batting serenely. The two went in for tea at 243 for 7. Four overs after the break, Clarke finally cracked. After 81 lovely runs among the ruins, he stepped out to Kumble and was stranded as Dhoni whipped off the bails.

At 253 for 8, the posture of every Indian watching the match on television changed. They now relaxed and slouched as victory was a few overs away. Yet, cricket has a way of teasing even the most sincere of spectators, and it was nothing but a tease as Johnson and Stuart Clarke put on 73 runs in 12.5 overs with three sixes and half a dozen lusty blows to the boundary. The slam bang ended soon, as Pathan and R.P. took the last two wickets, even as Johnson walked off with a fifty. India had bowled out Australia for 340, winning the Perth Test by 72 runs. Irfan, R.P. and Ishant – a young inexperienced trio – had proved to be heroes. Had Zaheer, Munaf Patel and Sreesanth been fit, these youngsters might not have played or even made the touring party. Now they had turned in a performance that gave India one of its greatest victories of all time. The irony is that both Pathan and R.P. have faded away, while Ishant alone remains, and it has been a painstaking journey for him on the way to 200 Test wickets.

The improved behaviour at the WACA seemed like atonement for the awful incidents in Sydney. Clarke walked when he snicked

Ishant Sharma to Dhoni. Phil Jaques did not claim a catch that he was unsure of. When Lee went at Pathan with bumpers to his head, Pathan negotiated without losing the ability to acknowledge the bowler's excellence with a smile. Lee in turn saluted Pathan for his skill and courage. The Australian crowd too demonstrated good humour. Around six in the evening, as umpire Bowden turned down an appeal from Johnson for LBW against Dravid, the crowd responded with chants of 'We want Bucknor, we want Bucknor'.

The next day, the *Sydney Morning Herald* header read, 'India bring Australia back to earth'. It seemed like poetic justice after Sydney. India was the only Asian side to beat Australia in Perth, and for the second time, broke Australia's sequence of 16 consecutive Test wins. They had done it at Eden Gardens in 2001, and skewering Ponting's team at the WACA would have given them thrice the pleasure. Ram Mahesh in his dispatch expressed it all: 'There are moments in sport that are rewardingly cathartic, that seem to make worthwhile – even necessary – all that has preceded it, and on Saturday at the WACA, India experienced one such.'

WACA was one more evidence that fast bouncy tracks would no more give the hosts any advantage against India. Just as they had shown on the green top of Bullring and in the swinging conditions of Nottingham, India's efficient bowling combination had once again trumped the host. The years 2001–10 were when pace and spin came together for India; most times abroad it would be three pacemen from among Zaheer, Nehra, Sreesanth, Pathan and Agarkar and the fourth bowler would be the wrenching choice between Harbhajan and Kumble for the sole spinner's place. Add to this the fact that during this period India had rich left-arm pace resources. The wonderful Zaheer Khan, among the top five left-arm pacemen in the game's history, had through these exciting years the support of Ashish Nehra, Irfan Pathan and R.P. Singh. Around 60 per cent of the wickets claimed by Indian pacemen came from these four left-armers. Left-arm fast provided the variety and edge to India's bowling combination that they never had earlier.

Nobody would have looked askance if the Indians' celebrations were over the top but even in rejoicing, Kumble was different from Ponting, who had celebrated wildly after winning at Sydney. The Indians celebrated in moderation for Kumble wanted the team to focus on giving another outstanding performance at Adelaide. Sambit Bal noted, 'A less resilient side would have been shattered by the heart-breaking last-minute loss at Sydney and the other distractions it brought. India are fortunate to have a man of Anil Kumble's resolve and calm, and a bunch of steely senior players in the dressing room.' Kumble has called this victory the greatest win of his career, referring to the special bond within the team. Unlike come-from-behind miracles like Kolkata 2001 or Adelaide 2003, India had dominated every single day here, outplaying Australia session by session. There were no grand individual performances, just solid efforts from every batsman and bowler, safe wicketkeeping, good catching and complete commitment on the ground.

Many years later, sitting with Premachandran in his office, he recalled an anecdote that pleased him immensely. It was past 7 p.m. on the last day, everyone had left the WACA and only a couple of scribes were left behind filing their dispatches. Sitting just behind him, Mike Coward, the Australian journalist, told him, 'Something to tell the grandchildren, that we all watched an Indian fast bowler put an Aussie great through the wringer.' There could not be a more befitting end to this essay.

Test No. 1862: WACA, Perth, 16–19 January 2008: India (Toss) 330 in 98.2 overs (Rahul Dravid 93, Sachin Tendulkar 71; Mitchell Johnson 4-86, Brett Lee 3-71) and 294 in 80.4 overs (V.V.S. Laxman 79, Irfan Pathan 46; Stuart Clark 4-61, Lee 3-54) beat **Australia** 212 in 50 overs (Andrew Symonds 66, Adam Gilchrist 55; R.P. Singh 4-68, Ishant Sharma 2-34) and 340 in 86.5 overs (Michael Clarke 81, Johnson 50*; Pathan 3-54, Virender Sehwag 2-24) by 72 runs. **MotM:** Irfan Pathan.

Captains: Anil Kumble (India) and Ricky Ponting (Australia)

25

The Spirit of a Proud Team

India vs Sri Lanka, second Test, Galle International Stadium, 2008

After their World Cup win in March 1996, Sri Lankan cricket surged forward in the most remarkable manner. In the 12 years since Arjuna Ranatunga lifted the World Cup – and till this game in 2008 – visiting teams had won only 11 of the 61 Tests in Sri Lanka, and a victory against them in their own den was considered a special feat by the best of teams. Sri Lanka during this time had all-round strength and balance. The batting core was provided by the stalwarts Sanath Jayasuriya, Mahela Jayawardene and Kumara Sangakkara while Chaminda Vaas and Muttiah Muralitharan bowled Sri Lanka to victory with regularity.

The Galle Test, played between 31 July and 3 August 2008, was the second of a three-match series. India had suffered a crushing innings defeat in the first Test in Colombo, as Sri Lanka piled a mammoth 600 for 6 in their first innings with centuries from four batsmen. India's bowlers took a pounding: Zaheer 1 for 157, Ishant 2 for 124, Harbhajan 3 for 149 and skipper Kumble none for 121. India were then bowled out for 223 and 138. Muralitharan had match figures of 11 for 110, supported by the debutant mystery spinner Ajantha Mendis who had an eight-wicket haul. Mendis's carrom ball had a lethal novelty that nonplussed the best of the batsmen.

The skipper then exhorted the players to give their best in Galle, saying, 'We have no option but to win.' In his press conference on the eve of the match, Kumble said, 'There is definitely a lot of experience and resilience in this team. We will fall back on that resilience and I'm sure we will be able to put up a better show and get the right result here. We need to win this Test match.'

Galle was one of the most picturesque venues in the world before the tsunami flattened it in December 2004. It is a testimony to the indomitable human spirit that the Sri Lankans got it back in action in the shortest possible time. When the Indians played their game in 2008, it was still work in progress. The pitch, which had been covered and caked with layers of salt from the sea during the tsunami, had been dug out and relaid. A 400-year-old clock tower looked down upon the ground from the great height of the Dutch fort. The Indian Ocean could be seen on two sides of the ground. A friend, who was at Galle for the India–Sri Lanka Test in 2015 came back saying it was the most astoundingly scenic ground he had ever been to. Sitting in the pavilion, one is diagonally across the fort and can watch the sea on either side, the left side noticeably calmer and the other rough with waves lashing the rocks.

Both teams were greeted by a strange-looking new pitch that sported two very different halves. It looked dry and cracked at the city end and damp and flat at the fort end. India won the toss and was given a rollicking start by Sehwag who was supported splendidly by Gambhir, who had an early stroke of fortune when wicketkeeper Prasanna Jayawardene dived in front of slip and spilled a catch. The openers raced to 61 before the drinks break and in the next hour hammered 90 more runs. When Mendis came on in the eleventh over, Sehwag made his intent clear and the spinner was hit for a boundary in almost every over and also slogged for a six over mid-wicket. Muralitharan, brought on in the 18th over, was unable to slow things or trouble the batsmen. Twice in his second over, Sehwag spotted the doosra and smashed both for boundaries. India went to lunch at 151 for none, with Sehwag on 91 and Gambhir on 50. A lashing downpour accompanied by strong winds stopped play for hours after lunch. Only 15 more overs were possible that day, but India lost the momentum during that period. Sri Lanka fought back with the wickets of Gambhir, Dravid, Tendulkar and Ganguly as India finished the day on 214 for 4. Sehwag was the shining light, completing a brilliant century off just 87 balls. Most importantly, the swashbuckler was unbeaten.

Gambhir's wicket had come from a successful leg before referral. The Decision Review System (DRS) was being used for the first time in a series featuring India. Indian players and BCCI have consistently opposed the DRS saying it is not error-free, especially in its use of the ball-tracking system. Their experience with the DRS for the first (and till now the only) time in the series only hardened India's resistance to the DRS. The leg before decisions through the DRS did not inspire confidence while the judgement of when to call for reviews eluded India throughout this tour.

Dravid made only two before Mendis foxed him, but during that brief stay, Dravid overtook Gavaskar in the tally of overall Test runs. Next over, he inner-edged Mendis to forward short-leg, and walked before the umpire gave him out. He was actually not out, for the fielder caught the ball after it had deflected off his helmet. Not surprising, for Dravid was the man who walked when he was on 95 in his debut innings at Lord's.

The second day began with a little drama. The on-field umpire Rudi Koertzen – nicknamed Slow Death for the inch-by-inch raising of his index finger – had fallen ill and Mark Benson the TV umpire came out in his place with Billy Doctrove. The first hour belonged to India as Laxman and Sehwag added 49 runs in 13 overs. Sehwag continued at better than run-a-ball and his 150 came off 144 balls. When the fifth-wicket pair had put on exactly 100, Laxman departed for 39, deceived by a carrom ball from Mendis. Dinesh Karthik, playing in this series only because Dhoni had made himself unavailable, did not last long as Mendis trapped him lbw with another carrom ball. Sehwag, the only Indian untroubled by Mendis, then hit him for a straight six off a googly that he read early. Sehwag read Mendis and Murali better than anyone else and this coupled with his aggressive intent was an awesome combination. Kumble fell when Sehwag was eight short of his double-century. Harbhajan became Mendis's fifth victim of the innings while Sehwag was still on 192. When Zaheer fell to Muralitharan, Sehwag was on 195. With last man Ishant Sharma for company, Sehwag with a single here and a couple there, reached 200. The innings finished at 329 a few balls later with Ishant's dismissal, and Sehwag became only the second Indian – the first being Gavaskar – to carry his bat through the innings.

Sehwag is a remarkable man. In this innings, he refused a single on 199 because he did not want to expose Ishant to four balls of Murali – a simple way of communicating 'Team before self'. Not once did he hesitate to speak his mind. When he retired from international cricket, reporters asked him, 'Who is the best captain you played under?' He could have justifiably hedged the question, but Sehwag, without a second's hesitation, replied, 'Anil Kumble'. Why? Because he was the one who was always true and honest in his communication with colleagues, said Sehwag. This directness is the essence of the man.

His teammate Laxman thought Sehwag's Galle innings was one of his best. 'Ajantha Mendis and Murali troubled us all, but Viru was in the zone, in a class of his own. He not merely kept them at bay, but he toyed with the two of them. He played with a straight bat and very late while most of us played early to Mendis. While we tried to play him like an off spinner, Viru played him like a medium pacer who bowls a wicket-to-wicket line. He wasn't taking a big stride but waiting for the ball to come. And the way he played Murali through the offside was special. He would go deep into the crease, open the bat's face and hit him through the covers, playing against the turn. To play like that against Murali requires a lot of class.'

His innings at Galle reminded us of a similar double-century we saw at Chinnaswamy Stadium against Pakistan in 2005. Replying to Pakistan's mammoth 570, Sehwag batted as though he was in a different planet and plundered 201 off 262 balls. The only other Indian batsman to cross 50 was Laxman. The effect of Sehwag's batting on the crowd can only be experienced if one is in the stands. The spectators go into a trance; even the most analytical fans completely forget India's situation in the game and give themselves up completely to the joy of watching Sehwag's fireworks. He had the gift of transporting all the spectators to a special world of his own.

The rest of the day saw a keen contest between Sri Lankan batsmen and India's bowlers, Harbhajan Singh in particular. The Lankans got off to a poor start losing Michael Vandort in Zaheer Khan's first over to a sharp low catch by Dravid at third slip. Kumar Sangakkara joined Warnapura and the pair batted with great composure to put up an excellent partnership of 133, finding easy runs against Zaheer and Ishant but earning them against the spinners. Harbhajan, who had been lacklustre in recent outings outside India, suddenly found form. Usually the off spinner's morale drops if he does not taste blood early. Here, despite the long partnership, he did not flag and probed away unceasingly. Finally he broke through, getting Warnapura caught at short cover. From that point, he was on a roll. 137 for 2 became 144 for 3, as Harbhajan deceived Sangakkara into giving a return catch off the leading edge. Then, with a superb change of pace, bowling from round the wicket, he trapped Thilan Samaraweera leg before. Off the last ball of the same over, he dismissed Tillakaratne Dilshan for zero off a lovely ball that dipped, turned and bounced for a bat-pad catch taken by a diving Gambhir at forward short-leg. Sri Lanka were 215 for 5 at stumps, with Mahela Jayawardene holding one end with a well-compiled 46. It had been a riveting day's cricket.

On the third day, India claimed the remaining five wickets for 77 runs, Harbhajan finishing with 6 for 102 while Kumble took 3 for 81. Commentators and experts called it Harbhajan's finest performance overseas. Jayawardene made 86, carrying the batting with little support from the bottom half. India had taken a small lead of 37 runs, but in the context of this match and the uncertain nature of the pitch, a lead not to be sneered at. All depended now on how India would cope with Murali and Mendis and the kind of target they could set.

Sehwag and Gambhir put the fears to rest. Sehwag, forthright as ever, began by plundering boundaries off Nuwan Kulasekara. Jayawardene brought Murali into the attack in the sixth over and Sehwag clattered him for a boundary and a six off successive overs. India were going at five runs an over; the 50 came up in the 11th over. At drinks India were 69 off 14 overs. Sehwag reached 50 off 49 balls and in the next over got out to Vaas, as Dilshan took a sharp catch off a full-blooded drive. Dravid came out to join Gambhir and settled in comfortably with positive boundaries off both Murali and Mendis. Meanwhile, Gambhir was batting beautifully. He was always an assured player of spin, skipping out on quick feet or using the depth of the crease to go back and cut. Here in Galle, he tackled both the spinners with aplomb. India was on a healthy 144 when Gambhir finally went for 74; both openers had played their roles. Ram Mahesh in his column wrote, 'The importance of an opening pair that can attack fine bowling, not merely through skilful strokeplay but also through adept running, cannot be stressed enough... A feature of Gambhir's 74 was the placement of his off and cover-drives, several of them struck inside-out.'

During 2001–10, India's openers had an average of 49 runs for the first wicket, not only India's best ever, but better than what even opposition opening pairs averaged against India during this decade. Such an opening meant that India's fabulous middle order came to bat on a much firmer platform; the average partnerships for the second, third, fourth and fifth wickets during this period by India are better

than the average partnerships that the opposition put up. No wonder
then that India's first-innings average during this period is 10 runs more
than the average first-innings score by opposition teams against India.

The old firm of Dravid and Tendulkar then strengthened India's
position further in the hour before drinks with positive play. Tendulkar
jumped out and hit a googly from Mendis for four. The two were belting
a boundary every now and then. At drinks India had progressed to 185
for 2. Then the hard-working Vaas, bowling a crafty line slanting to off,
cracked Tendulkar's patience as he chased a wide delivery. India were
now 200 for 3. At the same score in the next over, Dravid fell to Murali,
a successful referral for lbw after Doctrove turned down the appeal.
Kaushik, the *Deccan Herald* correspondent, wrote, 'India received yet
another unkind cut from the review process being trialled in this series,'
and devoted a column highlighting the inconsistencies of the DRS. Bad
light ended play shortly thereafter and India rued losing two important
batsmen just before close. That evening Harbhajan told pressmen that
a target of 300 would be enough. Jayawardene responded, 'We'll get
400. If they get 500, we'll go and get 500. Nothing is difficult for us.'

Before play began on the fourth day, Waqar Younis on Ten Sports
television said, 'From here it's going to be a spinners' game. The cracks
are opening up.' Mendis and Muralitharan opened proceedings to
Ganguly and Laxman. Just when it seemed the early period of play
was negotiated, Laxman was defeated by the carrom ball from Mendis,
which pitched middle and hit Laxman on his back pad in front of
offstump. India were 220 for 5, which effectively meant a lead of 257.
Karthik joined Ganguly. He was having a wretched time both behind
and in front of the stumps and it must have been an awful feeling to
hear people saying, 'Oh, if only Dhoni were playing.'

Perhaps that was on Karthik's mind that morning as he walked out
and he decided to attack the bowling. He began with a reverse sweep
off Murali for a boundary and followed this with a six over long-on off
a Mendis googly. He then turned his attention to Murali and slog-swept

him to mid-wicket for a six. But it was too good to last. With India on 252, and his own score at 20, Karthik tried to repeat the slog-sweep, was beaten in the flight and holed out to deep mid-wicket. Off the last ball of the same over, Murali got Ganguly with a pearl. The offbreak, flighted on middle and off, drew Ganguly forward and out of his crease and then dipped and spun away. Prasanna whipped off the bails. In the next over, Kumble went leg before to Mendis and a ball later, Ishant was run out in a mix-up with Harbhajan. From 220 for 4, India had collapsed to 257 for 9. The last pair added 12 runs before Harbhajan was dismissed. It was ironic that Harbhajan had to score the runs that helped India reach the lead of 300, which he had said would be adequate.

The Lankan openers had around 10 overs to negotiate before lunch. India began with Dravid dropping a catch at third slip in Zaheer's first over. Yet, all thoughts that the dropped catch was an ill omen were misplaced, as India's pace bowlers broke the back of Lanka's batting within just three overs. Ishant began the damage. From over the wicket, a perfect ball pitched on leg and middle and seamed away from left-handed Warnapura, who edged it to Laxman at second slip. In the next over from Zaheer, Sangakkara was dismissed by a beautiful ball that landed on a perfect length, bounced and seamed away. The great batsman had to play at it and again Laxman at second slip pouched it. As Ram Mahesh put it, 'Zaheer's dismissal of Sangakkara deprived Sri Lanka of the man who could structure the chase.' The Lankans were 5 for 2 in the third over. It was then Ishant's turn. Jayawardene, hoping to stroke his way out of the hole, attempted a cut but could not keep it down, and Dravid made no mistake at gully this time. The innings was in tatters as Sri Lanka went to lunch at 24 for 3.

Samaraweera and Vandort resisted Zaheer, Ishant and Kumble for an hour after lunch, before the skipper brought on Harbhajan to bowl the last over before the drinks break. Bowling from round the wicket, the spinner trapped left-handed Vandort lbw off the last ball, a quicker one ball that held its line. The Indian spinners then bowled in tandem to

Dilshan and Samaraweera. Both batsmen put up a fight with strokeplay, Dilshan playing bustling strokes while the stylish Samaraweera executed some outstanding cover-drives. Samaraweera completed a fine half-century and Dilshan looked good on 34 as Sri Lanka went to tea at 109 for 4. Mention of Samaraweera will always bring memories of the horrendous terrorist attack on the Sri Lankan team bus in Lahore in March 2009. While most were uninjured, Samaraweera was the one who suffered a grievous injury as a bullet pierced his thigh. In a glorious testimony to his strength of character, Thilan Samaraweera returned to Test cricket after surgery and months of recuperation. Five of his 14 Test centuries were made after his remarkable comeback.

The first over after tea, Dilshan received a cracker from Ishant that burst and straightened from a perfect length. Caught on the crease, Dilshan edged it to the keeper. Scribes, commentators and his captain have said Ishant's spell at Galle reminded them of his spell to Ponting at Perth. Ram Mahesh wrote, 'Bowling with a rhythm reminiscent of his magnificent displays in Australia, Ishant did everything his captain asked of him.' Jamie Alter wrote, 'Ishant looked like getting a wicket off every ball in that spell and the other bowlers cashed in and ran through the tail... This spell was better than the one in Perth, because there was nothing in this pitch for the fast bowlers.'

India had now prised open the lower half of the Lankan order as their keeper Prasanna Jayawardene came out to join Samaraweera. But Ishant and Harbhajan were at their throats, knowing they were on the verge of a win. After seventeen scoreless balls, Prasanna lost his nerve and tried to slog Harbhajan. The mistimed hit ballooned up over mid-wicket where Ganguly ran back and caught it while tumbling over. Then Harbhajan proved too much for the tail. In his next over, he trapped Vaas leg before with a flighted ball that dipped and hit the batsman on his toe. 131 for 7. At the other end, Kumble replaced Ishant after a terrific five-over spell after tea, and struck straightaway, getting Kulasekara caught off the leading edge. As Samaraweera watched helplessly from the non-striker's end, Mendis departed next, caught at mid-on off Harbhajan. It was Harbhajan's fourth wicket of the innings, his first ten-wicket haul in an overseas match since 2002 at Kingston against West Indies. The off spinner had bowled with patience and guile in both innings, showing confidence in his own abilities as was evident in the way he varied his pace, trajectory and angles.

The match finally came to an end in the next over as Kumble calmly accepted a return catch from Muralitharan. The Sri Lankans had lasted less than 48 overs and wilted for 136. As the Indians hugged and collected stumps as souvenirs, their coach Kirsten came out to join them in celebration. 'Without warning the day combusted, producing so frenetic a procession between the dressing rooms and the middle that a round-trip operator would have done roaring business,' wrote Ram Mahesh to describe the rapidity with which wickets fell on the final day to bring the match to an early finish. Premachandran described India's turnaround aptly, 'India finished the first Test of a series like a man holding on to the edge of a cliff by his fingernails. A week later, they once again looked like world-beaters...'

The defining character of this Indian team was that it hurt badly when it lost. They took a lot of pride in playing for India and to play below their best or spoil their record through a careless session caused them a lot of pain. Their collective mission was to take India to the No. 1 position among Test-playing nations. This Indian team would never have the invincibility of Australia but it was registering wins regularly on every overseas tour. The comeback victory at Galle only added to this enviable record. Gary Kirsten had by now taken over as the coach. He and Paddy Upton formed a great bond with the Indian team. In the ensuing months, the team would take significant strides towards the pinnacle by beating Australia and England at home and notching up a series win in New Zealand. Galle epitomized the proud and resilient spirit of this team.

Test No. 1884: Galle International Stadium, 31 July 31–3 August 2008: India (Toss) 329 in 82 overs (Virender Sehwag 201*, Gautam Gambhir 56; Ajantha Mendis 6-117, Chaminda Vaas 2-74) and 269 in 76.2 overs (Gambhir 74, Sehwag 50; Mendis 4-92, Muttiah Muralitharan 3-107) beat **Sri Lanka** 292 in 93.3 overs (Mahela Jayawardene 86, Kumar Sangakkara 68; Harbhajan Singh 6-102, Anil Kumble 3-81) and 136 in 47.3 overs (Thilan Samaraweera 67*, Tillakaratne Dilshan 38, Harbhajan 4-51, Ishant Sharma 3-20) by 170 runs. **MotM:** Virender Sehwag.

Captains: Anil Kumble (India) and Mahela Jayawardene (Sri Lanka)

26

Winning It for Mumbai

India vs England, first Test, M.A. Chidambaram Stadium,
Chepauk, Chennai, 2008

'*Sachin Tendulkar's outrage over the terrorist murders in his home city of Mumbai has been the most enduring image of the Chennai Test. His defiant words, played endlessly on Indian television, have felt like an address to the nation. He speaks of the need to pull together in bad times until the good times return and his vehement final sentence ingrains itself in the memory of all who hear it. "I play for India," he spits. "Now more than ever."*' – David Hopps in the *Guardian*, 16 December 2008.

Never has a Test match been played under the shadow of such immense tragedy. The country was in mourning after the heinous 26/11 terrorist attacks in Mumbai that killed nearly 200 people and injured around 400, leaving the entire nation in grief and the citizens seething in anger. India, to proclaim that we would continue to live our lives undaunted, and with the belief that sports can be a source of succour, decided to go ahead with its Test series against England. England's cricketers honoured the martyrs of Mumbai in the best manner by agreeing to come. They went straight into the Test in Chennai without a practice match, Kevin Pietersen and his team setting a glorious example.

Barely a fortnight had passed since the tragedy when the Test began on 11 December. In a cauldron of emotions, as cricket lovers settled into their seats at Chepauk, Pietersen and Dhoni went out for the toss. Dileep Premachandran has written that the game began in an atmosphere of 'Presidential-style security' while Peter Roebuck more tolerantly wrote, 'By all accounts the security was tight but not oppressive.'

How can sportsmen focus on the game when a tragedy casts such a huge shadow? As we write this, India has just played a Test match against South Africa in Delhi as the horrific floods ravage Chennai. How could Ravichandran Ashwin bowl 50 overs to win a game while agonizing over the well-being of his family? At such times, sportsmen – very young men, most of the time – show amazing steel and character. Tendulkar, grieving for his beloved Mumbai, tells us how the cricketers coped with the trauma of 26/11. In *Playing It My Way*, he writes: 'When we assembled in Chennai for the first Test on 11 December we were still finding it difficult to concentrate on cricket. Our thoughts were with the victims of the attacks and everyone was talking about those traumatic three days. But we had a Test match on our hands and we felt it was important for all our fans that we should put in a good performance in Chennai.'

The Indian team had a settled look. Kumble had retired and seamlessly handed the reins to Dhoni. India's batting was its strength; openers Gambhir and Sehwag, the fabulous three in the middle order with Yuvraj taking Ganguly's place. The bowling unit looked balanced with Zaheer Khan and Ishant Sharma to bowl pace, Harbhajan Singh and Amit Mishra to bowl spin.

England had sent a full-strength contingent, with a fine opening pair in Andrew Strauss and Alastair Cook. The middle order had Kevin Pietersen at the peak of his form, the stylish Bell and the battling Collingwood. For great team balance they had Flintoff, the world-class all-rounder, and Matt Prior, the wicketkeeper-batsman. Pace bowlers James Anderson and Steve Harmison, debutant off spinner

Graeme Swann and left-arm spinner Monty Panesar gave variety and depth to their bowling. The two sides were evenly matched and any home advantage would be marginal. The Test had been shifted from Ahmedabad to Chennai at short notice and the groundsmen had limited time to prepare the pitch; the reddish playing strip was said to be uncertain. A cracker of a contest was what everyone predicted and Chepauk invariably was the venue of great cricket.

Although Cook and Strauss were playing a Test after four months, the two did well to take England to lunch at 63 for no loss. They continued resolutely and were only separated in the 40th over after a century partnership when Cook fell to Harbhajan. Strauss had not touched a bat for weeks, but the way he batted showed he was very much in the groove, making 123 off 233 balls, falling just before close. On the other hand, Ian Bell, Pietersen and Paul Collingwood fell cheaply. Pietersen perished to an ill-advised pull off Zaheer while Collingwood got a poor bat-pad decision from umpire Billy Bowden. Zaheer and Ishant used reverse swing while Amit Mishra, slow through the air and off the pitch, kept the pressure from his end. England ended the day at 229 for 5 and honours had been shared.

Next morning, in a crucial strike, Mishra got rid of Flintoff. Nightwatchman Anderson was obdurate and Matt Prior quite positive, but once they were separated there were no further partnerships. Meanwhile, the pitch had begun playing a trick or two. A ball from Harbhajan leapt off a length and Swann could only edge it to Dravid. England finished at 316.

India began poorly, losing Sehwag early. Then, in a sensational start to what would be a fine career, Swann got two wickets in his first over in Test cricket. Bowling with a lovely, clean action, Swann struck the pads of left-handed Gambhir off his third ball and right-handed Dravid off the last ball, both clean lbws. India was in strife at 37 for 3. Tendulkar and Laxman tried to repair the situation and took India to 98, when Laxman fell to Panesar, and immediately after, Tendulkar too departed for 37, falling to Flintoff – both batsmen caught and bowled. Before the day ended, Yuvraj was also out, driving loosely against Harmison, and India finished at 155 for 6.

Dhoni and Harbhajan played valuable hands on the third morning. Dhoni, a model of consistency in his last few innings, added another half-century while Harbhajan did his bit with 40. They took the score to 212, a partnership of 75 before Harbhajan fell to Panesar. The last three wickets fell for 29 runs. India had conceded a lead of 75, a costly one considering they would bat last on a pitch that had begun to acquire a crumbly look. The odd ball was leaping alarmingly and the uneven bounce and turn would only increase as the game progressed.

When England went in for their second knock, the Indians struck back to reduce the visitors to 42 for 3 by the 13th over. It included the wicket of Pietersen falling to his bête noire Yuvraj (the innocuous left-armer got Pietersen out quite a few times and was labelled a 'pie-chucker'). The joy was short-lived, as the rest of the day belonged to Strauss and Collingwood who batted with composure and determination to take England to 172 for 3. The two were unbeaten on 73 and 60 respectively, sharing a partnership of 129. England now held the upper hand, ahead by 247.

Analysing Strauss's superb batting, Dileep Premachandran wrote, 'On a slow pitch, where the odd ball leapt alarmingly throughout, he crafted a game plan that played to his strengths: the cut, whenever the ball was short, and the sweep to spin bowling of a full length, without risking the front-foot drive.' Collingwood, typical of the man, played a game built on sturdy temperament, playing spin very well. He was upbeat at the press conference that evening. 'The pitch has started to play a few tricks. It's crumbling, and the ball is not really coming on to the bat. This could prove vital when we bowl. We're hoping to get some reverse swing as well.' Gary Kirsten was asked if the match was now out of India's grasp. The South African replied, 'If that is the perception, we would certainly like to change that.' Not many were convinced, like S. Dinakar of *The Hindu*, who began his report saying, 'England holds all the aces in the first Test at Chepauk.'

The fourth day was again a day of contrasts. England's laborious progress in the first two sessions was followed by a most exhilarating blitzkrieg from Sehwag that lit up Chennai. England began the day with the intention of grinding India out of the game. Strauss and Collingwood added 72 off 26 overs in the pre-lunch session during which Strauss completed his second century of the match. Their plans went awry after lunch. They could only add 57 runs off 22.5 overs, while losing five wickets. For the first time in three and a half days, India had won a session. The only consolation for England was that Collingwood also completed his ton. In a post-match analysis, Michael Vaughan, the former England captain, called this the session where England let the game slip from their hands. Shortly after tea, Pietersen declared, setting India a target of 387 to get in 126 overs.

Only thrice in the history of the game had any team scored more in a winning chase but then Sehwag had this delightful unconcern about history. When he came out with Gambhir, a tornado was unleashed at Chepauk for the next 100 minutes. Anderson and Harmison did not know what hit them. If he slashed one fiercely over gully, he dismissed the other with an on-drive. Slash, drive, cut – as always, it was the wonderful combination of an uncluttered mind, matchless hand–eye coordination, a still head and the gift of timing and finding gaps. Fifty came off 5.3 overs. Sehwag raced to his own 50 off 32 balls; he had peppered the fence with six hits and sent spectators into raptures with two huge sixes, one an uppercut over point and the other a mighty biff over mid-wicket off a full toss from Panesar. At the drinks break, it looked like a one-day chase, with India 85 for no loss off 15 overs, with Sehwag on 61. Suddenly, everybody had forgotten a wearing fourth-evening pitch. So what if a few balls jumped or shot through, when Sehwag batted, such things were irrelevant. Pietersen thought he would get Sehwag on the cut but the buccaneer hit at least eight of his boundaries in the arc between point and third man. India raced past 100. Then Swann broke through. Sehwag first smote him for six over mid-wicket and two balls later, departed, ironically, not attempting a big hit but missing a delicate paddle sweep. An incandescent innings had come to an end. The entire crowd rose to acknowledge one of the most fascinating innings ever seen at Chepauk. Roebuck made the nuanced observation that Sehwag 'is an intelligent and consistent batsman who has managed to remain instinctive and creative. It is a most unusual combination.' In the space of 100 minutes and 23 overs, Sehwag had turned the equation upside down.

India went into the fifth day needing 256 off a possible 90 overs. The press still felt the odds were against India, and the morning papers reminded readers the highest ever winning score in India was 276 by the West Indies. Yet, that did not deter the crowds. On the last day, even though it was a working day, over 20,000 spectators poured into Chepauk. An unforgettable treat was in store for them. Although the day began poorly for India, as Dravid went in the third over, caught behind as a ball from Flintoff left him, Tendulkar walked in at 141 for 2 to a rousing reception, as always.

Gambhir on the other end was concentrating fiercely, determined to play every ball on merit, enjoying a couple of fortuitous boundaries between good shots; he crossed his fifty, while Tendulkar began to settle in. At the first drinks break, India were 180 for 2, having added 49 in the first hour off 12 overs. The break did no good to Gambhir who left as soon as play resumed; Collingwood caught his loose drive off Anderson neatly at gully. Laxman looked in silken touch as he played three gorgeous cover-drives and a straight-drive, as Tendulkar played second fiddle, secure in defence after having weathered the threat of Flintoff. India went to lunch at 213 for 3. The target was still 174 runs away; there were plenty of overs left, thanks to the Sehwag assault, but fourth innings are notoriously tricky. A couple of wickets and the lower middle order would come under immense pressure.

The lunch break proved expensive for India; the third over after lunch, India lost Laxman as an offbreak from Swann spun and spat at him. A catch to short-leg, and India were 224 for 4. In came Yuvraj, a nervous starter and vulnerable to spin. The target seemed a fair distance away. Suddenly, Tendulkar pulled out a couple of paddle sweeps and a thumping pull against the spinners. Yuvraj took heart and when his turn came, he hit three rousing boundaries – a punch into the off, a sweep and a lovely loft over mid-on. India went past 250. Pietersen effected a double change, Flintoff and Harmison replacing the spinners. Tendulkar survived a huge appeal for lbw from Harmison and also an inner-edge off Flintoff. The two aggressive bowlers, who went flat out in a burst on either side of drinks, gave Yuvraj a torrid time. The two batsmen survived that nervy period. More importantly, Tendulkar had gone past fifty. By and large, he had been immaculate, his wonderful technique helping him neutralize any threats the pitch threw up. India needed just over 100 now.

When the spinners came back, Yuvraj unleashed a majestic pull over mid-on for six to bring India close to 300. As tea approached, Yuvraj played an impulsive reverse sweep and missed. Tendulkar admonished him for the act. In his autobiography, he wrote, 'There was a time in his innings when he attempted to play the reverse sweep to Panesar and I walked up to him to tell him that all he needed to do was remain not out and finish the game. I reminded him of the Pakistan game at Chennai in 1999 and said I had been in a similar position before and remembered well how painful it was to lose from a winning position. Yuvraj reined himself in…'

As the players came out for the final session, the home crowd sent up a roar while the Barmy Army cheered the visitors. Yuvraj completed a fine fifty even as the new ball became due. When it arrived, there were a few close shaves, a difficult chance went down but India remained in control. Nothing exemplified this better than the way Yuvraj belted Anderson for two boundaries as he moved into his sixties – a cracking straight-drive and then dancing out to hit the fast bowler over mid-on.

India now needed less than 50 runs , and Pietersen began to switch his bowlers around. India was cantering to a win. Tendulkar was in his eighties and Yuvraj moved into his seventies as he put away a full toss from the dispirited Swann to the mid-wicket fence. With just 19 runs needed for a win, Tendulkar was still 12 runs from a century. He set this right in Panesar's over, with a delicate paddle – a beautiful sight on any day, and he played quite a few that day – and a splendid drive to cover. He moved to 97 while India needed 10 runs for a famous win. Yuvraj played the next over with exaggerated defence, waiting to allow Tendulkar to complete his century. An over later, it was Swann again. Yuvraj tickled him round for a single and the crowd was on its feet. Tendulkar was on 99, and India 383 for 4. Off Swann's third ball, Tendulkar played the sweep that ran away to the fine-leg boundary and raised his arms in triumph. Yuvraj bore down on Sachin and lifted him off his feet in a bear hug of delight, a moment of 'perfect symmetry' as *Cricinfo*'s Andrew McGlashan wrote, describing the perfect timing of Tendulkar's century and India's victory coming off the same ball.

If there was one thing constantly held against Tendulkar, it was that he had not piloted India to a victory in a fourth innings chase. He set that right in front of 35,000 deliriously happy spectators. Dileep Premachandran wrote, 'He's 35 years old and owns practically every batting record in the game, but you couldn't escape the feeling that this was probably Sachin Tendulkar's finest hour.' Dedicating his century to the people of Mumbai, Tendulkar said, 'I don't think by India winning or my scoring hundreds, people who have lost their dear and loved ones would feel better. It's a terrible loss and our hearts are with them. All I can say is that in whatever way we can contribute to make them feel better, we'll make that effort.'

Sehwag was voted Man of the Match for his game-changing knock, but the Test is remembered for Sachin. Premachandran explains this: 'Those who aren't Indian struggle to fathom exactly what Tendulkar means to so many millions, and it's doubtful whether even those who live here really comprehend just how much a part of the national consciousness he has become. He is such a unifying force, a personality capable of stirring the emotions in every nook and corner of a vast land. And in these times of distress and anger, it was so very appropriate that it would be Tendulkar who put the smiles back on at least a few faces.'

On the other hand, in some indefinable manner, Pietersen and his men had altered the way Indian spectators looked at a visiting English side. They had come straight into a Test without any practice, rusty after weeks of lay-off and yet not once did KP or his team trot out any excuse. They dominated the game till tea on the fourth day and competed almost till the end of a pulsating final day. Then, in a fine gesture, they donated 50 per cent of their match fees to the relief fund for victims of 26/11. Hopps in his dispatch for the *Guardian* wrote, '...England should reflect with satisfaction on the part they played in one of the most politically significant Tests in history.'

Once in a rare while, a Test match is played under the most emotional and difficult circumstances. When such a match also turns out to be an epic contest, it creates for itself a place in the minds and hearts of people.

Test No. 1898: M.A. Chidambaram Stadium, Chepauk, Chennai, 11–15 December 2008: England (Toss) 316 in 128.4 overs (Andrew Strauss 123, Matt Prior 53*; Harbhajan Singh 3-96, Amit Mishra 3-99) and 311/9 dec in 105.5 overs (Strauss 108, Paul Collingwood 108; Zaheer Khan 3-40, Ishant Sharma 3-57) lost to **India** 241 in 69.4 overs (M.S. Dhoni 53, Harbhajan 40; Andrew Flintoff 3-49, Monty Panesar 3-65) and 387/4 in 98.3 overs (Sachin Tendulkar 103*, Yuvraj Singh 85*; Graeme Swann 2-103) by six wickets. **MotM:** Virender Sehwag.

Captains: M.S. Dhoni (India) and Kevin Pietersen (England)

27

The Fourth-Innings Houdini

India vs Australia, first Test, I.S. Bindra Stadium, Mohali, 2010

Eight years after achieving their greatest ever Test victory at Kolkata, India became the No. 1 Test-playing nation in 2009. It had been a thrilling climb to the summit, with remarkable overseas victories in every Test-playing nation. After Chennai 2008, the Indian team enjoyed more success. They handed Australia a 2-0 defeat when they visited India in late 2008 and followed it up with a series win in New Zealand in early 2009. That was a superb tour – a great 10-wicket win at Hamilton followed by a stupendous rearguard to save the game at Napier to ensure a series win. When Sri Lanka visited India towards the end of 2009, India beat the visitors 2-0 and were anointed the No. 1 Test team. They retained that ranking through 2010 by beating Bangladesh, drawing a home series against South Africa and an away series against Sri Lanka. Now in October 2010, for the first time, India would play Australia from its perch as the world's No. 1 one Test team. This would be a two-Test series, with the first game in Mohali. The Aussies in transition had slipped to fourth in the ICC Test rankings, with stalwarts Warne, McGrath, Langer, Hayden, Martyn and Gilchrist all retired. Ponting was building a new side that he could then hand over to Michael Clarke.

Apart from India's already existing and formidable batting line-up, Suresh Raina, the livewire fielder and ODI specialist, was given a chance that year to establish himself in the Test middle order. The bowling looked well rounded with Zaheer and Ishant Sharma for pace and Harbhajan and left-armer Pragyan Ojha for spin. The fulcrum was Dhoni, one of the finest all-rounders in modern cricket – captain, keeper and No. 7 batsman – who was riding the crest of success at the time, with the ODI World Cup soon in the future too. The Australians' world-conquering days were in the past. However, Shane Watson and Simon Katich were a reliable opening combination and the middle order of Ponting, Clarke and Mike Hussey looked sound. The fast bowling was in the hands of Ben Hilfenhaus and left-armers Doug Bollinger and Mitchell Johnson. They had promising batting all-rounder Marcus North to provide balance but there could be no adequate replacement for the peerless Gilchrist. Whatever the relative strengths, when the two teams took the field, it would be an even contest.

Ponting gave Australia the early advantage by winning the toss. There were two distinct halves to the day's play. After Watson was dropped off the second ball of the match by Sehwag at gully, Zaheer broke through with a piece of intelligent planning and execution to trap Katich leg before. Ponting and Watson quickly consolidated and Dhoni tried all his bowlers, even Sehwag, to break through, but without success. Australia went to lunch at 101 for 1, and both batsmen continued in fluent vein after the break; runs were coming at over four an over. Ponting reached his 50 with a sequence of lovely boundaries, while a sedate Watson achieved his half-century a few overs later.

Just as Australia looked on top, on the stroke of drinks, the quicksilver Raina ran out Ponting. As Ponting left, Zaheer needled him, heated words were exchanged and umpire Billy Bowden had to intervene. On TV it did not make for good viewing. In the next three hours, India fought back by taking three wickets for 70 runs. Harbhajan, after a wayward start, bowled with discipline, Ojha was tight and Zaheer probed away. Clarke and Watson added just 18 runs in 12 overs. With tea three overs away, Clarke fell to Harbhajan, Dravid taking a sharp low catch at slip. The dour batting continued after tea as the spinners wheeled away accurately. After 80 overs, Australia were 215 for 3; Watson was in his nineties. Dhoni did not claim the new ball and instead brought Zaheer back who immediately provided a master class in reverse swing bowling. Off his third ball, he trapped Hussey lbw with one that reversed back to defeat the defensive prod. In his next over Zaheer bowled Marcus North, the next batsman, who let the ball go but it came back to dislodge the off bail. He could have had Tim Paine, the new batsman, in the same over too, but Dhoni spilled the low catch. Nonetheless, it was an exhibition of first-class bowling from the left-armer, probing and difficult. Australia ended the day at 224 for 5, with Watson unbeaten on 101.

On the second morning, Paine and Watson batted watchfully, adding just 25 runs off 14 overs. The old ball was still being used. Watson's innings finally came to an end when Gambhir at short-leg dove to catch an inside edge. He had batted 461 minutes to score 126 runs. When Johnson, a very useful No. 8 batsman, joined Paine, the latter shook himself into action with a boundary and a six off Harbhajan to get Australia past 300. Both batsmen now began to play shots against a tiring Indian attack, quickly scoring 82 runs together before Johnson was caught behind off Zaheer. With the score at 373, Australia lost Nathan Hauritz, and Dhoni finally took the second new ball – after 146 overs! Zaheer responded immediately with the wicket of Paine, and it was a pity he missed his century by eight runs. He never played a Test after that series, and the Mohali effort would remain his best. Bollinger finally fell to Ojha and Australia were all out for 427 after a marathon innings of 152.4 overs.

The scoreline did not bother Sehwag at all, as he began India's chase with a belter of a start. Boundaries thudded into the fence between third man and cover as he laid about Hilfenhaus and Bollinger. After 12 overs, India had scored 69 runs, at nearly six an over. Sehwag's batting has always infected writers, and one can imagine Peter English, the Australian journalist, being almost breathless as he typed, 'Sehwag started biffing through the offside, hitting two boundaries from a Doug Bollinger over, and then crashing three off Ben Hilfenhaus. Nathan Hauritz's first ball went over mid-off, his next sped along the ground in the same region for the same result, and the over cost 11.'

When Johnson got Gambhir out for 25, India were 80 for 1. Dravid came and played some lovely shots: a flowing cover-drive, a flick off pace, and an on-drive off spin. Then, like a shooting star, Sehwag was gone, caught off Johnson – 59 off 54 balls. The crowd went silent, while the Australians breathed a sigh of relief. Ishant came as nightwatchman. The day ended with India 110 for 2.

Next day, as though in preparation for his fourth-innings heroics, Ishant played the role of an obdurate, irritating nightwatchman to perfection. Even as Dravid played some lovely on-drives and a cover-drive off his back foot, Ishant frustrated the Aussies for a full hour till the first drinks break, when he offered no shot to left-armer Bollinger and lost his stumps. The score stood at 151 for 3. The Mohali crowd exulted, for the great man walked in. Tendulkar got into his stride with a cover-drive and a square-drive while Dravid played a gorgeous straight-drive, a steer and a back cut to complete his 50. India went to lunch at 191 for 3, and both continued untroubled after lunch and played lovely shots. A cover-drive on bended knee by Tendulkar was followed by a delicate late-cut from Dravid. Forty years ago radio commentator Ananda Rao in his nasal drone would have described it for his listeners as 'delectable'. The youthful *Cricinfo* commentator, however, typed 'Yummy!', bringing an instant smile to the faces of people following the game at their office desks. The 'Yummy' shot was followed by a spurt of three boundaries from Tendulkar, who pulled out the sweep and slog from his arsenal.

India finally lost Dravid for 77 against the run of play, as he edged a ball from Bollinger that left him. Raina, playing only his third Test, walked out to join Tendulkar. He had a nervous start against the bouncer and mistimed a couple of shots dangerously, but Tendulkar guided him through that period. Soon he hit a couple of his elegant drives through covers and negotiated successfully till tea. Post tea, Raina was in sublime touch, playing exquisite shots on both sides of the wicket. India cruised past 300 and Raina scored most of the runs, surviving a stumping just before he got to fifty. Tendulkar then played one of his best shots of the day, an off-drive off Hilfenhaus that was utterly sumptuous – a stride forward, the left elbow high as the ball was met with the full face of the bat. Soon, however, there was agony for Tendulkar and the fans as he fell just two short of a century after the drinks break, leg before as he played across the line to the off spin of North.

Dhoni, not Laxman, came out; Laxman's back had been troubling him and he was in no condition to bat. Dhoni and Raina treated Hauritz harshly but Ponting brought back Johnson who immediately had Dhoni caught by Watson in the slips. Next ball, he removed Harbhajan, also caught by Watson in the slips. The scoreboard read 382 for 7 and still no Laxman. Zaheer, after some anxious moments, threw it away with a wild heave against Hauritz. Laxman finally had to come out with Gambhir as his runner. At the other end, Johnson took his fifth wicket by whipping one through to catch Raina in front of the stumps. Raina's spunky innings of 86 and his partnership with Tendulkar had been precious. Laxman's bad back was evident as he failed to stretch forward and gave a catch off Hauritz. Play on the third day ended with India all out for 405.

The fourth day was packed with action as 14 wickets fell and left the match poised on knife edge. Watson and Katich put on 87 in just 18 overs; Watson showing murderous intent as he powered his way to a run-a-ball fifty. However, Ishant struck three quick blows and turned the game on its head. Watson attempted a pull but could only direct the ball onto his stumps; two balls later, Ponting pulled Ishant into the hands off Raina at square-leg. In his next over, Ishant got Clarke with a brute of a bouncer that reared up at the batsman's face, which could only be blindly fended to Dhoni. From 87 for no loss, to 96 for 3. Ishant's spell of six overs, on either side of lunch, was relentlessly hostile. As Ram Mahesh had said of another such spell by Ishant, he opened the Australian innings like a can of beans.

The spinners came on and with Australia on 138, Ojha was rewarded for accurate bowling as Katich was caught behind off a thin edge. Six overs later, Hussey was out to a poor decision, given leg before to a ball from Harbhajan that pitched outside his legstump bringing the score to 154 for 5. In his next over, North, out of his depth against the spinners, was caught at short-leg and Australia went to tea at 165 for 6. In the first over after tea, Paine fell to Ojha as Pujara, the substitute, took a sharp reflex catch at silly-point. Zaheer came back from the other end and produced another master class in reverse swing. First, he got Johnson with a ball, shiny side outside, that moved away late from the left-hander; the edge went safely to Dhoni. Next over, he went round the wicket to Hauritz, pitched the ball on middle and reverse-swung it to take the offstump. He finished the sensational spell with a perfect yorker to Hilfenhaus that knocked out middle, his Test wicket No. 250.

India had 216 to get in the fourth innings with plenty of time left. But a roller coaster of a day had more surprises. In the first over, Hilfenhaus claimed Gambhir leg before, another poor decision as replays showed a big inside-edge onto the pad. Tails up, Hilfenhaus and Bollinger steamed in to test the batsmen with sharp bouncers and movement off length balls. Sehwag and Dravid hit a few boundaries and the innings seemed to be back on an even keel at 31 for 1. But that was illusory. Bollinger pitched one on a length that moved away; Dravid reached forward to defend and edged it to Paine. The innings received its next jolt as Sehwag guided a rising ball meekly to gully, a strange dismissal that was contrary to Sehwag's character. 42 for 3. Raina came in and was out third ball as he fended a bouncer from Hilfenhaus to North. Zaheer, the nightwatchman, survived a dropped catch and play ended with India 55 for 4.

India needed 160 runs on the final day with six wickets in hand. Bryan Coverdale in his bulletin for *Cricinfo* wrote, 'There will be a winner. The hard part is predicting whom.' Tendulkar started the day with a neat off-drive for four and followed it with an on-drive to the ropes, but with only 16 runs added, nightwatchman Zaheer left, caught at slip off Hauritz. Laxman came out with Raina as his runner. He marched out briskly as always – Ian Chappell said he walked to bat like a drill sergeant – but his movements were going to be difficult. A surge in the scoring occurred when in one over from Hauritz, Tendulkar played a classy straight-drive and Laxman hit two boundaries, the first a front-foot drive through cover, the second a back-foot drive to the same region. Bollinger replaced Hauritz and bowled a testing over, even as Hilfenhaus was bowling superbly at the other end. Of course, Laxman did not hesitate to pull or cut when offered the short delivery. The score had moved to 119, when Tendulkar, in a lapse of judgement, lost his wicket to Bollinger attempting a strange-looking cut.

When Dhoni walked out to the middle, Ponting brought in Johnson. Dhoni survived two testing overs but in the next over was run out. When a batsman has a runner, confusion is always on the cards. On this occasion, Raina and Dhoni's stop–start running was fatal for the latter. Roebuck scathingly called Raina 'a runner...as dangerous to the Indian cause as any Australian bowler'. A ball later, Harbhajan too was out as a lifter from Bollinger went off his gloves to Ponting in the slips. India were 124 for 8 and everybody sensed an imminent Australian victory.

Ishant at the crease doesn't usually inspire much confidence, but the tall tail-ender was an obdurate man with a good temperament, who put a price on his wicket. At the other end stood a fourth-innings magician who had conjured victories for India out of nowhere. Just two months ago, despite a troubled back, Laxman had hit a century to take India to a win in Sri Lanka. Would the challenge today – 92 runs with two wickets in hand – prove to be beyond even this conjuror?

Inscrutable and imperturbable, Laxman had a plan. Ponting spread the field, offering him a single and Laxman accepted every time, taking a run off either the first or second ball in eight consecutive overs, trusting Ishant to negotiate the rest of the over. By lunch, Sharma had played

35 balls and was on 14 with two fours, while Laxman had played only 16 balls – together, they had added 38 runs.

The pattern continued after lunch. In the first eight overs after lunch, Ishant played 36 balls while Laxman faced only 12. Ponting's tactics of spreading the field for Laxman did not work as he calmly took singles off the first ball and handed strike to the tail-ender. The two had added 31 more runs by now, when Laxman played a stunning pull of great authority and then caressed a cover-drive on the rise off Watson. Then Sharma steered a couple of boundaries through the gully and survived a scary bouncer from the pacy Johnson. Seeing Johnson trouble Ishant in the 53rd over, Laxman changed tactics when he faced Johnson next, refusing singles till the fourth ball. If the tension and pressure was unbearable for the spectators and viewers on television, how must it have been for the players? Ishant played out the remaining two balls. The score had moved to 203 for 8. Back against Hilfenhaus, Laxman reverted to taking a single off the first ball. Next ball Ishant was out to a poor leg before decision, as the ball was clearly missing leg. He had helped Laxman take India from the brink of defeat to within sight of victory, with an 81-run partnership in nearly two hours and 22 overs. Ojha survived the rest of the over and Laxman took all of Johnson the next over.

With six more runs needed, Laxman wanted a single off the fifth ball of Hilfenhaus but Ojha was slow and indecisive, and the opportunity was lost. For the only time in public memory, the monk-like calm of Laxman cracked as he berated Ojha with expletives – immortalized in a now-famous image of Laxman raising his bat at Ojha. But a minute later, the 'man of peace' had calmed down, patted Ojha, apologized and smiled at him.

In Johnson's next over, India received an incredible stroke of fortune as the umpire turned down a shout for leg before. Ojha seemed gone, but Bowden decided there was an inside-edge. Amidst the excitement, Steve Smith tried to throw down the stumps, missed and India were gifted four overthrows. One to tie, two to win. As the clock showed

1.37 p.m., Ojha and Raina ran the two leg-byes that took India to victory. Laxman, Raina and Ojha embraced and all the Indian players rushed to the ground. The Houdini of fourth-innings victories had created another masterpiece.

Laxman had the wisdom to recognize that he could not score all the runs by himself and that the tail-enders must play their parts. His strategy therefore was to trust them with the responsibility and provide them with confidence. It was only when 12 runs were required and only when Johnson caused some bother to Ishant that Laxman shielded his partner. To navigate the team to a win with only the tail for company calls for great inner strength. Sambit Bal wrote after the match, 'The splendour and the gorgeousness of his batting sometimes distract Laxman's admirers from the mental strength that is such a big part of his game.' Ian Chappell, always a huge admirer, wrote, 'Laxman's contribution to India's breath-taking victory went way beyond the runs he scored… His ability to middle the ball 99 times out of a hundred stood him in good stead, as he was unable to shift his feet very far… You have to see V.V.S. Laxman bat to understand his magic.'

Between us, we watched the entire match live on TV and did not move from our seats during the ninth-wicket partnership. Therefore when Sunil Gavaskar told a TV channel 'I think it has got to be the greatest win and among the greatest achievements in Indian sports', one understood the spirit of that pronouncement. Next day, *The Hindu* ran an editorial, 'The real thing', in praise of Test cricket. The *Times of India* called Test cricket the 'acme of the game' and pertinently added, 'Now, if the BCCI takes one lesson from this match, let it be that bland one-day tours must be shelved in favour of Test match series of three or more games.' Harsha Bhogle put this in perspective in the opening sentences of his review of the series: 'I feel like I've been invited to dinner, been offered a drink and starter, and then been thanked in the doorway by the host for coming. Two-Test series are neither here nor there, especially between two quality teams. They create a sense of anticipation and suddenly they are gone.'

Test No. 1972: PCA Stadium, Mohali, 1–5 October 2010: Australia
(Toss) 428 in 151.4 overs (Shane Watson 126, Tim Paine 92; Zaheer
Khan 5-94, Harbhajan Singh 3-114) and 192 in 60.5 overs (Watson
56, Simon Katich 37; Ishant Sharma 3-34, Zaheer 3-43) lost to
India 405 in 108.1 overs (Sachin Tendulkar 98, Suresh Raina 86;
Mitchell Johnson 5-64, Doug Bollinger 2-49) and 216/9 in 58.4
overs (V.V.S. Laxman 73*, Tendulkar 38; Ben Hilfenhaus 4-57,
Bollinger 3-32) by one wicket. **MotM:** Zaheer Khan.

Captains: M.S. Dhoni (India) and Ricky Ponting (Australia)

28

Top of the World

India vs South Africa, second Test, Kingsmead, Durban, 2010

Kingsmead 1996 and Kingsmead 2010. As we begin the last of our essays, it may be a good time to look at how much the Indian team had changed between these years. Fourteen years ago, at the same Kingsmead ground in Durban, a meek Indian team had been crushed for 100 and 66 in two innings. Then Eden Gardens 2001 happened, and India beat Australia 2-1. Suddenly things fell into place: the team discovered a new spirit, a well of self-belief had been sprung and they went unafraid on tours, confident they could win anywhere and under any conditions, which they did: Leeds 2002, Adelaide 2003, Multan 2004, Johannesburg 2006, Kingston 2007, Nottingham 2007, Perth 2008, Galle 2008 and Hamilton 2009. The one common thread that connected all the achievements during these ten years was the resilience that the Indian team exhibited. Where earlier, after losing the first Test, India would lose heart and fade away, the modern Indian team fought ferociously when down. This team took pride in its performance and hurt badly when it lost. Other teams began to fear India the most at such times. They lost at Lord's and hit back at Headingley; they lost in Colombo and roared back in Galle; and heartbroken at Sydney, they were like tempered steel in Perth.

The team became the No. 1 Test side in ICC rankings in December 2009 and defended this position through 2010. It now faced South Africa in a three-Test series, and if it did well, would round off 2010 as the world's top-ranked Test team. The record in South Africa did not inspire much confidence; India had won only one Test in three visits to that country, and South Africa, with its fast, bouncy, seaming tracks and strong pace bowling, had always been India's biggest challenge. The first Test at Centurion Park confirmed these fears as India lost by an innings. The only notable takeaway was that Tendulkar hit a landmark hundred – the 50th Test century of his career. Despite scoring 459 in their second innings, India lost by an innings, such was the gulf in the first innings.

The teams then moved to Kingsmead in Durban, which like Melbourne has the tradition of hosting the Boxing Day Test when teams visited their country. Kingsmead, as Ram Mahesh told his readers, was 'a gull's flap from the ocean'. The belief was that swing bowlers got assistance from the south-westerly breeze and the change of tide, somewhat like the 'Freemantle Doctor' – the afternoon breeze from the River Swan at the WACA in Perth.

Yet, when the Indians arrived in Durban, it was not a light breeze but rain that greeted them. When they inspected the ground, they were, to quote Anand Vasu from his report, 'greeted by the greenest Kingsmead pitch in recent memory'. Rain on the first day teased the groundsmen with its stop–start antics and play was delayed by an hour. Dhoni lost the toss and Graeme Smith, smiling broadly, sent the Indians in. On that grassy fast pitch and in overcast conditions, he would unleash Dale Steyn, Morne Morkel, Tsotsobe and Jacques Kallis on the Indians. 'Lot of moisture on the track, and tough overhead conditions,' said Dhoni, admitting that his batsmen had a tough task ahead. To compound matters, India were without Gambhir, whose hand had not healed from the injury he suffered in the first Test. Murali Vijay replaced him. On the positive side, Zaheer, the leader of the bowling unit, was back. How important he was to this team! In his absence, Sreesanth and

Ishant looked inadequate but with Zaheer in their ears, from mid-off or mid-on, the two became totally different bowlers.

Sehwag who usually never took first strike, did so in this game to shield Vijay from the nerves of facing the first ball. Sehwag winced in pain, as Steyn's opening delivery kicked up and hit him on the glove. The two openers began to apply themselves against testing bowling in difficult conditions. The batsmen survived some unplayable deliveries and a dropped catch too even as Sehwag put Morkel away for a couple of boundaries. Steyn was finally rewarded for superb bowling in his sixth over when Sehwag on 25 edged a drive to second slip as an outswinger left him. Steyn struck again in his next over, getting Vijay caught behind for 19. India were stumbling at 48 for 2. Dravid and Tendulkar looked more assured than the openers and they also played a few fine shots, to wit, Rahul's straight-drive and Sachin's upper cut off Morkel. India went to lunch at 74 for 2. However, in the first over after lunch, Tendulkar perished, attempting a drive off a ball from left-armer Tsotsobe that he could have left alone. It was to be a feature of India's innings – each of the first eight batsmen spent time in the middle and got into double digits, but either threw it away or lost their wicket to South African brilliance. The pitch challenged the batsmen right through, even someone like Dravid who was applying himself. Laxman played gorgeous shots – a pull and a back-foot punch to cover off Tsotsobe, followed by a crashing off-drive and a hard, flat, pulled six off Steyn. But Steyn broke through when Dravid, in a moment of indecision, gloved an away-swinging ball to Boucher. India were reduced to 117 for 4. Pujara – who had replaced Raina for this Test – joined Laxman and received a searching examination from the world's best fast bowler. Spin had been introduced a little earlier and Laxman, in great form, latched on to a flat delivery to pull it perfectly to the square-leg boundary to reach 38.

He then succumbed to a moment of sheer brilliance: Steyn bowled short and Laxman drilled a perfectly timed pull to mid-wicket. By rights it should have struck the hoarding on the fence, but Tsotsobe dived, stretched and flung his right hand out to pluck an amazing catch out of thin air. Laxman was felled in full flight; he was the one batsman who had looked in command and his wicket ensured that the Indian innings would not prosper. Dhoni and Pujara grimly hung together, the latter slowly gaining confidence, not hesitating to hook or cut when the ball was banged short. Yet, he too threw it away, top-edging a pull off Tsotsobe to the keeper. By tea, India, at 168 for 6, seemed to have surrendered the advantage to South Africa. It was gloomy and overcast, the floodlights had come on and three overs after tea, play was called off for the day.

Next morning, the light was a far sight better than the first day. It was only a matter of time before Steyn dismissed Harbhajan, the thick edge travelled fast but a diving de Villiers at third slip took the catch with both hands. Steyn had his five-wicket haul in the innings. Zaheer fell to Morkel in the next over, and Dhoni realizing the innings would finish soon tried to get some runs. A top-edged hook was followed by a six over long-off but when he aimed a slash at Steyn, it ended up in Alviro Petersen's hands at deep point. India were all out for 205 when Sreesanth fell first ball to Morkel.

South Africa's openers began by taking a few boundaries off a wayward Sreesanth but in Zaheer's third over, Smith was caught behind of a ball of lovely length and line that moved away – Smith would remain, in cricketing parlance, Zaheer's 'bunny'. Amla came in at 23 for 1, and hit Sreesanth off successive balls to the cover boundary. Zaheer again provided India a breakthrough, bowling Petersen off his pads. 46 for 2. That brought Kallis and Amla together.

Ishant replaced Sreesanth, while after a spell of seven overs Zaheer made way for Sreesanth. Immediately, India received a huge stroke of fortune. Amla imperiously drove the first ball of Ishant to the cover boundary. The next ball was smashed back by the batsman but Sharma got his fingertips to it before it crashed into the stumps at the bowler's end. Kallis, backing up, was caught out of his ground. South Africa received another jolt in the next over, the result of a terrific delivery from Sreesanth, who could exasperate his captain with poor deliveries but also had the knack of bowling unplayable deliveries. De Villiers, not yet off the mark, got a lethal leg-cutter that pitched on off, bounced and took his glove on its way to Dhoni. That was lunch. South Africa were 74 for 4 and India had fought back.

Ashwell Prince and Amla had taken South Africa to 92 for 4 after lunch when Dhoni brought Harbhajan to bowl. In his second over, Harbhajan got Amla with a ball that pitched on the stumps and kept going straight. Amla missed the sweep and was leg before. Then Zaheer, who had come back into attack, got Prince with a splendidly conceived piece of bowling. After planting doubt in Prince's mind with balls going either way, he bowled one on a length that pinned the batsman on the crease. The ball held its line and bowled Prince off the inside-edge. The South African innings was in tatters at 100 for 6. Harbhajan then mopped up the tail, taking out Steyn, Harris and Tsotsobe. He had figures of 4 for 10. Ishant took Morkel but the credit for that wicket too should go to Harbhajan, who plucked an amazing catch on the fine-leg boundary after covering many yards. Dravid's catch to dismiss Steyn was the 200th catch of his Test career and one of his finest. As the edge flew between slip and keeper, Dravid dived to his left and behind Dhoni to pull off a stunning catch. It was a piece of brilliance that one can watch on YouTube with undiminished pleasure. Dravid's catching prowess, like his batting, was the result of lifelong practice. He told us: 'You would never ever have seen me without a ball when I was a child. I was always bouncing and catching it from any surface all day long. Tucked into this is the important point about practice with a tennis ball. If some of us learnt to catch cricket balls with soft hands, the answer lies in the fact that we practised with tennis balls that tend to bounce and pop out of the hands; we learnt to "give" as the ball came to us and this virtue remained with us when we caught cricket balls.'

Sehwag and Vijay opened India's second innings with the reassuring cushion of a 74-run lead, Sehwag banging Steyn for a boundary in his first over. He continued in that merry way, flicking Steyn for a boundary and for good measure flaying him again to point and glancing him for more boundaries. Just when it looked Sehwag would take the game away, Tsotsobe suckered him with a wide short ball that he edged to Boucher, out for a 31-ball 32. Sehwag's wicket sucked the momentum out of India's innings. The pitch was still helping the bowlers and sure enough, a brutal delivery from Morkel reared up at Vijay's head and he could only fend it to short-leg. Then Dravid, completely against character, played an extravagant waft at a ball from Tsotsobe to get caught. Steyn in his second spell struck first ball, getting Tendulkar who went for a drive to a ball that seemed right for the stroke but edged it to de Villiers at third slip. At 56 for 4, India were in danger of losing the ground they had gained before lunch.

It was midway in the session between lunch and tea, but already 18 wickets had fallen in the day. All 22 players had come to the crease at least once during the day. Laxman, whose first innings of 38 was easily the best of the match, carried that form into his second knock. He played an exquisite cover-drive off Kallis and followed this with a pull and whip to mid-wicket off the left-arm spinner Harris. Already Mike Haysman and Allan Donald were arguing on TV – Haysman saying Laxman was famous for his second-innings exploits and Donald saying one was 'bound to get a ball with one's name on it'. The wit on the *Cricinfo* commentary typed this after Donald's retort: 'I might know why Laxman seldom gets that ball in the second innings. Try writing Vangipurappu Venkata Sai Laxman on a ball. You will run out of space or ink or patience.' The day ended with India 165 ahead with six wickets in hand. Importantly, Laxman was not out on 23.

The third day began badly for India as they lost Pujara early to Morkel: 98 for 5. Crucially, Pujara had occupied 81 minutes at the crease and allowed Laxman to play freely at the other end. Steyn induced a couple of mishits from Laxman without causing grief. He then tested Dhoni with in-cutter and outswinger. Dhoni tried to attack his way out of trouble with a couple of boundaries but Steyn kept at him. After a superb four-over spell, Morkel replaced him. Laxman unfurled a square-drive off the back foot, all silken grace. Seeing that shot, one can understand why Ian Chappell was so moved by Laxman's extraordinary hand–eye coordination: 'If he'd been lost to cricket and become a doctor, as so nearly happened, he'd have been a brilliant surgeon.'

At the other end, Tsotsobe had Dhoni caught behind, pushing at a delivery that was slanted across him. Tsotsobe, one felt, was reaping 'soft wickets' because of the pressure created by Steyn and Morkel at the other end. A few balls later, Harbhajan's short stay ended, Kallis catching him off Morkel. 148 for 7, Laxman not out on 47 and once again left with the tail. Yet again – one loses count – Laxman forged an uncanny partnership with the tail. This time it was Zaheer, knuckling down to support Laxman. He faced more balls than Laxman, and had a few hits to the fence too. When they went back for lunch, the two had added 70 runs in 19 overs and taken India close to a 300-run lead. Zaheer fell in the second over after lunch to left-arm spinner Harris.

For those looking for interesting coincidences and statistical trivia, Zaheer and Laxman had added exactly 70 runs at the Wanderers too in that wonderful 2006 win. Zaheer, in a tribute to Laxman when his Eden Gardens' knock was rated the finest Test knock of the past 50 years, said, 'Laxman had great mental strength and a will to succeed. In tough situations he would somehow find an extra focus, a determination to do well. We believed that he could somehow save us. That was Laxman throughout his career.'

When Kallis bounced out Ishant, India became 222 for 9, and Laxman was nine short of a ton. Sreesanth survived but it was Laxman who got out. After sweeping Harris for a four and crossing over for a single, Laxman failed in an attempt to cut Steyn for the boundary that would have got him to his century. Boucher took the edge. Earlier in this book we called Viswanath's 97 not out against West Indies as the best 'non-hundred' by an Indian bat. This one ranks as high, for this too was achieved on a seamer-friendly track against high-quality fast bowling. Laxman has himself said Durban was among the toughest wickets he had ever played on. Dileep Premachandran, turning a pen thoughtfully between his fingers, told us that this knock would be among the greatest by an Indian in recent memory.

How did Laxman do this again and again? Sharda Ugra wrote, 'When Laxman takes the stage in his moment, he can conjure up the illusion that the crisis is not being tackled, it is being ignored. That fretting over it is all quite trivial. Like a genteel sorcerer pulling streams of silk out of a hat, his hands create gaps in the field that captains and bowlers cannot conceptualise, let alone attempt to cover.'

The stage was set: 303 to win, on a pitch where 30 wickets had fallen for just 564 runs. A tough task, but Kingsmead was the venue where South Africa had scored 340 to beat Australia in 2002. Smith and Petersen began with purpose, Smith as though wanting to put Zaheer out of the attack. After six overs the Proteas were 35 for none, Smith on 24 with five boundaries. Zaheer had gone for 24 off three overs. After 11 overs, the South Africans were 58 for no loss and Dhoni introduced Harbhajan. Off the first ball of Sreesanth's next over, also the last over before tea, Smith was dismissed. His mistimed pull spiralled high before settling into Dhoni's gloves.

After tea, Amla treated spectators to two lovely shots, a cover-drive and a straight-drive in an over from Sreesanth. However, Harbhajan struck in the following over, disposing of Petersen as the batsman failed to negotiate the bounce the off spinner generated. In Sreesanth's next over, Amla gave it away, attempting a cut off a wide delivery, short and swinging away, and edging it behind. From 63 for no loss, South Africa had slid to 82 for 3 in five overs. When bad light ended play, South Africa were 111 for 3, requiring 192 to win.

Day four began under blue skies and bright sunshine. Sreesanth and Harbhajan opened the attack against Kallis and de Villiers, and in the eighth over, the former produced a beast of a ball out of nowhere. From short of length, it leapt at Kallis's throat. Even as he arched his back to evade it, the ball was upon him and Kallis could do no more than glove it in a gentle arc to Sehwag at gully. There is a wicked YouTube clip that shows this in agonizing detail in slow motion. Sreesanth, wacky, weird, exasperating, but also bowler of the unplayable ball, getting de Villiers in the first innings, and Kallis in the second. Anand Vasu called this 'the ball of the series'.

In the first over after drinks, Harbhajan bowling round the wicket hit the pads of de Villiers, and though replays showed the ball would have gone over middle, South Africa copped a rough one from umpire Asad Rauf. They slid to 136 for 5. At the other end, Zaheer replaced Sreesanth. It was now the turn of umpire Steve Davis to hand out a poor lbw decision to send Boucher on his way. The wheels were coming off quickly. While Prince was intent on defence, Steyn was being worked over by Zaheer with a variation of length and movement both ways. After 25 minutes of this, Zaheer got his man with a full ball that was edged to Pujara at third slip. The *Cricinfo* commentator, relishing this duel, typed, 'The entire Steyn vs Zaheer contest has been riveting to watch. Zaheer gets the bragging rights here.'

Ishant and Sreesanth were now bowling in tandem. There was short-pitched bowling and chatter at the wicket too. A yorker was slipped in and there were more stares and glares. In the commentary this gave scope for some droll humour: 'These guys are good friends, I tell you!' Harris continued to be peppered with more bouncers, and not all were well directed. At lunch, South Africa were 180 for 7.

Zaheer was, after Wasim Akram, the best exponent of left-arm bowling from round the wicket and reverse swing. Straight after lunch, he scalped Harris with a perfect ball. Pitching on middle, it moved away to take the off stump's bail. Morkel and Prince resisted stoutly playing out the next 11 overs before Ishant claimed Morkel, caught behind off a ball that straightened after pitching. Two balls later it was all over as last man Tsotsobe was run out by the short-leg fielder Pujara.

India had pulled off a stunning victory in conditions that were tailor-made for the hosts. After the victory, Dhoni said, 'We will party in the night but not get drunk.' That statement conveyed a lot more. Four years ago in Johannesburg, the Indians celebrated in berserk fashion, pouring drinks over themselves and all the upholstery. This time their celebrations were calmer, for after all they were the No. 1 team in the world and had got used to winning regularly. Kirsten's and Upton's theory was that the Indian team's psyche was such that they produced their best performances in retaliation. There is evidence to support this only from 2001 onwards though, and not earlier. It began with Ganguly's team and was then demonstrated by the teams that were so ably led by Dravid, Kumble and Dhoni.

As Kingsmead emptied out that evening, the year was coming to a close. India could look back at 2010 with satisfaction. They had not lost a series during the year and they had retained their No. 1 Test ranking. As it turned out, it was the last overseas victory for Tendulkar, Sehwag and Zaheer. Though Laxman and Dravid were part of the win against West Indies in Jamaica in 2011, the winds of change had already started to take their effect, and India conceded their No.1 status to England after a 0-4 whitewash soon after winning the World Cup. It was the end of an era. There is still the unfinished business of winning a series in South Africa and Australia. Perhaps Kohli and the next generation of Indian cricketers would achieve that. It would be a fitting tribute to the wonderful teams of 2001–10.

Test No. 1987: Kingsmead, Durban, 26–29 December 2010:
India (Toss) 205 in 65.1 overs (V.V.S. Laxman 38, M.S. Dhoni 35; Dale Steyn 6-50, Lonwabo Tsotsobe 2-40) and 228 in 70.5 overs (Laxman 96, Virender Sehwag 32; Tsotsobe 3-43, Morne Morkel 3-47) beat **South Africa** 131 in 37.2 overs (Hashim Amla 33, Alviro Petersen 24; Harbhajan Singh 4-10, Zaheer Khan 3-36) and 215 in 72.3 overs (Ashwell Prince 39*, Graeme Smith 37; S. Sreesanth 3-45, Zaheer 3-57) by 87 runs. **MotM:** V.V.S. Laxman.

Captains: M.S. Dhoni (India) and Graeme Smith (South Africa)

Looking Back to Look Ahead

When the British brought the game to India, they did not imagine we would embrace it with such passion. Our love for the game since India began playing Test cricket was totally unconditional, especially in the first 40 years – India did not win a Test for 20 years after making their debut at Lord's in 1932, nor did India win a Test overseas till 1968. But Merchant, Amarnath, Hazare, Mankad, Pataudi, Durani, Borde and others remained hugely popular, and the stands overflowed when these cricketers played first-class cricket. Indian fans supported their team even when they weren't winning games. The first signs of progress were in the 1960s when India evolved from a coterie of talented individuals into a cohesive unit under Pataudi. With the arrival of a world-class spin quartet and a cordon of superb close-in catchers, India, during the 1970s, translated its undoubted potential into Test victories both at home and abroad.

For India, the 1983 World Cup win was a seminal moment. Limited-overs cricket impacted every aspect of the sport – fielding, running between wickets, innovative strokeplay, bowling variations – and contributed positively to a much more dynamic game in Tests. From an average run rate of around 2.4 runs an over in the 1960s, run rates rose over the next 30–40 years to over 3.3 runs an over. In the 1950s and 1960s, less than 60 per cent of the games ended in a result but in the period 2001–10 over 75 per cent of the Tests were decisive. For all our nostalgia and fondness for the wonderful amateurs who adorned our game, it is the talent, commitment, work ethic and dynamism of the modern-day professional cricketer that is mind-boggling. With one-day cricket capturing the imagination of everyone, it was no longer the game of cities and the middle class. Talent was unleashed from everywhere and some of India's best cricketers have emerged from small towns. The modern cricketer is not a defensive, attritional cricketer but a dynamic sportsman, representative of an aspirational environment.

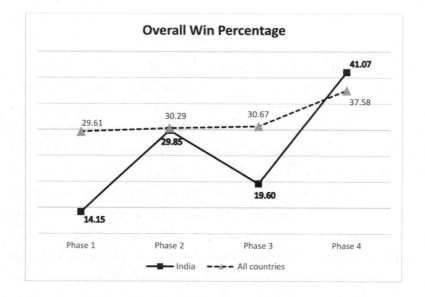

From 1932 to 2000, India only won 11 Tests out of 150 games played overseas, but in the years 2001–10, India won 22 Tests of the 62 they played abroad, and registered a victory in every Test-playing nation.

The impact of technology on sport in the last 20 years has been profound, and we've seen it in cricket too, be it in its use for umpiring or the quality of bats or the development of protective gear. Trumper and Nayudu would wonder, if they saw the game today, whether aliens were playing a vaguely familiar-looking game. Yet, the innate beauty and essence of the game has remained the same. That essence is the contest between bat and ball; the team that has the ability to consistently take

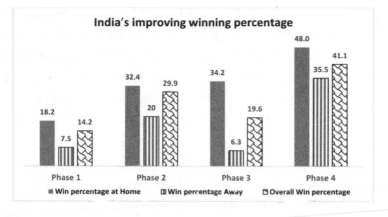

20 wickets will win Tests more often than others. We analysed data across these four eras to see if a clear pattern would emerge and indeed, the numbers revealed illuminating insights.

In the period till the late 1950s, India's Test cricketers, especially the batsmen, were still largely from West Zone. West Zone played most of their cricket on turf but despite their greater experience on turf, and their strong performances at home, technically sound batsmen like Hazare, Manjrekar and Borde were not successful abroad. Unlike at home, they often came to bat early against the new ball after the openers were dismissed quickly, on pitches that favoured seam and swing. This affected their performance and their overseas batting averages were inferior to their home averages. Manjrekar and Borde averaged less than 30 in away matches. Umrigar was the only batsmen of that period who had an away average over 40.

In the 1960s, the only other batsmen who batted well abroad and whose overseas average was in the high 30s were Pataudi and Sardesai. In much the same vein, till 1968, Indian bowlers did not have the wherewithal to get 20 wickets in a game regularly. On an average, they only took around 12 wickets per Test with spinners doing the bulk of the job. The spin bowling in that period was strong but success was limited due to indifferent fielding. It was finally in 1968 on the tour to New Zealand that India registered their first series victory abroad.

The arrival of Gavaskar, Viswanath and Amarnath, the brief but critical resurgence of Sardesai and a world-class close-catching cordon to support the magical spin quartet, is when things changed. For the first time, the 1970s saw Indian batsmen and bowlers – Gavaskar, Viswanath, Bedi, Chandra – figure among the world's top five in their respective categories. Spin still accounted for more than 70 per cent of the wickets abroad but the dismissals through catches jumped up to 60 per cent in the 1970s from 50 per cent in the earlier decades, a clear result of the superb close-catching support. India during this decade averaged nearly 14 wickets per game and won 30 per cent of the Tests they played.

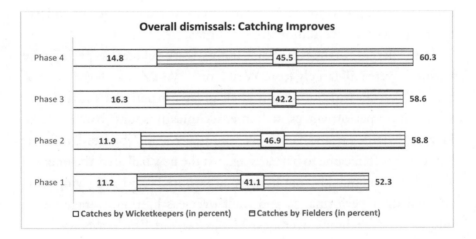

Overall dismissals: Catching Improves

	Catches by Wicketkeepers (in percent)	Catches by Fielders (in percent)	Total
Phase 4	14.8	45.5	60.3
Phase 3	16.3	42.2	58.6
Phase 2	11.9	46.9	58.8
Phase 1	11.2	41.1	52.3

Gavaskar brought a new dimension to batting. He was the first Indian to master foreign pitches and pace and had a storybook start in the Caribbean Islands in 1971. He is recognized as among the three greatest openers in Test history. His overseas average of 52.1 is only marginally less than Tendulkar's and Dravid's. While 13 of his 34 Test 100s came against the feared West Indian pace attacks of the 1970s and 1980s, Gavaskar has an unmatched average of 72.21 in the fourth innings. He carried India's batting like a colossus from his debut in 1971 till his retirement in 1987. Mohinder Amarnath is the only other Indian

Overall Figures – Batsmen > 20 Tests and Away Average > 40.0

Player	Span	Matches	Runs	Highest Score	Average	100	50	Average in Away Tests
S.R. Tendulkar	1989–2013	200	15,921	248*	53.78	51	68	54.74
R. Dravid	1996–2012	163	13,265	270	52.63	36	63	53.03
S.M. Gavaskar	1971–1987	125	10,122	236*	51.12	34	45	52.11
M. Amarnath	1969–1988	69	4,378	138	42.50	11	24	51.86
S.M. Patil	1980–1984	29	1,588	174	36.93	4	7	47.38
A.M. Rahane	2013–2015	22	1,619	147	44.97	6	7	46.37
V. Sehwag	2001–2013	103	8,503	319	49.43	23	31	44.65
G. Gambhir	2004–2014	56	4,046	206	42.58	9	21	43.61
V. Kohli	2011–2015	41	2,994	169	44.02	11	12	43.00
V.V.S. Laxman	1996–2012	134	8,781	281	45.97	17	56	42.49
S.C. Ganguly	1996–2008	113	7,212	239	42.17	16	35	41.56
P.R. Umrigar	1948–1962	59	3,631	223	42.22	12	14	40.76

batsman, apart from Tendulkar, Dravid and Gavaskar, with an overseas batting average above 50, thanks to his heroic exploits against hostile pace in West Indies and Pakistan. The batsman who comes closest to these four batsmen is Sandeep Patil with an average of 47.38, thanks to blistering centuries in Australia and England in the early 1980s.

The coming of Kapil coincided with the fading away of the spin quartet. Over the next two decades, India did not have the spinners to win matches abroad and although pacemen took more wickets, India was back to its 1960s' predicament of taking only an average of around 12 to 13 wickets per Test overseas. Nothing explains this better than a comparison with the 1970s. The spin quartet took an average of 9 wickets per game at a strike rate of 87 balls per wicket. But in the 1980–2000 period, spinners took an average of 4 wickets per game at a strike rate of 106 balls per wicket. During the same period, the pacemen – Kapil, Ghavri, Madan Lal, Chetan Sharma, Srinath and others – took around 8 wickets per game on average at a strike rate of 74 balls per wicket. India were able to win a few games abroad in the 1980s but in the 1990s they never came anywhere close to winning a game outside India, barring a solitary win each in Sri Lanka and Zimbabwe. As the 1990s came to a close, India had reconciled themselves to being tigers at home and lambs abroad; the public too chose to immerse itself in the glory of individual exploits of Tendulkar and gave individual records and milestones more importance than team achievements (except when the World Cup came up every four years).

The last phase, the golden decade of 2001–10, is therefore all the more remarkable. It came after the game had been desecrated by match-fixing; the team, after Kolkata 2001, realized what it was capable of and as captain, coach and senior players formed a most responsible and determined unit, they found the Gestalt magic of their 'whole being greater than the sum of their individual parts'. Sehwag arrived in 2001, and in 2002 was in a masterstroke catapulted to opener and the dynamic of the Indian batting changed completely. The Fab Four, coming to bat on a platform laid by Sehwag and opening his partner, became the most feared middle order in Test history. Finally, the bowling combination and balance was forged, especially for the away games. What Srinath started, Zaheer took to fruition as he allied forces with Nehra, Pathan, Sreesanth, Agarkar and R.P. Singh. The pacemen regularly snared nine wickets in away games; the spinners – Kumble and Harbhajan, mostly solo or occasionally as a team with support from Tendulkar and Sehwag – captured an average of six wickets per game. What this meant was that for the first time in 70 years, India was able to dismiss, on an average, 15 opposing batsmen in away games. The strike rate improved dramatically to around 65 balls per wicket from 90 balls per wicket in the 1990s. Thus, efficient bowling complemented fabulous batting, and voila, India began winning games regularly, in every cricketing nation.

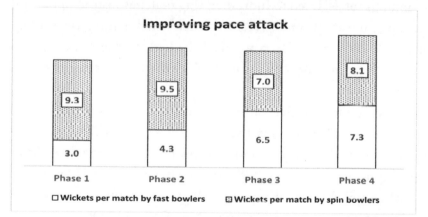

All the top-order batsmen – No. 1 to No. 6 – were averaging above 40 abroad with Tendulkar and Dravid hitting career averages of 54.7 and 53 respectively. India's average partnerships for the first five wickets during this period were not only the best ever, but wicket for wicket, better than what the opposition could score against India. The scoring rates all round the world had increased from 2.4 in the 1950s to 3.3 in the 2000s; India did not lag behind and in fact always had a jump-start, thanks to Sehwag, who gave India a blazing 4 to 5 runs an over

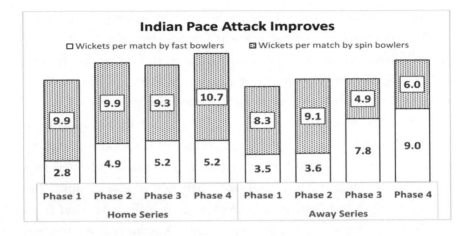

when he was at the crease. He scored his runs at an incredible 82 per 100 balls and the momentum he provided was the platform for huge first-innings totals. It led to India dictating matches instead of playing catch-up as in earlier times. When Wisden voted Sehwag the leading cricketer of 2009, Scyld Berry wrote, 'If he had an identical twin who batted at the same rate as Viru in 2009, India would score 600 in a day of 90 overs.'

Something precious that turned the scales on India's performances abroad during 2001–10 was the team spirit, the will to win and confidence that the captains and coaches instilled in the side. After regressing in the 1980s and 1990s to glorifying individual heroics of Gavaskar, Kapil, Azhar and Tendulkar, India and its players recognized the primacy of team success. Ganguly, Dravid, Kumble, Dhoni and now Kohli, all leaders who communicated only one goal: become the best team we can. There have been no larger-than-life ego clashes in these last 15 years as one had seen in earlier times. Selfless cricket also meant fearless cricket. Batting first on a green top in Leeds 2002 was a prime example of that. The other striking evidence of this confidence is that India inserted the opposition as an attacking option and not merely to avoid playing on a juiced-up track. In the same vein, when inserted by the opposition, the Indian team played with spirit and regularly turned the tables on them. During 2001–10, off the 26 occasions that India either inserted the opposition or were forced to bat first, they won on 11 occasions.

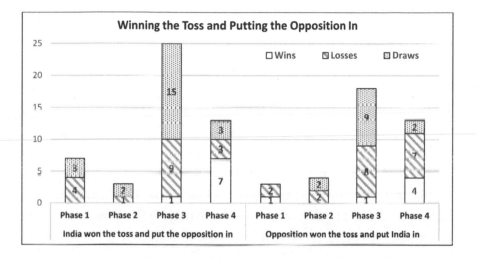

When Wisden nominated their World XI in 2008, as many as five players from India – Sehwag, Tendulkar, Dhoni, Harbhajan and Zaheer – found a place, and in their 2009 World XI, four Indian players – Schwag, Tendulkar, Dhoni and Gambhir – were included.

Our narrative comes to an almost natural closure with the 2010–11 season. It is an inflection point in Indian cricket as the Fabulous Four, Sehwag, Zaheer, Harbhajan and others were fading away after illustrious careers. India had to rebuild. They needed a new, stable opening pair as well as batsmen who could average 50; they again needed bowlers who could take wickets abroad. Even great teams like Australia and South Africa have taken time during such transitions. India too required that time; they have also endured the pain of 0-4 drubbings in England and Australia. Dhoni has made way for Kohli. The early signs since Kohli took over in 2014 indicate that the young captain is a clear-thinking leader with intent and passion. India are again on the upswing. A heartening performance in Australia in 2014 – though they lost 2-0 – and a series triumph in Sri Lanka and a home series win against South

Africa in 2015 augurs well. There are signs that a promising nucleus is emerging; between Kohli, Vijay, Rahane and Pujara, India has a batting outfit for all conditions. Ashwin is at the peak of his prowess and a proven match-winner. If he can bowl abroad as well as he has in the subcontinent and is supported by spinners Jadeja and Mishra and by the promising pace attack of Shami, Bhuvaneshwar, Ishant and Umesh Yadav, India will win overseas. Kohli with his positive intent is making it clear that he wants 20 wickets every time he steps on to a Test ground. He will have his sights set on a series win in South Africa and Australia, a feat no Indian team has achieved. It is once again an exciting period for India and its young guns.

Meanwhile, the effects of T20 on our cricketers cannot be ignored. While truly versatile and talented cricketers like Kohli, Rahane and Ashwin can adapt to all formats, and have in fact raised their cricket by bringing in strengths from their T20 experience, lesser cricketers could be permanently damaged. How will young batsmen brought up on T20 learn to build an innings; what about the technique to patiently negotiate hostile seam bowling conditions or the skill to play on difficult dusty turners? What about leaving the swinging ball outside offstump? In the last few years, Indian batsmen have struggled as much against spin (be it Nathan Lyon, Rangana Herath or Moeen Ali) as against high-quality pace, be it Anderson in England or Johnson and Starc in Australia. The bowlers brought up on T20 face their own problems. Trained to bowl dot balls for containment, they do not have a repertoire or the practice to vary their length, line or spin in the longer game. Spinners need to play matches to hone the art of flight, drift and variations in spin, but T20 has frozen that. The domestic calendar is subservient to the packed international calendar and therefore top players don't play the longer version of domestic cricket any longer. While fielding and boundary-line catching have improved unrecognizably, close catching conversely has not improved, as the shorter version of the game hardly has a role for short-leg or silly-point. Unless the pitch plays a part – a raging turner or a green seaming wicket – the game is tilting the way of batsmen. Even when bowlers beat batsmen, the edge carries to the fence because of the monstrous bats. The compressed willows have a bow and an edge so thick and formidable that bowlers are fodder for the cannon.

Limited-overs game has the money. India is the economic fulcrum and the public in India seem to enjoy the frenetic whirligig compressed into a few hours. Two years ago, we argued that Test cricket would survive; that in fact cricket would survive only if Test cricket survived. We pointed out that the crowds in Melbourne, Trent Bridge and Lord's for Test matches were undiminished; that Boxing Day Tests at Melbourne and Durban were marquee events in those nations' sporting calendar.

We are less sure now. Unless Test cricket survives and thrives in India, it will not have a future. Ask any cricketer and he will tell you in complete earnestness that Test cricket is the ultimate challenge. Ask him what hurts and he will recall the 0-4 hiding at England and the 0-4 routing in Australia in 2012–13. Ask him to recall similar painful matches from India's bilateral one-day series, and he will be hard-pressed to recall one. There is a permanence to Test cricket that cannot be expected from the 50- or 20-over bilateral games. The World Cup tournaments in the 50-overs version and the T20 version are absolutely brilliant and certainly have a critical salience, but bilateral one-day games are meaningless, without the lasting impact and relevance that come from Tests.

Of course, the public too has to buy this. When Amla and de Villiers batted for hours against Ashwin and Jadeja on a turner at Nagpur in November 2014, hardly scoring a run but demonstrating tremendous skills to stay and save a game, they made for edge-of-the-seat viewing, but for how many? How many would watch this sort of a game, or would they prefer the thrills of an IPL jamboree?

We have a problem, and we cannot wish it away. In this age of TV watching, sponsorship money and media hype, who will watch Tests, even if they produce results? If crowds do not come to the grounds, can the present team of players and support staff be a sustainable proposition? What must we do to ensure Test cricket does not merely survive but thrive? The best answers to these questions will come from the committed and ambitious cricketer who believes Test cricket is the acme of the game. Someone like Kohli, who is committed to Test cricket and excels in every format of the game, will have as many good ideas as a recently retired Dravid or the older thinkers like Venkataraghavan and Bedi.

We set the ball rolling here with a few suggestions and if some of them seem desperate that only means we have a desperate problem: (i) play Test cricket in the more traditional centres, where there is a better chance of the public coming to watch the longer version, while reserving the limited-overs games for other venues; (ii) do not telecast the Test match live in the city (at least till noon) where it is being played; so if there is a game at Chinnaswamy Stadium, the match will not be beamed live into homes in Bengaluru; (iii) have a cap of 125 overs for the first innings of the Test match as this will leave at least two days for the teams to go for a result; (iv) all players must participate in a minimum number of first-class games in a season to qualify for national Test selection; (v) give children under the age of 15 free admission to Test matches when accompanied by parents; (vi) designate certain dates in the calendar for Test matches as a tradition: Pongal at the Chidambaram Stadium, 1 January at Eden Gardens, and so on, just as Australia and South Africa have designated Boxing Day Tests.

From a perspective of building capable Test teams, some thoughts could be around the possibility of players being selected for Test cricket only after playing a certain number of longer-version first-class games. Thus, a hugely talented player like Shreyas Iyer would know that only his exploits in Ranji Trophy and Duleep Trophy will land him in a Test squad, while his IPL exploits can get him a place in the ODI and T20 squads. If there are some very talented opening batsmen and spinners whose technical abilities could get eroded by limited-overs games, BCCI could keep them exclusively for Tests but compensate them with a handsome contract so that they do not lose out on the lucrative limited-overs cricket. The most knowledgeable coaches and cricketers have emphasized that the players must learn the basic skills before venturing into innovations. Thus batsmen must first learn to use their feet well to play back and forward, learn balance, wrist-work, correct grip and back-lift. This thorough grounding is necessary before they attempt the 'dilscoop' or the reverse sweep; so the thousands of youngsters and more importantly their pushy and ambitious parents must be made to watch the longer version of the game (lure them to the ground with whatever incentives necessary) to appreciate that a limited-overs career will in fact be more likely if the youngster has a good grip of the longer version. As Venkataraghavan told us, Richards, Lloyd, Greenidge and Tendulkar were perfectly prepared by the longer version and that is why they were so good at the shorter version.

Finally, for India to spot and groom promising Test players, the IPL or the Junior World Cup is not the place to search. It has to be the performances in three-day games in domestic tournaments and the matches that the India 'A' and India Under-19 squads play at home and under a variety of testing conditions abroad. Selection to these squads will come on the back of consistent performances in Ranji Trophy and Dulcep Trophy games. It is the exposure and examination of promising talent in these longer-version games against international opposition that will give us our next crop of quality Test players.

Last Word

Sharda Ugra

The bewitching list that makes up India's great Test matches in this book contains for the reader both collective history and individual memory. In among the 28 terrific Tests are 13 away victories; the first three clustered together from 1971 to 1979, two in the 1980s and the next eight from 2000 onwards. To a generation growing up in the 1990s and the headiness of the Tendulkar era, away Test victories were – never mind rare – as good as invisible. As the decade wore on, the solitary Test won in July 1993 at the SSC in Colombo became a mirage – was it really there? Did it really happen?

The onset of the new millennium under India's golden generation marked the start of a mission to be better, more durable travellers. India, under Sourav Ganguly, remained tough to beat at home and became handsomely competitive overseas. Thirteen Test wins outside home in six decades were, in the first decade of the 2000s, followed by 19 under Ganguly and Rahul Dravid. Goodbye, bad memories of 1990s' away tours. Don't come back. Not even in a bonsai-replica pop-up of the same.

But they did. For a hairy period of three years – between June 2011 and December 2014, when in 32 Tests,* India won 11 of 15 at home

---

* http://stats.espncricinfo.com/ci/engine/team/6.html?class=1;spanmax2=30+Nov+2014;spanmin2=10+Jul+2011;spanval2=span;template=results;type=team

and lost 13 off 17 away. Among those results lay a particularly painful home series defeat to England, the first in three decades. It was the result of creating overcooked turning wickets at home, which would work against most touring teams. Against England with Graeme Swann and Monty Panesar and a line-up of batsmen far more adept at handling the turning ball than India's successors to Dravid and VVS, that plan fell face forward. Bring on gloomsville.

Fortunately, that remained bonsai-sized too; India's twin troughs at the time – 4-0, 4-0 in England and Australia – were the fallout of the rapid fading of the batting quartet and the ageing of its golden generation, the roots of its travelling turnaround. As its most accomplished batsmen have moved away from the game, India has moved on, too - to a road rarely contemplated, which is where we are today.

If the Ganguly era was built around and dominated by the scoreboard pressure of bat-once bat-big, India's Test cricket mulls over an altered identity. Its Test team today acknowledges that as much as the batsmen are lionized, it's the bowlers who own the roar. That India's bowling strengths are best applied when the batsmen are made to do a slightly larger share of heavy lifting themselves, with five specialists packed in rather than a safer six. Followed by an optimistic all-rounder thrown into the line-up. Not all the time, every time, but wherever that tactic is deemed fit and must be responded to with confidence.

It began during Dhoni's last full series as captain on the 2014 tour of England. It led to the mirthful heist that became a rare Indian Test victory at Lord's, only the second time in 17 Tests. Indian cricket's New Deal has achieved its full expression and reward for Dhoni's successor in Sri Lanka. If a leader has to be identified for this fresh approach to India's Test cricket, it is Virat Kohli. And Adelaide 2014 marks the formal inauguration of what promises to be an age of exploration and discovery for the Indian Test team. In a heady chase of 364, in which India fell short by 48 runs, Kohli led the way in a full-on, frontal charge. He produced his second century of the Test, and was to say later that it was the only way to tackle the Australians and send out a message. In going for the win, his team and he, Kohli said, were not afraid of losing.

Post-Adelaide, Dhoni was to return as captain, the five-bowler formula was abandoned for two Tests and the series lost. Formally appointed as India's new Test match captain after Dhoni's mid-series Test retirement, Kohli was able to put the New Deal to full use on the tour of Sri Lanka and has remained wedded to the gamble. The group of Indian cricketers who usually call themselves the 'labour class' – that is, the bowlers – have been given a special pedestal. The search for the non-negotiable holy grail of 'Twenty Wickets' has now been firmly established as the starting point for every tour and every game on that tour. On this mission, the current team director Ravi Shastri, a hard-bitten competitor from the 1980s himself, is brother-in-arms with Kohli. The batsmen will set the foundations in Tests, they believe, but the bowlers will make you fly. Now that Dhoni has retired, this has meant pitchforking all variety of 'all-rounders' into the No. 7 slot and talk of an attack with 'four and a half' bowlers – and being able to take all the jokes that follow. But Kohli and Shastri do know that when they can pull it off, the biggest reward and the last laugh will be theirs and their team's alone. What Kohli, Shastri and Co. would like to achieve is what no Indian team has been able to do – win a series in Australia and South Africa.

At home, however, India are yet to break out of their post 2011 response to the Eight-Oh – post-England 2012, tempered somewhat by the opposition that comes visiting. Teams without spinning options are being greeted with underwatered crumblers that produce template games ending in three days. Remember Indian takeaway food in Britain? In which everything tastes the same but is categorized as korma/masala/vindaloo depending on how many spoons of chilli they contain. An Indian wicket is being cooked these days on an identical principle, whether it is in Mohali, Nagpur or Chennai. The fundamental, diverse nature of our wickets is being diluted – or rather spiced up – to a simple, single formula. An explanation that 'results matter' may silence intemperate questions. A greater introspection of such a habit would suggest though, that cookie-cutter tracks show no respect to either India's new batsmen or its young bowlers. On whom India's fans have invested so much of their post-2015 optimism.

Who knows how India's New Deal with Test cricket and its general change of course eventually goes. Cricket is itself living in an age of bubbling upheaval and constant flux. T20 has whittled away at the Test capabilities of smaller nations and the clutch of countries committed to the game's longest and most beguiling form are getting smaller. Yet, as long as India has its sharpest, hippest, coolest tattooed young players believe in the value of Test match success and regard it as their individual final frontier, we must count our blessings and fasten our seat belts.

Tests that Missed the Cut

1. **Test No. 614: M.A. Chidambaram Stadium, Chepauk, Madras, 13–18 January 1967: India** 404 in 143.2 overs (Chandu Borde 125, Farokh Engineer 109; Lance Gibbs 3-87, Wes Hall 2-68) and 323 in 105.4 overs (Ajit Wadekar 67, V. Subramanya 61; Charlie Griffith 4-61, Gibbs 4-96) drew with **West Indies** 406 in 132 overs (Garry Sobers 95, Rohan Kanhai 77; Bhagwat Chandrasekhar 4-130, Rusi Surti 3-68) and 270/7 in 93 overs (Sobers 74*, Griffith 40*, Bishan Singh Bedi 4-81, Erapalli Prasanna 3-106).
   Captains: M.A.K. Pataudi, Jr. (India) and Garry Sobers (West Indies)

2. **Test No. 626: Brisbane Cricket Ground, 19–24 January 1968: Australia** 379 in 112.2 overs (Doug Walters 93, Bill Lawry 64; Rusi Surti 3-102, Bapu Nadkarni 2-34) and 294 in 83.4 overs (Ian Redpath 79, Walters 62*; Erapalli Prasanna 6-104, Surti 3-59) beat **India** 279 in 100 overs (M.A.K. Pataudi 74, M.L. Jaisimha 74; Bob Cowper 3-31, Eric Freeman 3-56) and 355 in 107 overs (Jaisimha 101, Surti 64; Cowper 4-104, John Gleeson 3-50) by 39 runs.
   Captains: M.A.K. Pataudi Jnr (India) and Bill Lawry (Australia)

3. **Test No. 869: M.A. Chidambaram Stadium, Chepauk, Madras, 15–20 January 1980: Pakistan** 272 in 73.4 overs (Majid Khan 56, Sadiq Mohammad 46; Kapil Dev 4-90, Karsan Ghavri 3-93) and 233 in 66.4 overs (Wasim Raja 57, Javed Miandad 52; Kapil 7-56,

Dilip Doshi 2-42) lost to **India** 430 in 134.2 overs (Sunil Gavaskar 166, Kapil 84; Imran Khan 5-114, Iqbal Qasim 3-81) and 78/0 in 13 overs (Chauhan 46*, Gavaskar 29*) by 10 wickets.
Captains: Sunil Gavaskar (India) and Asif Iqbal (Pakistan)

4. **Test No. 1047: Leeds, Headingley, 19–23 June 1986: India** 272 in 104.2 overs (Dilip Vengsarkar 61, Kiran More 36*; Derek Pringle 3-47, Graham Dilley 3-54) and 237 in 76.3 overs (Vengsarkar 102*, Kapil Dev 31; John Lever 4-64, Pringle 4-73) beat **England** 102 in 45.1 overs (Bill Athey 32; Roger Binny 5-40, Madan Lal 3-18) and 128 in 63.3 overs (Mike Gatting 31*, Chris Smith 28; Maninder Singh 4-26, Binny 2-18) by 279 runs. **MotM:** Dilip Vengsarkar.
Captains: Kapil Dev (India) and Mike Gatting (England)

5. **Test No. 1073: M. Chinnaswamy Stadium, Bangalore, 13–17 March 1987: Pakistan** (Toss) 116 in 49.2 overs (Saleem Malik 33, Rameez Raja 22; Maninder Singh 7-27, Kapil Dev 2-23) and 249 in 94.5 overs (Rameez 47, Saleem Yousuf 41*; Ravi Shastri 4-69, Maninder 3-99) beat **India** 145 in 64 overs (Dilip Vengsarkar 50, Sunil Gavaskar 21, K. Srikkanth 21; Iqbal Qasim 5-48, Tauseef Ahmed 5-54) and 204 in 93.5 overs (Gavaskar 96, Mohammad Azharuddin 26; Qasim 4-73, Tauseef 4-85) by 16 runs. **MotM:** Sunil Gavaskar.
Captains: Kapil Dev (India) and Imran Khan (Pakistan)

6. **Test No. 1344: Green Park, Kanpur, 8–12 December 1996: India** 237 in 100.1 overs (Sachin Tendulkar 61, W.V. Raman 57; Paul Adams 6-55, Hansie Cronje 2-11) and 400/7 dec in 126 overs (Mohammad Azharuddin 163, Rahul Dravid 56; Fanie de Villiers 2-58, Lance Klusener 2-72) beat **South Africa** 177 in 72.3 overs (Gary Kirsten 43, Pat Symcox 23*; Anil Kumble 4-71, Javagal Srinath 3-42) and 180 in 96.1 overs (Cronje 50, Klusener 34*; Srinath 3-38, Sunil Joshi 3-66) by 280 runs. **MotM:** Mohammad Azharuddin.
Captains: Sachin Tendulkar (India) and Hansie Cronje (South Africa)

7. **Test No. 1443: Feroz Shah Kotla, Delhi, 4–7 February 1999: India** 252 in 91.5 overs (Mohammad Azharuddin 67, S. Ramesh 60; Saqlain Mushtaq 5-94, Mushtaq Ahmed 2-64) and 339 in 113.4 overs (Ramesh 96, Sourav Ganguly 62*; Saqlain 5-122, Wasim Akram 3-43) beat **Pakistan** 172 in 64.3 overs (Shahid Afridi 32, Saleem Malik 31; Anil Kumble 4-75, Harbhajan Singh 3-30) and 207 in 60.3 overs (Saeed Anwar 69, Afridi 41; Kumble 10-74) by 212 runs. **MotM**: Anil Kumble.
   Captains: Mohammad Azharuddin (India) and Wasim Akram (Pakistan)

8. **Test No. 1697: Rawalpindi Cricket Stadium, 13–16 April 2004: Pakistan** 224 in 72.5 overs (Mohammad Sami 49, Yasir Hameed 26; L. Balaji 4-63, Irfan Pathan 2-49) and 245 in 54 overs (Asim Kamal 60*, Yousuf Youhana 48; Anil Kumble 4-47, Balaji 3-108) lost to **India** 600 in 177.2 overs (Rahul Dravid 270, Sourav Ganguly 77; Shoaib Akhtar 3-47, Imran Farhat 2-69) by an innings and 131 runs. **MotM**: Rahul Dravid.
   Captains: Sourav Ganguly (India) and Inzamam-ul-Haq (Pakistan)

9. **Test No. 1915: Seddon Park, Hamilton, 18–21 March 2009: New Zealand** 279 in 78.2 overs (Daniel Vettori 118, Jesse Ryder 102; Ishant Sharma 4-73, Munaf Patel 3-60) and 279 in 102.3 overs (Brendon McCullum 84, Daniel Flynn 67; Harbhajan Singh 6-63, Munaf 2-60) lost to **India** 520 in 152.4 overs (Sachin Tendulkar 160, Gautam Gambhir 72; Chris Martin 3-98, Iain O'Brien 3-103) and 39/0 in 5.2 overs (Gambhir 30*) by 10 wickets. **MotM**: Sachin Tendulkar.
   Captains: M.S. Dhoni (India) and Daniel Vettori (New Zealand)

References and Bibliography

Part 1: 1947 to 1969   Hope Takes Root

1. Pataudi, M.A.K. (1969). *Tiger's Tale*. London. Stanley Paul. Pp. 9–18, 104–06, 114–16, 122, 142–44.
2. Mukherjee, S. (1968). *The Romance of Indian Cricket*. Delhi. Hind Pocket Books. Pp 44–62, 85–100.
3. Bose, M. (1990). *A History of Indian Cricket*. London. Andre Deutsch. Pp. 183–88.
4. Bala, R. (2004). *The Covers Are Off*. New Delhi. Rupa & Co. Pp. 47–49, 55–57, 68.
5. Menon, S. (Ed). (2015). *Wisden India Almanack 2015*. Bloomsbury India. Pp. 65–67.
6. Ramaswami, N.S. (1975). *From Porbander to Wadekar*. New Delhi. Abhinav Publications. Pp. 111–13.
7. Conversation with Rajdeep Sardesai. 14 and 17 October 2015.
8. Conversation with S. Venkataraghavan. 26 January 2013, 15 December 2013 and 31 December 2015.

Chapter 1: Fourth-Innings Heroes

1. Special Correspondent (4 February 1949). The Bombay Test | Chances of India's victory. *The Hindu*, p. 8.
2. Special Correspondent (5 February 1949). Fifth Test at Bombay | West Indies 235 for 6 | Tourists start shakily. *The Hindu*, p. 8.
3. Special Correspondent (6 February 1949). West Indies all out for 286 | India

132 for 5 at close. *The Hindu*, p. 8.

4. Special Correspondent (7 February 1949). West Indies lead India | Home side dismissed for 193 runs. *The Hindu*, p. 8.

5. Special Correspondent. (8 February 1949). West Indies all out for 267 | India 90 for 3 at close. *The Hindu*, p. 8.

6. Special Correspondent (9 February 1949). West Indies win Rubber | Exciting finish to final Test | India baulked of victory by 6 runs. *The Hindu*, p. 8.

7. Gurunathan, S.K. (12 February 1949). With the West Indies Cricketers. *Sport & Pastime*, pp. 4, 9.

8. (1950). Fifth Test Match India v West Indies 1948–49. Retrieved from http://www.espncricinfo.com/wisdenalmanack/content/story/almanack/year. html?year=1950

9. Ramchand, P. (8 October 2002). Weekes proves the difference: 1948–49. Retrieved from http://www.espncricinfo.com/ci/content/story/122015.html

10. Lynch, S. (2013, June 8). Stollmeyer's Stories. Retrieved from http://www. espncricinfo.com/magazine/content/story/639415.html

11. Mukherjee, S. (1968). *The Romance of Indian Cricket*. Delhi. Hind Pocket Books. Pp 52–57, 138.

12. Conversation with Chandu Borde. 31 July 2015 and 16 August 2015.

13. Conversation with Mohinder Amarnath. 2 October 2015.

Chapter 2: Beating the World's Best

1. Gurunathan, S.K. (19 December 1959). Second Test at Kanpur| Wicket will help spin attack. *The Hindu*, p. 12.

2. Gurunathan, S.K. (20 December 1959). India score only 152| Davidson and Benaud excel. *The Hindu*, p. 10.

3. Gurunathan, S.K. (21 December 1959). Patel hero of the day | Takes 9 wkts for 60 runs. *The Hindu*, p. 10.

4. Gurunathan, S.K. (22 December 1959). India fightback| Borde and Baig bat well| Superb innings by Contractor. *The Hindu*, p. 8.

5. Gurunathan, S.K. (23 December 1959). Contractor's dismissal in second innings. *The Hindu*, p. 10.

6. Gurunathan, S.K. (24 December 1959). India score 291 runs| Davidson takes 7 wkts. *The Hindu*, p. 8.

7. Gurunathan, S.K. (25 December 1959). India's great triumph in Kanpur Test. *The Hindu*, pp. 1, 10.

8. PTI (25 December 1959). President's felicitations to team. *The Hindu*, p. 10.

9. PTI (25 December 1959). Amarnath's tribute. *The Hindu*, p. 10.
10. Gurunathan, S.K. (2 January 1960). A great Test triumph. *Sport & Pastime*, pp. 15, 16.
11. (1961). Second Test Match India v Australia. Retrieved from http://www.espncricinfo.com/wisdenalmanack/content/story/152737.html
12. Ramaswami, N. S. (1975). *From Porbander to Wadekar*. New Delhi. Abhinav Publications Pp 78; 137-140.
13. Ramchand, P. (24 December 1999). The miracle at Kanpur – 40 years on. Retrieved from http://www.espncricinfo.com/ci/content/story/79156.html
14. Singh, Yajurvindra (2003). G.S. Ramchand: Wisden Asia Cricket Obituary. Retrieved from http://www.espncricinfo.com/india/content/player/33062.html
15. Amarnath, R. (2004). *Lala Amarnath: The Making Of a Legend*. New Delhi. Rupa & Co.
16. Conversation with Chandu Borde. 31 July 2015 and 16 August 2015.
17. Conversation with Mohinder Amarnath. 2 October 2015.

Chapter 3: Cliffhanger

1. Special Correspondent (10 October 1964). Second Test at Bombay. *The Hindu*, p. 11.
2. Special Correspondent (11 October 1964). Jarman and Veivers consolidate position | Burge's glorious knock: Bright batting by Australia. *The Hindu*, p. 8.
3. Special Correspondent (12 October 1964). Manjrekar and Jaisimha in century stand | Chandrasekhar bags four wickets. *The Hindu*, p. 10.
4. Special Correspondent (13 October 1964). Sparkling knock by Pataudi | Veivers good bowling; Fast scoring by Lawry. *The Hindu*, p. 14.
5. (14 October 1964). Bombay Test | O'Neill not to play. *The Hindu*, p. 10.
6. Special Correspondent (15 October 1964). India need 180 for victory | Nadkarni and Chandrasekhar spin out Australia. *The Hindu*, p. 15.
7. Special Correspondent (17 October 1964). Exciting victory for India | Pataudi and Manjrekar's stand paves way for triumph. *The Hindu*, p. 10.
8. Fingleton, J.H. (18 October 1964). India's victory | Australian Press's praise. *The Hindu*, p. 8.
9. Sundaresan, P.N. (31 October 1964). Memorable day for Indian cricket. *Sport & Pastime*, pp. 19, 20, 36, 37.
10. (1965). Second Test India v Australia. Retrieved from http://www.espncricinfo.

com/wisdenalmanack/content/story/152843.html

11. Ramchand, P. (2004). *The Gentle Executioners*. Delhi. Konark Publishers. Pp. 111.

12. Bala, R. (2004). *The Covers Are Off*. New Delhi. Rupa & Co. P. 111.

13. Wadekar, A.L. (1973). *My Cricketing Years*. New Delhi. Rupa & Co. P. 30.

14. Pataudi, M.A.K. (1969). *Tiger's Tale*. London. Stanley Paul. Pp. 13, 48–50.

15. Mukherjee, S. (1968). *The Romance of Indian Cricket*. Delhi. Hind Pocket Books. Pp. 160–63.

16. Ramnarayan, V. (2014). *Third Man: Recollections From a Life in Cricket*. New Delhi. Westland. Pp. 182–87.

17. Conversation with Chandu Borde. 31 July 2015 and 16 August 2015.

18. Conversation with Salim Durani. 1 October 2008.

19. Conversation with Rajdeep Sardesai. 14 and 17 October 2015.

20. Email exchange with Raju Bharatan. 17 October 2015 and 27 December 2015.

Chapter 4: Rising From the Dead

1. Swamy, C.S.A. (15 March 1965). Borde, Sardesai lead India's fightback. *The Indian Express*, p. 12.

2. Swamy, C.S.A. (16 March 1965). Dramatic turn on final day: N.Z. escape defeat | Brilliant 200 n.o. by Sardesai. *The Indian Express*, p. 12.

3. Swamy, C.S.A. (14 March 1965). India succumb to pace attack, follow on. *The Indian Express*, p. 8.

4. Special Correspondent (12 March 1965). Third Test from today. *The Hindu*, p. 11.

5. Special Correspondent (13 March 1965). Unbeaten century by Dowling. *The Hindu*, p. 10.

6. Special Correspondent (14 March 1965). New Zealand on top in Bombay test | India forced to follow-on; 16 wickets fall in a day. *The Hindu*, p. 8.

7. Special Correspondent (15 March 1965). Borde's glorious century | Sardesai concerned in two valuable stands. *The Hindu*, p. 10.

8. Special Correspondent (16 March 1965). Dramatic draw at Bombay| Time robs India of victory. *The Hindu*, p. 10.

9. Sundaresan, P.N. (3 April 1965). With the New Zealand cricketers | Time to tourists' rescue. *Sport & Pastime*, pp. 16, 17.

10. Gurunathan, S.K. (3 April 1965). From defeat to glory. *Sport & Pastime*, p. 18.

11. (1966). Third Test India v New Zealand. Retrieved from http://www. espncricinfo.com/wisdenalmanack/content/story/153706.html

12. Giridhar, S. and Raghunath, V.J. (2014). *Mid-Wicket Tales: From Trumper to Tendulkar.* New Delhi. Sage.

13. Bailey, T. (1976). *Sir Garry: A Biography.* Kolkata. Collins. Pp. 107–8.

14. Pataudi, M.A.K. (1969). *Tiger's Tale.* : London. Stanley Paul. Pp. 51–52.

15. Menon, S. (Ed.) (2015) *Wisden India Almanack 2015.* Bloomsbury India. Pp. 65–67.

16. Conversation with Chandu Borde. 31 July 2015 and 16 August 2015.

17. Conversation with Salim Durani. 1 October 2008.

18. Conversation with Rajdeep Sardesai. 14 and 17 October 2015.

19. Conversation with S. Venkataraghavan. 26 January 2013, 15 December 2013 and 31 December 2015.

Part 2: 1970 to 1980 – A Heady Feeling

1. Bharatan, R. (1977). *Indian Cricket: The Vital Phase.* New Delhi. Bell Books/ Vikas Publishing House. Pp. 9–14.

2. Menon, S. (2011). *Bishan: Portrait of a Cricketer.* Gurgaon. Penguin. P. 27.

3. Pataudi, M.A.K. (1969). *Tiger's Tale.* London. Stanley Paul. Pp. 75, 99.

4. Bose, M. (2006). *The Magic of Indian Cricket: Cricket and Society in India.* Oxon. Routledge. P. 237.

5. Giridhar, S. and Raghunath, V.J. (2014). *Mid-wicket Tales: From Trumper to Tendulkar.* New Delhi. Sage. Pp. 52–53.

6. Bala, R. (2004). *The Covers Are Off.* New Delhi. Rupa & Co.

7. Conversation with Bishan Singh Bedi. 14 July 2015 and 26 August 2015.

8. Conversation with S. Venkataraghavan. 26 January 2013 and 15 December 2013.

Chapter 5: Garry, We Are Enforcing the Follow-On

1. Rutnagur, D.J. (1972). First Test match West Indies v India. Retrieved from http://www.espncricinfo.com/wisdenalmanack/content/story/150252.html

2. Jones, B.R. (18 February 1971). Indian spin attack may prove decisive. *The Hindu,* p. 12.

3. Jones, B.R. (20 February 1971). India loses three quick wkts after being asked to bat. *The Hindu,* p. 12.

4. Jones, B.R. (21 February 1971). Unbeaten century by Sardesai | India 270

for 8 at lunch. *The Hindu*, p. 12.

5. Jones, B.R. (22 February 1971). Brilliant 212 by Sardesai | Century stand with Prasanna. *The Hindu*, p. 12.

6. Jones, B.R. (22 February 1971). Sardesai cracks pressbox panes. *The Hindu*, p. 12.

7. Jones, B.R. (23 February 1971). West Indies 133 for 3 at lunch. *The Hindu*, p. 12.

8. Jones, B.R. (24 February 1971). Good batting by Kanhai and Lloyd; West Indies rally. *The Hindu*, p. 12.

9. AFP (25 February 1971). Best piece of spin bowling. *The Hindu*, p. 12.

10. Jones, B.R. (25 February 1971). Kanhai (158 not out) and Sobers (93) foil India's victory bid. *The Hindu*, p. 12.

11. Cookiepictures (10 September 2015). An evening with Ajit Wadekar. Retrieved from https://www.youtube.com/watch?v=Zjs_I58fRO8&feature=youtu.be

12. Gavaskar, S.M. (1976). *Sunny Days*. New Delhi. Rupa & Co. Pp. 38–39, 46–47.

13. Bharatan, R. (1977). *Indian Cricket: The Vital Phase.* : New Delhi. Bell Books/ Vikas Publishing House. Pp. 56–58.

14. Ramnarayan, V. (2014). *Third Man: Recollections from a life in cricket*. New Delhi. Westland. Pp. 179–81.

15. Conversation with S Venkataraghavan. 26 January 2013, 15 December 2013 and 31 December 2015.

16. Conversation with Rajdeep Sardesai. 14 and 17 October 2015.

Chapter 6: A New Era Is Born

1. AP and Reuters (11 March 1971). Windies are cornered. *The Indian Express*, p. 12.

2. PTI (10 March 1971). Another century by Sardesai | Bowled, not leg before. *The Indian Express*, p. 12.

3. PTI (12 March 1971). Don't relax, says Merchant. *The Indian Express*, p. 12.

4. Rutnagur, D. (9 March 1971). Sardesai, Gavaskar among runs again. *The Indian Express*, p. 12.

5. Rutnagur, D. (12 March 1971). Wadekar & his boys write a golden chapter. *The Indian Express*, p. 12.

6. Jones, B.R. (7 March 1971). West Indies loses quick Wkts.; 86 for 4 at Lunch. *The Hindu*, p. 12.

7.   Jones, B.R. (8 March 1971). Mankad & Gavaskar give good start: India 186 for 4. *The Hindu*, p. 12.

8.   PTI (8 March 1971). Sensational start. *The Hindu*, p. 12.

9.   Jones, B.R. (9 March 1971). Another fine knock by Sardesai: 96-run stand with Gavaskar. *The Hindu*, p. 12.

10. (10 March 1971). Sardesai hits century again: India gains 138-run lead. *The Hindu*, p. 12.

11. Jones, B.R. (11 March 1971). Noreiga bags nine wickets: West Indies' sudden slump. *The Hindu*, p. 12.

12. Jones, B.R. (12 March 1971). India's first ever Test victory over W. Indies. *The Hindu*, p. 14.

13. Rutnagur, D.J. (1972). Second Test match West Indies v India. Retrieved from http://www.espncricinfo.com/wisdenalmanack/content/story/150253.html

14. Gollapudi, N. (n.d). Dancing in the lion's den. Retrieved from http://www.espncricinfo.com/magazine/content/story/326340.html

15. Ramchand, P. (9 March 2002). A watershed victory in Indian cricket. Retrieved from http://www.espncricinfo.com/india/content/story/118703.html

16. Ramchand, P. (6 March 2001). Thirty years after his debut, Gavaskar's legacy endures. http://www.espncricinfo.com/india/content/story/104673.html

17. Wadekar, A.L. (1973). *My Cricketing Years*. New Delhi. Rupa & Co. Pp. 68–71.

18. Bose, M. (2006). *The Magic of Indian Cricket: Cricket and Society in India*. Oxon. Routledge. P. 177.

19. Bose, M. (1990). *A History of Indian Cricket*. London. Andre Deutsch. Pp. 193–95.

20. Bharatan, R. (1977). *Indian Cricket: The Vital Phase*. New Delhi. Bell Books/ Vikas Publishing House. Pp. 37–44.

21. Giridhar, S. and Raghunath, V.J. (2014). *Mid-wicket Tales: From Trumper to Tendulkar*. New Delhi. Sage. P. 229.

22. Ramnarayan, V. (2014). *Third Man: Recollections From a Life in Cricket*. New Delhi. Westland. Pp. 192–95.

23. Conversation with Bishan Singh Bedi. 14 July 2015 and 26 August 2015.

24. Conversation with S. Venkataraghavan. 26 January 2013, 15 December 2013 and 31 December 2015.

25. Conversation with Salim Durani. 1 October 2008.

26. Conversation with Rajdeep Sardesai. 14 and 17 October 2015.

Chapter 7: Magical, Marvellous Chandra

1. AP (24 August 1971). India need 97 runs for victory | Chandrashekar sends England reeling. *The Indian Express*, p. 18.
2. Miller, K. (26 August 1971). Well done India | A historic triumph. *The Indian Express*, p. 12.
3. AP (26 August 1971). Raves from Fleet Street. *The Indian Express*, p. 12.
4. AFP and Reuters (19 August 1971). Oval pitch may suit the Indian spinners. *The Hindu*, p. 12.
5. AP (20 August 1971). England again recovers to total 355. *The Hindu*, p. 14.
6. AP (22 August 1971). Fighting knocks by Solkar, Sardesai and Engineer. *The Hindu*, p. 14.
7. (24 August 1971). Chandrashekar routs England: India needs 97 to win. *The Hindu*, p. 14.
8. PTI (26 August 1971). Indian Cricket's finest hour | India wins first ever series in England. *The Hindu*, pp. 1, 14.
9. Yardley, N.W.D. (26 August 1971). It was a surprise to Illingworth. *The Hindu*, p. 14.
10. (1972). First Test match England v India. Retrieved from http://www.espncricinfo.com/wisdenalmanack/content/story/153791.html
11. (1972). Third Test match England v India. Retrieved from http://www.espncricinfo.com/wisdenalmanack/content/story/153793.html
12. Williamson, M. (2011, August 13). India's day of glory. Retrieved from http://www.espncricinfo.com/magazine/content/story/527248.html
13. Swanton, E.W. (1983). *As I said at the time*. Retrieved from http://static.espncricinfo.com/db/ARCHIVE/1970S/1971/IND_IN_ENG/IND_ENG_T3D5_24AUG1971_MR
14. Wadekar, A.L. (1973). *My Cricketing Years*. New Delhi. Rupa & Co. Pp. 114–19.
15. Menon, S. (2011). *Bishan: Portrait of a Cricketer*. Gurgaon. Penguin. P. 34.
16. Bose, M. (1990). *A history of Indian Cricket*. London. Andre Deutsch. Pp. 1–15.
17. Underwood, D. (1975). *Beating the Bat.* : London. Stanley Paul. Pp. 48–49.
18. Sunil Rao. (30 November 2010). India vs England – B S Chandrasekhar. Retrieved from https://www.youtube.com/watch?v=iGZyjxee54Y
19. Realty Merchant (6 August 2015). Indian Cricket team's first Test Series win in England 1971. Retrieved from https://www.youtube.com/watch?v=4HfZHrz6o1U

20. Tangible Emotions (5 November 2012). England v India: Test Series (1971). Retrieved from https://www.youtube.com/watch?v=6r1XiDSOcig
21. Conversation with Rajdeep Sardesai. 14 and 17 October 2015.
22. Conversation with S. Venkataraghavan. 26 January 2013, 15 December 2013 and 31 December 2015.

Chapter 8: Eden and Euphoria

1. UNI (25 December 1974). Kallicharan suffers a minor injury. *The Times of India*, p. 9.
2. Prabhu, K.N. (27 December 1974). Pataudi should help middle-order batting. *The Times of India*, p. 9.
3. Prabhu, K.N. (28 December 1974). India's poor batting display. *The Times of India*, p. 1.
4. Prabhu, K.N. (29 December 1974). Madan Lal star of the day. *The Times of India*, p. 1.
5. Prabhu, K.N. (30 December 1974). Vishwanath's superb innings. *The Times of India*, p. 1.
6. Prabhu, K.N. (31 December 1974). Our spinners not getting enough support on field. *The Times of India*, p. 9.
7. Prabhu, K.N. (1 January 1975). India have a fighting chance. *The Times of India*, p. 1.
8. PTI. (1975, January 2). Congratulations from President, PM. *The Times of India*.
9. UNI (2 January 1975). Pataudi burns his fingers. *The Times of India*, p. 8.
10. PTI (2 January 1975). Pataudi expresses happiness. *The Times of India*, p. 8.
11. PTI (2 January 1975). Vishwanath climbs to top of batting averages. *The Times of India*, p. 8.
12. Hendricks, R. (30 December 1974). India still have a long way to go in third Test. *The Indian Express*, p. 12.
13. Hendricks, R. (1 January 1975). Vishwanath completes superb century. *The Indian Express*, p. 12.
14. Hendricks, R. (2 January 1975). West Indians dance to Chandra's tune. *The Indian Express*, p. 12.
15. Hendricks, R. (31 December 1974). Much will depend on Vishwanath. *The Indian Express*, p. 10.
16. PTI (2 January 1975). Lloyd's dismissal was turning point. *The Indian Express*, p. 12.

17. UNI and PTI (27 December 1974). Holder replaces Boyce in West Indies team. *The Hindu*, p. 12.

18. (28 December 1974). Sound knocks by Visvanath & Madan Lal: Roberts strikes again. *The Hindu*, p. 12.

19. PTI (29 December 1974). Madan Lal puts India back in the match: Fredericks hits century. *The Hindu*, p. 8.

20. UNI and PTI (30 December 1974). Fighting innings by Visvanath & Engineer. *The Hindu*, p. 12.

21. PTI. (31 December 1974). Calcutta Test interestingly poised. *The Hindu*, p. 12.

22. PTI (1 January 1975). Calcutta Test poised for keen finish: Gallant century by Visvanath. *The Hindu*, p. 12.

23. (2 January 1975).Chandrashekar & Bedi bowl India to victory. *The Hindu*, p. 10.

24. Rutnagur, D.J. (1976). Third Test match India v West Indies. Retrieved from http://www.espncricinfo.com/wisdenalmanack/content/story/153470.html

25. Rutnagur, D.J. (1976). The West Indies in India and Pakistan and Sri Lanka, 1974–75. Retrieved from http://www.espncricinfo.com/wisdenalmanack/content/story/154333.html

26. Menon, S. (2011). *Bishan: Portrait of a Cricketer*. Gurgaon. Penguin. Pp. 50, 99.

27. Bharatan, R. (1977). *Indian Cricket: The Vital Phase*. New Delhi. Bell Books/ Vikas Publishing House. Pp. 226–27.

28. Bala, R. (2004). *The Covers Are Off*. New Delhi. Rupa & Co. Pp. 135–36

29. Pataudi, M.A.K. (1969). *Tiger's Tale*. London. Stanley Paul. P. 123.

30. Giridhar, S. and Raghunath, V.J. (2014). *Mid-wicket Tales: From Trumper to Tendulkar*. New Delhi. Sage. P. 234.

31. Prasanna, E.A.S. (1978). *One more over*. New Delhi. Rupa & Co. Pp. 55–56.

32. Conversation with Bishan Singh Bedi. 14 July 2015 and 26 August 2015.

33. Conversation with S. Venkataraghavan. 26 January 2013, 15 December 2013 and 31 December 2015.

Chapter 9: Emulating the Invincibles

1. Reuters (6 April 1976). Andy Roberts rested for two tests. *The Times of India*, p. 11.

2. Mama B.B. (6 April 1976) Richards completes 1,000. *The Times of India*, p. 11.

3. Prabhu, K.N. (7 April 1976). India have a chance of drawing level: two changes likely. *The Times of India*, p. 13.

4. Prabhu, K.N. (8 April 1976). Chandrashekar claims all three wickets in pre-lunch session. *The Times of India*, p. 11.

5. Prabhu, K.N. (13 April 1976). Kallicharan upsets India's restrictive plan. *The Times of India*, p. 11.

6. Staff Reporter (14 April 1976). India's feat rates higher than that of Bradman's team. *The Times of India*, p. 11.

7. Prabhu, K.N. (15 April 1976). Lloyd under fire from fickle fans for defensive approach. *The Times of India*, p. 11.

8. Cozier, T. (13 April 1976). Gavaskar hammers another century. *The Indian Express*, p. 14.

9. Cozier, T. (12 April 1976). Holding's bowling will be cherished. *The Indian Express*, p. 12.

10. Cozier, T. (15 April 1976). India's historic win. *The Indian Express*, p. 14.

11. Cozier, T. (13 April 1976). Just like a wall. *The Indian Express*, p. 14.

12. Cozier, T. (12 April 1976). Kallicharan hits century, Windies hold whip hand. *The Indian Express*, p. 12.

13. Jones, B.R. (7 April 1976). Change in venue will be to India's advantage. *The Hindu*, p. 10.

14. Jones, B.R. (8 April 1976). Richards and Lloyd in century stand. *The Hindu*, p. 10.

15. Jones, B.R. (9 April 1976). Richards' third century of series. *The Hindu*, p. 14.

16. Jones, B.R. (9 April 1976). India off to poor start: W. Indies all out for 359. *The Hindu*, p. 14.

17. Samachar (10 April 1976). India struggles for runs. *The Hindu*, p. 9.

18. Jones, B.R. (11 April 1976). India all out for 228: Holding bags six wickets. *The Hindu*, p. 12.

19. Jones, B.R. (12 April 1976). Unbeaten 103 by Kallicharan: India 58 for no wkt. at tea. *The Hindu*, p. 12.

20. Jones, B.R. (13 April 1976). India wins third Test | Centuries by Gavaskar and Visvanath: Mohinder bats well. *The Hindu*, pp. 1, 12.

21. AFP (14 April 1976). Well judged scoring rate. *The Hindu*, p. 12.

22. (14 April 1976). Lloyd blames his bowlers. *The Hindu*, p. 12.

23. Jones, B.R. (14 April 1976). India registers historic victory: Patel's sparkling knock. *The Hindu*, p. 12.

24. (1977). Third Test match West Indies v India. Retrieved from http://www.espncricinfo.com/wisdenalmanack/content/story/153022.html

25. (1977). India in the West Indies in 1976. Retrieved from http://www. espncricinfo.com/wisdenalmanack/content/story/153020.html

26. Krishnan, S. (2001, April 12). Twenty five years later, the Queens Park Oval triumph still lingers on. Retrieved from http://www.espncricinfo.com/india/ content/story/95171.html

27. Prabhu, K.N. (April 2002). The great chase. Retrieved from http://www. espncricinfo.com/magazine/content/story/244014.html

28. Gavaskar, S.M. (1976). *Sunny Days.* : New Delhi. Rupa & Co. Pp. 222–23.

29. Tangible Emotions (5 November 2012). West Indies v India: Test Series (1976). Retrieved from https://www.youtube.com/watch?v=06O8Kgvz0ec

30. Conversation with Bishan Singh Bedi. 14 July 2015 and 26 August 2015.

31. Conversation with S. Venkataraghavan. 26 January 2013, 15 December 2013 and 31 December 2015.

Chapter 10: That Monumental Chase

1. Reuters. (28 August 1979). England make three changes. *The Times of India*, p. 11.

2. (31 August 1979). Gooch and Willey rescue England from poor start: Test. *The Times of India*, p. 11.

3. Reuters (30 August 1979). Plenty to play for in final test. *The Times of India*, p. 11.

4. UNI (1 September 1979). Plucky 62 by Vishwanath as India struggle in Test. *The Times of India*, p. 7.

5. (2 September 1979). England assume control of second test: Boycott bats well. *The Times of India*, p. 7.

6. (4 September 1979). Gavaskar and Chauhan get heads down to Herculean task. *The Times of India*, p. 11.

7. Reuters (5 September 1979). Gavaskar raises vision of victory. *The Times of India*, p. 11.

8. Reuters (6 September 1979). Gavaskar rates 57 at Manchester in 1971 as his best. *The Times of India*, p. 11.

9. Rutnagur, D. (4 September 1979). Boycott hits century: India face uphill task. *The Indian Express*, p. 12.

10. Rutnagur, D. (2 September 1979). England progress to a strong position. *The Indian Express*, p. 18.

11. Rutnagur, D. (5 September 1979). Tantalising Test: India fail to win narrowly. *The Indian Express*, p. 6.

12. Rutnagur, D. (3 September 1979). Will Venkat be retained? *The Indian Express*, p. 14.

13. Bala, R. (30 August 1979). This England team can be beaten. *The Hindu*, p. 14.

14. Bala, R. (31 August 1979). Stubborn unbeaten 79 by Gooch. *The Hindu*, p. 14.

15. Bala, R. (1 September 1979). England all out 305: India in poor way. *The Hindu*, p. 14.

16. Bala, R. (2 September 1979). England on top: Good knock by Boycott. *The Hindu*, p. 14.

17. Bala, R. (3 September 1979). India needs resolute batting to save Test. *The Hindu*, p. 14.

18. Bala, R. (4 September 1979). England sets India big victory target. *The Hindu*, p. 14.

19. Bala, R. (5 September 1979). Victory eludes India by 9 runs: Gavaskar hits glorious 221. *The Hindu*, p. 14.

20. Special Correspondent. (8 September 1979). Sunny sets on the Empire | Gavaskar scales new heights. *Sportstar*, pp. 6, 7.

21. Vaidya, S. (8 September 1979). The Botham blitz. *The Sportstar*, p. 7.

22. Marlar, R. (8 September 1979). The over that will haunt Brearley. *The Sportstar*, p. 7.

23. Cooper, T. (1980). Fourth Test match England v India. Retrieved from http://www.espncricinfo.com/wisdenalmanack/content/story/153030.html

24. Preston, N. (1980). India in England. Retrieved from http://www.espncricinfo.com/wisdenalmanack/content/story/155222.html

25. Williamson, M. (5 September 2015). When Sunny made 438 look gettable. Retrieved from http://www.espncricinfo.com/magazine/content/story/917805.html

26. Cricketcountry (11 September 2013). Sunil Gavaskar's epic 221 vs England at the Oval in 1979, Yajurvindra Singh recalls. Retrieved from https://www.youtube.com/watch?v=DHLIDNBKx-U

27. Prasanna, E.A.S. (1978). *One More Over*. New Delhi. Rupa & Co. P. 107.

28. Brearley, M. (2001). *The Art of Captaincy*. : London. Channel New Edition. P. 138.

29. Boycott, G. (2009). *The Best XI*. London. Penguin. Pp. 229–31.

30. Starsports (24 July 2011). Sunil Gavaskar 221 vs England. Retrieved from https://www.youtube.com/watch?v=ETOjd_qH2JY.

31. Conversation with Bishan Singh Bedi. 14 July 2015 and 26 August 2015.

32. Conversation with S. Venkataraghavan. 26 January 2013, 15 December 2013 and 31 December 2015.

Chapter 11: Fiercer than the Ashes

1. Prabhu, K.N. (5 December 1979). Everything came right for Asif at the end. *The Times of India*, p. 11.
2. Sriman, R. (5 December 1979). Wasim Raja helps Pakistan weather Kapil's electrifying jolts. *The Times of India*, p. 11.
3. Prabhu, K. N. (7 December 1979). Indian attack was a two-man affair. *The Times of India*, p. 11.
4. Sriman, R. (7 December 1979). Pakistan in a commanding position in the second test. *The Times of India*, p. 11.
5. Sriman, R. (10 December 1979). India's epic fightback on final-day against Pakistan. *The Times of India*, p. 11.
6. Special Correspondent (4 December 1979). Sikhandar Bakht in Pak Team for Delhi Test. *The Hindu*, p. 14.
7. Special Correspondent (5 December 1979). Wasim Raja leads rally after Kapil Dev rocks Pakistan. *The Hindu*, p. 14.
8. Special Correspondent (6 December 1979). Majid's sporting gesture | Sikhandar Bakht excels on pace bowlers' day. *The Hindu*, p. 14.
9. Special Correspondent (7 December 1979). Indian bowlers fall short of expectations. *The Hindu*, p. 14.
10. Special Correspondent (8 December 1979). Difficult but not impossible task ahead for Indian batsmen. *The Hindu*, p. 14.
11. Special Correspondent (9 December 1979). Interesting final day's play in prospect. *The Hindu*, p. 14.
12. Sports Reporter (1979, December 10). 'It was a Fair Verdict' – Asif. *The Hindu*, p. 14.
13. Special Correspondent (10 December 1979). Exhilarating Delhi Test drawn: Vengsarkar's marathon 146 N.O. *The Hindu*, p. 14.
14. Mohan, R. (15 December 1979). A Capital show. *Sportstar*, pp. 4, 5.
15. (1981). Second test match India v Pakistan. Retrieved from http://www.espncricinfo.com/wisdenalmanack/content/story/153826.html
16. Guha, R. (1994). *Spin and Other Turns: Indian Cricket's Coming of Age*. New Delhi. Penguin. P. 78.
17. Guha, R. (2005). *The States of Indian Cricket: Anecdotal Histories*. Delhi. Permanent Black. Pp. 237–38.

Part 3: 1981 to 2000 – Everyone's Game

1. Mazumdar, B. (12 April 2012). How cricket was sold in India. Retrieved from http://www.openthemagazine.com/article/sports/how-cricket-was-sold-in-india

2. Ugra, S. (27 March 2011). Satellite television. Retrieved from http://www.espncricinfo.com/page2/content/story/505206.html

3. Narayan, M. (22 March 2015). Million dollar middle-ager. Retrieved from http://www.wisdenindia.com/cricket-article/million-dollar-middle-ager/156192

4. Guha, R. (1 October 2014). The march of a national game. Retrieved from http://www.caravanmagazine.in/print/4769

5. Bose, M. (2006). *The Magic of Indian Cricket: Cricket and Society in India*. Oxon. Routledge. P. 237.

6. Bala, R. (2004). *The Covers Are Off*. New Delhi. Rupa & Co. Pp. 13, 174–83

7. Conversation with S. Venkataraghavan. 26 January 2013 and 15 December 2013.

8. Conversation with R. Mohan. 29 September 2015 and 1 November 2015.

9. Conversation with Dileep Premachandran. 16 October 2015.

Chapter 12: Fury and Ecstasy

1. Niran (6 February 1981). Australian Journal. *The Times of India*, p. 11.

2. Prabhu, K.N. (7 February 1981). Melbourne Test could help India level the series. *The Times of India*, p. 11.

3. Prabhu, K.N. (8 February 1981). Hello Listeners, This is Alan. *The Times of India*, p. SMVI.

4. Sports Correspondent (9 February 1981). An unnecessary risk? *The Times of India*, p. 11.

5. Prabhu, K.N. (10 February 1981). Gavaskar, Chauhan lead Indian rally with a century stand. *The Times of India*, p. 11.

6. Cricket correspondent (11 February 1981). Ugly situation averted. *The Times of India*, p. 11.

7. Prabhu, K.N. (11 February 1981). India's epic win. *The Times of India*, p. 1.

8. Mohan, R. (7 February 1981). Spinners will hold sway in Melbourne Test. *The Hindu*, p. 14.

9. Mohan, R. (8 February 1981). Visvanath (114) stands firm amid India's slump. *The Hindu*, p. 14.

10. Mohan, R. (9 February 1981). Chappell & Border play masterly knocks. *The Hindu*, p. 14.
11. Mohan, R. (10 February 1981). Facing a Herculean task: Gavaskar, Chauhan open on confident note. *The Hindu*, p. 14.
12. Mohan, R. (11 February 1981). India fritters away good start & Australia needs 119 runs with 7 Wkts left to win. *The Hindu*, p. 14.
13. Reuters and AP (11 February 1981). Benaud hails Lillee's feat. *The Hindu*, p. 14.
14. Special Correspondent (11 February 1981). Indian Team Manager averts serious incident, *The Hindu*, p. 14.
15. Editorial (12 February 1981). Honours even. *The Hindu*, p. 8.
16. Mohan, R. (12 February 1981). Tornado Kapil hits Australia: India pulls off incredible 59-Run victory. *The Hindu*, p. 14.
17. PTI (12 February 1981). First Indian team to square series. *The Hindu*, p. 14.
18. Mohan, R. (21 February 1981). Miracle at Melbourne, *Sportstar*, pp. 5, 6, 8, 9.
19. (21 February 1981). The Three Prophets. *The Sportstar*, p. 11.
20. Rutnagur, D.J. (1982). Third Test match Australia v India. Retrieved from http://www.espncricinfo.com/wisdenalmanack/content/story/152230.html
21. Mohan, R. (1 March 2009). Chappell throws it away. Retrieved from http://www.espncricinfo.com/magazine/content/story/390865.html
22. Monga, S. (25 December 2011). Shivlal Yadav returns to familiar ground. Retrieved from http://www.espncricinfo.com/magazine/content/story/546793.html
23. Williamson, M. (5 March 2005). When Sunny spat the dummy. Retrieved from http://www.espncricinfo.com/magazine/content/story/145850.html
24. The Third Umpire (11 September 2009). Aus vs Ind, 3rd Test, Melbourne 1981 – Ind 1st innings. Retrieved from https://www.youtube.com/watch?v=YpZu41Olf8g
25. The Third Umpire (14 September 2009). Aus vs Ind, 3rd Test, Melbourne 1981 – Ind 2nd innings. Retrieved from https://www.youtube.com/watch?v=LNhvKkPaVvY
26. 10anujrathi10 (8 August 2011). Kapil Dev 5-28 vs Aus Melbourne 1980–81. Retrieved from https://www.youtube.com/watch?v=o2SoSL9pU8U

Chapter 13: Lords of Lord's

1. Cricket Correspondent (17 March 1986). Which way will the pendulum swing? *The Hindu*, p. 14.
2. Mohan, R. (5 June 1986). India has the capacity to call the shots. *The Hindu*, p. 15.
3. Mohan, R. (6 June 1986). Gooch plays the waiting game to a nicety. *The Hindu*, p. 14.
4. Mohan, R. (7 June 1986). India comes up with a competent display. *The Hindu*, p. 14.
5. Mohan, R. (8 June 1986). Vengsarkar makes it a hat-trick at Lord's. *The Hindu*, p. 14.
6. Mohan, R. (9 June 1986). India fails to take firm grip on Test. *The Hindu*, p. 14.
7. Mohan, R. (10 June 1986). Kapil Dev's inspired spell puts India on road to victory. *The Hindu*, p. 14.
8. Mohan, R. (11 June 1986). India makes history at Lord's. *The Hindu*, p. 14.
9. Cricket Correspondent. (11 June 1986). Kapil Dev delighted to have jinx out of the way. *The Hindu*, p. 14.
10. Marlar, R. (21 June 1986). Laudable show at the Lord's. *The Sportstar*, pp. 54, 55, 56.
11. Wright, G. (1987). The Indians in England. Retrieved from http://www. espncricinfo.com/wisdenalmanack/content/story/153073.html
12. Wright, G. (1987). First test match England v India. Retrieved from http:// www.espncricinfo.com/wisdenalmanack/content/story/151960.html
13. Pye, S. (10 July 2014). Recalling England's defeat to India in the first Test at Lord's in 1986. Retrieved from http://www.theguardian.com/sport/that-1980s-sports-blog/2014/jul/10/england-india-first-test-lords-1986-gower
14. Reggie (14 January 2008). CLASSIC: INDIA vs ENGLAND 1986 LORDS TEST -1/3. Retrieved from http://www.dailymotion.com/video/x41m3w_classic-india-v-s-england-1986-lord_sport
15. Reggie (14 January 2008). CLASSIC: INDIA vs ENGLAND 1986 LORDS TEST -2/3. Retrieved from http://www.dailymotion.com/video/x41m9y_classic-india-v-s-england-1986-lord_news
16. Reggie (14 January 2008). CLASSIC: INDIA vs ENGLAND 1986 LORDS TEST -3/3. Retrieved from http://www.dailymotion.com/video/x41mgj_classic-india-v-s-england-1986-lord_sport
17. Conversation with Krishnamachari Srikkanth. 19 October 2015.

Chapter 14: It's a Tie!

1. Cricket Correspondent (18 September 1986). Pitch may prove spinners' paradise. *The Hindu*, p. 14.
2. Cricket Correspondent (19 September 1986). Boon (122), Jones grind Indian attack. *The Hindu*, p. 14.
3. Cricket Correspondent (20 September 1986). Border plays with customary efficiency: Jones comes of age as a Test batsman. *The Hindu*, p. 14.
4. Cricket Correspondent (21 September 1986). Misplaced batting priorities put India in a spot. *The Hindu*, p. 14.
5. Cricket Correspondent (22 September 1986). Kapil Dev, tailenders save India from embarrassment. *The Hindu*, p. 14.
6. Cricket Correspondent (23 September 1986). A memorable victory for cricket. *The Hindu*, p. 14.
7. Mohan, R. (4 October 1986). The foursome made it a memorable one. *The Sportstar*, pp. 10–12.
8. Coward, M. (4 October 1986). The suspense beats a Hitchcock thriller. *The Sportstar*, pp. 6–7, 9–10.
9. Mohan, R. (1988). The Australians in India 1986–87. Retrieved from http://www.espncricinfo.com/wisdenalmanack/content/story/153092.html
10. Ramchand, P. (22 September 2000). Tied Test II – 14 years on. Retrieved from http://www.espncricinfo.com/ci/content/story/94590.html
11. Mohan, R. (1988). First Test match India v Australia. Retrieved from http://www.espncricinfo.com/wisdenalmanack/content/story/151994.html
12. (October 1986). The second tied Test. Retrieved from http://www.espncricinfo.com/ci/content/story/142862.html
13. Miller, A. (13 October 2004). Tied Test marked the renaissance of Australian cricket. Retrieved from http://www.espncricinfo.com/magazine/content/story/142306.html
14. Fingleton, J.H. (1961). *The Greatest Test of Them All*. Sydney. Collins.
15. Cornered Tiger 1992. (3 June 2011). The 2nd Tied Test India vs Australia 1986. Retrieved from https://www.youtube.com/watch?v=LIFtb_Yh9R8
16. Conversation with R. Mohan. 29 September 2015 and 1 November 2015.
17. Conversation with Mohinder Amarnath. 2 October 2015.
18. Conversation with Krishnamachari Srikkanth. 19 October 2015.

Chapter 15: Trumping with Pace

1. Mohan, R. (20 November 1996). Fasten your seat belts for some great action. *The Hindu*, p. 22.
2. Viswanath, G. (20 November 1996). Brown pitch puts South Africa in a quandary. *The Hindu*, p. 22.
3. Mohan, R. (21 November 1996). South Africa seizes the initiative. *The Hindu*, p. 22.
4. Viswanath, G. (21 November 1996). A matter of strategy. *The Hindu*, p. 22.
5. Special Correspondent (22 November 1996). We are back in the game. *The Hindu*, p. 22.
6. Viswanath, G. (22 November 1996). Donald does one better than Pollock. *The Hindu*, p. 22.
7. Mohan, R. (22 November 1996). South Africa draws parity inspite of the umpiring. *The Hindu*, p. 22.
8. Viswanath, G. (23 November 1996). I have to continue with the task, says Laxman. *The Hindu*, p. 22.
9. Mohan, R. (23 November 1996). Laxman revives India's hopes. *The Hindu*, p. 22.
10. Mohan, R. (24 November 1996). Fiery Srinath bowls India to a great win. *The Hindu*, p. 22.
11. Viswanath, G. (24 November 1996). Cronje, Tendulkar stress need to improve batting. *The Hindu*, p. 22.
12. Viswanath, G. (7 December 1996). Srinath breathes fire. *The Sportstar*, pp. 8–12.
13. Bryden, C. (1998). South Africa in India 1996-97. Retrieved from http://www.espncricinfo.com/wisdenalmanack/content/story/153314.html
14. Bryden, C. (1998). First Test match India v South Africa. Retrieved from http://www.espncricinfo.com/wisdenalmanack/content/story/153931.html
15. Mukherji, A. (19 December 2013). 14 greatest bowling spells in India–South Africa Tests. Retrieved from http://www.cricketcountry.com/articles/14-greatest-bowling-spells-in-india-south-africa-tests-77054
16. CricClassics (26 July 2013). Javagal Srinath 6 for 21 vs South Africa 1st Test 1996–97 Ahmedabad. Retrieved from https://www.youtube.com/watch?v=5LwiY9luvd0
17. Tendulkar, S.R. (2014). *Playing It My Way*. London. Hodder & Stoughton. Pp. 79–80.

18. Conversation with Venkatesh Prasad. 26 September 2015.
19. Conversation with Sunil Joshi. 23 August 2015.

Chapter 16: Clash of the Titans

1. (1999). The Australians in India, 1997–98. Retrieved from http://www.espncricinfo.com/wisdenalmanack/content/story/153376.html
2. (1999). India versus Australia. Retrieved from http://www.espncricinfo.com/wisdenalmanack/content/story/153377.html
3. Chappell, I.S. (15 November 2009). Tendulkar outwits Warne. Retrieved from http://www.espncricinfo.com/magazine/content/story/419065.html
4. Sachin Tendulkar Centuries and Best Innings. (2013, June 11). Sachin Tendulkar 15th Test Century: 155* vs Australia, Chennai 1998. Retrieved from https://www.youtube.com/watch?v=otPZnUJWf5g
5. Haigh, G. (2012). *On Warne*. Melbourne. Penguin. P. 193.
6. Tendulkar, S.R. (2014). *Playing It My Way*. London. Hodder & Stoughton. Pp. 91–93.

Chapter 17: A Hero's Heartbreak

1. Viswanath, G. (28 January 1999). Another 'Friendship series' set to take off: No quarter will be asked nor given. *The Hindu*, p. 22.
2. Rajan, V. S. (29 January 1999). Resurgence of South Zone players. *The Hindu*, p. 22.
3. Viswanath, G. (29 January 1999). Kumble bags 6 wickets, India calls the shots on opening day. *The Hindu*, p. 22.
4. Viswanath, G. (30 January 1999). Saqlain claims five wickets, Pakistan wrests initiative. *The Hindu*, p. 22.
5. Ahmed, Q. (30 January 30). Kumble and Saqlain will decide the outcome. *The Hindu*, p. 22.
6. Rajan, V.S. (31 January 1999). Afridi proves a point. *The Hindu*, p. 22.
7. Viswanath, G. (31 January 1999). Afridi, Prasad hold centrestage, a thrilling climax in the offing. *The Hindu*, p. 22.
8. Viswanath, G. (1 February 1999). Saqlain proves too crafty for Indians, Tendulkar's brilliance just not enough. *The Hindu*, p. 22.
9. Rajan, V.S. (1 February 1999). Tendulkar inconsolable. *The Hindu*, p. 22.
10. (1 February 1999). Sachin's ton in vain as Pak wins thriller. *The Hindu*, p. 1.
11. Ahmed, Q. (1 February 1999). A befitting climax. *The Hindu*, p. 22.

12. Viswanath, G. (1999, February 13). Gripping till the end. *Sportstar*, pp. 10–12, 14–15.
13. (2000). The Pakistanis in India, 1998–99. Retrieved from http://www.espncricinfo.com/wisdenalmanack/content/story/153417.html
14. (2000). First test match India v Pakistan. Retrieved from http://www.espncricinfo.com/wisdenalmanack/content/story/151936.html
15. (28 January–1 February 1999). India v Pakistan, first Test at Chennai: *Cricinfo* report. Retrieved from http://static.cricinfo.com/db/ARCHIVE/1998-99/PAK_IN_IND/SCORECARDS/PAK_IND_T1_28JAN-01FEB1999_CI_MR.html
16. Bal, S. (26 July 2009). Chennai applauds Pakistan. Retrieved from http://www.espncricinfo.com/magazine/content/story/410452.html
17. Brijnath, R. (2003). Batting for a billion. Retrieved from http://www.espncricinfo.com/wisdenalmanack/content/story/154917.html
18. Jeremy Behrens (4 May 2012). Sachin Tendulkar 136 vs Pakistan 1999 Chennai. Retrieved from https://www.youtube.com/watch?v=PQk-8JzRZv4
19. Guha, R. (2011). *A Corner of a Foreign Field*. London. Pan Macmillan. Pp. 408–413.
20. Tendulkar, S.R. (2014). *Playing It My way*. London. Hodder & Stoughton. Pp. 102–03.
21. Giridhar, S. and Raghunath, V.J. (2014). *Mid-Wicket Tales: From Trumper to Tendulkar*. New Delhi. Sage. P. 164.
22. Conversation with Venkatesh Prasad. 26 September 2015.

Part 4: 2001 to 2010 – The Rise to the Top

1. Wright, J. (2006). *John Wright's Indian summers*. New Delhi. Penguin Viking. Pp. 231, 240.
2. Guha, R. (2011). The leading cricketer of the world, 2010 Sachin Tendulkar. Retrieved from http://www.espncricinfo.com/wisdenalmanack/content/story/518339.html
3. Bala, R. (2004). *The covers are off*. New Delhi. Rupa & Co. Pp. 221–233.
4. Conversation with Venkatesh Prasad, 26 September 2015.
5. Conversation with Sharda Ugra, 27 December 2014 and 3 October 2015.
6. Conversation with R. Mohan. 29 September 2015 and 1 November 2015.
7. Conversation with Mohinder Amarnath. 2 October 2015.
8. Conversation with Anand Vasu. 6 October 2015.
9. Conversation with Dileep Premachandran. 16 October 2015.

Chapter 18: The Greatest Game Ever

1. Lokapally, V. (10 March 2001). Optimism takes a backseat as Indians take on the cruising Aussies. *The Hindu*, p. 19.
2. Gilchrist, A. (11 March 2001). Australia has special respect for Eden Gardens. *The Hindu*, p. 19.
3. Conn, M. (12 March 2001). Flair and confidence propel him to glory. *The Hindu*, p. 23.
4. Special Correspondent (12 March 2001). A special metamorphosis. *The Hindu*, p. 23.
5. (12 March 2001). Prasanna lauds effort. *The Hindu*, p. 23.
6. Conn, M. (13 March 2001). Steve Waugh saps India's soul, McGrath breaks the heart. *The Hindu*, p. 23.
7. Lokapally, V. (13 March 2001). Inept Indians in a hurry to hug humiliation, Steve strides to an amazing century with a tail for company. *The Hindu*, p. 23.
8. Conn, M. (14 March 2001). Steve Waugh determined to keep pressure on India. *The Hindu*, p. 27.
9. Lokapally, V. (14 March 2001). India lives to fight another day thanks to Laxman's sensational symphony. *The Hindu*, p. 27.
10. Srikkanth, K. (14 March 2001). Indians have to show some character. *The Hindu*, p. 27.
11. Menon, M. (15 March 2001). Records fall like nine pins. *The Hindu*, p. 23.
12. Conn, M. (15 March 2001). Laxman's sublime knock brings Kangaroos back to earth. *The Hindu*, p. 23.
13. Lokapally, V. (15 March 2001). Extra ordinary turn around in India's fortunes as Laxman and Dravid transcend time, tame the Aussie attack. *The Hindu*, p. 23.
14. Lokapally, V. (16 March 2001). Harbhajan, Tendulkar trip up the Kangaroos, India does the incredible. *The Hindu*, p. 27.
15. Menon, M. (16 March 2001). India defies odds at Eden Gardens. *The Hindu*, p. 27.
16. Conn, M. (16 March 2001). The greatest win ever. *The Hindu*, p. 27.
17. Srikkanth, K. (16 March 2001). A victory for Test cricket. *The Hindu*, p. 27.
18. (16 March 2001). India ends Aussie winning streak. *The Hindu*, p. 1.
19. Lokapally, V. (24 March 2001). Amazing turnaround | The team's victory mattered most. *Sportstar*, pp. 10–15.
20. Vasu, A. (15 March 2001). Laxman, Harbhajan script sensational Indian victory. Retrieved from http://www.espncricinfo.com/ci/content/story/105091.html

21. Vasu, A. (14 March 2001). Laxman carves a place for himself in history at the Eden Gardens. Retrieved from http://www.espncricinfo.com/ci/content/story/105061.html

22. Vasu, A. (13 March 2001). Laxman holds centre stage but India still face uphill task. Retrieved from http://www.espncricinfo.com/ci/content/story/105015.html

23. Vasu, A. (12 March 2001). Steve Waugh stands tall as India flicker and fade out. Retrieved from http://www.espncricinfo.com/ci/content/story/104974.html

24. Vasu, A. (11 March 2001). Harbhajan makes history as India restrict Aussies. Retrieved from http://www.espncricinfo.com/ci/content/story/104928.html

25. Bhattacharya, R. (2013). Two southern gentlemen. Retrieved from http://www.espncricinfo.com/wisdenalmanack/content/story/679115.html

26. Ray, M. (2002). Classical Kolkata. Retrieved from http://www.espncricinfo.com/travel/content/story/478582.html

27. Gollapudi, N. (13 September 2011). What's common to Headingley '81 and Kolkata '01? Retrieved from http://www.espncricinfo.com/magazine/content/story/529377.html

28. The cricket monthly (January 2016). 281-degree panorama. Retrieved from http://www.thecricketmonthly.com/story/953093/281-degree-panorama

29. Trevor Byers Cricket (29 July 2010). Australia vs India @ Kolkata 2001 'The Greatest Test Match of All Time' – Full Match Highlights. Retrieved from https://www.youtube.com/watch?v=mQGTXhqVmCQ

30. Cricket Religion (14 March 2012). VVS Laxman and Rahul Dravid 376-run Partnership vs Australia – Kolkata 2001. Retrieved from https://www.youtube.com/watch?v=8y-hIfNrlk8

31. Explore www.Krazy4brands.in (26 October 2011). Very Very Special Laxman unforgettable 281 vs Australia at Eden Gardens, Kolkata. Retrieved from https://www.youtube.com/watch?v=4z7gkC1-0wU

32. Hindustan Times Leadership Summit (25 November 2014). Sourav Ganguly and V.V.S. Laxman Sharing some Secrets of Indian Team. Retrieved from https://www.youtube.com/watch?v=KI_kZzFcvRw

33. Wright, J. (2006). *John Wright's Indian summers*. New Delhi. Penguin Viking. Pp. 45–60.

34. Conversation with Venkatesh Prasad. 26 September 2015.

35. Conversation with Sharda Ugra. 27 December 2014 and 3 October 2015.

Chapter 19: The Ascent Begins

1. Bhattacharya, R. (2003). The Indians in England 2002. Retrieved from http://www.espncricinfo.com/wisdenalmanack/content/story/154968.html

2. Aldred, T. (2003) Third Test England v India. Retrieved from http://www.espncricinfo.com/wisdenalmanack/content/story/154971.html

3. Prasanna, E.A.S. (27 August 2002). India were wise in playing the spinners. Retrieved from http://www.espncricinfo.com/india/content/story/112379.html

4. Dellor, Ralph (26 August 2002). India complete victory by an innings and 46 runs. Retrieved from http://www.espncricinfo.com/ci/content/story/112359.html

5. Vasu, A. (23 August 2002). Ganguly, Tendulkar, Dravid serve a dish to be savoured. Retrieved from http://www.espncricinfo.com/ci/content/story/112301.html

6. Dellor, Ralph (22 August 2002). Dravid leads India to commanding position at close of day. Retrieved from http://www.espncricinfo.com/ci/content/story/112263.html

7. Weaver, P. (23 August 2002). Fletcher arrows in on bowling deficiencies. Retrieved from http://www.theguardian.com/sport/2002/aug/23/cricket.indiainengland2002

8. Hopps, D. (23 August 2002). India adopts the Boycott approach. Retrieved from http://www.theguardian.com/sport/2002/aug/23/cricket.indiainengland20021

9. Hopps, D. (23 August 2002). Ganguly gamble pays off as England suffer torture by a thousand hits. Retrieved from http://www.theguardian.com/sport/2002/aug/24/cricket.indiainengland2002

10. Bhattacharya, R. (23 August 2002). Little Master overhauls the Don. Retrieved from http://www.theguardian.com/sport/2002/aug/24/cricket.indiainengland2002

11. Marks, V. (24 August 2002). England face uphill survival battle. Retrieved from http://www.theguardian.com/sport/2002/aug/25/cricket.indiainengland2002

12. (25 August 2002). Defiant Hussain requires innings of a lifetime. Retrieved from http://www.theguardian.com/sport/2002/aug/26/cricket.indiainengland2002

13. (26 August 2002). England tumble to Kumble. Retrieved from http://www.theguardian.com/sport/2002/aug/26/cricket.indiainengland2002

14. Viswanath, G. (23 August 2002). A priceless effort by Dravid.

Retrieved from http://www.thehindu.com/thehindu/2002/08/23/
stories/2002082305921900.htm

15. Viswanath, G. (25 August 2002). India on clear victory path. Retrieved from http://www.thehindu.com/thehindu/2002/08/25/ stories/2002082506531900.htm

16. Viswanath, G. (26 August 2002). Hussain, Stewart keep India at bay. Retrieved from http://www.thehindu.com/thehindu/2002/08/26/ stories/2002082605122100.htm

17. Viswanath, G. (27 August 2002). It's jubilation time as Indians draw level. Retrieved from http://www.thehindu.com/thehindu/2002/08/27/ stories/2002082705252100.htm

18. Viswanath, G. (28 August 2002). Kumble keeps up a great tradition. Retrieved from http://www.thehindu.com/thehindu/2002/08/28/ stories/2002082802321900.htm

19. Star Sports (11 August 2011). Rahul Dravid 148 versus England. Retrieved from https://www.youtube.com/watch?v=aFDF3xcifYg

20. Wright, J. (2006). *John Wright's Indian Summers*. New Delhi. Penguin/ Viking. Pp. 97–100.

21. Boycott, G. (2009). *The Best XI*. London. Penguin. P. 241.

22. Conversation with Rahul Dravid. 25 February 2013.

Chapter 20: Only the Second Time in History

1. Special Correspondent (12 December 2003). Harbhajan's costly blunder. *The Hindu*, p. 23.

2. Roebuck, P. (12 December 2003). India needs to sustain its effort for five days. *The Hindu*, p. 23.

3. Lokapally, V. (12 December 2003). Injury rules out Zaheer and Harbhajan; A no-holds-barred contest in the offing. *The Hindu*, p. 23.

4. Menon, M. (12 December 2003). All about the Adelaide Oval. *The Hindu*, p. 23.

5. (13 December 2003). A hard day's toil for Indians, 'Punter' Ponting turns plunderer. *The Hindu*, p. 19.

6. Srikkanth, K. (13 December 2003). Advantage Australia. *The Hindu*, p. 19.

7. Chappell, G. (14 December 2003). What's wrong with Tendulkar? *The Hindu*, p. 17.

8. Lokapally, V. (14 December 2003). Ponting completes double century, Laxman and Dravid offer India some hope. *The Hindu*, p. 17.

9. PTI (14 December 2003). Pascoe sees red. *The Hindu*, p. 17.
10. Special Correspondent (15 December 2003). It was nice to bat the way we did. *The Hindu*, p. 19.
11. Srikkanth, K. (15 December 2003). Memories of another day. *The Hindu*, p. 19.
12. Lokapally, V. (15 December 2003). Australian bowling limitations exposed; Dravid, Laxman turn Adelaide into Garden of Eden. *The Hindu*, p. 19.
13. Lokapally, V. (16 December 2003). India has a great chance to make history, Awesome Agarkar rocks Australia. *The Hindu*, p. 21.
14. Chappell, G. (16 December 2003). What a difference a day makes. *The Hindu*, p. 21.
15. Lokapally, V. (17 December 2003). Dravid savours the magic moment; After 22 years a Test victory down under. *The Hindu*, p. 21.
16. Lokapally, V. (27 December 2003). Turning the tables and how. *The Sportstar*, pp. 10, 12, 14 and 15.
17. Bal, S. (2005). The Indians in Australia 2003–04. Retrieved from http://www.espncricinfo.com/wisdenalmanack/content/story/237384.html
18. Bal, S. (2005). Second Test Australia v India. Retrieved from http://www.espncricinfo.com/wisdenalmanack/content/story/237393.html
19. Bhattacharya, R. (2013). Two southern gentlemen. Retrieved from http://www.espncricinfo.com/wisdenalmanack/content/story/679115.html
20. Premachandran, D. (27 September 2009). Dravid conquers Adelaide. Retrieved from http://www.espncricinfo.com/magazine/content/story/426847.html
21. Premachandran, D. (23 January 2008). A modern epic. Retrieved from http://www.espncricinfo.com/ausvind/content/story/332903.html
22. Bal, S. (16 December 2003). 'Rahul batted like God,' says Sourav. Retrieved from http://www.espncricinfo.com/ci/content/story/125867.html
23. Roebuck, P. (15 December 2003). Courage under fire, now it's game on. Retrieved from http://www.smh.com.au/articles/2003/12/14/1071336815290.html
24. Roebuck, P. (16 December 2003). United they stand: visitors use collective will to stage great comeback. Retrieved from http://www.smh.com.au/articles/2003/12/15/1071336893788.html
25. Roebuck, P. (17 December 2003). One man took the garlands, but this comeback was an amazing team effort. Retrieved from http://www.smh.com.au/articles/2003/12/16/1071336963044.html
26. Saltau, C. (17 December 2003). Dravid slays Goliath. Retrieved from http://www.smh.com.au/articles/2003/12/16/1071336963050.html

27. Saltau, C. (15 December 2003). Dravid sends a message: remember Calcutta? Retrieved from http://www.theage.com.au/articles/2003/12/14/1071336812538.html?from=storyrhs
28. AAP (15 December 2003). Dravid, Laxman lead Indian fightback. Retrieved from http://www.smh.com.au/articles/2003/12/14/1071336800737.html
29. Bhattacharya, S. (18 December 2003). It's our bolly game, not yours. Retrieved from http://www.smh.com.au/articles/2003/12/17/1071337025983.html
30. Culley, J. (17 December 2003). Was this Test cricket's greatest comeback? Retrieved from http://www.independent.co.uk/sport/cricket/was-this-test-crickets-greatest-comeback-82866.html
31. Roebuck, P. (29 December 2003). New Wizards in Oz. Retrieved from http://indiatoday.intoday.in/story/fearless-play-by-team-india-brought-down-the-mighty-australians-peter-roebuck/1/204793.html
32. Roebuck, P. (17 December 2003). A win for unity and commitment. *The Hindu*, p. 21.
33. Mkabhijit2 (9 April 2011). Dravid 233 Laxman 148 Australia Adelaide 2003. Retrieved from https://www.youtube.com/watch?v=WYbsmiT5jL8
34. loduuu1 (5 December 2013). Ajit Agarkar 6/41 vs Australia 2003 Adelaide Test. Retrieved from https://www.youtube.com/watch?v=4y7v_jJCrSA
35. Wright, J. (2006). *John Wright's Indian Summers*. New Delhi. Penguin Viking. Pp. 160–65.
36. Memon, A. (14 December 2003). Real life epic. Retrieved from http://timesofindia.indiatimes.com/cricket/Real-life-epic/articleshow/358495.cms?
37. Memon, A. (17 December 2003). Retrieved from http://timesofindia.indiatimes.com/cricket/India-brought-about-the-rebirth-of-never-say-die/articleshow/363301.cms?curpg=2
38. Editorial (17 December 2003). Retrieved from http://timesofindia.indiatimes.com/edit-page/TODAYS-EDITORIALBRShining-India/articleshow/362881.cms?

Chapter 21: The Nawab of Multan

1. Special Correspondent (28 March 2004). Back to where it all began. *The Hindu*, p. 19.
2. Dinakar, S. (28 March 2004). Rahul Dravid to lead | Yet another challenge for India. *The Hindu*, p. 19.
3. Special Correspondent (29 March 2004). For my parents and fiancee. *The Hindu*, p. 23.

4. Dinakar, S. (29 March 2004). Sehwag sizzles with unbeaten 228. *The Hindu*, p. 23.

5. Special Correspondent (30 March 2004). Caught unawares by the timing. *The Hindu*, p. 1.

6. Dinakar, S. (30 March 2004). Sehwag is the Sultan of Multan. *The Hindu*, p. 21.

7. Dinakar, S. (31 March 2004). Hameed falls in the 90s again; A wonderful opportunity for India. *The Hindu*, p. 23.

8. Khan, M. (1 April 2004). Dravid's declaration a big shock. *The Hindu*, p. 23.

9. Dinakar, S. (1 April 2004). Youhana delays the inevitable, India on the verge of historic win. *The Hindu*, p. 23.

10. Dinakar, S. (2 April 2004). India keeps date with destiny. *The Hindu*, p. 23.

11. Editorial (2 April 2004). A Test of character. *The Hindu*, p. 10.

12. (2 April 2004). India completes historic win in Multan. *The Hindu*, p. 1.

13. Marqusee, M. (2 April 2004). Inzamam and the interplay of opposites. *The Hindu*, p. 23.

14. Dinakar, S. (10 April 2004). A match of many firsts. *The Sportstar*, pp. 15–19.

15. Bhattacharya, R. (2005). The Indians in Pakistan 2004. Retrieved from http://www.espncricinfo.com/wisdenalmanack/content/story/238003.html

16. Bhattacharya, R. (2005). First Test Pakistan v India. Retrieved from http://www.espncricinfo.com/wisdenalmanack/content/story/238011.html

17. Bal, S. (1 April 2004). Aspiring to greatness. Retrieved from http://www.espncricinfo.com/sri-lanka-v-india-2015/content/story/134073.html

18. Premachandran, D. (31 March 2004). Triumph and defeat. Retrieved from http://www.espncricinfo.com/ci/content/story/140532.html

19. Bal, S. (29 March 2004). Departures from the past. Retrieved from http://www.espncricinfo.com/ci/content/story/140480.html

20. Samiuddin, Osman.(28 March 2004). Listless and helpless. Retrieved from http://www.espncricinfo.com/magazine/content/story/140584.html

21. Samiuddin, Osman (30 March 2004). Ghost stadiums. Retrieved from http://www.espncricinfo.com/magazine/content/story/140524.html

22. Bhattacharya, R. (2012). *Pundits from Pakistan*. New Delhi. Penguin Books. Pp. 167–212.

23. Wright, J. (2006). *John Wright's Indian summers*. New Delhi. Penguin/ Viking. Pp. 97, 106–07, 180-85.

24. Tendulkar, S.R. (2014). *Playing It My Way*. London. Hodder & Stoughton. P. 155.

25. Bose, M. (2006). *The Magic of Indian Cricket: Cricket and Society in India.* : Oxon. Routledge. P. 243.
26. Laxman, V.V.S. (23 October 2015). Virender Sehwag – a Heart of Gold, caring and giving. Retrieved from http://www.cricketcountry.com/articles/vvs-laxman-virender-sehwag-a-heart-of-gold-caring-and-giving-344176

Chapter 22: Beating Them in the Bullring

1. Richards, B.A. (15 December 2006). The eternal asset. *The Hindu*, p. 23.
2. Dinakar, S. (15 December 2006). Bullring is set for showdown, S. Africa starts favourite; India unconcerned about underdog tag. *The Hindu*, p. 23.
3. Dinakar, S. (16 December 2006). Cautious start by India on a rain-hit day. *The Hindu*, p. 19.
4. Special Correspondent (16 December 2006). A brave decision. *The Hindu*, p. 19.
5. Dinakar, S. (17 December 2006). India gives South Africa a taste of its own medicine. *The Hindu*, p. 19.
6. Dinakar, S. (18 December 2006). South African top order fails yet again. *The Hindu*, p. 19.
7. Special Correspondent (18 December 2006). Previous experience helped. *The Hindu*, p. 19.
8. Special Correspondent (19 December 2006). A great win, says Dravid. *The Hindu*, p. 19.
9. Dinakar, S. (19 December 2006). India scripts a sensational win. *The Hindu*, p. 19.
10. Dinakar, S. (23 December 2006). Indian bowlers hold sway. *The Sportstar*, pp. 36–37.
11. Manthorp, N. (2007). Series review, South Africa v India. Retrieved from http://www.espncricinfo.com/wisdenalmanack/content/story/291145.html
12. Manthorp, N. (2007). First Test South Africa v India. Retrieved from http://www.espncricinfo.com/wisdenalmanack/content/story/291153.html
13. Gollapudi, N. (18 December 2006). How the Wanderers was won. Retrieved from http://www.espncricinfo.com/rsavind/content/story/273278.html
14. (18 December 2006). India-South Africa, 1st Test Match 3rd Day, S. African Wickets. Retrieved from https://www.youtube.com/watch?v=7KH3_AtQhqA
15. cric572 (16 December 2006). India vs South Africa Test 1 Day 2 – Wickets. Retrieved from https://www.youtube.com/watch?v=uBm7b7YEXNY
16. PTI (19 December 2006). Team praised in Lok Sabha. Retrieved from

http://timesofindia.indiatimes.com/Team-India-praised-in-Lok-Sabha/articleshow/852875.cms?

17. Bobilli Vijay Kumar (18 December 2006). India on verge of historic win. Retrieved from http://timesofindia.indiatimes.com/India-on-verge-of-historic-win-in-SA/articleshow/828208.cms?

Chapter 23: Steel, Not Jelly

1. Special Correspondent (27 July 2007). Criticism of middle-order inevitable: Dravid | It felt as much as a victory: Vaughan. *The Hindu*, p. 25.
2. Ram Mahesh, S. (28 July 2007). India wrests control on Day One. *The Hindu*, p. 25.
3. Ram Mahesh, S. (29 July 2007). Indian top-order backs up the bowlers to put the team in command. *The Hindu*, p. 21.
4. Ram Mahesh, S. (30 July 2007). India's batsmen pile on the runs. *The Hindu*, p. 21.
5. Ram Mahesh, S. (27 July 2007). India's bowlers may hold the key. *The Hindu*, p. 25.
6. Corbett, T. (29 July 2007). Pressure getting to Sidebottom. *The Hindu*, p. 21.
7. Special Correspondent (30 July 2007). Sachin is the best: Donald. *The Hindu*, p. 21.
8. Special Correspondent (31 July 2007). India on the verge of victory as Zaheer strikes | Chattering away without rancour. *The Hindu*, pp. 1, 23.
9. Ram Mahesh, S. (31 July 2007). India on the threshold of victory. *The Hindu*, p. 23.
10. PTI (31 July 2007). Taufel 'upset' about Tendulkar decision. *The Hindu*, p. 23.
11. Ram Mahesh, S. (1 August 2007). India plays out a few nervy moments; wraps up test. *The Hindu*, p. 23.
12. Special Correspondent (1 August 2007). Jelly bean incident blown out of proportion | Jelly bean incident spurred me on. *The Hindu*, pp. 22–23.
13. Brijnath, R. (1 August 2007). Tendulkar wears pressure with a quiet dignity. *The Hindu*, p. 22.
14. Ram Mahesh, S. (11 August 2007). Leftie Zaheer gets it right. *The Sportstar*, pp. 7–10.
15. Hussain, N. (2008). Series review India v England 2007. Retrieved from http://www.espncricinfo.com/wisdenalmanack/content/story/374215.html
16. Shastri, R. (2008). Second Test England v India. Retrieved from http://www.espncricinfo.com/wisdenalmanack/content/story/374217.html

17. Brearley, M.J. (29 July 2007). Vaughan's strange field-placings give Indians the edge. Retrieved from http://www.theguardian.com/sport/2007/jul/29/cricket.englandcricketseries3

18. Booth, L. (31 July 2007). England choke on their jelly beans as Zaheer savours sweet revenge. Retrieved from http://www.theguardian.com/sport/2007/jul/31/cricket.englandcricketseries5

19. Selvey, M. (31 July 2007). Zaheer tears through England as brave defence crumbles. Retrieved from http://www.theguardian.com/sport/2007/jul/31/cricket.englandcricketseries2

20. Premachandran, D. (1 August 2007). Zak attack: how Zaheer gave India some fast love. Retrieved from http://www.theguardian.com/sport/2007/aug/01/cricket.englandcricketseries6

21. Bal, S. (31 July 2007). A double celebration. Retrieved from http://www.espncricinfo.com/engvind/content/story/304624.html

22. Conversation with Venkatesh Prasad. 26 September 2015.

Chapter 24: Poetic Justice

1. Ram Mahesh, S. (15 January 2008). Australians on threshold of a new mark. *The Hindu*, p. 22.

2. Special Correspondent (17 January 2008). The shot was on, says Dravid. *The Hindu*, p. 27.

3. Ram Mahesh, S. (17 January 2008). Australia's late surge earns it ascendancy. *The Hindu*, p. 27.

4. Special Correspondent (18 January 2008). It was a crucial wicket, says Anil Kumble. *The Hindu*, p. 25.

5. Ram Mahesh, S. (18 January 2008). An eventful day sees India wrest control. *The Hindu*, p. 25.

6. Special Correspondent. (19 January 2008). I enjoy playing under pressure. *The Hindu*, p. 21.

7. Ram Mahesh, S. (19 January 2008). It's all happening at the WACA! *The Hindu*, p. 21.

8. Roebuck, P. (19 January 2008). Kumble – A man for all seasons. *The Hindu*, p. 21.

9. Special Correspondent (20 January 2008). This will probably rate as one of our best wins, says Kumble. *The Hindu*, p. 19.

10. Ram Mahesh, S. (20 January 2008). India halts Australian juggernaut once again. *The Hindu*, p. 19.

11. Ram Mahesh, S. (20 January 2008). India reverses Austalia's winning run. Young pacemen and veteran batsmen team up at Perth to deny Ponting's men new world record. *The Hindu*, p. 1.

12. Ram Mahesh, S. (26 January 2008). Busting stereotypes. *The Sportstar*, pp. 4–7.

13. Baum, G. (2008). Series review Australia v India 2007–08. Retrieved from http://www.espncricinfo.com/wisdenalmanack/content/story/365665.html

14. Baum, G. (2008). Third Test Australia v India. Retrieved from http://www.espncricinfo.com/wisdenalmanack/content/story/365671.html

15. Vaidyanathan, S. (20 January 2008). Ishant savours spell to Ponting. Retrieved from http://www.espncricinfo.com/ausvind/content/story/332404.html

16. Vaidyanathan, S. (19 January 2008). Smells like team spirit. Retrieved from http://www.espncricinfo.com/ausvind/content/story/332305.html

17. Chappell, I.S. (20 January 2008). New life for a young rivalry. Retrieved from http://www.espncricinfo.com/magazine/content/story/332318.html

18. Roebuck. P. (16 January 2008). Nothing to be gained raking over the ashes. Retrieved from http://www.smh.com.au/news/cricket/nothing-to-be-gained-raking-over-the-ashes/2008/01/15/1200159449929.html

19. Roebuck, P. (18 January 2008). One puff and India are back. Retrieved from http://www.smh.com.au/news/cricket/one-puff-and-india-are-back/2008/01/17/1200419971704.html

20. Roebuck, P. (21 January 2008). Losers? Think again Australia. Retrieved from http://www.smh.com.au/news/cricket/losers-think-again-australia/2008/01/20/1200764081746.html

21. Brown, A. (20 January 2008). Test of history awaits. Retrieved from http://www.theage.com.au/news/cricket/test-of-history-awaits/2008/01/18/1200620211422.html

22. Baum, G. (19 January 2008). Its spirit (at times) willing, the query remains: is Australia able? Retrieved from http://www.theage.com.au/news/cricket/its-spirit-at-times-willing-the-query-remains-is-australiaable/ 2008/01/18/1200620211425.html

23. English, P. (19 October 2008). Australia's cracks finally exposed. Retrieved from http://www.espncricinfo.com/ausvind/content/story/332276.html

24. English, P. (19 October 2008). Kumble questions Australia's spirit. Retrieved from http://www.espncricinfo.com/ausvind/content/story/329405.html

25. Bal, S. (19 October 2008). A great rivalry revived. Retrieved from http://www.espncricinfo.com/ausvind/content/story/332312.html

26. Premachandran, D. (19 October 2008). Inspired India end Australia's streak. Retrieved from http://www.espncricinfo.com/ausvind/content/story/332219.html

27. Roebuck, P. (22 October 2008). A tale of two captains. Retrieved from http://www.espncricinfo.com/magazine/content/story/374905.html

28. Thinkpadx60 (19 January 2008). Cricket: 3rd Test Australia v India Day 3 Perth Highlights. Retrieved from https://www.youtube.com/watch?v=QiI1IySKRPQ

29. Thinkpadx60 (19 January 2008). Cricket: 3rd Test Australia v India Day 4 Perth Highlights. Retrieved from https://www.youtube.com/watch?v=9LEjJKZWDNo

30. Conversation with Dileep Premachandran. 16 October 2015.

Chapter 25: The Spirit of a Proud Team

1. Ram Mahesh, S. (1 August 2008). Virender Sehwag at his belligerent best. Retrieved from http://www.thehindu.com/todays-paper/tp-sports/virender-sehwag-at-his-belligerent-best/article1306226.ece

2. Ram Mahesh, S. (2 August 2008). India battles back through Harbhajan Singh. Retrieved from http://www.thehindu.com/todays-paper/tp-sports/india-battles-back-through-harbhajan-singh/article1306834.ece

3. Ram Mahesh, S. (3 August 2008). Fine batting sees India inch ahead. Retrieved from http://www.thehindu.com/todays-paper/tp-sports/fine-batting-sees-india-inch-ahead/article1307447.ece

4. Ram Mahesh, S. (4 August 2008). India scripts remarkable victory. Retrieved from http://www.thehindu.com/todays-paper/tp-sports/india-scripts-a-remarkable-victory/article1307967.ece

5. Ram Mahesh, S. (5 August 2008). A curious but fascinating Test match. Retrieved from http://www.thehindu.com/todays-paper/tp-sports/a-curious-but-fascinating-test-match/article1308101.ece

6. Monga, S. (3 August 2008). Ishant inspires India to series levelling win. Retrieved from http://www.espncricinfo.com/slvind/content/story/363482.html

7. Premachandran, D. (2 August 2008). India haul themselves from the precipice. Retrieved from http://www.espncricinfo.com/slvind/content/story/363528.html

8. Alter, J. (3 August 2008). Ishant runs on Ubuntu. Retrieved from http://www.espncricinfo.com/slvind/content/story/363532.html

9. Bal, S. (11 August 2008). High scores. Retrieved from http://www.espncricinfo.com/magazine/content/story/364613.html

10. Bal, S. (4 August 2008). Another look at reviews. Retrieved from http://www.espncricinfo.com/magazine/content/story/363578.html

11. Bal, S. (1 August 2008). Sublime Sehwag on a different plane. Retrieved from http://www.espncricinfo.com/slvind/content/story/363256.html

12. Monga, S. (31 July 2008). Honours even despite Sehwag century. Retrieved from http://www.espncricinfo.com/slvind/content/story/363071.html

13. Bal, S. (2 August 2008). Dravid's dismissal adds familiar twist. Retrieved from http://www.espncricinfo.com/slvind/content/story/363403.html

14. Alter, J. (2 August 2008). Gambhir proves Test credentials. Retrieved from http://www.espncricinfo.com/slvind/content/story/363406.html

15. Cricinfo staff (5 August 2008). Fightback started with Kumble – Kirsten. Retrieved from http://www.espncricinfo.com/slvind/content/story/363759.html

16. Kaushik, R. (5 August 2008). Sehwag his own master. Retrieved from http://archive.deccanherald.com/deccanherald.com/Content/Aug52008/sports2008080482776.asp

17. Kaushik, R. (4 August 2008). India hit back in style. Retrieved from http://archive.deccanherald.com/deccanherald.com/Content/Aug42008/sports2008080382569.asp

18. Kaushik, R. (4 August 2008). India seize advantage. Retrieved from http://archive.deccanherald.com/deccanherald.com/Content/Aug32008/sports2008080282416.asp

19. Kaushik, R. (2 August 2008). Umpire review system | lbw under scanner. Retrieved from http://archive.deccanherald.com/deccanherald.com/Content/Aug22008/sports2008080282330.asp

20. Kaushik, R. (1 August 2008). Sehwag saves the day. Retrieved from http://archive.deccanherald.com/deccanherald.com/Content/Aug12008/sports2008080182124.asp

21. Laxman, V.V.S. (23 October 2015). Virender Sehwag – a Heart of Gold, caring and giving. Retrieved from http://www.cricketcountry.com/articles/vvs-laxman-virender-sehwag-a-heart-of-gold-caring-and-giving-344176

Chapter 26: Winning it for Mumbai

1. Dinakar, S. (11 December 2008). The stage is set for an intriguing contest. *The Hindu*, p. 19.

2. Sports Reporter (11 December 2008). A good game is what we owe the nation at this juncture, says Dhoni. *The Hindu*, p. 19.

3. Dinakar, S. (12 December 2008). Strauss composes a patient century. *The Hindu*, p. 21.

4. Dinakar, S. (13 December 2008). India's top order batsmen fail to get going. *The Hindu*, p. 21.

5. Sridhar, N. (12 December 2008). I was comfortable out there: Strauss. *The Hindu*, p. 20.

6. Diwan, K. (13 December 2008). Swann thrilled with his dream start. *The Hindu*, p. 20.

7. Diwan, K. (14 December 2008). Strauss has set a great example. *The Hindu*, p. 20.

8. Dinakar, S. (14 December 2008). England in a commanding position. *The Hindu*, p. 21.

9. Dinakar, S. (15 December 2008). Buccaneer Sehwag sets up India's chase. *The Hindu*, p. 21.

10. Diwan, K. (15 December 2008). All four results seem possible. *The Hindu*, p. 20.

11. Dinakar, S. (16 December 2008). Historic win for India | Tendulkar, Yuvraj guide India to a superb win. *The Hindu*, pp. 1, 19.

12. Lokapally, V. (16 December 2008). Just cannot keep Sehwag down. *The Hindu*, p. 20.

13. Diwan, K. (16 December 2008). Tendulkar dedicates his knock to all Indians. *The Hindu*, p. 18.

14. Diwan, K. (20 December 2008). A masterful display it was. *Sportstar*, pp. 4–6.

15. Hopps, D. (2009). Series review India v England 2008-09. Retrieved from http://www.espncricinfo.com/wisdenalmanack/content/story/430971.html

16. Premachandran, D. (2009). First Test India v England 2008-09. Retrieved from http://www.espncricinfo.com/wisdenalmanack/content/story/430984.html

17. Roebuck, P. (17 December 2008) Win-win situation. Retrieved from http://www.espncricinfo.com/magazine/content/story/382487.html

18. Bal, S. (15 December 2008). A triumph of belief. Retrieved from http://www.espncricinfo.com/magazine/content/story/382326.html

19. McGlashan, A. (15 December 2008). Sehwag sets up intriguing final day. Retrieved from http://www.espncricinfo.com/indveng/content/story/382228.html

20. McGlashan, A. (15 December 2008). Tendulkar century sets up famous win. Retrieved from http://www.espncricinfo.com/indveng/content/story/382035. html

21. Shastri, R. (2009). The leading cricketer of the world, 2008 Virender Sehwag. Retrieved from http://www.espncricinfo.com/wisdenalmanack/content/ story/398689.html

22. Berry, S. (2010). The leading cricketer of the world, 2009 Virender Sehwag. Retrieved from http://www.espncricinfo.com/wisdenalmanack/content/ story/455921.html

23. Tendulkar, S.R. (2014). *Playing It My Way*. London. Hodder & Stoughton. P. 200.

24. Hopps, D. (16 December 2008). Tendulkar's ton sinks England and soothes India's Mumbai torment. Retrieved from http://www.theguardian.com/ sport/2008/dec/15/india-win-chennai-test

25. Premachandran, D. (15 December 2008). Superstar Tendulkar writes the perfect script. Retrieved from http://www.espncricinfo.com/magazine/ content/story/382314.html

26. ESPNcricinfo commentary (15 December 2008). Retrieved from http:// www.espncricinfo.com/indveng/engine/match/361050.html?innings=1; view=commentary

Chapter 27: The Fourth-Innings Houdini

1. Special Correspondent (1 October 2010). No extra pressure on us: Dhoni. *The Hindu*, p. 21.

2. Ram Mahesh, S. (1 October 2010). Another engrossing series between equals looms. *The Hindu*, p. 21.

3. Special Correspondent (2 October 2010). Test is evenly poised, says Watson. *The Hindu*, p. 25.

4. Ram Mahesh, S. (2 October 2010). Watson stands firm with a chancy century. *The Hindu*, p. 25.

5. Special Correspondent (3 October 2010). Zaheer deserves a lot of credit. *The Hindu*, p. 15.

6. Ram Mahesh, S. (3 October 2010). Patient Paine proves to be a pain for India. *The Hindu*, p. 15.

7. Special Correspondent (4 October 2010). Dravid disappointed at letting Australia back into the game. *The Hindu*, p. 19.

8. Ram Mahesh, S. (4 October 2010). Chaotic collapse hands Australia the advantage. *The Hindu*, p. 19.

9. Ram Mahesh, S. (5 October 2010). Ishant, Hilfenhaus share day's honours. *The Hindu*, p. 17.

10. Special Correspondent (5 October 2010). We sense victory, says Hilfenhaus. *The Hindu*, p. 16.

11. Ram Mahesh, S. (6 October 2010). Laxman special derails Australia. *The Hindu*, p. 17.

12. (6 October 2010). Laxman magic sees India home in thriller. *The Hindu*, p. 1.

13. Special Correspondent (6 October 2010). Hurts more than Kolkata 2001, Ponting. *The Hindu*, p. 17.

14. Editorial (6 October 2010). The real thing. *The Hindu*, p. 10.

15. Shekar, N. (6 October 2010). Killing them softly. *The Hindu*, p. 17.

16. Ram Mahesh, S. (21 October 2010). Very, very special knock. *The Sportstar*, pp. 24–25.

17. Monga, S. (5 October 2010). India's Atlas, Australia's nemesis. Retrieved from http://www.espncricinfo.com/india-v-australia-2010/content/story/480096.html

18. Chappell, I.S. (10 October 2010). The magic of VVS. Retrieved from http://www.espncricinfo.com/magazine/content/story/480644.html

19. Roebuck, P. (7 October 2010). The genius and the doubter. Retrieved from http://www.espncricinfo.com/magazine/content/story/480205.html

20. Bal, S. (6 October 2010). The steel beneath the silk. Retrieved from http://www.espncricinfo.com/magazine/content/story/480141.html

21. Bhogle, H. (15 October 2010). Australia finds the boot on the other foot. Retrieved from http://www.espncricinfo.com/magazine/content/story/481715.html

22. Coverdale, B. (5 October 2010). Magical Laxman seals thrilling one-wicket win. Retrieved from http://www.espncricinfo.com/india-v-australia-2010/content/story/479976.html

23. English, P. (3 October 2010). Virender Sehwag surges to set up India. Retrieved from http://www.espncricinfo.com/india-v-australia-2010/content/current/story/479524.html

24. Edit Page Comment (6 October 2010). Cricket Returns. Retrieved from http://timesofindia.indiatimes.com/edit-page/Cricket-Returns/articleshow/6692666.cms?

25. ESPNcricinfo commentary (1, 3 and 5 October 2010). Retrieved from http://www.espncricinfo.com/india-v-australia-2010/engine/match/464526.html?innings=1;view=commentary

Chapter 28: Top of the World

1. Ram Mahesh, S. (26 December 2010). South Africa keen on wrapping up series in Durban. *The Hindu*, p. 17.
2. Ram Mahesh, S. (27 December 2010). Steyn has India hopping and jumping again. *The Hindu*, p. 19.
3. Ram Mahesh, S. (28 December 2010). Advantage yo-yos between South Africa and India. *The Hindu*, p. 21.
4. Ram Mahesh, S. (29 December 2010). Laxman knock puts India marginally ahead. *The Hindu*, p. 21.
5. Ram Mahesh, S. (30 December 2010). Bowlers give India famous win. *The Hindu*, p. 23.
6. Sports Reporter (30 December 2010). India bounces back, levels series. *The Hindu*, p. 1.
7. Ram Mahesh, S. (13 January 2011). Durban conquered. *The Sportstar*, pp. 9 & 10.
8. Manthorp, N. (2011). Series review South Africa v India. Retrieved from http://www.espncricinfo.com/wisdenalmanack/content/story/518551.html
9. Vasu, A. (2011). Second test South Africa v India. Retrieved from http://www.espncricinfo.com/wisdenalmanack/content/story/518553.html
10. Monga, S. (30 December 2010). 'Durban among toughest wickets I've played' – Laxman. Retrieved from http://www.espncricinfo.com/south-africa-v-india-2010/content/story/494810.html
11. Monga, S. and Gollapudi, N. (30 December 2010). India exorcise demons of 1996. Retrieved from http://www.espncricinfo.com/south-africa-v-india-2010/content/story/494682.html
12. Chopra, A. (30 December 2010). The secret of Zaheer's success. Retrieved from http://www.espncricinfo.com/magazine/content/story/494724.html
13. The cricket monthly (January 2016). 281-degree panorama. Retrieved from http://www.thecricketmonthly.com/story/953093/281-degree-panorama
14. ESPNcricinfo commentary (27–28 December 2010). Retrieved from http://www.espncricinfo.com/wisdenalmanack/content/story/518553.html
15. Conversation with Dileep Premachandran. 16 October 2015.
16. Conversation with Rahul Dravid. 25 February 2013.

Index

juggernaut

THE APP FOR INDIAN READERS

Fresh, original books tailored for mobile and for India. Starting at ₹10.

juggernaut.in

1

CRAFTED
FOR MOBILE
READING

*Thought you would never read a book
on mobile? Let us prove you wrong.*

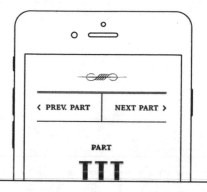

Beautiful Typography

The quality of print transferred
to your mobile. Forget ugly PDFs.

Customizable Reading

Read in the font size, spacing
and background of your liking.

2
AN EXTENSIVE LIBRARY

Including fresh, new, original Juggernaut books from the likes of Sunny Leone, Praveen Swami, Husain Haqqani, Umera Ahmed, Rujuta Diwekar and lots more. Plus, books from partner publishers and loads of free classics. Whichever genre you like, there's a book waiting for you.

DON'T JUST READ; INTERACT

We're changing the reading experience from passive to active.

juggernaut.in

Ask authors questions

Get all your answers from the horse's mouth.
Juggernaut authors actually reply to every
question they can.

Rate and review

Let everyone know of your favourite reads or
critique the finer points of a book – you will be
heard in a community of like-minded readers.

Gift books to friends

For a book-lover, there's no nicer gift than
a book personally picked. You can even
do it anonymously if you like.

Enjoy new book formats

Discover serials released in parts over
time, picture books including comics,
and story-bundles at discounted rates.
And coming soon, audiobooks.

4

LOWEST PRICES & ONE-TAP BUYING

Books start at ₹10 with regular discounts and free previews.

juggernaut.in

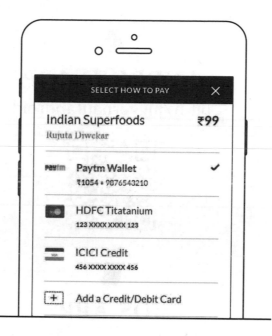

Paytm Wallet, Cards & Apple Payments

On Android, just add a Paytm Wallet once and buy any book with one tap. On iOS, pay with one tap with your iTunes-linked debit/credit card.

Click the QR Code with a QR scanner app
or type the link into the Internet browser
on your phone to download the app.

ANDROID APP

bit.ly/juggernautandroid

iOS APP

bit.ly/juggernautios

For our complete catalogue, visit www.juggernaut.in
To submit your book, send a synopsis and two
sample chapters to books@juggernaut.in
For all other queries, write to contact@juggernaut.in